RENEWALS 458-4574

DATE DUE

**WITHDRAWN
UTSA Libraries**

THE PITFALLS OF LIBERAL DEMOCRACY AND
LATE NATIONALISM IN SOUTH AFRICA

The Pitfalls of Liberal Democracy and Late Nationalism in South Africa

Mueni wa Muiu

THE PITFALLS OF LIBERAL DEMOCRACY AND LATE NATIONALISM IN SOUTH AFRICA
Copyright © Mueni wa Muiu, 2008.

All rights reserved.

First published in 2008 by PALGRAVE MACMILLAN® in the United States a division of St. Martin's Press LLC, 175 Fifth Avenue, New York, NY 10010.

Where this book is distributed in the UK, Europe and the rest of the world, this is by Palgrave Macmillan, a division of Macmillan Publishers Limited, registered in England, company number 785998, of Houndmills, Basingstoke, Hampshire RG21 6XS.

Palgrave Macmillan is the global academic imprint of the above companies and has companies and representatives throughout the world.

Palgrave® and Macmillan® are registered trademarks in the United States, the United Kingdom, Europe and other countries.

ISBN-13: 978–0-230–60815–3
ISBN-10: 0–230–60815–9

Library of Congress Cataloging-in-Publication Data

Muiu, Mueni wa.
 The pitfalls of liberal democracy and late nationalism in South Africa / Mueni wa Muiu.
    p. cm.
 Includes bibliographical references and index.
 ISBN 0-230-60815-9
 1. South Africa-Politics and government. 2. South Africa-Race relations. 3. Blacks-South Africa-Politics and government. 4. Afrikaners-South Africa-Politics and government. 5. Apartheid-South Africa-History. 6. Liberalism-South Africa-History. 7. Democracy-South Africa-History. 8. Nationalism-South Africa-History. 9. Social change-South Africa-History. 10. South Africa-Economic conditions. I. Title.

DT1798.M85 2008
320.540968–dc22   2008017290

A catalogue record of the book is available from the British Library.

Design by Scribe Inc.

First edition: December 2008

10 9 8 7 6 5 4 3 2 1

Printed in the United States of America.

My loves:
Muiu wa Muvya, Yoeli wa Muiu, Munyiva wa Muvya, Sosu wa Muiu, Katungwa wa Kisilu, Mwakudua wa Mwachofi, and Vilivu wa Muiu

Contents

Acknowledgments		ix
Abbreviations		xi
Key Terms		xiii
Introduction		1
1	The African Imagined Community, 1867–1948	21
2	An Afrikaner Imagined Community, 1867–1948	47
3	The Impact of Apartheid on African and Afrikaner Nationalisms, 1948–1994	63
4	"Home" as Depicted in Selected African and Afrikaner Novels and Short Stories	89
5	Changes in South Africa's Economy, 1976–1994	107
6	The Negotiations for a Democratic South Africa, 1990–1994	131
7	A Work in Progress: Social and Economic Policy Changes by the ANC, 1994–2006	151
Conclusion: South Africa: Toward Democracy and Development		179
Notes		189
Bibliography		219
Index		237

Acknowledgments

In writing this book many people helped me. Special thanks to Michael Nwanze and Robert Edgar. My deep gratitude to my sister Kalondu who provided me with a home in which I could work in peace and quiet. Without her this study would not have been possible. I am grateful to the staff of Winston Salem State University copy center. I would also like to thank Jackie Foutz at the media and marketing division of WSSU for doing the graphics for the book cover. Thanks is also due to Lungisile Ntsebeza, Benny Bunsee, Lawrence Sakarai—the trio whose constructive criticism and passion made the research worth while; my African Studies "family" supported me throughout the process; my sister Muthike who encouraged me, my brother Luveni whose courage and drive inspired me to work hard while appreciating the simple things that life has to offer. "Merci" to Guy for his encouragement and support, as well as for his contribution to improving the manuscript; my children Muthoki and Musumbi have kept me on my toes. I am grateful to the editors at Palgrave McMillan for everything they did to improve the quality of this manuscript. My deepest gratitude to my sister Kawinzi who first sparked my love for reading long before I knew how to read. But it is really Mwaitu, my mother, who started it all by forcing me into the classroom; without her persistence, courage, and vision, this work could not have been completed. To her I owe the greatest gratitude. Needless to say neither she nor anyone mentioned above is responsible for the opinions expressed in the following pages.

Abbreviations

AAC	All African Convention
ANC	African National Congress
APLA	Azanian People's Liberation Army
APO	African People's Organization
AWB	Afrikaner Weerstand Beweging
AZAPO	Azanian People's Organization
BCM	Black Consciousness Movement
BPC	Black People's Convention
CODESA	Convention for a Democratic South Africa
COSAG	Concerned South Africans Group
COSATU	Congress of South African Trade Unions
CP	Conservative Party
DP	Democratic Party
DRC	Dutch Reformed Church
FAK	Federasie van Afrikaanse Kultuurverenigings
FF	Freedom Front
GEAR	Growth, Employment and Redistribution
HDP	Historically Disadvantaged People or Communities; people or communities discriminated against on the basis of race and marginalized and excluded politically, economically and socially within the South African state under the apartheid regime.
HDIs	Historically Disadvantaged Institutions; formerly black [including African, Indian and Colored] universities and technical colleges (*technikons*) in South Africa.
ICU	Industrial and Commercial Workers Union
IFP	Inkatha Freedom Party

MDM	Mass Democratic Movement
NCAW	National Council of African Women
NP	National Party
NNP	New National Party
PAC	Pan Africanist Congress
PNP	Purified National Party
RDP	Reconstruction and Development Programme
SACP	South African Communist Party
SADF	South African Defense Force
SANDF	South African National Defense Force
SANNC	South African Native National Congress
SASO	South African Students Organization
UDF	United Democratic Front
DEIC	Dutch East India Company

Key Terms

Afrikaanse Handelsinstitut: Afrikaans Commercial Institute

Afrikaanse Pers: Afrikaner Press. Transvaal Nationalist Press group, publisher of *Die Vaderland*. Merged with Voortrekker Pers in 1972 to form the Perskor group

Afrikaner Broederbond: Afrikaner Brotherhood. Secret organization for Afrikaner males.

Apartheid: "Apart-ness" separation of the races

Boer(e): Literally, farmer used until the 1960s. In contemporary South Africa it is viewed as an insult.

Broedertwis: Literally, division between brothers

Bywoner: Afrikaner squatters, very poor

Gereformeerde Kerk: Reformed Church

Kaffir: Arabic for "unbeliever"; derogatory term used to refer to Africans

Kholwa: Zulu term used in Natal to refer to Africans who converted to Christianity

Nasionale Pers: National Press based in Cape Town

Ndiguni Topiya: Xhosa meaning "belonging to the church of Ethiopia"

Poqo: Xhosa meaning "alone," "pure" armed wing of the Pan Africanist Congress

Rapport: Report. Pro-NP verligte Sunday newspaper formed by the 1970 merger of *Die Beeld and Dagbreek*

Umkhonto we Sizwe: Xhosa meaning "spear of the nation," armed wing of the African National Congress

Verligte: Enlightened Afrikaner nationalist. A *verligte* in the 1990s was more enlightened (liberal) than one in 1960s.

Verkrampte: Conservative/reactionary Afrikaner nationalist. Like the *Verligte* they became less conservative/reactionary over time.

Voortrekker Pers: Literally, those who journeyed ahead. Alternative to Boy Scouts/Girl Guides created by the Broederbond and named after the people who undertook "The Great Trek."

Introduction

THIS STUDY INVESTIGATES THE CONNECTION BETWEEN LATE NATIONALISM and democracy, using South Africa as a case in point. I argue that liberal democracy in South Africa accommodated and left unresolved the contradictions of South African capitalism and the African National Congress's (ANC) multiracial nationalist debate. More specifically, the achievement of equal political rights in the new democracy was premised on the acceptance of unequal economic relations among different classes, genders, and races. Furthermore, the middle-class in all its multiracial and multiethnic diversity is threatened from above and below. Popular demands from below sometimes lead the middle class to partially satisfy the majority's economic and social demands. Pressures from various economic interests (particularly the business community) limit its room for maneuver. These pressures force the middle class to make compromises that are detrimental to the economic interests of the majority of the population. These realities will continue to inform the ANC and the economic and social policies of future African leaders as they try to transform South Africa. In short, this study seeks to understand South Africa's multiracial nationalism in the wake of the transition from apartheid to liberal democracy, without a simultaneous transformation of economic relations. This work also examines liberal democracy in contemporary South Africa and the challenges that face this unique experiment.

Unlike the French colonialists in Algeria or the British colonialists in Kenya and South Africa, both of whom had two passports and a home abroad to which they could return, the Afrikaners' only home is South Africa, which they share with the country's African majority. As a result, two distinct and competing nationalisms developed with a claim to the same land. Afrikaner nationalism, based on white supremacy, was exclusive, while African nationalism (as represented by the ANC) was multiracial, in other words, inclusive of all races and ethnic groups. It is important to note in this regard that exclusive nationalism led to apartheid while multiracial nationalism resulted in liberal democracy. It is crucial to analyze how and why these two nationalisms resulted in different types of political regimes. It is equally important to examine the shortcomings of multiracial nationalism and its transition to a post-colonial society. South Africa's transition to democracy in 1994 offers a unique opportunity to analyze and observe first-hand how South African nationalism (as an example of late nationalism) negotiated the quest for political and economic rights.

This transition to multiracial democracy can be viewed as the last wave of the democratization process in Africa that began in 1989. This process meant that former authoritarian regimes were opening up their democratic space as a result of internal and international pressures. The study of the South African case may also yield insights into how democracy can be consolidated.

The South African population is composed of Africans of different classes, ethnicities, and genders. The multiracial nationalism of the African National Congress, which recognizes and attempts to redress the political, economic, and social inequalities of a complex society, is that for which late nationalism stands. In contrast, the exclusive Afrikaner nationalism of the National Party represented economic and political power as a zero sum game and thus offered an example of colonial settler nationalism with no effective mechanisms for bridging important racial, ethnic, political, economic, and social divides within South African society. In this study, I will examine the National Party as an ideal example of this kind of nationalism.

In contrast, the ANC relied on liberal and moderate influences within the party and the country to provide a framework for negotiations for a democratic South Africa. Groups on the left of the political spectrum, such as the South African Communist Party (SACP) and the Pan Africanist Congress, also influenced liberal tradition by adding a class dimension. After the fall of the Soviet Union, the ANC supported liberal democracy for pragmatic reasons; no other viable alternative was available. ANC leaders had to seize the moment and negotiate. The Indian and Colored parties also influenced the ANC's liberal tradition by emphasizing the need for all oppressed groups to organize themselves based on a nonracial basis.

The choices of the ANC leadership were also influenced by trade union and other mass movements. These movements pressured the ANC leadership to voice their concerns. The ANC avoided controversial language by asking whites to "share" or "extend" the nation's wealth to the majority. By forming alliances with whites, Indians and people of mixed descent, the ANC presented itself as a liberal and moderate multiracial organization. As a result, it gathered supporters within and outside the country who viewed it as a moderate organization. In 1952, the ANC participated in several civil disobedience campaigns based on the strategy of passive resistance. Satyagraha, meaning "soul-free" or "soul-truth," was first introduced and applied in South Africa by Mahatma Gandhi. *Satyagraha* requires adherence to goals of love and mutual respect, and demands a willingness to suffer (if necessary) to achieve these goals.[1] The ANC tried to persuade the white minority that apartheid was morally wrong, but the regime remained "unimpressed by the moral principles implicit in passive resistance."[2] Ali Mazrui and Michael Tidy note further that political protests in public places in South Africa did not have a dramatic impact on apartheid since its agents (which included political leaders, the police, and the court system) did not have a guilty conscience over apartheid's repressive nature.[3]

The ANC's appeal to the white minority's sense of justice was unrealistic, given the state's leadership claim over the African majority. Heribert Adam has pointed out that one of the factors that led to this incorrect assessment by the ANC was "its Christian–liberal outlook and the bourgeois values of many African leaders, who received their education in missionary schools, hindered an early change of tactics even when their failure became obvious."[4] This influence led the ANC to believe that its sacrifices would impress the government. In 1955, a Congress of the People was organized by the ANC, the Indian Congress, the Congress of Democrats (whites), the Colored People's Organization, and the Congress of Trade Unions and adopted the Freedom Charter. According to the Freedom Charter, South Africa belongs to all who live in it. It adopted a Bill of Rights and "called for democratic majority rule, and inclusive nationalism that involved all races rather than a concern for an exclusive nationalism."[5] One positive result of the defiance campaign was an increased political awareness among Africans and ANC membership. Overall, however, passive resistance as a strategy for social and political change was a failure. The ANC leadership believed that it was morally superior to the National Party because it supported multiracialism. For the ANC, "democracy implied [a] representative government and the guaranteed freedom of all, including minorities, to enjoy not just political but cultural rights."[6] Multiracial democracy did not necessarily imply African control; it did, however, advocate for political equality in a pluralistic society. It also implied a political system based on majority rule.

As defined in the South African context, liberal democracy refers to equal rights before the law, freedom of association, movement, speech, and petition, representative government, and universal suffrage. The apartheid economy inherited by the new South Africa continues to rely on transnational and national firms. The management of these firms has been partially Africanized, but their objective remains the same, namely high profits based on cheap labor. As was the case during apartheid, a core group of entrepreneurs (a majority of which are white, some African and a few Indian), linked to domestic and foreign interests, control capital and the economy.

Liberal democracy in South Africa has three beneficiaries. The first, the capitalist class or bourgeoisie, includes South African and foreign transnational corporate interests of the European Union, Japan, and the United States. The transnational corporations and South African firms have access to cheap labor, vast sub regional and regional markets, and a large pool of natural resources; thus creating high profitability. These companies use South Africa as a springboard to penetrate markets in southern Africa and in the rest of the continent.

The second major beneficiary of liberal democracy in South Africa is the African middle class whose members are spread among the African National Congress and the Zulu-based Inkatha Freedom Party. This middle class is neither homogeneous nor static. It is a multiracial social group that is made up of different actors with diverse interests that are, at times, in conflict with one another; its composition changes depending on the interests at stake. The middle class is also characterized by higher standards of living, better economic opportunities, and higher levels of education compared to the rest of the population. The third beneficiary of liberal democracy in South Africa is the African people who are segmented by ethnicity, class, and gender. They can now vote and enjoy basic individual and political freedoms. As the majority of the population seeks to advance its economic rights, it exerts enormous political pressure on the middle class to deliver.

The triumph of multiracialism in South Africa contributed to a liberal democratic outcome. It established an example of the connection between late nationalism and democracy in that country. The present study compares two different and distinct nationalisms within the same country, reflecting the historical experiences of two distinct political waves: the first wave of political authoritarianism and the second and last wave, which led to democratization. The first national political wave in South Africa was marked by Afrikaner nationalism and the exclusionary system of apartheid. The second national political wave was marked by late nationalism, resulting in multiracial democracy. Apartheid is an example of the authoritarian political outcome of the first national wave. The present ANC-led democratic system, as an example of the late national wave, offers an interesting reversal of the assumption that democracy is a natural product of European nationalism. This study is not only about late nationalism; it is also an investigation into the shortcomings of liberal democracy in South Africa.

According to apartheid's classification, Africans were either "Bantu" "blacks" or "Natives" while people of mixed race were "Coloured" but Indian and whites retained their identities. In this study "Africans" will be used to refer to the various indigenous South African ethnic groups. "Biracial" or "mixed race" will be used to refer to people of mixed racial parentage. "Afrikaners" will be used to refer to whites of Dutch descent. "Black" includes Africans, Indians, and people of mixed descent. This study focuses on the period between 1976 and 2006. It views the Soweto revolt, which occurred on June 16,1976, as the beginning of apartheid's downfall. The revolt exposed cracks within apartheid, which the African majority continued to exploit until 1990, when all political prisoners were finally released. In order to examine the ANC's attempts at socioeconomic transformation, the study will end in 2006. In this study, the transition from apartheid to liberal democracy begins with the release of all political prisoners in 1990, although secret negotiations to dismantle apartheid between Mandela, the ANC in exile, government officials, and some members of the business community began as early as 1985. The transition process ended in 1994 with the first general elections in South Africa that resulted in a multiracial democracy. In the following section, we will specify the methodology adopted in this study and examine some of the perspectives used to analyze nationalism and the transition from apartheid to multiracial democracy in South Africa.

A Note on Methodology

The present study uses a multidisciplinary approach as well as a long-term historical perspective *a la* Fernand Braudel. Our multidisciplinary approach combines the key discipline of political science with history, economics (or more accurately, classical political economy), and literature. A long-term historical perspective is absolutely necessary to show how capitalism influenced the trajectory of African and Afrikaner nationalism in South Africa. Indeed one could argue that only such a perspective can truly show how nationalism developed in that country. Moreover, one cannot understand the process that led to the advent of liberal democracy in post apartheid South Africa without understanding the ANC's multiracial nationalism. Lastly, it is essential to use such a long-term historical perspective to clearly identify the actual beneficiaries of multiracial nationalism and liberal democracy in South Africa in terms of specific racial, class, and gender groups.

Perspectives on Nationalism and on South Africa's Transition from Apartheid to Liberal Democracy

Most of the literature on developing countries does not focus on late nationalism, that is, the last wave of nationalism in Africa. This wave refers to countries that won their independence in the 1990s, such as Namibia (1990), Eritrea (1993), and South Africa, which had been under British control until the creation of a united South Africa in 1910 when both the British and Afrikaners shared power. In 1948, the Afrikaners won the whites-only elections and introduced the policy of apartheid that was only abolished in 1994 with the victory of the African National Congress. Mention should also be made here of Western Sahara, a former Spanish colony claimed by Morocco, currently under United Nations mandate and supervision and whose international status is still undetermined. Note also that two other territories in Africa, the island of Mayotte in the Comoros archipelago and the island of Reunion in the Indian ocean, are still under French colonial tutelage. The general literature on the subject does not make the connection between nationalism and democracy. Most authors would agree that nationalism has generally led to the development of authoritarian political systems in the Third World (excluding India). Moreover, it should be noted that authoritarianism is not specific to third world countries. General Francisco Franco (Spain), Adolf Hitler (Germany), Antonio de Oliveira Salazar and Marcelo Caetano (Portugal), and Benito Mussolini (Italy) are just a few examples of authoritarian rulers in Western European countries. In Africa, the nationalist leaders mobilized their populations to fight against colonialism during the 1950s and 1960s. Once they defeated the colonial powers, these leaders progressively established one-party systems that monopolized political power, stifled dissent, and relied on coercion and repression to govern.

South Africa, where Britain and Dutch settlers fought over control of the territory, was not an exception. British and Afrikaner authoritarian governments ruled over Africans until 1948, when Afrikaner nationalists came to power. They established an apartheid state in which any rights, such as freedom of movement, access to property, and political rights (including voting), were denied to the Africans. The availability of an unlimited supply of cheap African labor for the benefit of the white minority was the most important issue.

Afrikaner nationalism, as embodied by the National Party (NP), aimed to save the white minority from the African majority. Afrikaners believed that the National Party was "democratic" because it held regular competitive elections for whites only. A parliamentary system was in place that allowed "free" speech as long as it did not radically challenge the regime. The National Party claimed that it was protecting the standard of living of the white minority. Furthermore, it represented a white minority, which it could identify based on race (if not culture), with the rest of the white race in the Western world. In this sense the white minority was "civilized" compared to the indigenous people. To its members, the National Party was "a volk bewiging—a people in movement, after all, fighting not for money or possession or territory or even privilege, but for the *life* of its people."[7]

The National Party presented itself as the protector of minority rights and a trustee of the African majority. For the National Party, separation of different groups based on ethnicity was "natural" because it ensured white survival; it was also presented as just. Each group would develop its own culture and be self-sufficient along separate lines. In defending apartheid, Prime Minister Verwoerd noted, "I am convinced that integration in a country like South Africa cannot succeed. I want justice for all groups not justice for one at the expense of the others." Further, Verwoerd urged Africans to *skep u eie toekoms, or* "[b]uild your on future."[8]

According to P. Eric Louw, apartheid is very different from segregation. The former accepts other ethnic groups' differences without master-servant relations. Segregation is based on white supremacy. It pretends to integrate diverse ethnic groups but in reality the white minority is always in control.[9] It is important to note that Afrikaners did not introduce segregation in South Africa. It was a "tradition" that was maintained by Europeans whenever they encountered people who belonged to other racial groups. Segregation also existed under the British Governor Theophilus Shepstone in Natal during the period 1845 to 1875. By 1887, Cecil Rhodes had initiated discriminatory laws, including residential permits and travel passes, for African male workers living on mining compounds. Afrikaners merely refined these laws when they came to power in 1948.

African and South African Nationalisms

Most of the literature on African nationalism dates back to the big national wave of the 1960s. It demonstrates how nationalism was conceptualized in the first wave. This literature also provides a historical background for the present study. According to Anton Lembede, African nationalism has six principles: humanity is viewed within its material conditions; there is a scientific basis to nationalism, which believes that every nation is unique and has a peculiar contribution to society; African nationalism must be based on history and on an economic structure. Lembede believed that indigenous African societies were based on communalism in which property belonged to the society as a whole. The chief acted as the trustee of the land. African political institutions were also democratic since ordinary people had a share in decision-making. Finally, African nationalism has an ethical basis in which morality is essential. Lembede saw "morality" as "the soul of society."[10] Thomas Hodgkin used the term "nationalist" to refer to individuals, organizations, or groups who called on Africans to fight against European colonialism.[11] According to Basil Davidson, African nationalism is a desire for personal emancipation, a search for equality, rights, self-respect, and full participation in the society. It is a continuous effort to rescue Africans from perceived inferiority as a result of colonialism.[12] The present study extends this definition to include the nature of the post-colonial state as it faces the challenge of addressing economic inequality in South Africa.

Frantz Fanon's theoretical framework, based on his analysis of the Algerian national struggle, focuses on the specific economic and political conditions that were to influence the outcome of the national struggle. In *The Wretched of the Earth*, Frantz Fanon defines the national bourgeoisie in developing countries in the following terms:

> The national middle class which takes over power at the end of the colonial regime is an underdeveloped middle class. It has practically no economic power.... the national middle class discovers its historic mission: that of intermediary. Seen through its eyes, its mission has nothing to do with transforming the nation-it consists, prosaically, of being the transmission line between the nation and a capitalism, rampant though camouflaged, which today puts on the mask of neo-colonialism. The national bourgeoisie will be quite content with the role of the Western bourgeoisie's business agent.... Because it is bereft of ideas, because it lives to itself and cuts itself off from the people..., the national middle class will have nothing better to do than to take on the role of manager for Western enterprise.... We may thus conclude that this bourgeoisie in miniature that thrusts itself into the forefront is condemned to mark time, accomplishing nothing.[13]

Thus, according to Fanon, the national bourgeoisie in the developing countries was not engaged in exploration or invention as was the bourgeoisie of the mother country; instead, the national bourgeoisie was content being the West's business agent. As a result, it wallowed in the luxuries and the decadence of the mother country's bourgeois life-style without having worked for it. This situation could have been reversed, had the national bourgeoisie turned to the people who had the capacity to transform the newly independent countries. However, this would have involved the repudiation of capital, which was a risk that the national bourgeoisie was unwilling to take. The national bourgeoisie's capital was never re-invested in productive ventures. Instead, it was spent on conspicuous consumption items such as houses or cars.[14] Similarly, the national bourgeoisie could never fulfill its historical role as midwife of capitalism because it lacked any degree of economic power and was utterly dependent on the former colonial powers.

Fanon noted that there were three main reasons why middle (or bourgeois) class nationalism was an impediment to radical transformation. First, it was an underdeveloped middle class that lacked economic power.[15] Second, the nature of the colonial economy, which was set up to empower the colonial ruling class, did not encourage its development. Third, this class failed because it chose to exclude the majority of the population instead of drawing on them and their resources for governance. In other words, the national bourgeoisie did not rebel against and break away from its colonial legacy. In Fanon's view, the national liberation project should have included a revolutionary transformation of the political system and the socioeconomic infrastructure.

The only way the national bourgeoisie could have acted as a real agent of change was by following a revolutionary path. Its activities as intermediary could not lead to industrialization.[16] Such a development could only occur through the involvement of the population in an economy geared toward internal production and satisfying the majority's basic socioeconomic needs, such as access to health care, food, and shelter.

Viewed in this way, nationalism could have become a truly liberating force for sub-economic transformation. Fanon argued that two developments had to occur before this kind of outcome could have been achieved. First, the people had to challenge and fight the interests of the middle class, or the latter had to follow a revolutionary path involving the rest of the population. Second, the middle class had to be involved in both the production of ideas as well as goods and services, in other words, economic production.[17]

Fanon linked nationalism to development and democracy. According to him, democracy could only be achieved once the middle class joined the working class and the peasantry in the nationalist project, thus achieving a radical break from the colonial past. Democracy could also develop if the middle class joined with other bourgeois capitalist classes. The middle class had to become *national* like its counterpart in Europe, which was engaged in both material and intellectual production. Fanon's definition of the national bourgeoisie is used in this study.

In South Africa the national bourgeoisie is primarily made up of the white minority. The middle class that Fanon analyzed also exists in South Africa. It is made up of some Africans, Indians, people of mixed descent, and whites. It is also made up of a small section of the African National Congress, Inkatha Freedom Party, and the New National Party. This middle class enjoys a higher standard of living, better education, and higher economic and social status than the majority of the population. These diverse groups and individuals benefit as associates of the white national bourgeoisie and from national and foreign capitalism. The middle-class plays the role of an *agent*, or intermediary/go-between, in this relationship.[18] It is not a mere victim since it has political power, which it can use to manipulate the other classes, including (if necessary) the white national bourgeoisie. The primary responsibility of the middle-class is to keep the majority of the population in check so that capitalism can operate in a free and stable environment.

Amilcar Cabral analyzed the conditions in Guinea-Bissau much as Fanon did in the case of Algeria. Cabral writes about an ongoing national liberation struggle against the colonial Portuguese regime in Guinea-Bissau. In *Revolution in Guinea*, Cabral identified the following social classes: a small proletariat, peasants, and rural and urban petty bourgeoisie. Cabral divided the petty bourgeoisie into three groups. The first, comprised of higher officials and some liberal professions, made compromises with colonialism. The second was composed of wage-earners who were "employed in commerce and [as] dock workers."[19] The working class had some nationalist tendencies that connected it with the liberation struggle, but could only succeed by forming an alliance with the peasants and petty bourgeoisie. The third group was made up of *declasses,* or classless people, and was divided into two groups: beggars and prostitutes made up the first group and young jobless people in urban areas comprised the second group. Because colonialism did not allow the development of a national bourgeoisie, the petty bourgeoisie was the only hope for organizing the peasants. In order to lead a national liberation, this class had to abandon its interests and identify with the masses. In other words, the petty bourgeoisie would have to commit class suicide in order to build a socialist state.[20] This development would have allowed the petty bourgeoisie to connect with the working class's needs and with the process of national liberation. To lead, the petty bourgeoisie had to *Return to the Source*, which, for Cabral, meant returning to the masses as part of building a socialist society.[21]

Similar to Fanon, Cabral noted the petty bourgeoisie's lack of economic power. It was a service class, "that is to say a class not directly involved in the process of production does not possess the economic base to guarantee the taking over of power."[22] Hence, this class had to renounce its historical role as a service class by addressing the basic needs of the people. Viewed in this way, nationalism was an approach to solving society's economic, political, and social problems. Although Guinea Bissau is different from South Africa in terms of size, economy, class composition, and colonial history, Cabral's study enriches the present one by demonstrating the differences between revolutionary nationalism and neocolonial society. It is also an example of a different type of nationalism that followed the early wave. Unlike Cabral's, the present study demonstrates that a country does not have to be socialist to develop economically and politically.

Dan O' Meara divides the literature on Afrikaner nationalism into three parts. The early literature in Afrikaans was written by Afrikaner nationalists. It constructed their political and cultural mythology. The leading author of such works was G. D. Scholtz. According to O'Meara, Afrikaner history could be understood by looking at the role of Calvinism and the constant struggles in which the group engaged with both the British and the indigenous African people. It was the resistance to all these attacks, "on Afrikaner identity (*eie*), and the history of suffering occasioned by these struggles, which forged the Afrikaner volk."[23] Johann Gottlieb Fichte defines a *volk* "as the totality of man living together in society and constantly [developing himself] naturally and spiritually, wholly subject to a special law through which the Divine develops with him."[24] A strong identity of "us" shapes the *volk's* boundaries. According to this nationalist perspective, the Afrikaner *volk* was elevated to a special place on earth like that occupied by the Israelites in the bible. "Devine Will forged Afrikanerdom into a discrete organic unity and converted it into its special instrument."[25]

According to O'Meara, the second view of Afrikaner nationalism is written in English by liberal historians. L. M. Thompson, who is the leading critic in this genre, notes that Afrikaner historiography has failed to "present the facts fairly and draw valid conclusions from them." As a result, there is a "diseased" national outlook in which the "capacity for formulating and pursuing a rational goal becomes vitiated by illusion."[26] Thompson assumes that his own view is untainted. O'Meara notes that in questioning these myths, many historians take Afrikaner unity for granted, never questioning its presentation. Their criticism is based on moral issues, instead. C. W. de Kiewet presents Afrikaners as a community that evolved in isolation in the eighteenth century. De Villiers, who presents Afrikaners as having developed out of fear both from Africans and the British, does not improve on de Kiewet.[27] De Villiers argues that Afrikaners formed a closed society that was hostile to outside ideas. Liberal authors who are opposed to the National Party have also written about Afrikaner nationalism. In this vein, O'Meara notes that such authors, like Leo Marquard, have failed to read what the Afrikaners write about themselves.

P. Eric Louw divides the academic literature on apartheid into liberal, Marxist and Afrikaner nationalist. Liberal authors viewed Afrikaners as racist bigots because of the influence of the frontier tradition, which forced them to live in isolation. Apartheid was viewed as a product of primitive people: "Because liberals viewed ethnic mobilization as a backward anachronism in the modern world, they made no attempt to actually engage with Afrikaner nationalist thinking."[28] Marxist and neo-Marxists focused on the development of capitalism in South Africa. Some like Slovo, Wolpe, and Yudelman argued that capitalism had profited from racism in South Africa. Marxists and neo-Marxists also focused on cheap labor and the class dimensions of South Africa's capitalist economy. Several debates arose between Marxists and liberals over the nature of apartheid. According to Louw, these two perspectives did not engage with the Afrikaner nationalists. The following were the core concerns of the Afrikaner nationalist perspective:

- Anglos subjugated Afrikaners. Establishing an Afrikaner-controlled state was seen as a way to end both Afrikaner impoverishment (at the hands of Anglo capitalism) and the destruction of Afrikaner culture/language (by Anglo cultural imperialism).

- Afrikaners feared future subjugation at the hands of black people. Such subjugation was seen as the likely outcome of demographic shifts (triggered by World War II), combined with post-World War II international reconfigurations. Apartheid was designed to counter this threat of black subjugation.[29]

Edwin Munger compares African to Afrikaner nationalism. According to his argument, charismatic leadership is the first phase of nationalism. In the second phase, the elite extends its ideas to include economic issues with a social class structure. The final phase of nationalism is marked by organized political parties, a feeling of national identity, and interactions with other countries.[30] Gail Gerhart highlights the ideological differences between the ANC, BCM, and the PAC. Her study focuses on the apartheid state, which the present one extends to post-apartheid South Africa. Gerhart analyzes the ideological roots of African nationalism by focusing on the leaderships of the ANC, Pan Africanist Congress (PAC), and Black Consciousness Movement (BCM). She divides African nationalists into realists (moderate assimilationists) and rebels (non assimilationists). Peter Walshe traces the rise of African nationalism in South Africa to the first half of the nineteenth century. According to him, Christianity and Western education played a major role in creating an African elite that challenged European colonialism. This elite used peaceful methods to agitate for its rights. Because of missionary influence, this elite believed in the sense of justice and fair play in the British liberal system. John Dube (ANC president) declared that Africans were going to place "hopeful reliance in the sense of common justice and love of freedom so innate in the British character" to fight for their rights.[31] According to Walshe's argument, non-racialism was practical because the interdependent nature of the economy made it impossible for different races to be independent of one another.

BENEDICT ANDERSON'S IMAGINED COMMUNITIES

Cultural studies have influenced the study of nationalism in three ways. By looking at cultural representation, some authors have found a different way of defining and understanding nationalism. These authors also looked at diverse groups within a society to understand how they are represented within the nationalist movement. "For nationalism to do its work, ordinary people need to see themselves as the bearers of an identity centered elsewhere, imagine themselves as an abstract community."[32] This is not just about subjective cultural identification, but it helps one to articulate how these abstract and real communities work. Viewed in this way, nationalism emerges as an "invention," part of what Benedict Anderson described as "imagined communities." The way the nation is represented and authorized forms the core of cultural studies. The present project is interested in the study of the cultural representation of apartheid as "exclusionary" and "separate" in comparison to the representation of South African nationalism as "multiracial" and its use of democracy to forge a new South African community. According to Benedict Anderson, the nation is "an imagined political community-and imagined as both inherently limited and sovereign. It is *imagined* because the members of even the smallest nation will never know most of their fellow-members, meet them, or even hear of them." Modern national communities imagined themselves in a distinct way, yet "in the minds of each lives the image of their communion."[33] According to Ernest Gellner, "Nationalism is not the awakening of nations to self-consciousness: it *invents* nations where they do not exist."[34] These communities are imagined as limited because each has its own boundaries, which separates it from others regardless of size. Nations are also:

> sovereign because the concept was born in an age in which enlightenment and revolution were destroying the legitimacy of the divinely-ordained, hierarchical dynastic realm. Coming to maturity at a stage of human history when even the most devout adherents of any universal religion were inescapably confronted with the living *pluralism* of such religions, and the allomorphism between each faith's ontological claims and territorial stretch, nations dream of being free, and, if under God, directly so. The gage and emblem of this freedom is the sovereign state.[35]

Finally, "it is imagined as a *community*, because, regardless of the actual inequality and exploitation that may prevail in each, the nation is always conceived as a deep, horizontal comradeship."[36]

Anderson presents four historical models of imagined communities. The Creole communities of the Americas developed the first national model between 1760 and 1830. They shared the language of the rulers, but not the privileges. Creole birth restricted the mobility of the functionaries in the imperial bureaucracies. Regardless of their bureaucratic performance, their administrative journey was restricted to the colony. But, journeying as clerks, teachers, or businessmen, they met other Creoles who shared this experience and knowledge of the colony. These travelers thought of the places that they visited through as "home"; this shaped and defined the way they imagined themselves and their communities. Newspapers that reported local events and interests also reinforced this sense of community. According to Anderson "neither economic interest, Liberalism, nor Enlightenment could, or did, create *in themselves* the *kind*, or shape, of imagined community to be defended from these regimes' depredations; to put it another way, none provided the framework of a new consciousness-the scarcely seen periphery of its vision-as opposed to centre-field objects of its admiration or disgust."[37] It was Creole print men who were crucial in shaping how the community imagined itself. One could read about important events or figures in the community. The local news reports caught the imagination of the readers as they began thinking of themselves as cohesive and distinct.

Anderson places the second model between 1820 and 1920, when national print-languages developed in Europe. For the first time, languages spoken and used by people in their daily lives were used in print. They replaced Latin as the sacred language of the previous religious communities. In Austro-Hungary, the dynasty chose German to replace Latin as a unifying language.[38] German was chosen for its vast literature and culture. Speakers of vernacular languages realized that they "were entitled to their place in a fraternity of equals."[39] Dictionaries and other books on grammar appeared, accelerating pride in these languages as a basis of community. Unlike Latin, print languages spread across regions and class because they were languages that people used every day. The main actors in this process were professionals, land owners, nobles/aristocrats, schools, and universities. But this so-called "populist" development had its own relations of power. Only those who could read (nobles, aristocrats, and land owners) could access print media, leaving out poor and illiterate groups. Additionally, the adoption of a particular dialect that became identified as proper English or German gave its speakers added power and influence.

The third model of imagined communities is described as "official nationalism." It developed over the last half of the nineteenth century. Empires used official languages first to nationalize the empire at home and then to unify it with its different colonies. It made nations out of their diverse ethnic and linguistic groups. Official nationalism sought to naturalize dynastic power and fit the empire into the nation. Dominant empires used new languages to administer their regions without abandoning their power. The state and its educational system were the core actors in this model. For example, the Baltic provinces were subjected to active Russification. This was a violent, totalitarian policy of forcing people to adopt Russian through schools and university systems.[40] There were revolts against Russification. In the colonies, imperial powers such as Britain focused on anglicization policies. According to Anderson, official nationalism was a reaction to the previous populist European linguistic nationalism and that of the Creoles in the Americas.

Anderson calls the fourth model of imagined community the "last Wave" dating from the post World War II period to the present. Nation-states replaced empires and dynasties in the last wave. The states involved in this stage were mostly non-European, even though European languages remained as the languages of the state. According to Anderson, three factors contributed to the rise of imagined communities that contested the legitimacy of colonial rule. First, better communication made it possible for people to be exposed to new ideas such as equality and self-determination and to better communicate with each other. Second, for administrative purposes, colonial powers needed personnel proficient in vernacular languages. Given the sizes of the colonies, it was no longer feasible to solely have European administrators. As a result, local vernacular language speakers had to be trained as administrators. Western education produced a bilingual intelligentsia that played a most important role due to the absence of local bourgeoisies.[41]

African and Afrikaner nationalisms fall into what Anderson calls the "last wave" model of nationalism. According to his argument, "the last wave of nationalism, most of them in the colonial territories of Asia and Africa, was in its origins a response to the new style of global imperialism made possible by the achievement of industrial capitalism."[42] British industrial demand for labor shaped nationalism in South Africa. This demand continued under apartheid. Between 1918 and 1948, Afrikaners concentrated on improving their cultural, economic, and social status through various organizations. Their grievances against the British brought them close to the bilingual intellectuals of the colonies. To progress culturally, economically, or politically in British-controlled South Africa, Afrikaners had to be bilingual. In 1948, the Afrikaner nationalist party won political control over the state. This can be viewed as the climax of Afrikaner nationalism. A bilingual intelligentsia that rejected and challenged British colonialism and apartheid and its exclusionary form of racial nationalism also fueled South African nationalism.

In 1959, the apartheid government introduced the "Promotion of Bantu Self-Government Act." According to this Act, 87 percent of the land belonged to the white minority while the remaining 13 percent was allocated to the African majority.[43] To this end, the Transkei Bantustan was granted self-government in 1963. The state needed to train Africans to administer the Bantustans. It also needed them for unskilled labor. As Africans of all classes traveled from one region to another, they met others who also suffered from the same exclusionary policies and regulations in the name of racism.

The apartheid regime designed Bantustan policy to separate Africans from the white minority. It was also intended to separate the various African ethnic groups from each other. Instead, this policy became the focus of African resistance against white domination. It contributed in its own way in defining an "imagined community" that was governed by the white minority's exclusionary rules and the daily rituals of oppression. Political violence, school boycotts, rent strikes, and police presence in most African townships influenced the way Africans imagined their community. Africans faced oppression in the private and public spheres where they were condemned to menial jobs, poverty, and lower standards in housing and schooling. This common oppression sharpened their sense of community. The present study aims at understanding how this experience with racism led the ANC to culturally represent its desired community as "multiracial" and to use democracy to forge this new South African community.

Anderson's framework highlights the role of print capitalism, vernacular language, the novel, education, and bilingual intelligentsia in facilitating the process through which people "imagined" their communities. One of the functions of the Afrikaner cultural movements was to produce literature in Afrikaans. This helped shape how they imagined themselves. Education was very important in facilitating an imagined community because it emphasized the Afrikaners' duty to protect the country. It also determined who their "enemies" were by emphasizing common suffering. According to Afrikaner education and mythology, South Africa was a "white man's country." Among the Africans, colonial education was a chronicle of past military defeats at the hands of either the Afrikaners or the British. Africans were represented as people without culture and history who were dependent on whites. The social structure where whites were represented as superior to Africans was reproduced through educational institutions. Colonial education also raised the level of frustration among Africans because their social mobilization was limited under apartheid.[44] Education highlighted their sense of oppression and exclusion, which contributed to how Africans imagined their nation as inclusive as opposed to apartheid's exclusive nation.

The present study investigates the connection between late nationalism and democracy, using South Africa as a case in point. It uses Benedict Anderson's framework. According to this author, late nationalism developed after the Second World War when colonialism was under attack. In the case of South Africa, this period covers the climax of Afrikaner nationalism when it came to power in 1948. It continues until the early 1990s with the last wave of democratization that included Eritrea, Namibia, and South Africa. This wave occurred under different circumstances. Thus, after the fall of the Communist Block, capitalism remained the sole economic system; as a result, globalization and intense economic competition between various actors followed. In order to connect late nationalism to democracy, we need to review some of the approaches of the authors on the subject.

South Africa's Transition from Apartheid to Multiracial Democracy

In an edited volume on transitions from authoritarian rule to democracy and the prospects for democracy in Southern Europe and Latin America, Guillermo O'Donnell and Philippe C. Schmitter define transitions as the "interval from one political regime to another."[45] The transitions are limited by the historical setting of the particular actors involved as well as by the actors' interests. The various trajectories of transitions, whether through negotiation, revolution, or war, also determine how democracy is consolidated in a post-authoritarian society. Transitions by pact-making are based on the experiences of Southern Europe, Latin America and Eastern Europe. During a transition, political leaders make deals about the order of a future society. Guillermo O'Donnell and Phillipe C. Schmitter define pacts as

> [an] explicit, but not always publicly explicated or justified, agreement among a select set of actors which seeks to define (or better, redefine) rules governing the exercise of power on the basis of mutual guarantees for the "vital interests" of those entering into it . . . At the core of a pact lies a negotiated compromise under which actors agree to forgo or underutilize their capacity to harm each other by extending guarantees not to threaten each other's corporate autonomies or vital interests.[46]

Transitions by pact-making best explain South Africa's transition from apartheid and authoritarian rule to multiracial liberal democracy. These transitions are mostly elite-based. They may be made temporarily to allow the elite to negotiate or in a permanent manner if the elite decide to adopt them after the negotiations. They involve negotiations between authoritarian regimes and left-wing parties. The latter makes compromises to the right to accommodate the outgoing regime. Pacts are biased against popular participation because the people's needs are neither taken into account nor represented (as was the case in Chile). Transitions by pact-making are viewed as a way of achieving democracy by undemocratic means because they limit the issues and actors involved in the process. Democratization through pacts involves a bargain over alternative institutions between the party in power and its opponents. This type of transition is important for divided societies such as South Africa.

According to Pierre du Toit, competing parties within South Africa were so dependent on each other that no particular one could dominate the transition. Incentives and rewards had to be used to encourage compromises. But since each party's needs were different from the other, all parties had to agree on a pact. The moderate center from the ANC and the NP was active in this process by eliminating extremist forces such as the far right and the Pan Africanist Congress (PAC). A pact was also important in South Africa because together, the ANC, the NP, and Inkatha Freedom Party (IFP) held "the balance of terror in South African politics."[47] Each party had enough constituents to make peace impossible. The NP could draw on its economic resources to block economic growth, while both the ANC and IFP could make peace elusive by advocating violence. As a result of their mutual dependence, these parties had to form a pact, which forced them to work toward a common goal.

Van Zyl Slabbert's *The Quest for Democracy: South Africa in Transition* rejects the approaches developed by theorists of democratic modernization that emphasize certain institutional and structural conditions for democracy. According to him, the preconditions might instead actually be outcomes of democracy. Slabbert's approach looks at the following:

> The critical role of key *political actors* and their *strategic choices* concerning democracy, democratization and each other; to locate these choices within the context of *opportunities and obstacles* that have to be exploited or overcome; and then plot a *probable outcome* to the process. In this way structural factors are seen as interacting with strategic choices of key actors rather than predetermining them, which provides a more reliable picture of the dynamics of transition.[48]

Van Zyl Slabbert argues that the debate on democracy in the world scene followed two trends. The first trend was the presence of free enterprise economies and an emerging common belief on the value of democracy. In this type of democracy, competitors follow established "rules of the game" which are codified by a constitution that protects people's rights. Slabbert identifies four models of transitions. According to the first model, a pact is made between domestic actors and those outside the regime such as leaders within the international community. In this model of transition, leaders agree that the regime needs to be transformed as a result of political, economic, and social pressure. The second model is based on transition that is carried out as a result of some form of imposition by one particular force. It can be an outside force such as investors, the military, or strong opposition within the regime. The third model states that regimes can reform as a result of mass pressure from popular movements. Finally, within the fourth model, regimes can carry out a transition as a result of a revolution that replaces the old regime. The author argues that the type of transition that a regime carries out determines the outcomes of democracy. According to Slabbert, transitions that focus on pacts between leaders rather than bottom-up processes based on reform or revolution are more likely to stabilize into a democratic system.

According to Van Zyl Slabbert, there were "planned/unplanned as well as internal/external pressures for change" in South Africa. Unplanned pressures included population increase among Africans in urban centers, placing pressure on the government to provide services. Planned internal pressures refer to the political uprisings of the late 1970s and early to mid-1980s. The end of the Cold War, which meant that South Africa could no longer use the spread of Communism to obtain U.S. support, was an example of unplanned external pressure.

The international community's isolation of South Africa is an example of planned external pressures that forced the state to negotiate. Slabbert focused on the problems that the negotiators would encounter during the negotiation process. The first problem dealt with normalization or liberalization, which meant extending rights to groups that were excluded by the previous regime. The other problem had to do with *democratization*, which meant that previously excluded groups had to be involved in various levels of decision-making in the new regime. Slabbert's main concern was with the problems of normalization and democratization. According to Slabbert, successful consolidation of democracy depended on four agreements amongst the main actors. These include "a civil-military pact; an economic contract; an agreement on redistribution and development; and consensus on a new democratic constitution."[49]

Drawing on the work of Michel Foucault, Edward Said, and Robert Cox, Rita Abrahmsen shows how development discourse has constructed the third world as underdeveloped, and thereby normalized and legitimized the right of the North (developed) to intervene in, control, and develop the South (underdeveloped). According to Abrahmsen, the 'good governance' discourse is merely the latest reproduction of the 'dream of development' and similarly entitles the North to develop and democratize the South in its image. The South becomes the object of the North's development activities. Development discourse thus emerges as crucial to an understanding of recent transitions to multi-party democracy in Africa. Abrahamsen further argues that many newly elected governments in Africa face two irreconcilable constituencies: external donors and creditors and their poor domestic majorities. While African governments are crucially dependent on each for their financial survival and re-election respectively, they cannot satisfy both at the same time; the first casualty of this dilemma is the democratic process itself. She argues that the form of democracy demanded by donors and creditors (including the Bretton Woods institutions) offers African incumbents and elites the possibility of holding on to or capturing power without having to satisfy demands for social welfare and economic redistribution at home. In this sense, says Abrahamsen, a *de facto* alliance occurs between the African elites and the donors and creditors: they share a broadly similar conceptualization of democracy that centers on political rights and economic liberalism.[50]

Drawing on the work of O'Donnell and Schmitter on Latin America, Abrahamsen makes some observations that are quite relevant to the South African situation. Discussing 'democratic pacts' as a specific feature of transition processes in Latin America (and South Africa), she notes that such pacts were negotiated among established, highly hierarchical elites and aimed at reassuring traditional dominant classes that their vital interests would not be jeopardized under democracy (including amnesty from prosecution). But at the same time, such democratic pacts may serve as a vehicle through which elements of the previous authoritarian regime continue to influence the new democracy. In this manner, pacts may entail the marginalization of popular demands for improved living standards or allow fairly minimal and gradual transformation in gross social and economic inequalities. In South Africa, the gradual transition from the initial populist economic and social transformation program *(Reconstruction and Development Programme)* to the World Bank and IMF inspired GEAR *(Growth, Employment and Redistribution)* program in 1996, perfectly illustrates this situation.

OUTLINE

In this study, I will use Benedict Anderson's *Imagined Communities* to analyze African and Afrikaner nationalism in South Africa. According to Anderson, capitalism, through a capitalist economy, a centralized state, schools, print media and Western educated elites that later challenged colonialism, greatly influenced how nationalism developed. The role of educational institutions, churches, and language in shaping nationalism is also examined. I will also use Frantz Fanon's analysis of the national bourgeoisie in *The Wretched of the Earth* to analyze the problem faced by the liberal democratic experiment in South Africa. Chapter 1 provides a historical overview of the economic, cultural, political, and racial factors that contributed to the development of African nationalism from 1867 to 1948. Chapter 2 looks at Afrikaner nationalism from 1867 to 1948. It seeks to answer the following questions: Which factors contributed to the development of Afrikaner nationalism? What role did intellectuals play in this process? Did women play a pivotal role in the Afrikaner nation? I will also examine the similarities and differences between African and Afrikaner nationalisms in Chapter 2. Chapter 3 focuses on the impact of apartheid on both African and Afrikaner nationalisms. It shows how apartheid established the exclusive character of the nationalism of the National Party, provoking different types of African nationalist reactions dominated by the African National Congress. This chapter also examines both the ANC and NP's respective conception and definition of the South African community and political economy, as well as their views on the role of class, gender, and race. I discuss their conceptions of inter-racial and inter-class relations from 1948 to 1994. In Chapter 4, critical perspectives on both African and Afrikaner nationalisms presented in novels and short stories are examined. As social critics, novelists present another perspective on nationalism that differs from the mainstream version. Through their characters, authors reveal apartheid's daily impact on average citizens. These authors' works force the reader to understand the pain of being evicted the pain of being fired from a job; life in *Sheebens* (local bars based in townships); or how nationalism hurts those it claims to protect.

In Chapter 5 we analyze the changes experienced by the South African capitalist economy, the contradictory demands of this economy, and how these demands contributed to the development of a new NP debate that reflected a loss of faith in apartheid. Economic sanctions alone could not have resulted in the regime's fall. These sanctions became lethal when they were combined with disagreements over the accumulation process within the Afrikaner ruling class, increased domestic and international opposition, and the fall of the Portuguese colonial regimes in Angola and Mozambique. Slowly, a regime that had seemed all-powerful and invincible began to crack. In Chapter 6 we examine the process of negotiations for a democratic South Africa, raising the following questions: Who were the main actors? What demands were made? How were these negotiations viewed nationally and internationally? This chapter also examines the conflicting interests of key supporters and of the apartheid regime's critics. In the process, we also analyze key compromises made between the National Party and the African National Congress. Chapter 7 reviews the ANC's attempt at affecting economic and social change for the benefit of different racial, class, and gender groups in post apartheid South Africa. The main argument in this chapter is that the "historic compromise" between the African National Congress and the National Party (reminiscent of Antonio Gramsci's *Compromesso storico*) will continue to affect South Africa's attempts at socio-economic transformation. These compromises include an economy that is almost exclusively under the white minority and foreign business control and an economy that is marked by minimal and very slow land reform based on a willing seller/buyer premise, an unreformed justice system, and a security apparatus and government policies that privilege the market over social needs. Chapter 8 includes empirical and theoretical conclusions on the relationship between African and Afrikaner Nationalisms, as well as on the pitfalls of liberal democracy.

Conclusion

We have reviewed Frantz Fanon's *The Wretched of the Earth* and Benedict Anderson's *Imagined Communities*. In both, we have seen the crucial role of the middle class in the development of nationalism. Fanon emphasized the need for the middle class to reject its colonial legacy by following a revolutionary path, which would link it to the popular masses as well as to development. Anderson demonstrates how capitalism fueled nationalism by enabling diverse members of communities to "imagine" their common destiny even though they may not have met every member of the community. This process of "imagining" is made possible by print-media, communication, and the development of the middle class.

The ANC and the role of the NP's elite in the transition are best explained by pact-making. Transitions by pact-making focus on the role of external and internal actors during transitions. The United States, the European Union, and the former Soviet Union were crucial in deciding the trajectory of South Africa's democratic transition. The World Bank and the International Monetary Fund were also pivotal in determining the type of economy South Africa would eventually adopt. Furthermore, local business interests also influenced the transition. In the next chapter we will examine the trajectory of African nationalism.

CHAPTER 1

THE AFRICAN IMAGINED COMMUNITY, 1867–1948

Certainly ours is a hard lot, for when we remain in our heathen state, we are blamed and when we follow the white people's customs we are found fault with. What shall we do?

—*Ilanga*

The missionaries had negatively labeled the traditional ways, calling them paths of darkness, paganism and worshipping false deities like *uMvelinqangi* (the one who was present at the beginning) and *uNkulunkulu* (the Great one).

—Thula Bopela and Daluxolo Luthuli, *Unkhonto we Sizwe: Fighting for a Divided People.*

INTRODUCTION

IN THIS CHAPTER WE WILL TRACE THE INTELLECTUAL DEVELOPMENT OF THE African conceptualization of imagined national communities. We will do so by examining the factors that influenced the Africans' conception of community, its specific characteristics, relations with other communities and how relations among groups within the community affected its development. For the sake of clarity, this chapter is divided into five sections. In the first section, the European views of Africans are traced up to 1910. Section two looks at the impact of missionary activities on the development of this imagined community between 1867 and 1910. Section three examines political representations of the community by analyzing the role of the African National Congress from 1912 to 1948. Part four looks at gender roles in the African imagined community. A short conclusion concludes this chapter.

European Constructions of Africans, 1867–1910

Various African indigenous groups occupied the southern tip of Africa before the arrival of the Dutch in 1652. These were the Khoisan and Khoikhoi, in the Cape; and Tswana-Sotho-Pedi in the northern area; and the Nguni (Zulu and Xhosa) in the east and the south (present day Natal, East and Central Cape, and Swaziland). Once the Cape of Good Hope was established as a colonial outpost in 1652, any group of people that challenged this assumption was deemed "the natural enemies of the Europeans in South Africa."[1] Most of the early accounts of Southern Africa are by travelers, missionaries, or ship wrecked sailors. These accounts refer to Africans as "Hottentots," "savages," "Bushmen," "Natives," "Negro," and "Heathen." The term "Kaffir" appears in the early travel accounts of missionaries' and other people. It became popular during slavery and is believed to have been introduced through the slave trade. "Kaffir" became a generic term designating a pagan deemed unworthy of human dignity and rights.

The first encounter between Dutch colonizers and the indigenous community resulted in master/slave relations. Progressively, these relations became competitive and hostile, as Dutch colonizers encroached on indigenous land. To Britain, Southern Africa was a backward agricultural country, until the discovery of diamonds in 1867 transformed this view. The British government was determined to control South Africa's wealth. Its companies invested in the mines while the government sought to strengthen its control over the region. This was made possible by promoting the idea of empire, which was also becoming popular at home. Though Britain had been an empire for a long time, during this period "empire" meant founding colonies. The creation of a "Greater Britain" meant the extension of British culture, as well as political and economic control over "native" countries. As the wealthiest country, Britain regarded itself as the world's leader: "to develop and enlarge the empire was for such people a crusade against ignorance and backwardness and corrupt native governments and the many failings of the lesser breeds without the law."[2] The idea of empire was in conflict with the Africans' imagined community since they already occupied the territory claimed by the British.

By the late 18th century African images were of great interest in European middle class circles with an interest in Africa. Debates on Africa reached a wider audience because of the invention of the print-media, and the wide diffusion of newspapers, journals, books, and pamphlets. These debates projected African images that justified European domination.[3] Debates also focused on the role of Africa as the antithesis of Europe. Africa came to represent all that Europe was not, for example, it was "uncivilized," ruled by "emotion" and "eroticism" rather than "reason" and "rationalism." The outlook and perspectives of European missionaries, colonialists, geographers, and scientists were influenced by these debates. These people depicted Africa as a passive object waiting to be "reborn" and re-energized through various European forces. Reports about the Cape depicted vast empty lands and wildlife ready to be "taken."[4] Each of these debates and images had their aims, "and together, by virtue of both their form and their content, they established the dark continent as a metaphysical stage on which various white crusaders struck moral pastures."[5]

European perception of Africa shaped imperial policy, but also informed the African community. As a result, it developed within set racial boundaries. Britain first got interested in the Cape when it took it over as a result of its war with France in 1795. John Barrow, the founder of the Royal Geographical Society, wrote an *Account of Travels into the Interior of Southern Africa in the Years 1797 and 1798* (1801–1804). To Barrow, the land lacked "civilization" because it was left in its natural state. It needed to be demarcated and fenced out in an orderly way. Space in the Cape had to be organized to reflect European "civilization."[6] According to Barrow the land needed a "civilized" power to control it since the Dutch were presumed to have lost their "Europeaness." Barrow's book provided a map of the Cape, which presented it to Britain for the taking. Each contour of the land was set out, the valleys, mountains, and rivers divided with sharp lines marked in red. The map was devoid of any inhabitants. This map denied Africans their claim to the land. Barrow's book was also an eyewitness of the "degeneration" of the Dutch under the influence of the rugged African environment. Africans were portrayed generally as passive and dependent beings.

Barrow believed that the Dutch had mistreated "nature's innocents" through extermination instead of elevating them to a higher level of civilization through forced cultivation. Barrow depicted Africans as children who danced whenever their passions moved them and slept in beds "like the nest of an Ostrich." They were low "on the scale of humanity" but also raw material for the civilizing project.[7] Barrows' account shaped the views of the missionaries. In these representations, certain features were associated with intelligence and civilization. For example, Buffon looked at hair, stature and physiognomy and declared that white was "the real and natural color of man."[8] The rest of humanity came to be judged based on these standards. The shape of the skull was also used to demonstrate that Africans were closer to apes. Blumenberg used African's skull shapes to support his claim that the Ethiopian was the "lowliest deviation from the most beautiful" Caucasian type"[9] Following in Blumenberg's footsteps, the Dutch scholar Camper devised a scale that correlated the shape of the skull to physical looks and mental ability. His scale moved from dog to ape to "Negro" to the European and the idealized beauty in Greek sculpture. Thus, Camper inscribed the stereotypic bodily contours of non-Europeans on the European imagination. "His sample African profile, for instance, a distinctly bestial representation, was to become standard in nineteenth century texts on racial difference; significantly, these texts gave prominence to images of black South Africans"[10]

Georges Cuvier, a Swiss comparative anatomist, developed a scale to examine the perfection of intellect as well as the moral core of a person. He did so by measuring the degree of a person's dependence on external sensations based on the proportion of the mid-cranial area to that of the face. This test revealed either one's ability to reason and self control or lack of both. On this count, the "Negro" stood between the "most ferocious apes and the Europeans, who were themselves superseded by men and deities of ancient Greek sculpture."[11] Cuvier believed that self-control and intelligence were underdeveloped among indigenous people. Through these views and images, a particular way of knowing that justified domination was set in place. According to Jean and John Comaroff,

> the great chain of being, a vertical scale, had been set on its side, becoming also a linear history of human progress from the peripheral regions of the earth to its north European core. The hard facts of organic form, it seemed, could now explain and determine the place of men in the world.[12]

These writings influenced travelers to South Africa. For example, Cuvier's account provided information on the "Bushmen" as pygmy "plunderers" who "lurk[ed]" in the complicit woods and bushes."[13] This description was drawn from Lichtenstein. It is later found in Reverend Edwards' "eyewitness" account of 1886.[14] "The Interplay of other epithets in The Animal Kingdom-Hottentots as degraded and disgusting, or as swarthy, filthy, and greasy-may be traced to Lichtenstein."[15] These conceptions also took in gender within the distinct parameters set by the reorganization of production and the age of the industrial revolution during which exploitation of other people based on race or sex was believed to be "natural." Women were presented as hysterical, weak and stupid in these images. Reason and intelligence were men's faculties. This view of women in Europe was extended to Africa.

In *Animal Kingdom*, Cuvier described Saartje Bartman, the "Hottentot Venus," as an "essential black" from the Cape Colony. She was of Khoi ancestry and was exhibited in both England and France until her death in Paris in 1815. Her body ended up on Cuvier's table, where he dissected her and described her "organ of generation" which in its excessive development of the *Labia Minora* was held to set her kind apart "from the rest of humanity."[16] Barrow had also written of the genital aberrations of Khoisan women. According to Jean and John Comaroff, the obsession with Africa as an erotic place and of its female as the ultimate representation of that eroticism was set in place as biological study. Africa was therefore reduced to an African female waiting for the white man to rescue "her."[17]

These popular beliefs about Africa were plagued by contradictions. For example, the liberal ideology was based on "equality" between mankind, but its foundation (capitalist production) was based on the material exploitation of difference and inequality. As a result of these conceptions, Africa came to represent a place of "savagery" and "degenerates" where nature was depicted as man's enemy. The African "savage" was the obverse of the European "civilized" man. The latter was assertive and aggressive always, on the move and therefore determining his destiny. The African was a passive object who was there to be made into whatever the civilized man decided he could be. In South Africa, sometimes missionaries presented this image by establishing the African as the "degenerate" other, then "they would take hold of him in a transforming grasp that would harness his brute potential, making him into a lowlier, artless version of themselves."[18] South Africa was presented as both "savage nature" and innocent. These images were not constant. They changed depending on the issues involved. For example, prior to the rise of capitalism, Africans were depicted in a positive light worthy of the civilizing mission. Afterwards, with the introduction of colonialism, labor shortage, European racial propaganda, which denigrated Africans, accelerated.

European beliefs about Africa also influenced imagined communities in South Africa. Dutch settlers believed in white supremacy—the belief that the white race was superior to all the other races. Europeans held all the high positions in the Dutch East India Company. They also had slaves. Since the number of freed slaves was so small, they never acquired enough wealth to challenge European hegemony. Furthermore (as Richard Elphick and Hermann Giliomee demonstrate), poor Europeans, free Africans, Khoi and people of mixed race competed for the same positions in society thus making unity impossible. Another factor that reinforced white supremacy were the ties of the European with their fellow poor whites. A poor white was entitled to the same respect as a rich one. New laws were introduced representing whites as distinct from all the other races while burdening other racial groups with legal barriers, thus placing them in disadvantaged positions.[19] According to Elphick and Giliomee, white supremacy was not a coherent policy. Instead, it developed out of stereotypes regarding the different races. A tax report of the Cape Society in 1800 demonstrates that by this period the term "non-European" was emerging in European imaginings of their community. The list noted: "one of the European who were permanent inhabitants, one of ex-company servants, and one of those who belong to the Free Corps [for mixed-race people] as well as the free blacks, Bastards and other Hottentots that live on their own and are not in the service of others."[20] These diverse groups were not lumped together by a uniform ideology that led to the development of white supremacy; rather, they were bound by the assumption that *Europeans* were "unique and special."[21] As a result of this belief, Europeans occupied the best positions in the economy, society and political structure of the Cape society. Some members of other racial groups who were 'light' enough to "pass" for Europeans became some of the most respected leaders of Cape society.

White supremacy was also enforced because of the position of white women in the society as its moral markers. As a result, European men who had love affairs with "natives" could not marry them, nor could they accept their children. If they did, they were ostracized from society. Europeans who chose to live among Africans were also ostracized for living among "Heathens." In Cape society, two groups of people who constantly challenged white supremacy developed. These were "free Africans," whom Europeans saw as competitors who took over their positions, and the "Bastards." Free Africans were often educated in European culture, but were discriminated against on the bases of their color. "Bastards" were children resulting from intercourse between Europeans and all the other races. Culturally and linguistically, these 'Bastards' imagined themselves as Dutch. Both groups occupied ambiguous positions in the emerging imagined community.[22] By the beginning of the 19th century, color in the Cape came to be used as reversion against slaves as well as free Africans' culture and their "heathen" beliefs. To be European or white was associated with Christianity and civilization while other races were considered "savages." These traits marked imagined communities that later emerged. For example the imagined community of whites was marked by exclusive and rigid racial boundaries, while the African imagined community was informed by patronizing missionary and Victorian humanitarian values that emphasized man's universality.[23]

Relations between Africans and Europeans were also shaped by the material forces present in South Africa during this period. For example, with the rise of capitalism, journals, pamphlets, books, newspapers, and other forms of print media became sites of increased debates that privileged race. One of the popular stories in these newspapers focused on concerns of settlers about labor shortages. Other stories dealt with cases about Africans "stealing" from whites. There were also stories about Africans who were punished for committing crimes against whites. For example, on 4 July 1833, the *Grahamstown Journal*, a conservative paper, wrote a story on an African accused of murder. The accused was marched across town with onlookers on each side of the street. According to the account the accused sat on his coffin and conducted himself "with a steady composure and a firmness yet decency of demeanor that was highly becoming, "as the procession moved off preceded and followed by a guard from his majesty's 75th Regiment' in the direction of death. At the gallows the African lost his composure and "trembled excessively" as he "gazed at the awful preparations around him with that dismay they were so well calculated to inspire."[24] The story goes on to describe how in prison the accused had converted to the Christian God. At the hanging, the missionary stood by to watch over the accused who was to be hanged for murdering a British colonialist. When the corpse was limp, it was taken to be examined by a surgeon. The image of the whole spectacle was powerful: an anonymous African hanged by the state while a missionary (the society's moral marker) as well as colonialists and a number of "Blacks" looked on. Even in death, the African was nameless and therefore unimportant. What is crucial in this narrative is the complete domination of colonial forces over Africans.

In South Africa, racist propaganda that popularized beliefs of Africans as "lazy" and "thieves" increased with the discovery of minerals in the Transvaal in the later 19th century. Such racist propaganda aimed at establishing the view that the African was not worthy of equal rights with the white man, therefore justifying domination.[25] Based on this view African labor would lay the foundation of the colony without its economic benefits. Colonial settlers never engaged in manual labor, a tradition that persists in contemporary South Africa. After spending six months at the diamond mines in 1871, Sir Charles Paston observed that "it is quite sufficient for them [whites] to sit under an awning and sort, leaving the Kaffirs to perform all the other stages of work."[26] These racist beliefs structured state and civil society. They also consolidated the capitalist economy by making it more efficient through the ready availability of unlimited supply of cheap labor. As a result, the white minority community increasingly represented Africans in a negative manner. Not only was the skin color of Africans under attack, but their morality was also questioned. They were typically depicted as bloodthirsty murderers. Europeans killed "Kaffirs," but Africans "murdered" Europeans.[27]

In South Africa, race determined a person's professional specialization and job category. For example, whites were "thinkers" while Africans were manual laborers. G. R. Peppercorne (Natal's magistrate from 1850 to 1852), marveled at the success of cheap African labor: "in no other country in the world could an adult be found washing women's clothes, taking care of babies and carrying out general housework duties."[28] A narrow distinction was made between economic and moral needs. For example, a Natal Commission set out to investigate labor shortage ordered all Africans to be decently dressed, therefore forcing Africans into the European economy as laborers to provide for the new 'needs'. Such racial division of labor also boosted the European economy. Missionaries also preached against nakedness: to be 'civilized' one had to dress.[29] Africans were not passive during this process. They refused to be "objects" by resisting forced labor. Zulu and Xhosa men refused to work in the mines, forcing agents to seek labor outside South Africa. Most workers ran away from mines. Resistance took many forms. For example, workers could 'go slow' when they produced the bare minimum in spite of the pressure. They also refused to follow orders by faking illness. Some workers organized rebellions or simply ran away and out of the colonial system.

In these colonial debates Africans were presented as the "other" (uncivilized) in opposition to Whites who were presented as the epitome of civilization. According to Edward Said, this notion of the "other" has four essential features: (1) the geographical, cultural, economic, and political differences are created; (2) it involves relations of unequal power; (3) the dominant group establishes the standard of evaluation for both groups and in this way privileges itself; and (4) the differences are "naturalized in discourse."[30] Darwinism (a popular theory during this period) also justified domination. In 1852, Cole wrote that "the fate of the Black man . . . [will be that] his race is exterminated. The Kaffir's time is well-nigh come."[31] Speaking of the Xhosa, Steadman (an Englishman), noted that their very sight produced in a white man the worst reaction. African communities were also represented as disorganized. They could only be "saved" by the arrival of the white man whose presence ensured "peace" between different antagonistic and feuding ethnic groups. According to this view, the African character was the major obstacle to "civilization." In 1852, a Commission of Inquiry that was created in Natal to investigate African tradition reflected this view. Africans needed a strong power to rule them because if left to themselves, they would engage in warfare and mischief. According to this belief, Africans were superstitious and warlike. The only thing they understood was brute force.

As "ethnic/tribal other," African "tribes" had to be kept in constant tension to prevent the development of a national consciousness and to ensure white control. The Natal Commission expressed its fear that the "alleged disunion and tribal jealousy existing among the Kafirs within the district, is not a source of safety to be depended upon by the white inhabitants."[32] According to the report "tribal jealousy" was ending because different "tribes" were intermarrying. These "evils" could only be eliminated once the colonial government diminished the political power of African chiefs because they held their people in "bondage." As a result, Africans would never make any "progress" without colonial control. Such control was "good" for Africans since it "civilized" them. Uncivilized Africans could also endanger whites since the latter could not control them.[33]

Whites imagined themselves as a "single nation," the 'ruling class' that was also "civilized."[34] Accordingly, as the dominant group, whites had the power to name and classify Africans. For example, African men who served in the police, informers, servants or as manual laborers in the army were all "boys." Europeans called Africans by their first names regardless of the latter's age. This power to label the indigenous people developed into an "ethnic"—or better yet into a "tribal"—classificatory system. Certain African groups were viewed as better security guards or mine workers, while others were seen as good farm workers yet others were classified as lazy and cheeky.

To justify the brutalization of African labor, whites had to dehumanize them. The white minority presented Africans as uncivilized, hostile savages and therefore unworthy of the same rights as "civilized" men. Based on this belief, employment would have a civilizing effect on Africans. [35] Africans in South African cities were the only group who lived in "locations" which reminiscent of a (temporary) movie set. Locations could be moved any time the white minority deemed it necessary.[36] These residential patterns reinforced the relations of unequal power between Africans and whites. The latter could control African movement, residential premises, as well as burial sites. Colonial agents, which included government officials and missionaries, represented private property as a sign of "civilization." According to J. X. Merriman, a Cape Liberal politician because of private land tenure, "lazy" Africans would no longer discourage others from engaging in colonial labor. It would also force Africans to work so as to fulfill created wants such as the need to dress, and to purchase kitchen utensils such iron pots and pans. Based on this belief, Africans who owned land were seen as "lazy," but once settlers took it over, these Africans became "industrious." Unemployed Africans were "vagrants," "lazy," "loafers," while Europeans who were out of work were simply "unemployed."[37] By 1910, this image of Africans was entrenched in both the African and Afrikaner communities. The African community developed out of an attempt to counter this image, while the goal of the white community was to impose its values on the African imagined community. These beliefs and images also affected how whites defined their community. Because they were dealing with "savages" who were not entitled to equal rights, all sense of guilt was removed from the white community.

THE AFRICAN WORLD

As represented in European debates and images the African imagined community was not static. It was dynamic and influenced by different societal forces, classes and conflicts. It was also based on unequal power and gender relations between leaders and the people. Each member of the community played a specific role. Early accounts about Africans do not tell us what names they used to describe and represent themselves. Their identities were based on the family, the clan, and the ethnic group as well as on kinship relations. From the 1860's onwards, Africans were referred to as "native," or "Bantu" in the literature. Literate Africans who had gone to school used "Kaffir" to distinguish themselves from illiterate Africans. For example, a report on the social and legal problems that the African elite faced that appeared in the *Natal Witness* noted that, among other issues, they were discriminated against by "anti-civilization kaffirs." As Christians-and thus no longer bound by native laws, this African elite also demanded to have equal rights with the white minority.[38]

Christian African converts distanced themselves from the "anti-civilisation Kaffirs." They imagined their community as worthy of rights that were not available to

"Kaffirs." These "natives" imagined themselves as juniors among the civilized. They were sure of their departure from "the black race" but not of their acceptance by whites. This precarious position was expressed in March 1863, when the proceedings of a meeting of "natives" were reported in the *Natal Witness*; the main speaker was Johannes, who said,

> We are here met to attempt to decide a question which I will endeavor to put as clearly as I can. We have left the race of our forefathers; we have left the black race and have clung to the whites. We imitate them in everything we can. We feel we are in the midst of a civilised people, and that when we became converts to their faith we belonged to them. It was as a stone thrown into the water, impossible to return . . . We have all been well received-not as dogs, but as people. We have been protected since, and are happy. One thing alone detracts from our security. The law by which our cases are decided is only fit to be eaten by vultures. Who will say Kaffir law is good, when we see thousands flying every day from it to the refuge of the wings of the Englishman? The question for us to decide is whether we will have Kaffir or English law? We have left the black race— it is impossible to return. Let us represent this evil to our superiors. Let us tell them we have left the black race, and belong to them. Will they send us back to barbarity? They may send our bodies, but, our spirits they cannot send.[39]

"Johannes" did not have an African name. The "Kaffir" whom Johannes represented as "uncivilized" believed the African elite class was composed of degenerates. To the Xhosa people, this elite was *Amaquoboka* (people having a hole) because they opened a hole in the Xhosa nation to whites.[40] According to Theophilus Shepstone, the governor of Natal, "the semi-civilised class of [Africans] is looked upon by the mass of the native population as degraded and degenerate."[41] In 1914, when the First World War broke out, Africans offered their services to fight alongside British soldiers. They were recruited for non-combatant positions. During the war, Africans were exposed to other colonized people from the continent and Asia. From this period onwards, Africans used "Native" interchangeably with "African" for self-identification.

In 1923, the South African National Native Congress changed its name to the African National Congress. This change resulted from the experiences of Africans throughout the world. A crucial factor was the improvement of communication, which enabled Africans in South Africa to interact with other Africans on the continent. For example, those Africans who had studied in the United States also shaped the imagined community as a result of their interaction with Africans in America. As a result of similar experiences with colonialism and slavery, they began imagining a community based on a common race. South Africa's Africans thus came to identify themselves as "Africans." Africans represented whites as "whites" when they included all whites, or "Boers" to specifically refer to Afrikaners. This imagined community increasingly changed in the late 1940s to reflect the transformation brought about by a permanent African middle class in urban areas. The interaction of this African middle class with other races, notably Indians, whites and people of mixed descent, also changed how Africans represented themselves. Alliances across race emphasized common suffering rather than one's race, hence "multi-racial" "Black," "non-white" replaced "African" as a means of self-identification. Other forces (such as religion) were also at work in shaping the African community.

THE MISSIONARY

In a conversation between J.W Colenso, who was the first Church of England Bishop of Natal, and African converts in 1854, the latter advised him that "in order to commence a mission, do not promulgate laws about such things, but begin to teach. For a missionary must be like an experienced hunter. He must not show himself, and frighten the game away: but he must get around them, and so catch them."[42]

Indeed, the missionary was like "an experienced hunter" who knew his target and the best methods to entrap them. Missionaries were the only members of the white race who lived permanently among Africans. From the African perspective, they were viewed as "inside outsiders."[43] As Thiven Reddy has argued, missionaries were insiders because they lived among Africans. They could spy on them and pass the information on to colonial agents. But from the African perspective they were still "outsiders" because they were foreigners. In villages where missionaries lived, the people were more likely to buy European goods, provide labor without coercion and be generally civil to colonial powers. For example, such villages did not rise against colonial rule, which demonstrates the impact of missionary preaching among Africans. Furthermore, missionaries were best placed to spy for colonial powers. They informed the colonial authorities on any suspicious activities within these villages, as well as any conversations held between them and African chiefs. As a result, the Cape colonial government supported missionary activities because they also contributed to "the Westernization of the Bantu."[44]

Many of the changes brought about by missionary activity such as rudimentary education, European crafts, individualism, and the gradual transformation of the community into a labor reservoir facilitated colonial domination. For example, African peoples adopted western Christianity as a protest against the power of the African elite. Commoners challenged the authority of their leaders, thereby opening up their societies to foreign control. As a result of missionary presence, the family structure also changed from extended to the nuclear family. The concept of time, as well as gender relations and the arrangement of space within the home also changed.[45] By 1861, the impact of missionary activities on the African imagined community was apparent. For example, in Natal the American Board of Missions produced a religious newspaper in Zulu called *Ikwezi*; it survived until 1868 when it was succeeded by *Ubaqa*. *Ubaqa* survived from 1877 to 1883.[46] These newspapers became the preferred mode of communication among the small class of Africans with elementary education. This class, which came to be known as *Kholwa* (literally, believers) among the Zulu, set the contours of the community.

Missionaries also believed that they were representing different nations and tribes and, as such, reinforced and recreated ethnic boundaries. For example, Reverend Moffat worked among the "Tswana," and Reverend Owen among the "Zulu." Yet, missionaries believed that whites were a homogenous group. According to Thiven Reddy, missionaries saw themselves as "representing ethnic nations in their important role as mediators between the expansionist colonial administration and the selected chiefs."[47] Differences were created where they did not exist before. For example, the Xhosa and the Zulu, whose languages are similar, became distinct tribes, as different from one another as Europeans and Africans.

These recreations of identity affected the imagined community in several ways. Christian converts imagined their community along ethnic and Christian lines rather than racial ones. This imagining had its contradictions. On the one hand, it emphasized a Christian brotherhood that also included whites. On the other, it reinforced ethnic identities and divided the believers from the "heathens" while marginalizing African women in the community. Unequal relations of power between Africans and missionaries influenced the imagined community. Missionaries believed themselves to be trustees over Africans until the Africans were civilized enough to join white society. Secondly, missionaries "knew" the bible and were therefore constructed as superior to Africans who learned from them. Third, most of the missionaries originated from the lowest classes of their societies. They often had no formal education and, as Patrick Brantlinger argues, these missionaries found Africa attractive because of their humble roots.[48] As a result of missionary education and activities, African Christians internalized these views by representing themselves as the leaders of their community. They also accepted white tutelage and worked within these relations of power. Missionary education provided another representational aspect of the imagined community. The school became the most aggressive agent in transforming the African community. This impact did not escape Africans who objected to a local missionary school being started in their area in 1887: "They had no children to send to school. Their wives would be drawn away from their husbands, and mothers would be drawn away from their children, to go and wear dresses and become women of the lowest type, thereby bringing trouble and misery upon their families. The children tending the gardens and watching the stock would neglect their work and run away to school, so that the crops would be destroyed. Children who were educated and became Christians despised their parents."[49]

Lovedale, a missionary institution established in 1841 to train Africans, shaped the boundaries of the African imagined community. Emerging from Lovedale was a bilingual elite that threatened the colonial community. This elite imagined its community as part of the British empire. John Tengo Jabavu (1859–1921), editor of the Lovedale mission journal, *Isigidimi: Sama Xhosa* (Xhosa Express), later founded the first African independent newspaper, *Imvo Zabantsundu* (African Opinion). *Imvo* campaigned against Sprigg's government Parliamentary Registration Act of 1887, which disenfranchised Africans in the eastern Cape. Jabavu's editorial column claimed that the Bill would "establish the ascendancy of the Dutch in the colony for ever" by disenfranchising the English party's "devoted allies."[50] Like the missionaries, the elite was involved in a civilizing project. For example, Elijah Makiwane, editor of *Isgidimi Samaxosa*—the Xhosa version of the *Kaffir Express* between 1876 and 1881—opposed polygyny. Makiwane believed he was participating in the "noble effort of raising a barbarous or semi-barbarous people to a civilized state, or turning a conquered people to contented and even enthusiastic citizens."[51] To all the parties involved, "civilizing" Africans did not mean the same thing. For example, the African elite believed that to civilize Africans meant to uplift them from their semi-barbarous state. For missionaries, civilization meant the implementation of "Christianity, the abandonment of traditionalism, and education; the colonists meant mainly the elimination of those obstacles that inhabited the flow of Africans into the labour market."[52]

By late 1879, the western educated African elite realized that it would lead the next stage of liberation. This elite founded the Native Education Association in 1880, the South African Aborigine Association (Imbumba Yama Afrika) in 1882, and the Native Electoral Association in 1884. Although the majority of the members were Xhosa speaking, the associations were non-ethnic, reflecting the growth of an African consciousness.

The African imagined community was shaped by dominant relations of power in the society that emphasized its inferior status in all its dimensions. Jabavu noted, "We not only preach loyalty, but we preach subordination to superiors. The Kaffir, he maintained, was no leveler or democrat; he believed in caste and the principle that "some are born to rule and others to be ruled."[53] Jabavu used the term Kaffir to refer to all Africans regardless of class. When the Afrikaner Bond party challenged the African franchise in the Cape between 1882 and 1888, Jabavu urged the African elite to unite. The African elite was to make all efforts so that the privileges of education and "of being treated as free subjects of the greatest ruler in the world are not taken from them."[54]

According to Jabavu's *Imvo* editorial of March 18, 1901, Cape Africans were broken into three class distinctions. The first, the westernized Africans, were the school people. Africans who were not completely westernized but aspired to become so made up the second class. This was the working class, often the mine workers. The working class did not have high levels of education to entitle them to the privileges of the elite. They also lived temporarily in cities before returning to their villages after the end of their contracts. But this working class was closer to the elite than the "raw" Africans who were still wrapped in indigenous institutions: "the raw element . . . the only class that . . . properly be subjected to . . . benevolent discipline."[55] Jabavu believed that Africans who were not fully assimilated into Western society needed legislation to assist them in the process. This is not an unusual belief in communities that are dominated by a minority in which a certain body of knowledge is viewed as natural. According to Trinh Minh-ha, "You can no doubt capture, tame, and appropriate it to yourself, for language as a form of knowing will always provide you with your other. One of the conceits of anthropology lies in its positivist dream of a neutralized language that strips off all its singularity to become nature's exact, unmisted reflection."[56] Once this belief is made available to the community, it is understood as objective to the point that even the dominated people accept it as natural. The Africans' definition of their community as a subordinate group constantly reacted to developments in the settler community. For example, Africans created their own national anthem to counter the Boers' *Die Stem* and the King's national anthem. *Nkosi Sikelel iAfrika* (God bless Africa) is a song of liberation. It speaks of unity of struggle across class, ethnicity, or gender boundaries. *Nkosi* sounds like a Christian song, and, indeed, it is one. It calls on the holy spirit to intervene (Woza Moya Oyingewele!) on behalf of the "Setshaba sa Jesus!" (the nation of Jesus). It was composed at Lovedale College in the 1890s. *Nkosi* reflected the type of imagined community that the African elite desired. Africans adopted this anthem throughout Southern Africa.

The African elite faced two contradictions. First, the majority of Africans ostracized the elite because of its idolization of Western culture. The other contradiction lay in the elite's inability to move into civilized society. Yet, the elite was also "alienated from the tribal structure of chiefs, headmen (*abanumzana*), and commoners."[57]

The colonial government used Africans who remained within indigenous institutions against the elite (especially in Natal). According to the elite, such hostility could only lead to backwardness. In 1891, *Inkanyiso* noted that "the result [of this] is that civilisation is retarded because there is no difference made in the treatment of *kholwas* and that of Kraal Kaffirs."[58] Sol Plaatje's Native Life is a good example of the role the African elite played as the voice of the majority. As an educated African, Plaatje appeals to the British public against the injustices of the 1913 Land Act. The term Kraal Kaffirs (Red People) was used by the civilized, western educated elite to refer to illiterate Africans. The latter believed that Kraal Kaffirs were unworthy of any rights. Whites despised the African elite and referred to them ironically as gentleman Kaffirs, as they were only gentleman in theory since they did not enjoy equal rights with the white minority.[59] The white minority also used the term gentleman because it believed that the African elite was too arrogant for manual labor, but not adequately trained in important professional skills that mattered to settlers such as agriculture and carpentry. The tensions between the African elite and the Red People shaped the African imagined community in two ways. First, the African elite used all the methods at its disposal to persuade whites to assimilate this elite into civilized society. Secondly, the African elite distanced itself from the Kraal Africans to prove to whites that it was duly civilized, and therefore, worthy of equal rights. As a result, this African elite was unable to empathize with the African people.

In the 1890s the living conditions of the Africans significantly deteriorated. For example, in Natal, various taxes were imposed on Africans without a corresponding increase in wages. Communication between Africans and the colonial government, which had been open under Governor Shepstone, was now restricted. Various permits were required of African chiefs before they could meet with the Secretary of Native Affairs. A deep cleavage developed between chiefs and commoners because the needs of the latter were no longer met. The denial of political rights to the Kholwa class added to these problems. According to David Welsh, "their [African] leaders saw clearly the contradictions upon which justifications of the unequal society rested: Africans were 'barbarous' and therefore not entitled to civic rights; but évolué [civilized] Africans were mostly rascals, prone to crime and receptive to seditious doctrines that questioned the white man's right to supremacy."[60]

These contradictions were also expressed in *Ilanga*: "certainly ours is a hard lot, for when we remain in our heathen state, we are blamed and when we follow the white people's customs we are found fault with. What shall we do?"[61] Africans expected Europeans to lead them to a better life. Instead, the latter despised Africans, thus resulting in a degree of frustration among the elite.

The imagined community also changed as a result of increased racism, job discrimination, and economic difficulties. For example, some of the elite began imagining a community without white trusteeship by increasingly challenging white supremacy. A general feeling of the need to be self-sufficient developed among the African elite. In 1884, Nehemiah Tile, who broke away from the Wesleyan Church, established the first exclusively African church in Thembuland (Transkei). In 1898, Jabavu Mzimba broke away from the Free Church to found the African Presbyterian Church, which grew into a stable African independent church that drew numerous members from diverse organizations. Independent African churches operated on the assumption that Africans had to control their destiny, thus contributing to the rise of political consciousness within the community. These churches were self-sufficient; they were not mere African copies of European churches. To do so, Africans needed their own churches and leaders who could fulfill their needs and interests.[62]

The attempt of African Christians to break out of white paternalistic control was called Ethiopianism. In African history, Ethiopia has a special place because it was never colonized. Ethiopia represents history, honor and courage, especially because of its defeat of Italy at the battle of Adowa in 1896. Ethiopia's king Menelik had united Africans in the face of colonial encroachment and created a modern state that acted as the standard-bearer of African freedom. In this imagined community, Ethiopia represented everything that was positive about Africans: pride, tradition and African unity. As early as the first century, Ethiopia was also an African home for Christianity. Choosing the African faith was a way for these Africans to identify with the rest of the continent. Africans observed that missionary Christian moral standards differed from their own. African independent churches aimed at resolving these contradictions. Their goal was to link theory to practice by teaching Christian principles based on African history and tradition. They began questioning the role of the missionaries in colonizing their country and believed that independence could only be achieved once Africans rejected white paternalism. Their rallying cry was "Africa for Africans."[63]

Political and spiritual issues contributed to the development of Ethiopianism. This Christian belief sensitized Africans to their economic and social conditions and demonstrated that African leaders were divorced from their people because their organizations did not have a popular following. Ethiopianism appealed to large numbers of people who were left out by these organizations because of the latter's emphasis on Western Christianity and white trusteeship. Western Churches' Victorian and Cape liberal values were also irrelevant to African needs. For example, African demands for land and self-determination contradicted the elites' desire for assimilation in white society even as unequal partners. Among the *Kholwa* class, both separatists and moderates aimed at advancing African interests. The supporters of Ethiopianism were migrants and the less educated laborers who did not benefit from the new economy. Their movement opposed all aspects of white supremacy. The political and nationalist consciousnesses of Africans were raised as they met each other in various meetings organized under the auspices of the Church. African nationalism "emerged out of the rise and subsequent demise of the African peasantry and the blossoming of the separatist churches."[64]

The capitalist economy that developed in the early 1870s disrupted many indigenous institutions. In the confusion that followed, Africans tried to explain their world, to understand the changes and to reach back to what they had lost. Sol T.

Plaatje wrote the first novel about Africans set in the 1830s.⁶⁵ *Mhudi* was written in 1917 but published by Lovedale Press in 1930. Although Plaatje spoke Tswana, he wrote *Mhudi* in English. It was an epic love tale about two Barolong lovers. Mhudi and Ra—Thaga made their journeys through the hinterland. There, they met with the Ndebele and Boers. The novel demonstrated how Africans initially dealt with the Boers as equals. It also highlighted the African art of government through various debates. *Mhudi* projected a confident past based on common African history. It used history to present an image of the present and the future, which contradicted the racial egalitarianism of white supremacy. It also challenged white supremacy's claim that Africans did not have a common history. *Mhudi* was a prophetic novel that foreshadowed the preoccupations of some Black Consciousness writers of the 1970s.

Poets also wrote about the African past and contrasted it with life in the city. In *Ezinkomponi* ("On the Gold Mines,"), which was originally written in 1945 in Zulu, Benedict Wallet Vilakazi wrote,

> Rumble on, machines of the gold mines
> Thunder from first light to sun's sinking:
> Ah, stop plaguing me, I'll wake up.
> Rumble on, machines, and drown out
> The groans of the black working men
>
> Whose bodies ache with throbbing weals
> Struck by the thuds of the stifling air,
> On their limbs the stink of sweat and dirt:
> Sapped of the vigour of their loins.
> Be careful, though I go unarmed today
> There was a time when from these worn-out arms
> Long-bladed spears were flung far and wide
>
> Whose whirling dimmed the whole earth;
> They shook the empire of the she Elephant*
> [Queen Victoria]
> Thinned out Paul's [president Kruger]**
> boers—then I was struck down.
> Now I am forever dreaming, child of iron,
> That this earth of my forefathers once again
> Will be restored to the rightful Black hands . . . ⁶⁶

As noted in Vilakazi's poem, during this period "black" was becoming popular as a way of African self-identification. Vilakazi uses "rightful Black hands . . ." to refer to the indigenous inhabitants of the land who will eventually repossess it. In spite of divisions within urban Africans, Vilakazi presents them as united by a common history. This helped counter the Afrikaner claim that African ethnic groups were irreconcilable and not members of the same community. It was within this historical context that a national African consciousness emerged. Africans began imagining their community as people who were free from white minority.

Africans relied on the support of liberals as well as on petitions to present their case to the state. These efforts were fruitless. Instead, in 1897, Cecil Rhodes promised "equal rights for every white man south of the Zambezi."[67] In 1900, he promised equal rights to all civilized men South of the Zambezi. The elite imagined their community as "civilized." Thus, it urged Africans to support the British against Afrikaners during the 1899–1902 Anglo-Boer war. Among other reasons, the war was also sparked by the need for African labor, which could only be secured by a centralized state that united all the various parts of the country. When confronted by Africans, Britain protected both its interests and those of Afrikaners'. This process resulted in limits on African rights, control over African labor and the entrenchment of white supremacy throughout the country. In 1910 the Union of South Africa was created as a political entity independent from Britain. Africans were excluded from the new state and its resources except as providers of labor. This exclusion reinforced the African imagined community. To address it, the elite founded the South African National Native Congress in 1912.

POLITICAL REPRESENTATIONS OF THE AFRICAN COMMUNITY: 1912–1948

Africans refused to be subjected to white domination. The African elite, which included some aristocratic families and Western educated people, created the South African Native National Congress (SANNC) in 1912. This party was created to unify Africans in their fight for equality with the white minority. The thinking of its leaders was shaped by missionaries and British humanitarian values based on the superiority of the white race. In an interview with the *Times*, Pixley Seme said that social equality between whites and Africans was impossible and that he believed the "rule of the English to be a good thing for the African, bringing civilization and higher development."[68] The aim of SANNC was not to overthrow the state "in the name of the black majority as a whole."[69] The 1919 Constitution of the SANNC stipulated no higher aim than the peaceful elimination of racial segregation and equal treatment of the African elite in all sectors of the economy. It also demanded "civilized" (i.e equal) pay for the African elite. This class dimension was expressed during the 1920 civil disobedience campaign of the SANNC in Pretoria, which called on train conductors to allow its members' access to first class cars. A prominent Cape politician, D. D. T. Jabavu, noted at a Natal mission conference in 1920 that

> [railway] waiting rooms are made to accommodate the rawest blanketed heathens; and the more decent native has either to use them and annex vermin or to do without shelter in biting wintry weather.[70]

Jabavu used the term "native" to distinguish the African elite from the rest of the population. This identification was important in shaping relations between the elite and the "rawest blanketed Heathens" (i.e. the "natives").

European liberalism and Christian philanthropy influenced the political ideology of the SANNC. Liberalism emphasized gradual change of the system, based on the belief that Africans had to "develop" to a certain level of "civilization." According to this view, Africans would be accepted in white society once they had "reached" a certain level of civilization. As the dominant ruling group, the white minority was in a position to decide when Africans would be "ready" to join the "civilized community." The SANNC operated within these unequal relations of power. According to its first president, John Langa Langalibalele Dube, once Africans proved their "loyalty" to the Crown, they would be treated as equals. Instead of using Western education as a weapon to fight for freedom, the African elite used it to mitigate conflict between the colonial authorities and the majority of the people. For example, during the 1906 Bambata rebellion against the poll tax, *ILanga lase Natal* (the newspaper that catered to the elite) appealed to Kholwas: "Pay up your poll tax first and explain to the people why the government found it necessary to impose this tax."[71] Africans had to move slowly and cautiously to win their rights. According to Dube, western education was crucial in preparing Africans for equality with the white minority; only then will "the African beg his rightful place in the land of his fathers."[72] In a letter to Prime Minister Botha, Dube wrote, "we make no protest against the principle of separation so far as it can be fairly and practically carried out."[73] This belief shaped the African imagined community as represented by SANNC in its early period.

In 1917, the leadership of the SANNC moved from its original base in the Cape Province. Thus, moderate Cape-educated or Natal-born leaders such as Dube while no revolutionaries, had dominated Congress during its first six years. Transvaal leaders such as S. M. Makgatho were definitely more assertive. These leaders were drawn from the rank-and-file of the party. They believed that one did not need to "beg" whites to be included in the broader South African society. Thus the SANNC demanded the one shilling a day pay "which accompanied the wave of African strikes in Johannesburg that year [1917]."[74] Rather than using biblical language to demand for their rights, the leaders of the SANNC resorted to African history to inspire the people and provide a counter-history to the official state version. Under the SANNC leadership, the African imagined community developed within a history that emphasized a process of dispossession, which was explained in terms "of white political and economic hegemony."[75]

In the 1920s, the SANNC became more assertive as a result of African peoples' disillusionment with poor living standards (especially after the First World War), lack of job opportunities, discrimination, and increased hostility of the state against African demands. However, the SANNC continued to use passive resistance tactics to achieve equality. The association of the SANNC with the Industrial and Commercial Workers' Union of South Africa (ICU) stated,

> We are fed up with the white man's camouflage, his hypocrisy, his policy of pinpricks in the land of our forefathers. I am appealing to the racial consciousness of the radical aboriginal to use all means to rouse the African race to wake from their long sleep of many a decade . . . when those in authority become so unreasonably notorious . . . disregard that authority, be blind and damn the consequences.[76]

In 1926, ICU leader Clements Kadalie noted,

> We natives ... have always given the game away ... we are dealing with rascals, the Europeans are rascals ... There is no native problem but a European problem of weakness, greed and robbery.[77]

According to Kadalie, the ANC was too close to white liberals who were thus able to control their activities, an opinion shared by the working class within the ANC. This influenced the development of the African imagined community, which became more assertive by staging demonstrations and strikes. World events such as the first Pan-African Conference in 1919 may also have influenced the SANNC. There was a growing consciousness among Africans that they belonged to the wider African community. Presumably to mark the dawn of a new era, in 1923 the SANNC changed its name to the African National Congress.

In 1928, ANC president James Gumede developed a close relationship with the Communist Party. The CP believed that change in South Africa would follow in two stages. A nationalist bourgeoisie would lead the first stage. This bourgeoisie would deracialize the system. It would also act as an economic bourgeoisie by providing the material basis of the revolution. The second stage would lead to a socialist state. This association changed the African imagined community in several ways. First, Congress called for a Black Republic based on majority rule. Second, the struggle in South Africa was viewed as a wider struggle against colonialism. To Gumede, it included all the colonized people of Africa and Asia. A leadership struggle between Gumede and Pixley ka Izaka Seme in 1930 ended in the victory of the latter and the ANC moved to the right and into inaction.

The representation of the African imagined community by the ANC underwent important changes in the 1940s. First, there was a general feeling within the organization that it needed to address the basic needs of the African masses, notably high price of staple foods such as "mealies" (maize and beans). Housing was poor but expensive. In 1943, the ANC Constitution was rewritten. The "House of Chiefs" clause that privileged chiefs over commoners in the initial Constitution was removed. During this period, the number of African women increased in the cities, with a concomitant increase in their economic and political strength that could not be ignored. As a result, the ANC gave women members' equal status with men within the organization. Furthermore, most of the young members of the ANC were dissatisfied with its right-wing orientation, inaction and lack of direction.

Secondly, in 1943 the revolutionary nationalism of the African independent churches was revisited by the founding of the Congress Youth League, Anton Muziwakhe Lembede was its leading political thinker. He introduced the ideology of Africanism. According to Africanism, the struggle in South Africa was a struggle for the national liberation of the African people as a whole, rather than a class struggle or a multi-racial fight against apartheid. In Africanism the imagined community was defined as African. This community did not have to be assimilated into the white minority state. Africans free of mental colonization would operate at all levels of the imagined community. Lembede, who was also the first president of the league, believed in an evolutionary nationalism that urged Africans to accept their color as a God-given, positive aspect of their identity. He was appalled by the moral decay that prevailed among Africans living in urban areas particularly in Johannesburg. Such moral decay created an African who lacked self-esteem, who worshipped and idolized everything that was white by adopting foreign ideologies. As a result, the African developed a "pathological state of mind."[78] To be liberated, Africans had to overcome the psychological impact of oppression by accepting their Africanness. The league demanded self-determination, including an African leadership. It did not trust the white-dominated Communist Party, which was suspected by the Youth League to control and manipulate the ANC behind the scenes. As a result the CYL was in conflict with the ANC leadership. This conflict resulted in the 1959 split of the ANC into two different political parties: Pan Africanist Congress that followed the League's original ideal of Africanism, and the ANC that followed the ideals of liberalism and multiracial democracy.

At its 1949 annual conference, the ANC committed itself to implementing the Programme of Action. According to this Programme, the ANC would fight for self-determination and political independence by ending all forms of racial segregation, although it did not state the means by which these goals were to be achieved. At that time, the ANC leadership was a blend of the moderate old guard and of young radicals. Z. K. Matthews, a middle class member of the old guard from the Cape province joined the party's executive after the 1949 elections. Z. K. Mathews and his son Joseph, had a major intellectual influence on the evolution of the ANC. In particular, the preservation (alongside a distinctly confrontationist strategy) of a conciliatory and racially inclusive form of nationalist ideology, owes much to the Mathews's influence.

As a result of the disagreement between the conservatives and radicals, four factions developed within the African community. The first one was represented by the CYL radical leadership, which believed in African self-determination, mental decolonization as well as economic control. These radicals defined South Africa as an African country that required an African leadership rather than a multiracial one. While some within this group disagreed on some of the ideals to be achieved, all agreed on tactics, i.e that change would come about through mass demonstrations, strikes and boycotts. The second faction was represented by people within the movement such as the Mathews who believed that only gradual action would bring about change in South Africa. This camp viewed South Africa as a multiracial country, but was divided between those who favored relations with the Communist Party and those who opposed such relations. None of these groups engaged in any form of armed struggle. When the ANC adopted the Freedom Charter in 1955, multiracial democracy supporters became Charterists. This divide led to a split with the founding of the Pan Africanist Congress in 1959; it also influenced the emergence of the Black Consciousness Movement in the early 1970s.

The Charterists influenced the African imagined community in several ways. For example, they emphasized the multiracial dimension of the community rather than its Africaness. As a result, white liberals supported the ANC. According to Jeremy Seekings, "this strengthened ANC commitment to an English–speaking multiracial society. Mandela noted this influence when saying the ANC owed its origins to English missionaries, and in the process we have become black Englishmen . . . [and] it may well be the black man's hostility and contempt for the Afrikaner has also been influenced by the well-known hostility and contempt of the Englishman for this group."[79] The African National Congress was only "African" in name since it was open to all races who opposed racism. It internalized the mainstream discourse of the other because at first it identified its followers as Native, and later as Black further reinforcing its loss of identity with Africa, since the Afrikaners had laid claim over Africa by identifying themselves as such. Congress also accepted the white minority's definition of South Africa as an outpost of Europe rather than its being an integral part of the rest of the continent. Since that time, the African imagined Community in South Africa has been dominated by Charterists.

Gender

Power relations within the community also shaped gender relations. For example, missionary representations of the African suffering woman united missionaries and colonialists against polygamy. In 1863, a writer in the *Natal Witness* spoke of the alliance between the missionary and the labour-needing colonists, to alleviate the sufferings of the native woman. He suggested that "both were interested in ending a custom which materially interferes with the object for which they have respectively left their mother country."[80] In 1877, a former legislative council member James W. Winter wrote a pamphlet on *Lobola* called "Gigantic Inhumanity, of Women Slavery in Natal." Winter cited alleged cases of cruelty under the kinship system. To abolish polygamy, missionaries preached against it. In their view, African customs such as polygamy and traditional medicine were an obstacle to civilization.

The government saw itself as an agent of civilization that would free African women from the oppression of tradition. In reality, it eroded some of their rights. Prior to colonialism, women enjoyed a degree of freedom within indigenous systems that respected their property rights. Single or married women could also acquire property independent from their fathers or husbands. Women were independent of men because they were often economically self-sufficient. This economic power may have been in the form of land or cattle given for Lobola (bridewealth). For example, whenever they were paid for acting as midwives, women kept the proceeds for themselves. A Zulu chief explained the position of women in indigenous Zululand:

> There were for instance women inyangas [medicine women] and *Izangomas* [diviners] who acquired property. Diligent women also weaved mats and other handicrafts and accumulated first goats and with goats, cattle and that became their property. It is a definite fallacy that women had no property in Zulu society. A father could give property to his daughter and that became her property. There are instances where a husband also bequeaths cattle and other property to his childless wife.[81]

The colonial government curtailed women's freedom to be diviners by forcing herbalists to be licensed at a cost of 3 pounds. Missionaries provided another representation of African women. According to David Welsh, "A wife who by her industry produces corn enough to maintain her family, and with surplus to barter a cow, that cow with its increase is looked upon as her property separate from the estate of her husband."[82] Women's economic independence was eroded since missionaries believed women were sold.

The government believed that it was protecting women from "abuse," toward this end, it gave shelter to girls who ran way from forced marriages. It also encouraged them to report cases of 'abuse'. As more cases were reported, the government promised to make the concerned parties appear in court before the marriage, but this regulation was never enforced. According to the government once, a girl reached the age of twenty no consent was required from the parents. Most girls were too afraid to report their parents guilty of forced marriages. Missionaries offered shelter for African women who ran away from this "oppression." The Rev. T. L. Dohne of the Berlin Mission recommended to the 1852–53 Commission that lobola be abolished:

> The abolition of that sinful, and thus unlawful, trade, would put a most efficient check upon the Kaffirs unrestrained desire for cattle, make the females free and available for service, and every kind of improvement, civil and moral, exercising also an influence upon males, to bring them out for work, as the existence of that trade is a certain cause of keeping many at home.[83]

By protecting women's interests, the colonial state saw itself as improving their position in society. For example, the government determined the number of cows that were to be given in lobola under the pretense that it was freeing women. In the process, it perverted the function of lobola. Parents lost control over their daughters to the state, and if the marriage failed, they could not return a portion of the lobola. In reality, the government had reduced marriage to a matter of buying and selling by arbitrarily fixing the amount of lobola that couples could give thus further complicating the conditions that women faced. Instead of freeing women, colonial authorities added another layer of duties and another level of oppression. They also introduced new restrictions. For example, women were now confined to the home as mothers, daughters and wives who played a passive role in the community. The introduction of the plough in farming exposed men to cash economy's benefits such as regular wages, and technology. Since men were forced out of the home either to work in the mines or in the plantations, or to perform public works, women were burdened with additional duties.

The 1874 Native law in Natal introduced new restrictions on women's freedoms. This law, introduced by the government as a way of "civilizing" Africans, was in fact a gross distortion of traditional law. According to this law women were subordinate to men. H. J. Simons observed about a similar code that was introduced later that it stereotypes a concept of feminine inferiority unknown in traditional society. In fact, Zulu women had property rights before English women had any. Apparently missionaries forgot this important aspect in their conception of lobola. Missionaries believed the "suffering" of African women benefited African men, characterized as "lazy" because of the extra labor that women provided. As heads of households, men owned all property. In the eyes of colonial administrators, African women were minors who did not have any rights whatsoever. Women could no longer inherit property as they had done before. Controlling African women was very important for the colonial state in order to curtail their power. As mothers, women passed their cultural knowledge to their children, once they became Christians, these women lost that ability, therefore aiding the colonial government without planning to do so. The introduction of Western schools also reduced the power of women to influence their children. This right was denied to both believers and non-believers. A member of parliament asked,

> Whilst she lived a supposed Christian life with her husband under the operation of Christian Law her husband may have acquired property. When he dies why should she be abandoned under Native Law when she ought to inherit her husband's property, having been married by Christian rites?[84]

According to the Secretary of Native Affairs, the husband's heir was meant to provide for the woman. The Attorney-General of Natal saw no problem in denying African women property rights. According to him, "it simply means, if she has no property, that she is very likely to take service, and if it produces female servants it would be a very good thing."[85] Under the new law, women had to give all their earnings to the head of the household. They had to get their husbands' or sons' permission to travel. Once a woman in an urban area divorced her husband or became a widow, she was deported to the reserve. The new racial stratification placed African women at the bottom of a pyramid whose tip was occupied by white men, followed by white women, Indians, people of mixed descent, and African men.

Missionary education was crucial in reshaping African women's social identity. The introduction of Western education had its own contradictions: on the one hand, it empowered women by providing them with some means of supporting themselves. On the other hand, education introduced another layer of subordination. It reinforced the public/private divide that was introduced by the colonial government, and it also reinforced women's subordinate position since "decent" ones had to be married to Christian men. In the colonial system, women were either daughters, wives, or mothers, but they were never independent persons who could think by themselves. By the late 1860s, missionaries in Natal realized that semi-educated women had not proved to be the best wives for the Native leaders trained by the Missionaries. The overall improvement of Africans also depended on raising the status of African women, who were to be trained as Christian wives and mothers. A girls' school founded in 1869 had a special course for runaway girls who had escaped from polygamous marriages.

The introduction of Western education also reinforced class cleavages among African women. Elite women had more rights than the "red" women (those who rejected Westernization). This small educated class had access to better professions in the new economy, which contributed to improve its standard of living and social status. Women had a dual role in the capitalist economy, as both workers and producers of future laborers. Once the role of women as producers ended, they ceased to be of any use to the state. However, all African women were not oppressed in the same way. Their economic and social status determined their level of oppression. A rural, landless woman was not oppressed in the same way as a landowner, nurse, or maid. Rural women were the worst hit by unemployment, marital abuse, and hunger. Even within the rural community, women were divided along class lines. Some were squatters on white farms, farm workers or maids. Women were oppressed on several levels: as Africans, as women, and as poor peasants. As a result, change would occur only through the transformation of relations of production rather than through changes in men's attitudes.

Capitalism added another layer of restraints and duties in the subordinate position of women. For example, taxes imposed on African families influenced male/female relations, as male members left for different areas in search of labor. Women became heads of households for up to twelve months period, when men left for the mines. In this sense, women played a dual role in the economy. Migratory labor had contradictory effects. In some cases, it strengthened the women's position; for example, they were in a better position to resist the use of passes in Western Transvaal. Women in rural areas were in a better position to resist the use of passes than those in the city who relied on their jobs. On the other hand, women in rural areas were the last to be proletarianized because of their prolonged stay in the country side.

Colonial administrators variously identified African women as "Bantu," "Black," "Native," "kaffirs," or "worker." This representation came with a denial of rights. Women's construction of their own imagined community was an attempt to counter the state's representation. For example, women took the lead in resisting the use of passes through mass demonstrations, thus reconstructing their imagined community into an assertive one. Until then, African women had been perceived as weak and disorganized. Such mass demonstrations changed how African women were viewed in society—mostly as docile followers of their men. The anti-pass campaigns began the era of women participation in modern, non-ethnic political movements. Prior to the 1940s, women's organized activity focused on either church (based voluntary organizations-*Manyanos*) or on social welfare. Initially *Manyanos* dealt with domestic issues. Later on, as the state curtailed more African rights, women became more active in politics. Women used *Manyanos* to express their grievances in however confused a fashion, and as a way of redressing them.[86] *Manyanos* strengthened their ability to overcome the oppressive domestic conditions facing them. In a way they reinforced women's position in society as subordinates whose influence was limited to the domestic sphere. Such was the nature of Zenzele clubs, headed by Mrs Xuma or the National Council of African Women (NCAW), founded in 1933 to replace the Bantu League. The goal of the NCAW was to cater for the welfare of non-European women. It was an elitist organization that did not provide new avenues for women to develop independently of men. Its community was imagined according to white women's values. Joint inter-racial committees and liberal women's organizations became the model for these leaders.

In the 1940s, women's organizations became more political. In the cities, a small number of women joined the industrial workforce. For the first time in the country's history, there was a permanent African labor force in urban areas. African women were also more independent in cities than they had been in the rural areas. These women's position as wage-earners or as self-employed workers gave them some economic leverage, thereby, weakening patriarchal ties. Women became more politically and socially assertive as they organized themselves to fight against oppression, regardless of class and ethnic cleavages. For example, women became politicized through their involvement in popular movements such as bus boycotts or squatter movements.[87] These events influenced their imagined community. As they interacted with other races, African women began imagining their community as inclusive of all races. They became the most vocal group in demanding better wages, suffrage and housing. All these organizations' basic goal was Africans' freedom. During this period, a prominent African women middle class whose social mobility was blocked by racial discrimination developed. These women became the most vocal critics of apartheid. Realizing the political potential of African women, Congress founded the Women's League-based on the ANC's ideals of inclusive nationalism and multiracial democracy in 1948.

Conclusion

Various factors shaped the foundation upon which the African imagined community developed between 1867 and 1948. First, this community was imagined within racial boundaries based on the belief that Africans were inferior to whites. The African imagined community developed to counter this view by advocating an inclusive as opposed to the white's exclusive imagined community. Second, material conditions brought about by capitalism shaped some of the contours of this community. For example, class divisions were sharpened. A centralized state that introduced schools also determined how the community developed. Third, a western-educated elite that believed in assimilation into the white minority's society acted as the vanguard of the imagined community. This elite believed in "Onward! Upward! Into the higher places of civilization and Christianity—not backward into the slump of darkness nor downward into the abyss of antiquated tribal systems."[88] Having rejected its own culture, the African elite believed in everything British. This elite did not empathize with the African masses but sought instead to be accepted by the white minority.

Fourth, the imagined community was strengthened by the introduction of better communication and print capitalism that integrated diverse communities under a central authority. Better communication enabled Africans to move from one region to another; there, they met Africans who faced similar conditions. The capitalist print media, which included newspapers and journals, opened the world to literate Africans. This African elite could read about life in the empire (Britain and its colonies) as well as about the local white minority. This life based on freedom and equality was different from theirs. The more they read about it, the more they began questioning the conditions that they faced, most notably, oppression, poverty, and racial discrimination. Such questioning also strengthened their community, forcing the elite to mobilize the African people for social and political change.

Fifth, Christianity was an essential element of the imagined community. Only "civilized," (i.e., educated and Christian men) belonged to the imagined community. The African imagined community was variously affected by the different issues faced by the Africans. On other occasions, for example, when the ANC cooperated with the Communist Party, the community expanded to include members of other racial groups and women. Finally, the community's development was influenced and shaped by gender and gender relations.

FURTHER READINGS

Gerhart, Gail. *Black Power in South Africa: The Evolution of an Ideology*. Berkeley: University of California, 1978.

Magubane, Bernard. *The Making of a Racist State: British Imperialism and the Union of South Africa 1875–1910*. Trenton, NJ: Africa World Press, 1996.

Plaatje, Sol T. *Mhudi: An Epic of South African Native Life a Hundred Years Ago* Johannesburg: AD.Donker, 1989.

Sparks, Alistar, *The Mind of South Africa*. London: Mandarin, 1990.

Walker, Cherryl, ed. *Women and Gender in Southern Africa*. Cape Town: David Phillip, 1990.

Walshe, Peter. *The Rise of African Nationalism in South Africa*. London: C. Hurst, 1970

CHAPTER 2

AN AFRIKANER IMAGINED COMMUNITY, 1867–1948

> In spite of all the leaders of the Union having been ex-Boer War generals, South Africa was still a British country.
>
> —W. A. De Klerk, *The Puritans in Africa: A Story of Afikanerdom*

> The Boer nation can therefore understand the sufferings of the Bantu [blacks]. It is the same imperialism and capitalism, having them believe that the foreign is better than what is their own, which seeks to destroy their tribal life.
>
> —Cronje, *Tuiste*.

THIS CHAPTER TRACES THE EVOLUTION, THAT IS TO SAY THE, intellectual development of Afrikaner nationalism and, particularly, the formulations of the Afrikaners' definition of imagined national community. It does so by examining the changing formulations of community, the specific characteristics of the community, the relationship(s) it has with other communities, and how relations among groups within the community shaped it. The chapter is divided into four parts. Part I traces the construction of the Afrikaner imagined community from 1867 to 1914. The second part looks at political representation from 1914 to 1948, while part three examines gender representations. Part four consists of a comparative study of the intellectual development of both African and Afrikaner communities.

CONSTRUCTING THE AFRIKANER NATION

By the late eighteenth century, Cape society rested on two main assumptions: (1) that whites should be allowed to deal with other racial groups and slaves more or less as they saw fit, without government interference; and (2) that all whites were entitled to as much land as they wanted without paying for it.[1] In Peter Abrahams' *Wild Conquest*, the Afrikaner is represented as the essence of contradiction: in one hand, he carries the bible, and in the other, a rifle. Both tools mark his predicament in South

Africa. His existence in a strange environment boils down to "shoot first and speak afterwards. It's a good old Boer rule, Anna. Our forebears who had to fight the Kaffirs knew just how good it was."[2]

In early accounts of Cape society, whites were identified either as a European, immigrant, or settler regardless of their national origin. Those who farmed for the Dutch East India Company imagined themselves as *Burghers* (farmers). Once they left company work and lived as free citizens in the Cape colony, *Burghers* became *Free Burghers*. *Free Burghers* represented whites, who, as discussed previously, were entitled to certain rights, such as owning land and slaves. *Burghers* who preferred freedom from company rule moved into the interior. Once in the interior, these *Burghers* viewed themselves as *Trekboers* whose imagined community was shaped by experiences on the margins of the colony. A suitable English translation would be "Frontier Farmers." Members of the *Trekboer* imagined community also viewed themselves as indigenous, having permanently cut their ties with Holland and the Dutch East India Company. They adhered to a strict Calvinist Protestant ethic that privileged men as heads of the family.

The Afrikaner imagined community enshrined the master-servant relation present in Cape society into religious law. Thus, the *Trekboer* imagined community represented itself as Christian and therefore civilized. Afrikaner nationalists would later evoke the memories of the Great Trek to reinvent the Afrikaner imagined community. Certain authors, such as T.Dunbar Moodie, argue that Afrikaners believed themselves to be chosen by God. Andre Du Toit counters this argument by noting that the early settlers were not Calvinists though they were Christians. David Livingstone popularized the Calvinist ideal; later, the ideal was resurrected by nationalists who used it for purposes of political mobilization. Liberal thinkers and historians attributed the "savage-like" tendencies of the *Trekboers* to their isolation from the Cape Society's "civilizing" influence.[3]

The *Trekboer* is represented as a "new type of European" who opens up the African interior for "civilization." He is a "special" type of European who has been constructed by and within hostile "African conditions." According to Martin Legassick, the Trekboer's imagined community included exclusionary as well as inclusionary tendencies.[4] For example, because of the interdependent nature of the economy, *Trekboers* depended on their trade with Africans for their livelihood. However, there was no social interaction between the two groups outside of the master-servant relationship. Liberal historians trace the development of an Afrikaner imagined community to the isolation of this group from Western civilization. British scholars explain South African racism in terms of this lack of civilization. Some Afrikaner scholars argue that it is the "Africanness" of the *Trekboers* that justify their claim to be "indigenous" to Africa.[5] Furthermore, the Afrikaner imagined community has been shaped by conflicts between itself, Africans, and British forces. *Trekboers* became "settlers" following wars against the Africans in which they took over their land. The establishment of their own, independent states in the Orange Free State and Transvaal transformed the *Trekboer* imagined community from settlers to colonialists, since they were permanent dwellers who were entitled to rule over Africans. As colonialists, Afrikaners believed that they were a special, privileged community entitled to civilized rights such as a high standard of living, access to cheap labor, and an unlimited supply of slaves. According to this assumption, *Trekboers* were not only indigenous to Africa, but also superior to Africans. It is within these contours that what later came to be known as an "Afrikaner imagined community" developed.

By 1870, there was no clear meaning of Afrikaner. Afrikanders had been applied to slaves of mixed descent in the Cape and was detested by whites. Their language, Afrikaans, was a mixture of Dutch, Malay, and various African languages. Whites of Dutch ancestry began identifying themselves as Afrikaner in the late eighteenth century but the term had a colonial connotation rather than an ethnic one. It was used to distinguish whites of Dutch ancestry from the indigenous people and from other foreign-born whites. By 1872, Afrikaners were still thinking in terms of family or race rather than nation. Indeed, they were so divided that they appeared like different nations.[6] During the same period, the president of the South African Republic, T. E. Burghers, urged all whites in the country to belong to only one nationality: "de Afrikaansche." Afrikaansche was later used by the newspaper *Zuid Afrikaan* to include all whites, regardless of ethnicity or national origin.

Afrikaners also needed their own, distinct language to represent the reinvented identity. To disassociate it from its slave origins, attempts were made by the elite to "clean out" Afrikaans of its African and Malay influences. Afrikaans had to be presented as a Western language similar to French or English. Only then would the Afrikaners qualify as a white tribe in Africa, entitled to special rights because of their connection with Western civilization. Various publications began appearing in Afrikaans, for example, *Die Patriot—the Patriot*, a nationalist grammar, language, and school text book. An Afrikaans grammar book was published in 1876, a dictionary in 1917, and in 1919 the Bible was translated into Afrikaans.[7] This redefining of the Boer (initially used to designate whites of Dutch descent who were mostly farmers) imagined community was also reflected in political organizations. For example, in 1878, Onze Jan Hofmeyer founded the *Zuid Afrikaansche Boeren Beschermings Vereniging* (BBV) official newspaper. Its goal was the creation of a white South Africa in which both Afrikaner and British citizens shared the same nation. As an initiative of wealthy Afrikaners, this venture was supported by British capital.

By 1898, Afrikaner meant more than a "person of Dutch extraction, who believed in the advancement of the brandy market, protection to the corn farmer, and the repression of the native."[8] It represented a white community that identified itself as "indigenous" to South Africa as its only "home" unlike the British who retained their British nationality and could always leave for Britain. This self-identification of Afrikaners as indigenous is reflected in their artwork, national anthem, history, and novels. In official discourse, out of the four South African ethnic groups, only Afrikaners were allowed to identify with the continent, therefore denying Africans the right to represent themselves as such. The Afrikaner imagined community was increasingly redefined in ideological terms. The development of the Afrikaner imagined community was shaped by different debating societies in the western Cape that brought intellectuals and commercial farmers together. Schools and churches that exposed the community to strict Calvinist ideas also transformed this community. The church influenced the imagined community by presenting Afrikaners as a chosen people who were following God's divine will. According to this belief, Afrikaners were in the southern tip of Africa by God's choice and only God directed their affairs.[9] Their duty was to spread Western civilization by acting as trustees of the African majority. In this representation, religion and politics were united under the nationalist banner. Myths that represented Afrikaner heroes and the Vootrekkers expanding into "empty" land were popularized.[10] In these discourses, southern Africa was represented as a frontier in which the forces of civilization and barbarism battled each other. Civilization triumphed when savages were taught "their place" in the new society.

The *Trekboer* is represented as the "pioneer who opens up the frontier" to civilization. According to this belief, African communities are treated as homogenous, passive entities that are torn apart by internal conflict and awed by the invaders' superior military technology. African politics is taught through African chiefs, who are represented as despots ruling their people with an iron fist. In the "Frontier" tradition, the *Trekboer* became the primary framework to describe nineteenth century South African history. This self-identification was reinforced in school textbooks. Only children who were educated in Afrikaans and Afrikaner history could ensure the reproduction of future generations of white supremacists.[11]

The Afrikaner imagined community was also shaped by its intellectuals who produced a counter-ideology to challenge British economic control. Through their work after the war, Afrikaners imagined themselves as special people whose strength lay in isolation with the freedom to discriminate against Africans. Racial discrimination was not applied equally to all races. The Afrikaner imagined community accepted other whites depending on the circumstances. For example, Afrikaner and British interests converged in the need for African labor and the desire to maintain white supremacy. Though still discriminated against, people of mixed descent and Indians were treated more favorably than Africans. Race was the key determinant of power relations between all the social groups.

Because of an increase in landless Afrikaners (*bywoners*) in urban areas prior to 1910, Afrikaner imagined community's view of Africans changed and became more negative. *Bywoners* faced housing and job competition from Africans. Afrikaner nationalist leaders used race as the rallying point in an attempt to "save" these poor Afrikaners who lived in squalor alongside Africans. It was important to improve the economic and political conditions faced by *bywoners* because their poverty threatened the myth of white superiority. To maintain the position of *bywoners* as members of a civilized race, the Afrikaner imagined community represented Africans as criminals, heathens, kaffirs, or savages, who threatened the white race. This view was also crucial in ensuring disunity between *bywoners* and Africans. In segregated South Africa (1910 through 1948), the savage became a native who had rights only in "native" residential areas. By the mid-1940s the African was a Bantu who belonged to a tribe or nation without any rights in the South African state. This representation was further influenced by the material base of the economy.

As the need for African labor increased, so did the Afrikaners' attempt to represent Africans as the "other," namely foreigners in South Africa whose only raison d'etre was to be laborers for God's chosen race (the Afrikaners). This representation was based on unequal power relations between the white minority and Africans. Once

Africans represented themselves as such, their claim to South Africa could not be denied. It was this denial of Africans representing themselves as such that characterized the Afrikaner imagined community. In this debate, only Afrikaner claims were legitimate because they were the only group that was deemed to be indigenous to South Africa. In school textbooks, Afrikaner history claimed that Africans arrived in Southern Africa at the same time as the European colonialists. According to this view of history, both communities were foreign to the region, including Africans who arrived from the northern end of the continent. According to this perspective, Southern Africa was empty when the Europeans first arrived. Afrikaners imagined their community as white, entitling them to certain rights. It was imagined within a state that protected its members. British imperialism forced Afrikaners in an economically and culturally subordinate position within the South African nation. British imperialist ideals were implemented by Lord Milner, the Governor General of British Southern Africa from 1897 to 1905. Milner aimed at making South Africa totally British and at creating the proper conditions for racial capitalism. His policy encouraged the settlement of British citizens throughout the country, an efficient control over African labor, and the anglicization of South Africa. On the issue of African labor Milner noted,

> If the aboriginal natives are to come and go in large numbers in search of labour and to reside for considerable periods in the midst of a white community, there must be some passport system, else the place will be in pandemonium . . . It is absolutely essential to have some reasonable arrangements by which the incoming native can be identified, and his movements traced. Nor is it unjust, indeed it is necessary, that when he has freely entered into a contract he should be bound to observe the terms of it.[12]

Milner's vision led to a unified South Africa state led by a white oligarchy based on white supremacy and exclusive British rule. The goal of the South African state was to increase the standard of living of the white minority and make South Africa a "white man's country" As noted by W. A. De Klerk in such a scenario both Afrikaners and Africans were seen as indigenous and have-nots in British-dominated cities and urban areas.

Political Representation:
The National Party, 1914–1948

In 1914, General J. B. M. Hertzog and other Afrikaner nationalists founded the National Party (NP). According to John Fisher, the party's manifesto aimed toward five goals. First, it called for freedom of language and religion. Second, it demanded self-determination based on Afrikaner culture. Third, it opposed racial mixing. Fourth, it included other white immigrants as members of the imagined community, although some were favored over others. For example, whites of Dutch descent were privileged in terms of access to state support as well as housing, but Jews were discriminated against. German immigrants were privileged over British or Russian immigrants. Finally, the National Party called for a white nation under the trusteeship of British South Africans and Afrikaners. The open racism of the NP attracted *bywoners* and poor Afrikaner farmers who saw it as the only means of improving their economic standing in the community. Wealthy Afrikaner farmers were also attracted to the party because it promised to intervene in agriculture. By 1921, most of these farmers were its strongest supporters.

During this period, the Afrikaner imagined community underwent some changes. Afrikaner increasingly came to mean one who was white, spoke Afrikaans and belonged to one of the Afrikaner churches. The NP represented itself as the father of Afrikaners, especially the poor ones. The party would use the state to find work for the unemployed, create pension plans and old peoples' homes, and mitigate Communist influences on Afrikaner workers. It would also help increase the number of Afrikaners in the civil service.

The Afrikaner imagined community was also influenced by economic changes that faced South Africa after the Anglo-Boer war. After the war, Britain controlled the economy in general and the banking system in particular. As a result, debt forced most Afrikaner farmers into bankruptcy and into cities in search of jobs. In urban areas, secular values replaced religious influences. This transformed the Afrikaner patriarchal family. Men felt economically threatened as more women were forced into wage labor to make ends meet. As a result, families became more individualistic and egalitarian, thereby threatening the integrity and existence of the Afrikaner family. Even though they were faced by the divisive influences of urban centers, Afrikaner nationalist leaders organized the community to sustain its exclusiveness. They planned cultural events where Afrikaners met and discussed their common plight and organized language clubs as well as religious group gatherings. The role of this elite was to maintain the distinct cultural cohesiveness of Afrikanerdom in a cosmopolitan setting. The Afrikaner intellectuals shaped the community's contours. The NP sharpened its representation of Africans as enemies of civilization and of Afrikaner identity. In the 1924 elections, the NP asked Afrikaners to choose whether South Africa was going to be "one huge black compound kept for the benefit of the capitalists, or a prosperous white man's country."[13] According to P. Eric. Louw, the state that Hertzog envisioned did the following:

- Successfully guaranteed the supply of black migrant labor to the mines (and northern farmers), thereby building a tax base to pay for its Keynesian policies.

- Refined the administration of "black reserves" and increased the size of these reserves.

- Made urban segregation compulsory. This segregation legislation was driven by middle-class concerns about poor Afrikaners and nonwhites living together in slums that had grown up since the Boer war.

- Created working-class employment for Afrikaners in the state-owned railways, Iron & Steel Corporation, and secondary industries that mushroomed thanks to tariff protection.

- Facilitated the growth of an Afrikaner middle class by employing Afrikaners in the civil service as teachers.

- Tamed trade unions through an industrial conciliation system that delivered material benefits to white workers.

- Made Afrikaans a second national language (1925), replaced the British flag with a South African flag (1928), made Die Stem a national anthem alongside "God Save the King" (1934), and secured dominion status within the British Empire through the statue of Westminister (1931). Malan's NP argues this only served to obscure Britain's de facto hegemony.[14]

Hertzog's reforms did not ease the sense of alienation that Afrikaners felt in British-dominated cities and urban areas. W. A. De Klerk notes,

> They had been a defeated people. Their traditional society, in the process of defeat and post-war reconstruction, had been shaken to its foundations. . . . They had. . . . gathered in fringe areas of cities. They had already formed a wage-earning class; and alongside but also below them, another had been forming. It was black. The dominant white [Anglo] classes of the cities were no comfort, because they too were strange. The cities were still citadels of Anglo-Saxon culture and British economic power. The new immigrant Afrikaners were, in fact, strangers in their own country: hesitant, fearful of using their own language in shops and businesses, and confined very largely to the humbler areas and jobs. They were without the fine schools supported by the English churches, the institutions and amenities generally which the English took for granted. . . . They were exposed to rivalry of non-white South Africa. The increasing competition from black Africans, which took place primarily in the cities, affected them . . . [while] the established English middle class lived and worked in areas where the problems of color were items in the daily news. In spite of all the leaders of the Union having been ex-Boer War generals, South Africa was still a British country.[15]

The strong presence of Africans in cities and urban areas was represented as a sign of "disorder," a "return to barbarism" and the "end of white civilization." Having represented whites as a homogeneous group, the NP won the elections.

During the same campaign, J. B. M. Hertzog, D. F. Malan and Tielman Ross of the National Party issued the "Black Manifesto" which described what would happen if Smuts' policy of a segregated pro-British South Africa was adopted. For example, Africans would continue to threaten Afrikaners as they competed in the job market and access to various resources. According to the NP, Smuts' segregation policy was too soft on Africans. Throughout the document, the terms "a Kaffir Land," "black Kaffir state," and "a kaffir ocean" were liberally used. According to P. Eric Louw, the elections were about much more than keeping the "Kaffir in his place." Instead, he argues,

> Afrikaners perceived the UP's 'South Africanism' to mean a continuation of *de facto* Anglo domination within a unified state structured to serve Anglo corporate interests. Worse still, a UP state would serve the interests of a rapacious Anglo business sector demanding ever–greater quantities of labor. This encouraged black migration from

South Africa's "reserves," Mozambique, and British Africa. Such migration seemed to herald a new-looking industrialized South Africa, which would be increasingly urbanized, with cities demographically dominated by black people.[16]

Afrikaners believed that Smuts' United Party (UP) was controlled by the British. Nationalists claimed that their culture and history as a people would be lost if Smuts' policy succeeded.

Prominent leaders, including D. F. Malan, within the Afrikaner imagined community who wanted more economic power for the Afrikaners progressively changed the self-representation, and thus the development, of their community. These Afrikaners were influenced by white supremacy ideas emanating from Germany. According to these ideas, the pure race (*Boerevolk*) had to be maintained because that was God's will. Within this construction of the imagined community, the individual did not matter. What was important was the state that represented God's authority on earth. One of the Boerevolk proponents was Nicholas Diederichs, who put forward a view of nationalism that rejected liberalism and democracy. "Nationalism," he noted, "rejects this concept of freedom . . . on the grounds of its doctrine that the individual in itself is nothing, but only becomes itself in the nation as the highest community."[17] This discourse shaped the Afrikaner imagined community by privileging the state over the individual, and males over females. The Afrikaner imagined community became more exclusive, as religion, language, and culture were used to mold its boundaries.

The role of the Afrikaner brotherhood (*Afrikaner Broederbond*) was crucial in determining how the community developed. This organization was created in 1918 by a group of concerned Afrikaners who were worried about the difficult conditions faced by the community, notably its lack of economic power, the cultural influence of the British on Afrikaner culture, and the fate of *bywoners*. In 1919, the *Broederbond* became a secret society with membership by invitation only and open only to Afrikaner males of good Christian morals. These men, who were over thirty-five years of age, had chosen South Africa as their permanent home. The organization aimed at promoting Afrikaner language, religion, as well as Afrikaner self-determination at all levels of society. In the 1920s, the *Broederbond* organized several cultural organizations. It also created Afrikaner business firms such as an insurance business (Sanlam) and an Afrikaner people's bank bank (*Volkskaass*). The most important aspect of this process was the study of Afrikaans in schools. By the 1930s, the *Broederbond* had become the major force shaping the boundaries of the Afrikaner imagined community. The *Broederbond* (which also advised D. F.Malan) encouraged Afrikaners to help each other in all aspects of their lives. It also urged them to buy from Afrikaner businesses, employ each other, and engage in their own cultural activities.

In the 1930's, the first generation of Afrikaners born and raised in urban areas came of age; this Afrikaner generation's identity was shaped by the economic conditions prevailing in British-controlled capitalist South Africa. Intellectually, this generation was shaped by nationalist ideas emanating from Afrikaner universities such as Bloemfontein, Potchefstroom, Pretoria, and Stellenbosch. The Purified National Party (PNP) was created on July 1934 as a result of contradictions amongst advocates of stricter segregation, proponents of Afrikaner self-determination, individuals who pushed for greater control over African labor, and Hofmeyer's South African NP open to all whites. Most of the new party members were also critical of Hofmeyer's relationship with British capital. For D. F. Malan, the PNP president, all white South Africans were either Afrikaners or potential Afrikaners. Every village and city in the country had to be under Afrikaner control. The PNP wanted to regulate African labor by moving Africans into centralized locations. This representation implied a strict separation between the races as the only way that labor would be made accessible to Afrikaners. The Broederbond and the PNP helped organize the re-enactment of the Great Trek in August 1938, an event in which only Afrikaners were involved. The spectacle followed the Trekkers' original route. The wagons passed through Johannesburg, where "men and women gazed at the cumbersome vehicles that had cradled a nation, and were silent with adoration. . . . The Afrikaners on the Rand had made a pilgrimage to a new symbol of nationhood."[18] The symbol of Afrikaner unity, the ox-wagon, was re-invented. The procession ended with the inauguration of the Voortrekker Monument in Pretoria, where "women knelt in silent prayer." The image of women kneeling in silent prayer for the fatherland, maintains the supremacy of Afrikaner males. Women became the spiritual pillars of the new dispensation. Afrikaner women took part in the reenactment of the Trek as participants rather than leaders. The ceremony concluded with the singing of the Afrikaner national anthem, *Die Stem*. This spectacle represented Afrikaner nationalism as classless.

The PNP won the 1948 (whites-only) elections on a campaign platform fought on *Swart gevaar* (black danger). White workers who competed against African workers in the cities supported the National Party because they believed that it would halt the "black peril." To that aim, the PNP introduced *apartheid* (apartness). Apartheid was proposed as a departure from British integration policy, which lumped all races together economically but separated them geographically (via different residential areas). Apartheid theorists did not consider it racist because each group would develop free from the domination of others. British policy encouraged "horizontal domination" while apartheid presented an alternative "vertical separation" based on total partition. According to Louw, the apartheid ideal served Afrikaner interests in two ways: "First, its logic of cultural partition offered a means for Afrikaners to secure an autonomous space free of both Anglo domination and the potential domination of a black majority within a unified state. Second, it was argued, apartheid (or "apartness") involved ending white supremacy-that is, each group would be free of the domination of others, and hence able to develop its own way."[19]

Louw identified three challenges facing the National Party: foreign, materialist, and godless.

- Encoded into apartheid's founding texts was a rejection of godless capitalism, which (because it was driven by a single–minded pursuit of profit) was seen to ignore the "higher callings of community/cultural identity and community service, and to divide the nation into classes (which undermined the unity and welfare of the volk). Under Malan, Strijdom, and Verwoerd, this variant of anti-capitalism was a powerful subtext of Afrikaner nationalism. It began to weaken during Vorster's premiership, and was finally abandoned by P. W. Botha's NP.

- Fascism was rejected as unchristian, and during the 1940s, Malan 's BNP fought an intense struggle for its very political survival against pro-Nazi *Ossewabrandwag*/OB (Ox wagon guards). For a while, it was unclear which of the two—Malan's Christian nationalists or the OB—would emerge victorious.

- Communism was passionately disliked because it advocated atheism. Christian nationalists were deeply concerned that trade unions, led by communists like Solly Sachs, would recruit Afrikaners into "godless communism" and hence divide Afrikaans working class from the rest of the *volk*. Ardent anticommunism was a consistent feature of NP ideology. Hence, one of the first NP actions after coming to power was the 1950 suppression of communism Act. This was used to hound communists out of the trade union movement, while Christian nationalists built alternative trade unions to ensure the large Afrikaner working class was brought into the fold of a unified *volk*. This accorded with the NP's *Verzuiling* logic that national groups should have their own organizations, including trade unions.[20]

The leaders of the National Party introduced laws that made apartheid more efficient. The NP was successful because it convinced Afrikaners that only an interventionist state would end their unemployment and the humiliation of living in a British-dominated country. Such a state would limit African migration to cities and take control of the economy. Apartheid reinforced the belief that Africans were foreigners in South Africa by representing whites as civilized and, therefore, superior. The Afrikaner community imagined itself as a part of Europe, *yet in Africa but not of Africa*. Such a community would not succeed without the active participation of its women whom it sought to "protect" against such urban "vices" as communism. Poor Afrikaners also had to be extracted from city slums, where they lived alongside their African neighbors.

Gender

The Afrikaner imagined community was also shaped by gender relations. Women played a prominent role throughout its history. They set its moral tone by adhering to Christian teachings and the master-servant relations of white supremacy in the Cape colony. Afrikaner women resented equality between master and servant. Equality between master and servant would have resulted in African and women of mixed descent being equal to Afrikaner women, such equality lowered the privileged status of Afrikaner women in society.Their societal role as its moral boundary markers in their functions as teachers of their children or as police (monitoring agents) over inter-racial extramarital relations would be lost. Afrikaner women were prominent in the community as the keepers of its memory and pride. For example, in 1879, some wives encouraged their husbands to fight while mothers called on their sons to defend the land of their birth. As a result, Transvaal declared its independence from the British in 1880. Afrikaner memory immortalized this conflict as the first war of independence.

Initiated by the Afrikaner elite, gender politicization also contributed to the boundary setting of the Afrikaner-imagined community. This elite used the suffering of Afrikaner women and children in British concentration camps to re-invent the Afrikaner imagined community. As a result of starvation and disease, 4,100 women, 22,000 children, and 1,600 disabled men perished.[21] In this re-invention, Afrikaners were viewed as innocent, pure, and as God's chosen people. This construction of the community merged suffering with religion to demonstrate the plight of God's chosen people. According to this representation, God allowed his people to suffer as a way of teaching them their special place and mission on earth. Suffering and oppression were represented as the means through which God purified people. Within this discourse, suffering came to be seen as a virtue ora badge of honor and confirmation that the nation was chosen by God. Afrikaner poets were involved in shaping the contours of the imagined community. Totius's poem, *Rachel* (Rachel, mother of Joseph) follows this genre. It concludes,

> Thus I think of
> The Rachels of my land
> Who without home or house
> Were cruelly surprised-burnt
> Out of their homes
> Pushed into the veld.[22]

Not all women were victims during the Anglo/Boer war;most were freedom fighters, nurses, or workers. Afrikaner women were also willing to take up arms against the British.

Constant humiliation of Afrikaner women marked their existence under British domination, either in school—where they had to learn English—or at home, where they were the victims of the raids of British soldiers. Most often the first encounter of Afrikaner children with the British was humiliating. This mistreatment of Afrikaner children by the British was repeated over and over by Afrikaner mothers who never forgot the ill treatment. One child in Transvaal declared that she was learning English so that one day she could tell a Khaki (British soldier), "hands up."[23] Afrikaner women became the keepers of the memory of the nation. Of these women, James Ramsay MacDonald wrote,

> She it is who returns, forgiving nothing . . . She it is who has her heroes of the war; she it is who has her dead to mourn over. She it is who feels most keenly that all her sufferings, her weary waiting and her prayers have been naught.[24]

Because British soldiers burned Afrikaner homes and farms during the war, the latter were reduced to poverty. The women who remained behind as men left to fight had nothing to eat except *mealies* (maize and beans). Barring collaborators and some members of the elite, almost all Afrikaners suffered this humiliation. British brutality turned moderate Afrikaners into extreme nationalists. They preferred to leave their homes rather than fall under British authority. On a farm that was about to be burned by British soldiers, a young Afrikaner girl interrupted the preparations by "indignantly" playing "their national anthem to [the soldiers] on the piano."[25] The Afrikaner elite capitalized on the suffering of the Afrikaner people by using it for political mobilization purposes although the degree of suffering differed across gender and class lines. As a result, unity was created where previously it did not exist.

Lord Milner, who was Governor General of British Southern Africa, was the driving force behind British anglicization policy. Milner who firmly believed that South Africa was a white man's country, advocated a multi-pronged strategy of British domination. The first goal was to control the mining sector. A viable mining sector would only be made possible by introducing an educated workforce. Toward that goal, the government introduced British schools that forced Afrikaner women to relinquish their children to a British education that undermined their culture and language. To make South Africa a British country, Afrikaner education had to be replaced with a British oriented one. According to P. Eric Louw, Milner's anglicization policy also aimed at "denationalizing" Afrikaners for better control. Milner's mass migration of British citizens to South Africa, state-run schools, and the introduction of English as the official language all aimed at further the goal of anglicization. These policies contributed to disempower Afrikaner women as the cultural markers of their community. According to Milner,

> On the political side I attach the greatest importance of all to the increase of the British population . . . If, ten years hence, there are three men of British race to two of Dutch, the country will be safe and prosperous. If there are three of Dutch to two of British, we shall have perpetual difficulty . . . Next to the composition of the population, the thing which matters most is education. In the agricultural parts of the Cape Colony this needs to be completely overhauled . . . . In the new colonies the case will be easier to deal with provided we make English *the language of all higher education*. Dutch should only be used to teach English, and English to teach everything else. Language is important, but the tone and spirit of the teaching conveyed in it is even more important . . . I would attach especial importance to *school history books*.[26] (emphasis in the original)

Afrikaner women reconstructed Afrikaner nationalism in several ways. First they taught their children its basic tenets by acting as the guardians of Afrikaner history, culture, and tradition. Women were also the backbone of the Afrikaner family and ardent supporters of their men. For example, during the Anglo/Boer War, the husbands of Boer women who returned home were treated with contempt by those women whose husbands were still at the front. Resistance to British imperialism took many forms. For instance, a headmistress of a school in Bloemfontein refused to allow her students to perform in a competition in honor of the King of England. On another occasion, to celebrate the birthday of the former Transvaal president, Paul Kruger, women led children who carried Orange Free State and Transvaal flags and sang the Afrikaner freedom song, *Volkslied*. Women passed on the tradition of resistance to their children. Such transmission of traditions shaped how the community imagined itself.

Inter-class relations among Afrikaner women also shaped the Afrikaner imagined community. Middle-class women created various organizations to improve the conditions that faced the majority of Afrikaner women. For example, in the Cape colony, middle-class women founded ladies committees to help victims of the Anglo/ Boer war. The *Afrikaanse Chritelike Vrouwe Vereeniging* (Afrikaans Christian Women's Association, or ACUWA), founded in Cradock, addressed social welfare needs. The Association encouraged women and girls to value their language by speaking it. These women imagined their community in the tradition of European nationalism, through Afrikaner history. According to that tradition, Africans were not worthy of equal rights. Women were also active in self-sustaining projects that rejected liberal paternalism. They opposed liberal influence because they believed its paternalism prevented it from setting the boundaries of the imagined community. For these women being "an Afrikaner involved language, culture, as well as politics."[27]

The capitalist economy disrupted Afrikaner society. Previously, men in their capacity as heads of households acted as God's agents on earth. Their authority had to be obeyed. The place of women was in the home with the children. Wage labor transformed these relations. Following the Anglo-Boer war, most men were either out of work, in debt, or away from home in search of work. Women were forced into wage labor. This development had its own contradictions. For example, the introduction of the capitalist economy relieved Afrikaner women of some tasks. As the church took over responsibility for education, women no longer had to teach their children at home and were therefore left with free time for other activities. Another series of restraints was imposed on these women. Under the new power relations, women were treated as minors by both men and the state. As daughters, mothers, mistresses, sisters, and/or wives, women were also relegated to the "private" domain.

On the other hand, women gained a degree of freedom in the capitalist economy as many left rural patriarchal homes for secular cities. Most of the women who left for the cities were poor. In cities, they worked in factories, as prostitutes, or as maids. Sometimes these women sent remittances home. The urban experience gained by these women made them more assertive, as they became used to paying rent, taking care of themselves in strange environments, and living among people from different backgrounds and ideologies. In order to defend their rights and improve their working conditions, some women joined trade unions. The Transvaal Garment Workers Union campaigned for crèches (baby care centers), allowances for women for maternity benefits, and other special needs. A majority of the women worked in the textile industry, where they were protected under the civilized labor policy, which preserved better paying jobs for whites. In the cities, women discovered that the state privileged white men by paying men more, offering job benefits and higher level positions and allowing men to open bank accounts. Although white women were not oppressed to the same degree as African women, they were affected by the state's gender construction privileging white men at all levels. By the late 1940s, women moved into clerical work, as well as into service, professional, and industrial positions that had been vacated by white men. In the political sphere, the Purified National Party's think tank, the elitist Afrikaner Broederbond, was closed to women members.

The Afrikaner imagined community was also shaped by the experiences of women in the cities and urban areas, where they developed a distinct class consciousness. The community became more defensive as a way to "protect" women from Communist influences. Gender was mobilized in support of the nationalist cause. Thus, poor women, who at times worked as prostitutes in poor multiracial ghettoes, were used by the elite class as evidence of the decadence and moral decay of western civilization. The common experience shared by these women in terms of gender, ethnicity, and hiring practices led to the development of a common sense of identity. Women recommended other women for employment. As the practice developed, large numbers of female workers from the same area were employed at the same factories. This experience differed from the experiences of African male workers in the mines where individuals from different ethnic backgrounds were forced to live together to encourage a divide and rule policy for better control. Changes brought about by urbanization (such as better communication and education) also introduced class cleavages among Afrikaner women. The poor ones performed the worst jobs, while middle-class women had access to domestic help. Some middle-class women managed domestic labor, which gave them access to funds as well as some sense of freedom. Both classes were oppressed, though to different degrees. Middle-class women had to deal with patriarchy at a higher level with better-educated men than the ones working class women encountered. Some middle-class women were forced to stay home even though they were qualified to work in the public sphere. Others stayed home because they could not get the jobs they wanted, for example, in the legal and medical professions. Thus, class shaped the impact and contours of patriarchy. Middle-class women's organizations worked closely with the Dutch Reformed Church according to the premise that religion was not only for isolated individuals but also for members of a specific nation.[28] Afrikaner men also volunteered their services in women's organizations. Charity towards the poor was organized on the basis of need and ethnicity. These women's organizations built schools, hospitals, and helped place whites in jobs. When faced with a common enemy, Afrikaner women presented a united front.

During the re-enactment of the Great Trek in 1938, women laid the foundation of the Voortrekker Monument in Pretoria. Afrikaner women benefited from the new national myth as mothers who occupied a special place in the community. Women continued to play their role as cultural and racial boundary markers of the new nation without challenging its racist discourse. For example, they set up "Afrikaner women only" organizations that catered to their needs. Gender served the goals of the Afrikaner elite because it was used for political mobilization purposes, based on the belief that the imagined community was the protector of Afrikaner women. As mothers of the nation, their privileged position vis-a-vis Africans and people of mixed descent remained unchallenged. This construction fit within an Afrikaner nationalism that focused on the cycle of death and suffering based on the image of the strong Afrikaner woman.[29]

DIFFERENCES AND SIMILARITIES BETWEEN THE AFRICAN AND AFRIKANER IMAGINED COMMUNITIES

The African and Afrikaner imagined communities shared some similarities. In both, religion was important. Among Africans, religion opened the community up to the colonizing agents and missionaries who redefined its boundaries. Religion also introduced differences between believers and non-believers within the community, as well as alliances with white liberals. It was also crucial in moderating African militants, and it was within its confines that African independent churches emerged. These churches challenged white supremacy. Afrikaners used religion to close the community to outsiders. Only the white race was included in this imagining and, depending on the circumstances, only Afrikaners were members of the community.

The African imagined community was influenced by missionary education that introduced new values and needs. Western education negated African customs. The African elite aimed at assimilation in a white society, the highest level of civilization. For this elite, liberalism represented the ideal imagined community because of its paternalistic belief in man's equality. Built on this foundation, the African imagined community was inclusive of all races unlike the exclusive community of the white minority. The education of the Afrikaner imagined community aimed at presenting its members as exceptional Europeans, Africa's white tribe, which was indigenized by hostile African conditions. This explains the rejection of the term Boer and the adoption of Afrikaner for self-representation. This construction shaped the community's exclusive racial boundaries.

Class differences between both nationalisms also affected these imaginings. Middle-class Afrikaners empathized with poor ones. Since race was privileged over class, it was important to improve the living conditions of poor Afrikaners, which helped cement boundaries of the imagined community. The Afrikaner imagined community was influenced by the living conditions of the bywoners. In order to keep the bywoners from African and British influence, the elite had to keep reminding Afrikaners of how they were all victims of British imperialism. Gender was used to mobilize support of the nationalist cause without giving women the equality that came with this remembering. Congress did not appeal to gender to mobilize its followers as the Purified National Party did. Though different, both parties placed women in subordinate roles in their communities. Not until the late 1920s, did Congress mobilize the poor under the leadership of Gumede and the influence of the Communist Party. This explains the differences in emphasis between the African and Afrikaner nationalism in terms of their relation to the poor in their respective communities. Another similarity is the influence of the material conditions on both communities though with different results. Africans were forced into wage labor by the capitalist economy; additionally, they were forced to give up land and abide by a taxation policy. Among Afrikaners the capitalist economy provided more land and opportunities. However, the capitalist economy also introduced new layers of subordination in terms of gender relations. The representation of Africans as foreigners in South Africa, as well as thieves, lazy, and murderers sharpened with the increase in labor shortage. The poor economic conditions and hostility that confronted Africans in urban areas forced them to identify themselves as natives to strengthen their imagined community. Afrikaners who favored an imagined community inclusive of whites were defeated by the exclusionists. As a subordinate elite, Africans reacted to developments in the Afrikaner community, which explains why they rejected a race-conscious imagined community in favor of a multiracial one. The Charterists' conception of the imagined community triumphed over an African imagined community organized along racial lines. In essence, the Afrikaner community developed within exclusive racial boundaries while the African community was influenced by a form of Victorian humanitarianism and paternalistic liberalism that emphasized mankind's commonality without reference to race.

Conclusion

To sum up, we have observed that between 1867 and 1948, several factors shaped the development of an Afrikaner imagined community. First, it was imagined within racial barriers based on debates that represented Africans as the other and savages. According to this view, Afrikaners identified themselves as superior based on race. This identification came with certain rights, for example, a high standard of living. Second, the capitalist economy shaped the community by introducing different relations of power based on class. Divisions between poor and rich Afrikaners accelerated as a result of the Anglo-Boer war as well as the capitalist economy. This introduced landless byowners whose presence laid out the boundaries of the imagined community in distinct ways. For example, culture, language, and religion were added to the definition of the community. A centralized state that introduced schools also informed the community's imaginings. Afrikaners felt threatened by British education, which in turn encouraged them to emphasize their culture and language. As a result, they formed their own schools where both the Afrikaans language and Afrikaner history were taught. Third, a bilingual elite was crucial in mobilizing the majority of the people. Fourth, Christianity was essential. It was used to exclude heathens as well as to deny Africans any claim to the country. We also examined how gender was important in how the community imagined itself.

Further Readings

P. Eric Louw, *The Rise, Fall and Legacy of Apartheid*. Westport, Connecticut: Praeger, 2004.

W. A. De Klerk, *The Puritans in Africa: A Story of Afrikanerdom*. Harmondsworth: Penguin Books, 1975.

Leonard Thompson, *The Political Mythology of Apartheid*. New Haven: Yale University Press, 1985.

CHAPTER 3

THE IMPACT OF APARTHEID ON AFRICAN AND AFRIKANER NATIONALISMS, 1948–1994

> Their voices soared and the chamber filled with beautiful sounds that one didn't expect from the throats of men about to die. They had conquered fear, the fear of death, and there was nothing left to intimidate them anymore. Death is the final weapon of the oppressor. If you overcome the fear of death, then, and only then, do you become truly free.
>
> —Thula Bopela and Daluxolo Luthuli, *Umkhonto we Sizwe: Fighting for a divided People*

> You felt your blood rise as you stood up, and felt proud being black, and that is what Steve did to me.
>
> —Winnie Nomzamo Mandela

IN THIS CHAPTER, WE EXAMINE HOW APARTHEID MADE DISTINCT AND specific contributions to the exclusive character of the National Party's (NP) racial policies. We will also discuss how apartheid provoked different African nationalist debates within the Pan Africanist Congress (PAC), the Black Consciousness Movement (BCM), and the African National Congress (ANC) dominating that debate. This chapter is divided into four sections. The first section provides a characterization of apartheid and its evolution, goals and definition of the imagined community: it also examines how this characterization influenced apartheid's conception of nationalism. Section two looks at how apartheid elicited different nationalist reactions from the ANC, the PAC, and the BC. Although the Inkatha Freedom Party resorted to ANC symbols, it did not constitute a threat to the NP, nor did it provide a counter-nationalist debate because it officially operated openly within the framework of the apartheid regime. From this perspective, only the ANC, PAC, and BC are viewed as genuine and legitimate "liberation" organizations. Section three discusses conception and definition of the South African community, and its political economy of the ANC and the NP. Section four examines broader inter-racial and inter-class relations in South Africa up to 1994.

Institutional History of Apartheid

Studies that attempt to explain the emergence of apartheid exhibit two characteristics.[1] In the first set of explanations, history is perceived as a series of events that occur horizontally, in a linear movement. According to this perspective, segregation is understood as one particular event, and apartheid as another. On the bases of this reading, "apartheid' is fundamentally different from all other forms of segregation. For example, Stanley Trapido argues that apartheid replaced a representative regime "of established manufacturing and commercial interests timidly contemplating reform [with] a political order reflecting the concerns of a small group who were served better by the intensification of existing labour-repressive measures: farmers, financiers, small industrialists, and white workers threatened by African acquisition of industrial skills."[2]

Bernard Magubane further notes that apartheid constitutes a new stage during which the white minority's system of systematic economic exploitation and political oppression of Africans is entrenched. Other authors have argued that apartheid was exceptional in several respects: the small Afrikaner capitalist class that controlled the state: the openly racist state policy, the reproduction and maintaining of 'cheap labor" in the reserves; and "last but not least the increasingly repressive and discriminatory laws introduced by the Afrikaner, bureaucratic bourgeoisie. According to P. Eric Louw, apartheid (apartness) was, in theory, distinctly and discriminatory different from segregation. Apartheid called for total separation between the races. Unlike segregation, which was based on the premise of white supremacy, total separation did not imply master-servant relations and would allow each race to be in control of its own area. Thus, segregation was based on "horizontal domination" with whites as the master race while apartheid was based on "vertical separation" with each ethnic group in control of its own destiny. In practice, apartheid was a total failure. The NP and the *Broederbond* rejected "racial capitalism's ethnic ranking (placing Anglos on top; British imperialist hegemony; and the ethnic *"mengelmos"*) created by Anglo capitalism's importation of black migrants from across Southern Africa."[3] Afrikaner nationalists also opposed the importation of Chinese and Indian workers.

Afrikaners did not invent racial segregation in South Africa. It was a "tradition" upheld by whites, especially the British, who had ironed their skills in the craft against the Irish and later indigenous groups in the Americas. Leon Louw and Frances Kendall posit that to know the roots of apartheid in South Africa, one must look at the policies of the Dutch East India Company. In 1660, the company set the first apartheid law that separated *Khoisan* from *Burghers*. In 1663, the company introduced a law that legitimized separate schools, and imposed another law in 1678 banning mixed marriages. Sexual intercourse between the races was officially banned in 1681. During Theophilus Shepstone's governorship in Natal (1845 through 1875), racial separation was further entrenched into law as "Native Policy." It was this policy that Afrikaners further refined into apartheid by introducing the idea of total partition.

The second reading of apartheid looks at the relationship between politics (narrow state policy) and economics. Relations of production are privileged over politics. In this study apartheid is viewed as the logical outcome of earlier, British segregationist policies. Accordingly, apartheid was not fundamentally different from the preceding order. The only differences were the post-war conditions (when the number of Africans increased in urban centers, thus "threatening" Afrikaner privileges), intensified level of state violence and repression, and total partition.[4] Apartheid must be understood as the logical conclusion of racist European debates based on the belief that Africans were inferior to whites and, therefore unworthy of equal human, civil and political rights to those of the white minority.

The essence of apartheid was total economic, political and social control over Africans. It provided whites with "security" as well as "peace" and "stability" which could only be ensured if the different races were kept apart. Toward this goal, a *Population Registration Act* was introduced in 1950. This Act mandated that all citizens register their names, place of birth, and (most important of all), race in a national register. Individual entries were removed only upon death. Racial categorization was entrenched in the legal order. People did not exist as individuals but only as racially defined groups: for example, "Native," "Colored," or "White."

In spite of this "state dictionary," some people "passed" for other races. Thus, a "Colored" person could pass for white, while light-skinned Africans passed for "Colored." On the other hand, "Colored" could be reclassified as "Native," just as darker whites were classified as "Colored." Thus, racial boundaries were not rigid and static: they changed depending on the circumstances. Race also informed apartheid education. Thus, in 1954, the state outlawed missionary education for Africans. From then on, African education was administered by a Department of Bantu Education. Verwoerd explained the philosophy behind apartheid education:

> When I have control of Native Education I will reform it so that the Natives will be taught from childhood to realise that equality with Europeans is not for them. . . . People who believe in equality are not desirable teachers for Natives. . . . When my department controls Native education it will know for what class of higher education a Native is fitted, and whether he will have a chance in life to use his knowledge. . . . What is the use of teaching the Bantu child mathematics when it cannot use it in practice? This is quite absurd.[5]

The goal of apartheid education was to promote local and parochial "ethnic" and "tribal" identities to discourage the emergence of a national identity. In this regard, African inferiority was presented as quite "natural" and "normal."

Under apartheid, each racial group had separate educational institutions that reinforced the dominant master-servant relations of power. Educational institutions were also divided along ideological lines. These educational institutions played two roles. First, they legitimized and made concrete the notion of separate racial and ethnic groups in South Africa. They also reinforced the separatist ideology of the racist regime. In these institutions, young Afrikaners were trained for their "natural" leadership role in society. Africans were taught a history that was merely a chronology of military defeats at the hands of Europeans. Some Africans constructed an alternative body of knowledge that celebrated their own culture, history, and tradition, therefore, reversing and negating the impact of apartheid education. Mbulelo Vizihungo Mzamane describes how even in high school, teachers in Soweto had already constructed a different way of knowing what curriculum included a particular focus on African literature, history and culture for the benefit of the students. However, for the final exams, students had to recite the Afrikaner conception of African history in order to pass their exams.

Africans acted according to what was expected of "a good kaffir" in their daily activities. Their imagined community was reinforced within the confines of "bush colleges" where "school boycotts" were in most cases "the first lessons in political resistance."[6] As education became the main terrain and agency of resistance in the mid-1970s, its strategic value to the apartheid regime became evident.

During the apartheid era in South Africa, there were four English-medium, six Afrikaans, and only eight other universities in which Africans could study. Apartheid universities had a distinct ideological outlook. The Afrikaans' language universities were conservative and openly racist. A report drafted by M. Townsend in 1986 found that these universities produced personnel for the apartheid bureaucracy. Critical debate was discouraged. The NP elite was drawn from such institutions as the University of Stellenbosch, Rands-Afrikaans University, and the University of Pretoria, to name a few.

African universities were staffed with reactionary administrators with a very radical student body. Any discussions about exploitation or oppression were totally prohibited. As African students interacted with others from different areas who suffered under the same oppressive conditions, the boundaries of the African imagined community became sharper. The English-medium universities stood somewhere between the liberal and conservative extremes. Human, material and financial resources were distributed unequally among the various racial groups with African universities being the least well endowed.

Spatial organization based on race was a prominent feature of apartheid in every respect. According to its logic, Africans were an "asset" for the country because they were the laborers upon whom South Africa's economic foundation was constructed. From this perspective, apartheid was not meant to hurt Africans; instead it provided them with a better life. Furthermore, apartheid was a form of temporary white trusteeship aimed at progressively leading Africans towards political autonomy and self-government. Africans had to be patient and gradually they too would enjoy the same standard of living as Afrikaners. After all Africans and Afrikaners were not enemies. Thus, Prime Minister Malan justified apartheid in the following terms:

> I regard the Bantu not as strangers and not as a menace to the white people, but as our children for whose welfare we are responsible, and as an asset to the country. My government has no intention of depriving you of your rights or oppressing you. Nothing will be taken from you without giving you something better in its place. Your reserves will remain intact and where necessary will be enlarged. Your lands will be restored and your young men and women trained to improved methods of cultivation so that your reserves will be capable of supporting a larger population. What you want is a rehabilitation of your own national life, and not competition and intermixture and equality with the white man, in his particular part of the country.[7]

The NP viewed itself as the private and public mouthpiece and intermediary for the "Bantu," and claimed that it knew what was best for both rural and urban Africans. Like White liberals who acted as trustees for the Africans until they "developed" to the appropriate level of "civilization," apartheid rationalized African oppression in the belief that an "ideal" state would be set up for "natives" in the future. With this objective in mind, the apartheid regime passed the *Group Areas Act* in 1950, which specified what residential areas were reserved for which racial groups. More specifically, this act was used to force Africans out of areas that were viewed as 'black spots'. In some cases entire communities were forced to move from the only homes they knew.

For Africans, the *Group Areas Act* meant "the un-home," namely that condition between having a home and being homeless; for example, one can have a temporary house (possibly a shack) but it is not "home" because either the person is in transition or lives in fear because he or she can become homeless at any time. The condition of "un-home" is also experienced in exile because one's residence is only temporary, no matter how long a person lives abroad. The person always looks forward to returning home. *The Group Areas Act* increased the level of insecurity, fear, and violence in the private sphere because state agents could raid one's home at any time.

For the agents of apartheid, Sophiatown was one of the most uncontrolled African areas outside Johannesburg. Most Africans had succeeded in buying land before the 1923 *Urban Areas Act* that prohibited land sales. A cross-section of classes lived in Sophiatown including the unemployed, workers, and landlords, with the working class comprising the majority of the population. Various racial groups also lived in Sophiatown. According to the logic of the apartheid regime, Sophiatown was a slum, which bred thieves and rebels. It was seen as a threat to "order" and white security. Sophiatown was also a center of African resistance, which had to be destroyed. More importantly Sophiatown was difficult to police and therefore to control. However, Trevor Huddleston described Sophiatown as follows:

> Sophiatown is not, and never has been, a slum. There are no tenements: there is nothing really old: there are no dark cellars. Sometimes looking up at Sophiatown from Western Native Township, across the main road, I have felt I was looking at an Italian village somewhere in Umbria. For you do 'look up' at Sophiatown, and in the evening light, across the blue grey haze of smoke from braziers and chimneys against a saffron sky, you see close packed, red-roofed little houses. You see, moving up and down the hilly streets, people in groups: people with colorful clothes: people who, when you come up to them, are children playing, dancing and standing round the braziers. . . . In the evening, towards the early South African sunset, there is very little of the slum about Sophiatown.[8]

For Africans, Sophiatown was home. Miriam Tlali describes the area thusly: "Sophiatown. That beloved Sophiatown. As students we used to refer to it proudly as 'the centre of the metropolis.' And who could dispute it? The most talented African men and women from all walks of life—in spite of the hardships they had to encounter—came from Sophiatown."[9]

Apartheid was based on state-sponsored social violence, which meant tearing families and communities apart. Culturally diverse and vibrant areas such as District Six, in Cape Town, which was home to a cross-section of races with people of mixed descent as the majority, were destroyed. Some South African authors, such as Bloke Modisane, and Mandla Langa, have vividly used the characters in their novels to describe the sense of "un home" these experiences produced. Home for Africans represented insecurity and violence; in order to avoid state repression, African's were forced into constant movement, thereby influencing how the imagined community developed. The private sphere refers to the home, unpaid labor at home, or personal space while the public sphere refers to all activities that take place in the public domain, particularly those that relate to public policy and that involve the state. Politics were introduced in the home in various ways—including protesting for better services, reduced rents, or against removals—effectively merging the private with the public.

The pass system was used effectively to ensure that Africans remained in their assigned space. Passes contained the personal information of the carrier; they were visible symbols of oppression. Not only did passes control labor, but they also controlled the social well being of the native. Only three agencies could issue passes: the government, a white employer, and, before 1948, a traditional chief. Africans could only communicate with the state through its bureaucratic agents of control. As the dominated group, Africans negotiated the apartheid world through ethnicity, passes, raids, and constant police harassment intended to remind them of who was in charge.

Apartheid's spatial organization placed central business districts of all cities under strict white minority control. The non-whites lived on the cities' outskirts, separated from whites as well as from each other by "buffer zones" (which were either industrial areas, nuclear power sites, or some government property). Apartheid regarded whites as a national entity. Each racial group would develop according to its past history and tradition, which would eventually lead to self-reliance. The Minister of Labor, Schoeman, noted that apartheid meant that regardless of the level of development that was reached, Africans would never acquire equal rights (economic, political, or social) with the white minority. According to its advocates, apartheid was the best way for each community to develop peacefully; it was also seen as the fount of tradition, which maintained Africans in their indigenous setting. Since it was understood that Africans could only progress in this setting, apartheid was synonymous with development. According to this view, integration of the races would destroy African culture and customs while encouraging white supremacy.[10] Apartheid also afforded Africans with a degree of economic and political control. According to one of apartheid's leading theorists, C. A. Cronje:

> Afrikaners found themselves (in a polity created by Anglo imperialism) as a minority group surrounded by a majority who were culturally and racially different. He argued that given these circumstances, Afrikaners could never allow blacks to fully develop economically or politically because this would necessarily imply black domination over the Afrikaner minority. Cronje's Christian national solution to this dilemma was total-partition that is, apartheid would completely separate blacks and whites. Once this was done, argued Cronje, whites would no longer need to repress black interests and could actually assist blacks to develop their full potential in their separate black polities.[11]

Racial segregation legitimized the white minority's claim to South Africa's natural resources. For example, the 1913 Native Land Act gave the white minority 93 percent of the best land. In 1936, this figure changed: Africans got 13 percent of the land. As a result of this Act, most Africans became homeless and easy prey for cheap labor. Africans who had previously lived as tenants on white land were also homeless. Sol T. Plaatje's *Native Life* describes the fate of these Africans as they wandered from village to village in search of a place to graze their cows. Some could not even find burial places for their dead. In 1959, the Bantu Self-Government Act was introduced. Africans were deemed to be foreigners in South Africa where white minority hegemony had to be protected at all costs. The state reserved all skilled jobs for whites while using Africans as manual laborers. It allowed Africans "to nurse [the white's] baby, cook [the white's] dinner, drive [the white's] car. It does not permit him to do any of these things as a neighbour."[12] African male workers were confined to ethnic hostels without their families and social support systems. Labor was organized in such a way that it was always close to the needs of the white employers. According to the logic of apartheid, since Africans were not civilized, they had minimal needs that were not very different form basic "animal wants."[13]

Africans were not passive during this period. They used various methods to fight for their rights. Between 1949 and 1960, the ANC engaged in mass demonstrations. After it was banned alongside the PAC, African resistance went underground. It reemerged in the 1970s in the form of mass strikes and boycotts as well as through the Soweto revolt of June 16, 1976. The revolt shook apartheid to its core. Eventually, African resistance destroyed apartheid's myth of ensuring peace and security. South Africa's townships became arenas of contest regarding units of state power. After the uprising was quelled in 1977, political unrest continued throughout the country. For the first time in South Africa's history, state violence failed to ensure peace for thewhite minority. A crisis of the hegemony of racial rule developed. The uprising exacerbated the divisions already apparent within the Afrikaner ruling elite and set into motion a chain of events that ultimately forced the elite to introduce reforms.

From the 1960s, the Afrikaner ruling elite was divided between the *Verligte* (enlightened ones), who preferred change while controlling its progress, and the *Verkrampte* (those who preferred to modernize apartheid). This conflict reached its climax in 1982, with the founding of the Conservative Party. The *Verligte* camp put pressure on the state to dismantle apartheid. Other factors also contributed to the weakening of the apartheid regime. Foremost among these was the economic drain caused by the regime's wars in Angola and Mozambique, resulting in loss of support at home. Soweto began the reform process that finally culminated with South Africa's general elections. According to P. Eric Louw, between 1948 and 1990, apartheid changed but the following features remained constant from Malan to Botha.

- Afrikaners (as a small ethnic group) feared cultural swamping by global Anglo culture and black nationalism.

- A belief in verzuiling (own-ness)

- A belief that "apartness/separation" was just and Christian. This need to justify apartheid as being Christian was based on a deep Afrikaner religiosity that prevented the sorts of genocide seen in other societies.

- A passionate anticommunism (deemed the unchristian "other")

- A frikaner nationalists were legalists, obsessed with constitutionalism, the rule of law, and legally codifying every detail of their ideology. So whereas racist practices simply existed de facto before 1948, the NP made these de jure (something Anglo South Africans criticized as foolish, for drawing attention to practices best kept informal).

- A search for ways to secure Afrikaner self-determination.[14]

Faced with internal resistance, a slowing economy, and international criticism, the state began searching for ways to reform apartheid. Its ruling elite also realized that peace could not be attained through military means. Although the attacks of the ANC's armed wing, *Umkhonto we Sizwe*, were largely ineffective, they nevertheless succeeded in creating an environment in which the masses were seen as ungovernable, thus furthering the image that Africans threatened white security and foreign investment. After the violent reaction of the state against African children during the Soweto revolt, there was increased international pressure on the NP to dismantle apartheid. Throughout the history of modern South Africa, Western nations such as Britain, France, Germany, and the United States represented the apartheid regime as an extension of Western civilization in Africa. These countries' investment increased at the climax of state repression in the 1960s. The United States and Britain were the major sponsors of the regime. Their support came under attack in the 1970s and the 1980s, as mass anti-apartheid demonstrations swept throughout Europe. Only Scandinavian countries and the Soviet Union refused to support the regime.

The state's ideal of grand apartheid was failing. By 1979, the Homelands were a total failure. Several factors contributed to this. First, the economic drain caused by South Africa's wars in Angola and Mozambique was critical. Second, the Homelands were not economically self-sufficient. The state was spending vast sums of money to maintain separate institutions and bureaucracy. Third, no other country except South Africa recognized Homelands. Fourth, Homelands constituted a security threat to South Africa, especially through bush colleges and liberation movements. The Homelands further threatened the regime through their role as a rallying point for both Africans and people of mixed descent. Finally, the democratization wave sweeping Africa forced the ruling elite to begin reforming apartheid.

President Botha, who belonged to the *Verligte* camp urged white South Africans to get used to change in order to survive as a people. With that, Botha initiated the process of deracializing apartheid. In this undertaking, he faced five challenges. First, the large concentration of African population in the urban areas made it very difficult for the government to control its movements. Second, three Homelands (KwaZulu, Lebowa, and Gazankulu) refused independence, thereby undermining the whole rationale for the Homeland policy. Third, the independence of Mozambique in 1975 inspired most young Africans in South Africa to leave the country and join the ANC. It also gave hope to Africans in South Africa. Fourth, Afrikaner intellectuals grew increasingly disillusioned with apartheid and become convinced it could not work, especially because no one recognized Bantustans except the regime. Finally, the *verligte-verkramptes* cleavage was increasing because some Afrikaners began to believe that there was a large Afrikaner middle class, deeming apartheid no longer necessary. On the other hand, the Afrikaner working class believed that apartheid was still necessary to protect it. This disagreement led to a split in 1982. Apartheid had to be modified to face opposition. As such, the government extended limited rights to trade unions. It also allowed Indians and people of mixed descent representation in separate sections of Parliament. The reforms had a negative impact: they demonstrated that the system that had presented itself as omnipotent was in fact flawed and could be overthrown. Encouraged by the reforms, Africans ignored influx control laws by living wherever they desired.

Under President Botha, reforms still maintained the basic tenet of apartheid: majority rule was rejected because it would place Afrikaners at a disadvantage. Whichever reforms were carried out, they had to maintain the Afrikaners' *Verzuiling* (own-ness) and the rule of law. Reformers were searching for a way for Afrikaners to have their own separate state (self-determination). The reformers also wanted to retain the Homelands while creating new, racially homogenous areas but integrating all of them in a confederate type system that would deny Africans majority rule.[15] These reforms, which began with Prime Minister John Vorster and culminated with the release of Nelson Mandela by F. W. de Klerk in 1990, ended with the general elections of 1994.

THE NATIONAL PARTY

The NP came to power in 1948 with a majority of only five seats. To its members, the party was the standard-bearer of Western civilization that it would promote in Africa Afrikaners were bitter after years of control over their economic and cultural destinies by British imperialism. As a capitalist country under white minority control within the British empire, South Africa provided an outlet for labor, markets, and white European population. Afrikaners could only survive in a continent they barely knew by separating themselves from other racial groups. Prime Minister Malan aimed at controlling the economy, which was, at the time, under British domination. According to P. Eric Louw, "[Malan] was not especially concerned with the 'black issue,' and it is not even mentioned in his autobiography, which concentrates exclusively on his passion for uniting Afrikaners against Anglo domination. Formulating a policy toward blacks was never center stage under Malan, and only started to become significant from 1955 under Prime Minister Strijdom. During the 1930s to the 1950s, the NP and *Broederbond* were more focused upon creating 'own-ness' *(eiesoortigheid)* in relation to Anglos than in relation to blacks."[16]

The official policy of the NP was to man every level of the economy and bureaucracy with Afrikaners so as to end the humiliation of living under British domination. According to this view, only the NP could empower Afrikaners. Because of the way the party represented itself, it was able to mobilize support among English-speakers as well as among the white minority, which advocated authoritarianism and the political exclusion of the African majority. By 1977, the NP had increased its majority in Parliament to seventy-seven seats (up from five seats in 1948). In the eyes of the white minority, the NP was the party of white South Africa. There was no significant difference between English and Afrikaner attitudes when it came to dealing with Africans. Both believed that there were distinct differences between Africans and Europeans that made the latter superior.

According to the NP, no particular racial or ethnic group constituted the majority in South Africa. The country was made up of many nations: Afrikaners, British settlers, Africans (who, themselves, were divided into ten nations), coloureds (people of mixed descent), and Indians. When confronted by the other racial groups, the NP represented the white minority as one nation. Afrikaners constituted a privileged group among other white ethnic groups. As part of its divide-and-rule policy, the NP encouraged ethno-nationalism among Africans, and it also prevented alliances across race, class, and gender. Blacks (i.e. Africans, people of mixed descent, and Indians) challenged this belief by forming multiracial alliances such as that which formed the core of the ANC, the United Democratic Front, or the Mass Democratic Movement. Although the NP used socialist rhetoric to criticize British imperialism and specifically the South African capitalist economy, its goal was not to overthrow the existing capitalist order. Rather, the goal was to control it. The racial segregation policy of the NP was based on relations of power. Though all blacks were discriminated against, they were not all oppressed in the same manner. Only Africans were considered aliens in the land of their birth. Whites occupied the top of the pyramid, followed by Indians, and then people of mixed descent. Africans were at the bottom of the pyramid. White control of and supervision over other racial groups was entrenched into the system as the natural order of things.

Relations between the oppressed groups were also influenced by power. Indians discriminated against people of mixed descent and Africans, and vice versa. Indians were treated better than people of mixed descent who were more privileged than Africans. After the Soweto revolt most blacks began challenging apartheid's racial boundaries. Some blacks joined multiracial organizations like the United Democratic Front, which was created in 1983. Faced with internal resistance, international condemnation, and a slowing economy, the public opinion of the white minority was also changing during this period. This influenced the nationalist debate. A poll taken in 1984 revealed that an equal number of whites were in favor of government talks with the ANC as were against such talks.

The language of the National Party also shifted to reflect changes in its conception of nationalism. The crude and simplistic "us vs. them" dichotomy was refined when raw racism was replaced by a more sophisticated brand of racism. The NP increasingly used terms like group, culture, and rationality, instead of the term race. Thus, "races become cultural minorities, cultural minorities become political minorities, [and] political positions become cultural values."[17] People who did not belong to the minority culture were left out of policy debates. The NP used reason to argue that following the collapse of the Soviet Union, the age of ideology was over. According to the NP, the only option left for South Africa's leaders was to use reason as opposed to ideology to reach a political settlement. According to internal NP debates, some people within South Africa had not come to realize this fact. Speaking at the World Economic Forum in Davos in February of 1992, F. W. de Klerk stated that while "it is generally accepted today that communism is dead. . . . This message has not yet been brought home to all South Africans."[18] Furthermore, according to de Klerk, not everyone was able to grasp the fact that communism was over because some people still believed in outdated ideologies. Only a few people were able to participate in this political transition. As it had done throughout its history, the NP believed it was the voice of reason, knowledge, order, and the teacher that knew best.

The new language of the NP was also reflected in its demands during the negotiating process. It called for "consociationalism" in which group values (rather than race) would unite people on the basis of the particular groups' socio-economic status and cultural values. As if this ambiguity was not enough, identities between various political and cultural groups and political parties were established. F. W. de Klerk believed that he was representing a people. Addressing a Swiss audience, de Klerk noted, "We have this large Third World component, with the typical Third World problems which are slowly strangling the rest of Africa. We have them in our midst."[19] Though pretending to be different from the past, the new NP debate was framed within the same old paradigm: "we" represents the voice of reason, tolerance, development, and civilization while "them" is a negation of "us" and refers to those who threaten "our" values. As it had done in the past, the NP appealed to Western civilization because it was believed to understand its predicament well: "Some members of the population have come to a growing expectation that the envisaged restructuring of the constitutional system, will be coupled with an almost simultaneous ending of the relative backlog of the developing part of the population. . . . I am referring to . . . the pressure on First World standards by those who are not yet in a position to make that contribution to the economy that would justify their claims."[20]

In these debates, only white claims were seen as legitimate. The "others" (i.e. Africans) were seen as having unreasonably high expectations without having contributed to the economy and were considered to not be "ready." But this representation was plagued by contradictions. The NP conferred on the past to demonstrate its linkage with Western civilization as the engine of progress in South Africa. Yet, in the same breath, it urged Africans to forget the past. F. W. de Klerk, Gerrit Viljoen, Roelf Meyer, "Pik" Botha, Tertius Delport, Adriaan Vlok, and the entire core leadership of the NP made constant references to the need to forget the past. Along with this call, the NP argued that the present was a radical break from the past, to be understood as a "moment of truth" which provided a "window of opportunity."[21] People who refused to forget the past by failing to seize these opportunities based on reason were seen as the enemies of the transformation. All the groups that opposed the negotiation process were marginalized or silenced. Thus, Afrikaner conservatives were forced to register a separate political party, the *Afrikaner Eenheidsbeweging (AEB)*. The Inkatha Freedom Party was forced to register at the last minute when its leadership realized it did not have any other option left. These debates and the language used in them marked the negotiations between the ANC and the NP as moderates were brought to the center of the two parties in preparation for the general elections.

LIBERATION DEBATES:
THE ANC, THE PAC, AND THE BCM

Various counter-nationalist responses (by the ANC, PAC, and the BCM) relied on a "tradition" of African resistance to European invasion. These counter-nationalist discourses, which privileged African history, used the past to inspire their members to face the present. These various organizations did not use history in the same way. The PAC emphasized the early colonial phase to present whites as "settler-colonialists" who took African land by force. In this view, Africans were considered to be the indigenous owners of land and nativeness was important. Only Africans or other racial groups who accepted that South Africa was an African country were included in the nation. According to ANC's Freedom Charter, South Africa belonged to all who lived in it, both the blacks and the whites. To counter apartheid's ethnic divisions, the BCM believed that Indians and biracial people were included in the nation as blacks.

DEMANDS FOR EQUALITY:
THE ANC

According to Thiven Reddy, the counter-debates of the ANC, PAC, and the BCM can be divided into the ANC's demands for rights and equality and the PAC's conquest and psychological liberationist discourse, which was later endorsed by the BCM.[22] Apartheid represented a community that Africans wished to avoid at all costs. Throughout its history and through its mass demonstrations, petitions, and even when it advocated armed struggle, the ANC consistently exposed and criticized the evils of apartheid. The ANC's imagined community was inclusive, the exact opposite of apartheid. Even the PAC's imagined community was inclusive, as it included anyone who identified with Africa and as an African. This view privileged African culture and tradition over European culture and tradition. In essence, the ANC's multiracial debate developed as a reaction to apartheid. The goal of the ANC was to win equality for the African majority. Congress also demanded equal human, civil, and political rights and work, security, and equality for all. According to the ANC, its ideological belief has been the creed of African nationalism. It is not the concept of African nationalism expressed in reverse racism (which rejects the right of Afrikaners to be in South Africa). Instead it aimed at creating an inclusive society and a political system based on democracy rather than advancing a radical transformation of the system.

The efforts of the ANC were focused on the inclusion of the African majority in a post-apartheid South Africa. Non-racialism was practical because the interdependent nature of the economy made it impossible for the various racial groups to separate. Non-racialism also resulted from the ANC's Cape liberal tradition and from its relations with the South African Communist Party. The ANC operated across racial boundaries and represented itself as an essentially liberal and non-racial organization. Congress also attracted national and international support among those who viewed it as a moderate liberal party. For the ANC, "democracy implied [a] representative government and the guaranteed freedom of all, including minorities, to enjoy not just political but cultural rights."[23] Non-racial democracy did not necessarily imply African political and economic control, but merely political equality in a pluralistic society. The ANC also believed that South Africa's wealth belonged to its entire population. Once in power, ANC leaders planned to nationalize the economy by replacing the existing capitalist order with a socialist one. The new order would correct past injustices by setting a foundation for a more just society in which the economic needs of the African majority would be addressed. The ANC was weakened by the increased repression of the apartheid state, as well as by the failure of its strategy designed to appeal to the NP's sense of guilt and morality. First, the state infiltrated the ANC with informers. Second, the Treason Trials of 1957—1961 diverted its leadership from important activities. Third, factionalism increased within the organization to such an extent that it resulted in the failure of the Transvaal section of the ANC and the creation of the PAC. Finally, after its top leadership was imprisoned following the Rivonia Trials, its members were forced to go underground. The ANC then effectively collapsed. One could argue that had it not been for Winnie Mandela's resistance activities and the emergence of the Black Consciousness Movement, the ANC would have completely failed as an organization.

In 1960, the ANC was banned and thus forced into exile. As a result, it adopted a strategy of armed struggle in 1962. During the Rivonia Trials, Nelson Mandela explained that the ANC had turned to violence as a form of protest rather than as a way of forcing whites out of the country. The ANC also provided the masses with dedicated and responsible leadership. The goal of *Umkhonto We Sizwe* (the Spear of the Nation) was to engage in armed struggle against the state while avoiding civilian casualties. Despite the rhetoric of the ANC, *Umkhonto* volunteers were not well trained to face the formidable military might of the apartheid state. Furthermore, the so-called training in the Soviet Union did not teach the soldiers any relevant or useful skills. Like the ANC, *Umkhonto* was also infiltrated by state informers, which resulted in many instances of detention and torture. The armed propaganda of the ANC was also informed by the ANC's belief in non-violence. It emphasized the need for political leadership. Throughout the 1970s, "ANC strategy continued as if armed activity was the primary politicising agent."[24]

The ANC represented and spoke for the people. As the vanguard of the African majority's liberation, it was also its voice. The main focus of the ANC's liberation strategy was the African people as they were the most oppressed group in society. Thus, according to the 1969 Morogoro Declaration of the ANC: "Amongst other things it demands, in the first place, a maximal mobilization of the African people as a dispossessed and racially oppressed nation. This is the mainstream and it must not be diluted. It involves a stimulation and a deepening of national confidence, national pride and national assertiveness."[25] According to the ANC and its partner, the South African Communist Party, the liberation process in South Africa involved two stages. The first was a national revolution led by the ANC, which would be followed by a

Socialist revolution led by the South African Communist Party and the workers. As a result of the fall of the Soviet Union in 1989 (leaving the capitalist economy as the only alternative in the world economy) and the presence of major transnational corporations and multilateral aid institutions, the ANC was forced to abandon its nationalization polices. The ANC experienced a bleak period in exile from 1961 until the ban against it was lifted in 1990. While the ANC was in exile, the United Democratic Front (1983) and the Mass Democratic Movements (1988) voiced its ideals and took up its cause. Within the ANC, only Africans occupied the top executive positions until 1985 when such positions were opened to other races. The UDF was disbanded in 1990 following the return of the ANC.

SELF-DETERMINATION DEBATES: THE PAN AFRICANIST CONGRESS AND THE BLACK CONSCIOUSNESS MOVEMENT

The Pan Africanist Congress was created in 1959 when Africanists left the ANC over the issue of multiracialism and liberation strategies. In the eyes of the PAC, the ANC was a reformist organization that did not adequately cater to the needs of the Africans. Rather than promoting them, the *Freedom Charter* "sold out" African interests, and its multiracial perspective marginalized Africans. According to Robert Sobukwe, "Africans are asked, through their spineless leaders, not to 'embarrass' their 'friends' and 'allies' . . . [and] to 'water-down' their demands in order to accommodate all the Anti-Nat elements in the country; in short [the Africans were] asked to 'grin and bear it' so that [their] friends can continue 'to plead for us.' And we are told that in that we shall achieve freedom. What rubbish!"[26] The PAC rejected the notion that South Africa was exceptional in any way and argued that it experienced exactly the same type of colonialism, though longer in duration, as elsewhere on the continent. For the PAC, apartheid was unacceptable because it divided Africans and "nobody has the right to balkanize [the African's] land."[27]

As a political organization, the PAC was not homogeneous and was divided along ideological, class, and gender lines. Thus, there was a sharp divide between moderates and radicals: some members wanted to work with white organizations, like the Liberal Party, while others preferred an Africans-only party. In addition, disagreement arose between the leadership and the rank-and-file of the party over political strategy, specifically over how certain campaigns should be carried out.

There was an ideological convergence between the PAC and Ethiopianism. The dominant feature of Ethiopianism was the separation of Africans from whites on the basis of autonomy and self-reliance. One of the key weapons employed by a dominant group against an oppressed one is the supposed knowledge of the latter. Once a social group escapes from total control by the dominant group, this act becomes a weapon for liberation because the dominant group no longer has access to the oppressed people's knowledge base: it can only rely on spies who are notoriously unreliable. According to Bernice Reagan:

[Sometimes] it gets too hard to stay out in that society all the time. And that's when you find a place, and you try to bar the door and check all the people who come in. You come together to see what you can do about shouldering up all of your energies so that you and your kind can survive.... That space should be a nurturing space where you sift out what people are saying about you and decide who you really are. And you take the time to try to construct within yourself and within your community who you would be if you were running society.... [This is] nurturing, but it is also nationalism. At a certain stage, nationalism is crucial to a people if you are ever going to impact as a group in your own interest.[28]

The ideological roots of the PAC can be traced to Anton Muziwakhe Lembede. In his writings, Lembede urged Africans to liberate themselves mentally by accepting their race. He advocated self-determination for the Africans, under their own leadership. These ideas came to be known as "Africanism," and aimed at liberating Africans from foreign domination by uniting diverse ethnic groups under a single organization. The PAC also demanded human, civil, and political rights equal to those of whites.

According to the PAC, historically South Africa belonged exclusively to African people whom it represented and spoke for as "indigenous Africans." The PAC rejected the claims made by the white minority-that it had had settled on empty land. Consequently, the PAC did not need to provide any guarantees for minority rights. Only Africans had a legitimate claim and an inalienable right to South Africa. Members of the white minority who abandoned their claim to racial supremacy and who considered themselves to be Africans would be accepted as full members of the community. People of mixed descent were also considered to be Africans. The Africanist ideals of Anton Lembede and of the ANC youth league (CYL) were in total contradiction with those of the Freedom Charter. Change came only after the complete overthrow of the racist regime. According to Thiven Reddy, the PAC's imagined community in South Africa had two dimensions. First, Africans were seen as a racial group that refused apartheid's tribal identities. Secondly, the concept of African was understood in political terms: anyone who fully identified with a united Africa and who accepted the principle of majority rule was considered to be an Africans. This description included some Indians, people of mixed descent, and whites. During the 1960 Pass campaign, the PAC worked with the multiracial Liberal Party. For the PAC, repossession of the land from whites was an absolute prerequisite to the attainment of African freedom. Indeed, the PAC viewed South Africa as an essentially African country, closely connected to the rest of the continent through its history, culture, and tradition.

In 1960 the PAC was banned. The apartheid Minister of Justice justified the banning of both the ANC and the PAC (as well as the repression that followed) "on the ground that they were intent on 'generating revolution'.... [They] do not want peace and order... what they want is our country."[29] Two years later, the PAC moved its headquarters to Maseru. Most of the party members who remained in South Africa were either in prison or operating from underground. The PAC created a military wing, *Pogo* (*Xhosa* word meaning alone or pure). This organization traced its origins to the Ethiopianists whose members described themselves as *Ndingun Topiya*

Poqo (belonging to the Church of Ethiopia).[30] *Poqo* members instilled fear in the community by systematically targeting and killing agents of apartheid such as informers, policemen, and security agents. Most of *Poqo's* supporters were located in the Cape Peninsula, where influx control was most severe. The organization was also popular among migrant workers, although the educated elite held the leadership positions.

After both the ANC and the PAC were banned by the authorities, Africans experienced a political vacuum. However, the Black Consciousness Movement filled this vacuum in 1968. Ironically the BCM emerged in 1968 as a by-product of apartheid's segregated ethnic schools and colleges. The BCM re-invented a way of representing all non-Western groups in South Africa as "black," those who worked with the apartheid regime or continued to support it were represented as "Uncle Toms" or "collaborationists." Initially, the National Party viewed the BCM favorably because it believed it was driving a wedge between the small, missionary-educated African elite and the majority of the African people. In 1971, the pro-NP *Die Burger* noted that the BCM was:

> The product of disillusionment over the nice sounding phrases and ideas and programmes preached in the postwar years by the . . . Liberal school of thought. . . . The [BCM] people with whom this new thinking has taken root reject the condescension with which they have often been regarded by whites who represent themselves as their only friends. . . . [T]hey do not want to be objects of white politics any longer, but desire to determine their future themselves as people in their own right . . . [hence BCM] fits in well with the objectives of our relations policy.[31]

The BCM believed that South Africa was a black country in which whites would live as equals once they accepted this fact by abandoning any supremacist claims. The term black represented South Africans as well as other colonized people in Africa and Asia. According to the BCM, the liberation struggle in South Africa was part and parcel of the broader liberation struggle of third world countries in which the majority of the population was fighting off the colonial yoke imposed by a minority. The BCM represented all blacks whom it believed were victims of apartheid. Liberation could only be achieved by mobilizing Africans on the basis of group identity. BCM sympathizers formed the South African Students Organization (SASO), which believed that democracy in South Africa meant "one man-one vote." Like the ANC, SASO believed that a democratic South Africa should be based on non-racialism. But unlike the ANC, which believed in multiracialism, SASO believed that before South Africa could become democratic, blacks had to regroup and build their strength through their own, separate organizations.

Like Lembede's Africanism, the BCM believed that the freedom of blacks depended first and foremost on their own actions rather than on the benevolence of liberals. According to the BCM, blacks had to strengthen their own power base by building their own organizations. Thus, they could counter the divide and rule policies of the apartheid regime through their collaborative policies of unity. Black Consciousness (BC) emphasized the importance of psychological liberation of blacks from notions of inferiority and dependence resulting from centuries of oppression. BC aimed at restructuring the economy, as well as the social and political spheres by eliminating the worst elements of capitalism that dehumanized and exploited blacks. In post-apartheid South Africa, blacks would replace the capitalist system with a state economy based on communalism. Thus, political change was synonymous with economic transformation. In this discourse, the concept of black had two dimensions. First, the color black was intimately linked to specific socio-economic conditions (particularly to a low socio-economic status). Second, black combined the notion of oppression with the will to fight. As Steve Biko cogently remarked, "it will not be long before the blacks relate their poverty to their blackness in concrete terms. Because of the tradition forced onto the country, the poor people shall always be black people. It is not surprising, therefore, that the blacks should wish to rid themselves of a system that locks up the wealth of a country in the hands of a few."[32]

As an ideal movement, the BCM differed from the ANC in two ways. First, unlike the ANC's vague non-racial policy, the BCM had a philosophy that united its followers. Second, it introduced culture as a key element in and integral component of the liberation struggle. BCM re-invented the 1949 Congress Youth League discourse of psychologically decolonizing the African mind. BCM ideology also differed from that of the PAC since the latter did not identify culture as a key element in the liberation process. BCM political philosophy saw mental decolonization as the first priority in the African liberation struggle. Before anything else, Africans had to accept and value their Africanness, as well as their culture and tradition. Black consciousness required blacks–inclusive of Indians and people of mixed descent–to reject all value systems that made them aliens in their own land.[33] This was a revolutionary perspective, given the demoralized state of blacks resulting from the repressive policies of the apartheid regime.

BC demystified the image of the NP as an omnipotent, totalitarian state. Blacks were terrorized into submission and silence out of fear of state repression and violence through the repressive agencies of law, police, and security apparatus. BC challenged blacks to face their fear by negating it, thus illuminating that this constant fear was destroying them. According to Biko, blacks lived in two separate and distinct worlds. The first, in which they interact with whites in public, was passive and meek. However, in the private sphere, blacks expressed their hatred and vented their anger. This anger had to be re-directed against the system; but, a liberation ideology was needed to free blacks from this fear before they could confront the system.

Only once blacks have been freed of this fear would they be in a position to act:

> It is this fear that erodes the soul of black people in South Africa—a fear obviously built up deliberately by the system through a myriad of civil agents, be they post office attendants, police, CID [Central investigation Department] officials, army men in uniform, security police or even the occasional trigger-happy white farmer or store owner. It is a fear so basic in the considered actions of black people as to make it impossible for them to behave like people-let alone free people. From the attitude of a servant to his employer, to that of a black man being served by a white attendant at a shop, one sees this fear clearly showing through. How can people be prepared to put up a resistance against their overall

oppression if in their individual situations, they cannot insist on the observance of their manhood?[34]

Freedom from fear is revolutionary because it opens up a new terrain of resistance:

> Thus the native discovers that his life, his breath, his beating heart are the same as those of the settler. He finds out that the settler's skin is not of any more value than a native's skin; and it must be said that this discovery shakes the world in a very necessary manner. All the new, revolutionary assurance of the native stems from it. For if, my life is worth as much as the settler's, his glance no longer turns me into stone. I am no longer on tenterhooks in his presence; in fact, I don't give a damn for him. Not only does his presence no longer trouble me, but I am already preparing such efficient ambushes for him that soon there will be no way out but that of flight.[35]

BC provided a counter narrative to the NP version of history. For instance, it reminded blacks of past heroes such as Shaka Zulu and provided an alternative culture of resistance based on the black experience. Through its decolonization ideology and strategy, Black Consciousness shattered the self-representation of white supremacy as omnipotent and invincible. As part of this strategy, BC discouraged women from lightening their skins and from wearing Western make-up, calling on them to believe in their own beauty. BC also discouraged people from wearing tee-shirts with any texts or logos on them, as these were viewed as objects of capitalist exploitation. Different, more "hidden" ways of challenging the system were introduced. For example, absenteeism from work, foot dragging, and speaking in African languages unfamiliar to white supervisors represented "this everyday form of struggle."[36] As a result, a much more assertive and confident black community emerged, which prepared the youth to challenge the state during the Soweto revolt of 1976 as well as during the insurrections that followed.

BC has been criticized for representing blacks as homogeneous and as constituting another form of reverse racism. Liberals presented BC as anti-white because it "defined itself in opposition to white liberal institutions and criticised some liberal precepts, especially the notion of multiracialism."[37] Yet few deny that BC transformed the counter nationalist debate. BC provided blacks with a counter-ideology to apartheid that empowered black people to fight the state by decolonizing their minds. Unlike the ANC, which had little or no empathy with its popular base, BC genuinely empathized and was in sync with its black followers. Second, BCM introduced a "culture of resistance" as a powerful weapon for liberation. Finally, the BCM was the only movement that identified all Africans, Indians and people of mixed descent as black. This was revolutionary because it provided, for the first time, an alternative imagined community that exposed the regime's weaknesses and illegitimacy. Just before his untimely death at the hands of apartheid police in 1978, Steve Biko was working toward greater unity with the ANC. He hoped that all African liberation movements, notably the ANC, the PAC and the BCM, would be united under a single umbrella political organization against apartheid. It is interesting to note in this regard that in post-apartheid South Africa, the ANC government uses the

BC definition of black to refer to Africans, Indians, Malays, and people of mixed descent.

Two opposing conceptions of imagined community informed the nationalist discourse of the ANC and the NP: one was inclusive and multiracial while the other was exclusive and racialized. These conceptions of the imagined community shaped how each party defined the nation, its community, and the political economy. For example, for the ANC, "the people" represented every South African born in the country. The NP represented only whites (including European immigrants). According to the NP's conception of the imagined community, color was important since every policy was informed by race. In contrast to the exclusive nationalism of the NP, the ANC's imagined community was based on liberal, multiracial democracy.

Power relations between the ANC and the NP influenced the nationalist discourse. At first, the ANC dealt with the NP in a conciliatory language and manner. It used the language of a junior partner. In spite of the constant use of violence and repression by the NP against Africans through forced removals, pass regulations, and police brutality, the ANC used peaceful means such as petitions and mass demonstrations against the system. Until 1962, when it adopted armed struggle, ANC leaders operated under the premise that their moderation and good-will would eventually change the apartheid regime's racist policies. ANC leaders believed the immorality of apartheid would eventually turn its supporters away from the NP in favor of a multiracial democracy. Unfortunately, the ANC proved to be completely wrong. It only turned to armed struggle in the 1980s, after its peaceful methods (including passive resistance) proved to be a complete failure. By that time, the ANC was urging its followers to make South Africa ungovernable. Since its creation in 1912, the goal of the ANC was to be incorporated into the system through negotiations with the NP after it dismantled apartheid. The ANC was ready to share power with the National Party as early as 1950, but the latter refused. The 1969 Morogoro Document outlined step-by-step strategies to persuade the regime to engage in talks on the dismantling of apartheid.

Apartheid was based on state violence against Africans and on the fragmentation of the opposition movements. The state used every opportunity to incite violence between different African political movements. This forced division and rule tactic ingrained a culture of self-hatred as well as mistrust among Africans, thereby encouraging violence. A two-page pamphlet printed on a United Democratic Front letterhead declared the following: "We are calling all units for war. We have tolerated Azanian People's Organization (AZAPO) for long. They want to upstage our popularity in the community and they oppose all our campaigns."[38] Some activists from both parties blamed these attacks on the National Party. Others have noted that it was an effort to root out "radicals." The UDF denied any association with the pamphlet, but its diffusion increased the tense relations between its members and AZAPO. The Azanian Peoples' Organization was created on September 29–30, 1979 out of the BC tradition. Like the ANC, AZAPO fought against the fragmentation of Africans into various tribes and presented Africans as members of one nation.

Apartheid also shaped the nationalism of the ANC. From its inception in 1912, the ANC was created to counter both British colonialism and Afrikaner racial exclusiveness. At that time, the African elite wanted an organization that did not reflect either British or Afrikaner colonial policies and values. However, in the end, its members adopted British values. ANC members were "repelled by the brutal aggression of the British and the racial arrogance of the colonialists."[39] They were modernists who wanted to master the instruments of European culture and political institutions. Racism reinforced group cohesion and solidarity among ANC members. Caught between British paternalism and Afrikaner brutality, the ANC did not develop its own cultural symbols based on indigenous tradition. As a result of British influence and particularly missionary education, the African middle class looked up to British culture as its ideal. Its members were also suspicious of the way apartheid used African culture. Thus, culture was not used as an instrument of liberation and was not included in the ANC's definition of African nationalism.

The exclusion of culture from the ANC's imagined community was important because it kept the ANC alliance with the Communist Party in place. In the Marxist-Leninist tradition of the South African Communist Party, class relations superseded race. Class made sense on another level as well: since the alliance represented all South African racial and ethnic groups, which culture should be used? The ANC employed non-racialism instead of culture for political mobilization purposes. Even though Afrikaners were divided along class, gender, and ideological lines, they found a common symbol in language, religion, and culture. Africans lacked such symbols because of the influence of Western Christian values, which masked its racism through a paternalistic form of liberalism. Western Christianity taught Africans about mankind's brotherhood as well as tolerance and forgiveness. Liberals helped Africans understand that not all whites are racists. Finally, while communism privileged class relations over race, relations between white Communists and Africans were not devoid of paternalism. These influences contributed to the development of the ANC's policy of non-racialism.

As the dominant party, the NP was in the position to name all the other racial groups. Only Indians of various complexions maintained their original identity. For the NP, the white Afrikaner minority was the only group with a legitimate claim to South Africa. Thus, the NP denied the ANC the right to name its followers. The ANC never referred to its followers as Africans; instead, the ANC called them South Africans or the people. This self-denial of the right of naming itself or followers was a reflection of the relations of power existing between the NP and the ANC. Of all the opposition's discourses, only the PAC used African as a counter-identification to apartheid's naming privileges.

The history of apartheid also left Africans deeply suspicious of any organization that used race as a criterion for political mobilization. The ANC avoids identifying Africans as such, while the NP legitimized its claim to South Africa by using Afrikaner to refer to whites of Dutch descent. The ANC avoided exclusionary terms by focusing on non-racialism; people were mobilized on the basis of their socio-economic status rather than on their race. Once economic and social needs were met, there was no longer any need for a unifying ideology.

Additionally, the gulf between the African middle class and the African poor was so wide that the only common bond between the two was skin color. As Heribert

Adam and Kogila Moodley cogently remarked, most Africans go along with the status quo to make it in society. These authors argued that since these Africans depend on the white controlled economy, they are forced to engage in one form or another, "whether they like and admit it or not."[40] As a result, Africans are forced to aim for political power. Some ANC critics note that non-racialism was an empty slogan in which anyone could fit. In such a system, exploitation would continue because Africans would be under the false belief that they were liberated. In spite of its rhetoric, the ANC acted on the fundamental premise of apartheid by accepting the white liberals' presumed superiority over the Africans. The non-racial society advocated by the ANC was merely reproducing these old power relations. Unless each racial group underwent a thorough process of mental decolonization, relations of strict equality between social groups within a society traditionally and historically based on oppression and on relations of dominance/dependence would be impossible.[41]

Race, Class, and Gender

The liberation struggle was closely related to women's emancipation. Without empowering the women, liberation in South Africa would be meaningless.[42] Apartheid in South Africa was based on power relations between class, race, and gender. Gender refers to the social construction of sexual differences between men and women. The ideal white man was presented as a rugby player, an outdoor person, or in the military; he was, at times, educated. Among the Africans, "good" men were articulate, educated, and of middle class origin. In society or in the media, white women were presented as sexual objects. African women were also presented as sexual objects for white and African males: they were seen as the breeders of the society. In spite of racial segregation and apartheid laws, white men had access to both white and African women for sexual intercourse. African women were also maids who were not supposed to rise above their status. Criminals served longer jail terms for stealing than for rape, especially if the victim was not white. According to the motto "boys will be boys," violence among men was presented as something natural.[43] Some groups crossed the gendered boundaries set by the state. Thus, some women became involved in violent crimes, while gay people generally struggled to escape from state laws that punished them because of their sexual orientation.

Apartheid also shaped power relations within the white community. Just as the state was viewed as ordained by God, so was man's unquestioned authority within the family. A white woman's place in the family and state was to take care of the children under the man's authority. On the job market, white women were discriminated against. The government did not provide them with maternity leave and other job benefits. Those engaged in education could only be primary school teachers, whereas all principals were men. By 1986, married women were not given teaching contracts. There was only one white woman judge, three women members of Parliament, and a few senior army officers in charge of nursing and "the training of women recruits."[44] Women were not involved in the upper decision-making levels of the society, nor were they members of the NP's think-tank, the Broederbond.

Some white women's organizations, especially those linked to culture, language, and religion, were only opened to Afrikaner women. By the late 1970s, women demanded stricter punishment for rapists and the right to abortion. Women's organizations operated outside parliamentary party politics. Most of their leaders were from the middle class. Others, like the *Black Sash* and *End Conscription Campaign*, were drawn from a narrow base of women, mainly English-speaking, middle class professionals, wives of professionals, and highly educated women in major cities. White women were oppressed in terms of gender and class, and their organizations reflected this situation. Because of their inability to use their skills fully as lawyers, teachers, or doctors, white women were "a moral and intellectual condemnation of apartheid."[45]

White middle class women benefited from apartheid. They had access to African women's labor where the master-servant relations and the power dynamics of society were reproduced. Some middle class women did not have to work, which allowed them extra time for charity work. In general, white women represented themselves as superior to African women. White women saw themselves as the protector of and intermediaries for African women, and as persons who thought and spoke for these women. When dealing with the black women, white women united on the basis of race. This representation came under attack from African women in the early 1990s, but white women in South Africa continue to represent themselves in this manner. They organize conferences where a token number of African women are invited, and then proceed to discuss these women as though they were not present. Relations among white women were also influenced by power. For example, working class and middle class women did experience varying degrees of discrimination. Working class women had to compete with men for the same jobs yet their salaries were inferior to those that men received. White women living in rural areas were despised by women living in urban areas; urban women believed rural women to be backward as they were unfamiliar with city life.

By the late 1970s, political mobilization of African women increased significantly. Following *The Women's Charter* adopted in 1954 and the women's demands for the Freedom Charter compiled in 1955, African women demanded job opportunities, maternity benefits, day nurseries, equal pay for equal work, birth control clinics, universal education, and equal rights with men in property, marriage, and guardianship of children.[46] Unlike white women, who were oppressed in terms of class and gender, African women suffered from triple oppression: gender, class, and race. Up until the mid-1970s, daughters and wives of share-croppers or tenants on white farms worked alongside their brothers, fathers, and husbands without any financial compensation. Of all the racial groups, African women were the least educated and held the worst jobs. Initially, the liberation of women was inseparable from the national liberation struggle. In an interview in *Sechaba* (May 1981), Mavis Nhlapo of the ANC Women's Secretariat remarked thusly: "we do not actually pay much attention to these differences [between men and women] and these struggles, because we believe that in the main course of the struggle for national liberation, women will assert themselves and therefore will assume their rightful place in the struggle and in society."[47]

African middle class women organized without any particular goal in mind. Their organization was linked to the long-term goal of the liberation struggle. This struggle changed in 1985. Women's liberation came to be seen as synonymous with African liberation. No liberation would take place until African women were emancipated. In 1986, African women addressed major issues of concern. As the lowest-ranked social group within apartheid's hierarchy, African women demanded more education opportunities, which would in turn help them obtain better jobs. They also called on other women to engage in political mobilization and in regular and systematic information sharing activities. Transformation would only take place on the basis of their common oppression. As a result of the mobilization of women, the ANC recognized the importance of their specific conditions. To this end, it spoke out against their oppression. It also increased the number of women in certain party positions. Within the UDF, it was recognized that women needed to be organized to build up their confidence so that they could function in a liberated South Africa. Women also learned about their rights through mobilization, seminars, and clinics. Trade unions passed resolutions on women's rights and "their commitment to fighting to achieve these."[48]

Established women's organizations, such as the Federation of South African Women and groups linked to the ANC, NP, UDF, other housing organizations, the United Women's Congress, Transvaal Women, and Natal Women, were revived. Women mobilized because they felt that the other organizations were not meeting their needs in terms of better health care, child-care, and jobs. Unlike white women, African women had no birth control rights. The *Abortion and Sterilisation Act of 1975* (as amended in 1980) stipulated that before a person could be sterilized, the written consent of the guardian must be provided. The local magistrate was to make the decision if such a person could not be found. According to the magistrate, "notwithstanding the fact his view of sterilization is inevitably clouded by his racial prejudice (black overpopulation), the woman does not have a say whether she does or does not want to be sterilized. Her consent is not required."[49] Abortion was illegal except under very stringent conditions. African women turned to back alley doctors, where one out of every 200 of those who sought abortions died. "This happens to an estimated 140,000 women per year. The overwhelming majority of them are black."[50] Since only middle class women could afford to leave the country to obtain an abortion, poor women constituted the majority of the victims.

Women also organized against forced removals. Thus, in 1984 in Magopa, an African-owned farm in the Transvaal, women refused to be moved into the Bantustan of Bophuthatswana. Throughout the 1980s, the activism of African women increased. They organized "campaigns, networks of neighbourhood support, local demands that imply demands of national liberation, and immense courage in the face of the brutal, armed power of the state."[51] This mobilization reinforced the African imagined community by highlighting three factors. First, African women constituted a force within the society that could not be ignored; second, state brutality did not spare women; and third, the ANC fell far short of its stated goals in terms of improving the status of African women.

Housing was also a major concern for African women in the townships. By the late 1970s, most African families lived in houses or shacks meant for four, but ten to fifteen people were living in such households. According to Jeremy Seekings "by the end of 1982, there was an estimated shortage of 35,000 houses in Soweto and an estimated

23,000 families were living in 'Zozos,' easy to assemble instant accommodation."[52] By late 1986, these conditions had deteriorated as violence rocked the townships, not only threatening women's lives, but the lives of their children, as well. Motherhood became a rallying point against oppression. Using their common position in society as mothers, women were urged to rise against apartheid. Albertina Sisulu echoed this call by stating that, "no self-respecting woman can stand aside and say she is not involved while police are hunting other mothers' children like wild dogs in the townships. . . . A mother is a mother, black or white. Stand up and be counted with other women."[53]

In a similar vein, a UDF activist noted that "the struggle of national liberation is not only a struggle of our menfolk . . . join us, mothers who are still sitting."[54] This imagined community was inclusive both of other races as well as of men as partners in the liberation struggle. After the ban of all opposition political parties was lifted in 1990, women's organizations reemerged to express their needs. A Women's National Coalition demanded that the negotiating process and the constitution include a Bill of Rights where women's equality to men was protected. Against this background, African women continued to protest their exclusion from white feminist organizations on racial or class grounds. This challenge changed the nationalist discourse in three ways. First, it exposed the relations of power between women. Second, it brought women's issues to the center stage of the negotiating process. Third, it changed the dynamics of relations between white feminists and Africans as they all began imagining themselves as women on the basis of a set of complex relations such as class and race.

In 1991, controversy developed within South African women organizations. African women challenged the dominant position of white feminists as their self-appointed speakers. Throughout South Africa's history, white women represented themselves as the legitimate voice of African women; they knew what the latter needed just like the white male father figure understood his African children. A conflict developed. African women wanted to voice their own interests derived from the specific conditions they faced, particularly racial discrimination and poor economic living standards. White women wanted to dominate this process by determining what African women did and said. At a conference held in January 1991, African women challenged the relations of power that prevailed in women's organizations. The Women and Gender in Southern Africa Conference held at the University of Natal in Durban was organized by mostly white women academics. Except for a few African women academics, all women's groups without an intellectual background were excluded. Throughout the conference, African images were used, but African voices were not heard. One of the most controversial issues that arose between white feminists and Africans was the much-criticized conference's logo representing "a tiny-headed, naked and burdened other, 'present' only as object of scrutiny by the self-defining, theorising subject."[55]

In April 1992, various women's organizations united under The Women's National Coalition. The WNC represented many national and regional organizations. Women had long realized that the removal of white supremacy did not automatically end their oppression. The coalition brought a diverse group of women into the transition process. Unlike previous organizations, the WNC's sole purpose was to address women's issues. It did so by drawing up a women's Charter with five key issues: legal status, access to land, violence against women, health, and work. The Charter took into consideration the different cultures as well as class backgrounds of its members. The Coalition prepared women for the negotiating process through intense lobbying. For example, a Gender Advisory Committee was established at the Convention for a Democratic South Africa (CODESA). After CODESA, the Coalition demanded to have a representative present at all sessions. As a result, a women's lobby was created during the negotiation process with the aim of raising public awareness by informing women about their rights.

Conclusion

In this chapter, we have observed that apartheid influenced the nationalist discourse of the ANC and the NP in several ways. Apartheid's racial exclusiveness influenced the ANC's inclusive type of nationalism, which contradicted the regime's claim that South Africa was a white man's country. Relations of power within the NP influenced nationalism. The NP represented the ANC as a "terrorist" organization aimed at destroying the white minority's privileged position in the economy. Neither the ANC nor the NP were homogeneous; both were shaped by power relations based on class, gender, as well as race. The policies of the NP were based on the priorities and needs of Afrikaners. The party was led by an elite emanating from and controlled by the Afrikaner Broederbond.

The top leadership of the ANC was composed of African men while women occupied subordinate offices dealing with women's affairs. In both parties, the elite was divided into conservative and liberal factions. In the case of the NP, a sharp tension developed between the "militants" and the "moderates." Within the ANC, a rift developed between the African nationalists and Communists. Generational and ideological differences also informed these imaginings. These tensions led to the formation of the PAC, which provided a revolutionary counter discourse. When the ANC and PAC were banned, the Black Consciousness Movement filled the political vacuum.

Apartheid shaped the nationalism of these parties in different ways. The PAC mobilized its supporters by arguing that South Africa belonged to Africans as its indigenous people, while BC included all non-whites as blacks in its membership. Both BC and the PAC had clear political ideologies and strategies of economic, social, and political transformation. According to the ANC and the SACP, national liberation would be carried out in two stages. The first stage, called the national revolution, would be led by the ANC, while the SACP would lead the second stage, which would result in the advent of a socialist state. The ANC formulated an ideology for democracy and development in South Africa based on socialist principles. The ANC demanded that workers should own the land on which they worked. The party also demanded that the nation's wealth belong to the people and called for the nationalization of banks. After the fall of the Soviet Union in 1989, the ANC was in disarray because socialism came under attack. At that point, Congress decided to tone down its socialist rhetoric, thus leaving it without a clear and coherent ideology for democracy and development. This resulted in ideological weakness and confusion, leaving the ANC vulnerable and open to the advice of foreign states, transnational corporations, and international financial institutions. These entities steered the country on the path to a free-market economy and liberal democracy.

FURTHER READINGS

Harris, Allen. *Twelve Disciples of Nelson Mandela*, California Newsreel, 73 minutes, 2005, www.newsreel.org.

Mzimela, Sipho E. *Apartheid: South African Nazism.* New York: Vantage Press, 1983.

Pomeroy, William J. *Apartheid, Imperialism and African Freedom.* New York: International Publishers, 1986.

Reddy, Thiven. *Hegemony and Resistance: Contesting Identities in South Africa.* Burlington: Ashgate, 2000.

CHAPTER 4

"Home" as Depicted in Selected African and Afrikaner Novels and Short Stories

For example, you did not help me. Everybody. They preferred to sleep in their safety. But I ran too. And as the wind that blew against my face like the very sound of shame. The sound of victims laughing at victims. Feeding their victimness, until it becomes an obscene virtue. Is there ever an excuse for ignorance? And when victims spit upon victims, should they not be called fools?

—Njabulo Ndebele, "Fools"

Exile was not so much a geographical dislocation as a state of mind, something that consumed and branded and left one marked for life.

—Mandla Langa, "The Naked Song"

Introduction

As social critics, artists offered another perspective in the nationalist discourse where the imagined community was not as clear cut as the official definition. The official nationalist discourse represented the white minority as a homogenous group. The counter discourse offered alternative representation for blacks (BC), Africans (PAC), and the people (ANC). Artists represented communities informed by gender, class, and race. They also addressed the economic, political, and social issues that faced their characters. Some of these authors' characters exposed the fear and uncertainty of living under apartheid. In this chapter we will examine the role of artists in these representations. These fictional works provide a panorama of life under apartheid that was hidden from the official versions of the imagined community. What was life like during apartheid for the Afrikaner elite? *The Smell of Apples*, by Mark Behr, depicts the life of an Afrikaner elite family. In *The Hand that Kills*, by Sindiwe Magona, the plight of an African maid in a liberal Anglo home is exposed. Mtutuzeli Matshomba demonstrates the trauma of being homeless and the ability of apartheid to corrupt in in his short story, *My Friend the Outcast*. In all these works, the impact of apartheid on the individual is laid bare.

In "Fools," a short story by Njabulo Ndebele, the reader is introduced to the impact of apartheid on Africans during the climax of the regime's repression in the 1960s. The complexity of class, gender, and race comes through in Etienne van Heerden's *Ancestral Voices*. J. M. Coetzee's *Age of Iron* demonstrates the marginalized role of the social critic in apartheid's imagined community. In *Triomf*, a novel about poor Afrikaners, the National Party, and the new South Africa, the characters are not depicted as victims; they have choices and are in control of their lives. Thus, they are able to join another political party. The anxiety of the white minority in the "new" South Africa is aptly reflected in literature that is based on fear, such as *Disgrace*, by J. M. Coetzee and *House Gun* by Nadine Gordimer. Other works, like Seitlhamo Motshapi's poetry, reflect the unfulfilled dreams of Africans that have been replaced by deep class divisions and a sense of betrayal:

> I ask for bread
> my brother feeds me stone . . .
> hope is the hungry gruel
> at the glutted feet of the world
> that remembers me only
> in the clustered fly of the tv crew.[1]

Some authors, like Zakes Mda, are optimistic about post-apartheid South Africa. For the first time in history, African authors are able to make a living from writing. Change is taking place though at a slow pace. The complexity of life in post-apartheid South Africa is demonstrated in Mandla Langa's "The Naked Song." Marlene van Nierkerk's *Triomf* reveals the conditions in which poor Afrikaners live, while exposing the hypocrisy and failure of nationalism as promoted by the National Party. These different perspectives have some similarities. Firstly, they all address the concept of home during apartheid and after. Secondly, through their characters, these authors expose the conditions faced by marginalized people either as a homeless woman in "My Friend the Outcast"; the predicament of a young African man in white society in "The Hand that kills"; or the plight of the Afrikaner working class in *Triomf*.

The works discussed here were selected for various reasons. First, they represent the concept of home in such a way that exposes the contradictions of nationalism. Second, they all address class, gender and race issues. Finally, these works expose the role of the social critic in the nationalist conversation. The works were written both during the period of apartheid and after the period ended. The works begin during the 1970s; this marked the Soweto uprising and the demise of apartheid. Out of the eight works chosen, two are by women authors: one African (Sindiwe Magona) and the other by an Afrikaner (Marlene van Nierkerk). Four of the works are by Afrikaner authors and the other four are by Africans. These works are examined in chronological order. For clarity this chapter is divided into two parts. The first section discusses works set during apartheid. Part two looks at post-apartheid authors.

Apartheid Literature

In "Fools," by Njabulo S. Ndebele, private and public spheres are merged in the repressive conditions of apartheid South Africa during the 1960s. Whether through residential restrictions or job opportunities, the state controls all aspects of Africans' movement. Political activism is discouraged, while collaborators are made into heroes. There are no heroes in this story. This is a story about victims who have learned to accept their victim status as they laugh at their own despair. These are the "fools" that Ndebele depicts in his story. Zani, the political activist who is chased by an Afrikaner as other Africans look on, asks,

> What have I found anywhere? Everything seems so small. Am I that small too? Tell me. Have there been many years in which this smallness has turned into a tradition; many years of this crushing sleep of smallness? What is there to be done? It is so easy to make plans, and then everything comes crashing down because the proper act seems so rare. So many acts get done, and so few of them are proper. For example, you did not help me. Everybody. They preferred to sleep in their safety. But I ran too. And as the wind that blew against my face like the very sound of shame. The sound of victims laughing at victims. Feeding their victimness, until it becomes an obscene virtue. Is there ever an excuse for ignorance? And when victims spit upon victims, should they not be called fools?[2]

In this story, Afrikaners are depicted as Boers. As the dominating minority, they are everywhere; when Africans decide to have a picnic or a walk the Boer is there. The refusal to name the Afrikaner as such demonstrates the contradiction of his presence. He belongs, while at the same time he does not. He is not represented as having legitimate claims; he is a person who relies on violence to control Africans. Home cannot exist in these conditions. The Afrikaner must be forced to accept the presence of Africans in South Africa and their rightful claim to home. Thus, the characters only identify Afrikaners by their color and language but never by name. Africans cannot, however, ignore the Boer who constantly meddles in every aspect of the African's life.[3]

The Boer is represented as all powerful, a menacing presence that instills fear in Africans. The power of domination is demonstrated when a Boer beats a respected school principal in public. Not only does the Afrikaner discipline the principal but he is also the authority on how the latter should discipline the young man. The more the principal begs and tries to explain his predicament to the Boer, the more the latter beats him. Finally, both the principal and the Boer run after Zani, who escapes to the cornfields. The image of both oppressor and oppressed running after the agitator is powerful given the repressive state conditions of the 1960s when the state was trying to woo African moderates through the homeland system. Ironically, when both fail to catch Zani, the Boer turns on the principal again. Thus, the volatile nature of relations between the Afrikaners and their African collaborators is exposed.

The relationship between the two is not static; it changes depending on the issues at stake. As depicted above, the Afrikaner joins the teacher as they both run after the agitator, yet, when the agitator is unable to be caught, the Afrikaner turns back against the teacher. The principal, who was giving orders to the crowd prior to the arrival of the Afrikaner is forced to beg for mercy. The Boer tells the principal, "either way you will get a thorough beating. But at least with me you'll get home to your wife sooner."[4] "Please, my great king, please," pleaded the principal, "I was only trying to discipline that young man over there. It was all a mistake."

When the Afrikaner is done beating the principal, he turns his whip on the school teacher, Zamani, who had witnessed the whole scene. The juxtaposition between good and evil is revealed as African and Afrikaner confront each other. Good, as the better virtue, triumphs over evil. Afrikaners are depicted as the epitome of evil. The only form of communication that they have with Africans is through the whip. Passiveness is also represented as a virtue. Africans are depicted as good and patient people who will teach the Afrikaner this noble virtue. The presence of Africans and their passiveness in the face of Afrikaner brutality is a virtue that makes them strong. Africans are also depicted as "saints" who can withstand all forms of violence. Zamani describes the encounter in the following way: "He was the same substance as his whip. I offered no resistance as he lashed at me. I just stared at him. I struggled hard to absorb the searing pain, trying to say something without much understanding; the silence of desperate action. This would be the first silence that would carry meaning."[5] During the beating, Zamani begins to laugh and the Boer weeps. Zamani goes on: "The blows stopped; and I knew I had crushed him. I had crushed him with the sheer force of my presence. I was there, and would be there to the end of time; a perpetual symbol of his failure to have a world without me."[6] After the beating the Afrikaner leaves with his whip. Zamani says, "There he went; a member of a people whose sole gift to the world has been the perfection of hate."[7]

The only hope for a better life in this story is the presence of women characters, who run the homes and businesses, and support their men during crises. Similar to the men, they do not confront the system. They go about their business as a constant reminder to the men of how low they have fallen. In this representation, women are idealized; they are the brightest, the most understanding and loved greatly. Women are the pillars that hold society together when all others fall.

Women are also the pillar of Mtutuzeli's "My Friend the Outcast," which is about the trauma of apartheid, homelessness, despair and corruption.[8] The short story touches on class, gender, and race, demonstrating how in the apartheid discourse these identities are intertwined and related. This story personalizes the problems that individuals face because of unsympathetic policies that were imposed during apartheid. Mrs. Vusi is thrown out of her four-roomed house because a middle-class African has bribed a housing official. That night, two white police and three African police raid her home. Mrs. Vusi comments, "They got like mules and soon everything down to the last rag was in the street. When they finished, Beak Nose demanded the keys and the house was locked."[9] The narrator observes, "it was hard for all of us to accept that they were now homeless."

As depicted in this story, the African middle-class is not independent. It still identifies with the plight of the poor as noticed when the new owner decides against occupying the house. Instead, he advises Mrs. Vusi to go to the Social Services and liberal newspapers to tell her case to whoever will listen. The narrator describes the arrival of the new owner of the house: "The stranger arrived in a Chevair, which placed him among the fortunate of the sprawling location.... There was the air of confidence about him which is characteristic of those who have just found a way to keep their heads above the water. Most probably very recently married and badly in need of his own four-room. Dikeledi felt uneasy standing before him the way she felt when she faced a white man."[10] The plight of poor people is exposed in this story. When members of the middle-class need something they take it from the poor who lack power. Thus, the corrupt official who has been paid by the African takes Mrs. Vusi's house. There are good whites, like the social worker, who helps Mrs. Vusi; the liberal press, where Mrs. Vusi waits for someone to "hear" her story, is also touted as good. Home for Africans is plagued by fear and insecurity. Vusi declares, "South Africa! A cruel, cruel world with nothing but a slow death for us. I hate it, mfo, I hate it."

Race and gender play a role in all that happens to the characters. Mrs. Vusi is thrown out of her house because she is a poor African widow. The economic position that a person occupies in the community also determines the service he/she receives. The white housing official speaks kindly to the new tenant, though he despises him. The corrupt Superintendent longs for the "good old days when Bantus were Bantus and knew their place. Bring them out of the bush and teach them to read and write and they think they're smart enough to swear at the *baas*."[11] But Vusi's white boss is sympathetic. "Without demanding the usual 'proof' he gave [him] permission to attend to his affairs until they were settled and he assured him that would not affect his paypacket."[12]

Etienne Van Heerden also addresses the issue of home in apartheid South Africa, by looking at the plight of generations of biracial and Afrikaner families. The Moolmans are made up of two families: the "proper" family, white Afrikaners, and the *skaamfamilie*, the family of shame, family of guilt, the tainted family.[13] The real family is the white family, which is also the richest in Toorberg. Africans provide the backdrop to the story. In this story, home is depicted through the voices of dead ancestors and the legacy they have left for their families. For the Afrikaner family, home is like a shrine in which the ancestors' orders are obeyed. It is guarded with the bible in one hand and a gun in the other. Only Afrikaners are entitled to the benefits of home, such as, for example, proper burial grounds and ceremonies.

The family is divided along race and class lines. The white family acts as the overseer of the mixed-race one; it gives orders and they are obeyed. The white family also dictates where one is to be buried and that, too, is headed. Relations between the two families are intense. These families that share a love-hate relationship have been thrown together by fate. They share the same grounds, though the white family is materially better off than the mixed-race one. Home is represented as dangerous, a place that must be tamed by all means necessary. The concept of home is also contested: what is home to the white family is not the same as the conception of home for the mixed-race family. The white family alone has a legitimate claim to the home. Each member of the white family must pay the price of living in Africa, which includes maintaining the family history, defending it, and preventing blacks from forgetting their place. Home is also exclusive since it is open only to white families. Although the grandfather of the mixed-race family and the "Bushmen" settled on the land at the same time as the white family's grandfather (father Abel), only the latter's claims were recognized. One day the pastor/activist explains, "But when Founder Abel went to the Governor, he was the one who got the title-deeds. Because he was white, Meisie. . . . But who's stuck out on the Steifveld with a plot of prickly pears and a goat pen and a few rabbits? The Riets here, the Moolmans there."[14]

However, differences are submerged when the families are faced by outsiders. When Crazy Tilly's mixed-race child (Noah) falls into a well and gets stuck, Abel shoots him. He orders the well covered with cement. Both families are represented during the ordeal, yet neither family tells the investigating magistrate the truth. Both families unite for the sake of home and family. Throughout the story, women are depicted as the backbone of the two families. White women keep order in the absence of their husbands. They have a master-servant relationship with the mixed-race women. White women are given mixed-race maids as wedding presents. Afrikaner and mixed-race men speak highly of their women. They also treat them with respect. Women are viewed as the pillars of the family; they must support their families at all costs. Women who do not support their husbands are despised.

Home is also a contested terrain in the *Age of Iron* by J. M. Coetzee, which is based on the political violence that rocked South Africa between 1986 and 1989. *Age of Iron* revolves around characters in a Cape Town surburb. The main character is Mrs. Elizabeth Currie, a retired Professor of Classics, who is dying of cancer. Mrs. Currie is questioning the notion of home behind her protected bars as political violence sweeps the country.

In this story, Africans, whites, and mixed-race people are forced to live in a country that they cannot even agree on what its name should be. The concept of home has a different meaning for each character. Thus, for the homeless Mr. Vercueil and his dog, home is the layer of cardboard that they sleep on. For Florence and her children, home is in flames in the townships, violent as well as insecure. For Mrs Elizabeth Currie, home is lonely, a place where she must learn to live as a marginalized person. What is the *Age of Iron*? It is a period marked by courage as well as by the questioning of traditional beliefs. It is also the age of defiance. Mrs. Currie describes it thusly: "Children of iron, I thought. Florence herself, too, not unlike iron. The age of iron. After which comes the age of bronze. How long, how long, before the softer age return in their cycle, the age of clay, the age of the earth? A Spartan matron, iron-hearted, bearing warrior sons for the nation?"[15]

J. M. Coetzee's *Age of Iron* criticizes both the National Party, which has led the country through lies and propaganda, and the African nationalism that has sold its youth into violence as the only means of liberation. The future nation is represented as different from the present one. In such a nation all people will have to work. The name of the nation will also be changed: "South Africa: a bad-tempered old hound snoozing in the doorway, taking its time to die. And what an uninspired name for a country! Let us hope they change it when they make their fresh start."[16]

As depicted in this novel, the writer has lost his voice in South Africa. The state does not take the criticism of artists seriously. No one is listening to them. J. M. Coetzee's *Age of Iron* exemplifies this marginalization.[17] Mrs. Elizabeth Currie has a lot to say, but no one is paying any attention, not eve her maid. Most important is the relationship between writing and the political struggle. A recurring question emerges as the reader gets to know these characters: should artists keep writing even when no one is listening? What is the artist's role in a community that does not respect him/her? Elizabeth Currie's home becomes a refuge for Florence's son Bheki, his friend John, two daughters, Beauty and Hope, and finally for Mr. Vercueil and his dog. The South African nation is represented in this home: African, Afrikaner, people of mixed descent, and the Indian, who fixes the bars on the windows, are all present. At times, Mrs. Currie acts as the peace-maker between the boys and Mr. Vercueil; she is, however, marginalized in this endeavor, as well, as the boys chase Mr. Vercueil out of the house. The teenage boys who are fearless and arrogant have taken over the struggle against apartheid. These boys aim at eliminating apartheid. The political struggle is more important than their schooling. When Mrs. Currie urges Bheki to go to school, he responds, "What is more important, that apartheid must be destroyed or that I must go to school?"[18] She warns Florence, "Be careful: they may start by being careless of their own lives and end by being careless of everyone else's. What you admire in them is not necessarily what is best."[19] Florence admires the children because they fear *nothing*. She responds, "They are good children, they are like iron, we are proud of them."[20] Bheki is shot during a police raid in the township. John, Bheki's friend, uses the servant quarters on Mrs. Currie's compound as a refuge, but the police hunt him down and shoot him too. Florence leaves for Guguletu (a township on the suburbs of Cape Town) with her two daughters. Mrs. Currie is left in her home with her cats, Mr. Vercueil, and his dog. Finally, the cats also leave. Mrs. Currie complains about the boys to the police, but the police do not listen to her. We learn about her predicament in four letters to her daughter, who lives in America. The reader is left in suspense not knowing whether the letters written by Mrs. Currie will ever reach her daughter. Mrs. Currie does not demand anything from Mr. Vercueil, not even his word that he will mail these letters to her daughter. The dependency of Mrs. Currie on Mr. Vercueil is further exposed when he rescues her from her cancer. Mrs. Currie says, "I got back into bed, into the tunnel between the cold sheets. The curtains parted; he came in beside me. For the first time I smelled nothing. He took me in his arms and held me with mighty force, so that the breath went out of me in a rush. From that embrace there was no warmth to be had."[21]

As depicted in the *Age of Iron*, art has no role in the new South Africa because no one is listening. Mrs. Currie has no power over nationalism, whether as a critic, mediator, or as an observer. Mrs. Currie, who is depicted as the voice of reason in this story, is lonely and powerless. African and Afrikaner nationalisms are depicted as irrational forces that only listen to their respective supporters.

The Smell of Apples by Mark Behr is about the contradictions of home from the perspective of a Christian Afrikaner elite family.[22] Marnus (the narrator), is eleven years old. He tells the story through flash backs as an adult engaged in a losing war between South Africa and Angola in southern Angola. This is also set against political violence in the townships. His father, Johan, is a major-general in the South African Defence Force. His sister, Ilse, is a high school student. Leonora, his mother, was a famous singer before she married his father. Marnus' father is his hero. The life that Marnus loves changes when a Chilean general visits the family. The visitor, who is only known to Marnus and the family as Mr. Smith, has secret meetings with his father. *The Smell of Apples* is also about misrepresentations. It is cautious when addressing the contradictions of nationalism such as the discrepancy between how it depicts itself and how it is actually deployed in practice.

Home as represented here is meant only for Afrikaners. According to Johan, the English always run away. Afrikaners are the only ones who can save South Africa. Africans can never rule South Africa because they have failed in the rest of the continent. Besides, the brightest ones were taken to America to be slaves. Johan's ancestors escaped from Tanganyika when the blacks took it over. Afrikaners brought everything to South Africa, even the apples. Afrikaners are in South Africa because it is God's will.

Johan tells his son, "And this country was empty before our people arrived. *Everything, everything* you *see, we* built up from nothing. This is our place, given to us by God and we will look after it. Whatever the cost."[23] Johan and his family are God-fearing Afrikaners. He takes his family on vacations, goes fishing with his son, entertains his wife, and attends his children's school activities. He has only given his children hidings (spanking) once: Ilse for calling an African a Kaffir and Marnus for not responding to his father's call. The children know that they must not call Africans Kaffirs because they are also human. By all appearances, this is an ideal Afrikaner Christian family. Frikkie (Marnus' friend) is a fearless, energetic, and outgoing boy. But in the presence of Johan, Frikkie is afraid, nervous, and shy. Marnus discovers why Frikkie is terrified of his father, the morning he also wakes up to his father's deceit: this God-fearing nationalist is also Frikkie's rapist. This discovery shatters Marnus' life. He ceases to respect and adore his father. Marnus is glad that Frikkie will not tell. He thinks aloud: "If he didn't even want to tell me about Dad, then he'll *never* tell anyone. And it's right that way."[24] Class relations also shape these families. Leonora (Marnus's mother) is kind to Zelda who comes from a poor Afrikaner family. She gives Zelda old cloths, takes her on outings to expose her to culture and helps her pay for her son's hospital bill. Leonora also contributes blankets for Africans who live in the townships. She prefers Africans and coloreds who know their place.

Relations between men and women are based on power. Johan marries Leonora, who, at the time, was a successful singer. After their marriage, however, Johan forbids her to perform in public. He does not even allow her to listen to jazz because, according to him, it can only lead to evil. The only time when Leonara is able to enjoy jazz is in the car while driving her children to their school activities. The children promise her that they will not tell her secret to their father. This bright woman is reduced to entertaining guests. She endures long absences from her husband as he checks for trouble on South Africa's borders. She is no longer on speaking terms with her sister (Tannie), because, according to her husband, Tannie is a communist. Tannie believes in women's equality, which is taboo in South Africa where a woman's role was as a wife and/or beauty queen.

As a result of Leonora's marriage, her sister, Tannie Karla, had "seen enough of how Dad oppresses Mum to make sure she'd stay away from marriage for life. She'd never allow a man to tread her in the ground like Dad does to Mum."[25] Tannie is forced into exile in London. Ilse admires Tannie. Leonora tells her daughter not to throw her talents away. She must do what is expected of her, that is, marry and have children. People of mixed-race are depicted as violent and dependent drunks. Gloria, Frikkie's maid, is "cheeky" because she dresses in high heels and wears make-up as though she were a real madam. Africans are represented as breeders. Frikkie and Marnus order their maids around as though they were grownups. Poverty is hard on Africans and people of mixed-descent, but this does not concern middle class Afrikaners. Instead, they are appalled by the poor standard of living of the white family that lives close to the coloreds.

"The Hand That Kills" by Sindiwe Magona is also about deceit and the contradictions of home under apartheid. Lunga, Selina Korai's son, loves his home, which is located in a servant's quarter on Mr. and Mrs. Walker's compound. Lunga's mother works as a maid for the Walkers. Ever since he was a child, Lunga has only known the Walkers' home as his own. The Walkers know what is best for Lunga and Selina. Lunga has grown to accept what his mother tells him about the Walkers: "Occasionally, his mother made vague allusions. They would never want for anything. Mr. and Mrs. Walker had promised her that they would see that he get a good education; become a teacher. They would buy us a house in the township one day: when the time was right. Even if she were to die, her kind employers would never turn him away. This was their home, the Walkers were as good as parents to her. She was very lucky indeed. Both of them were."[26]

The Walkers raised Lunga as their own son. His home is 16 Tivoli Avenue in Newlands, a white Cape Town suburb. He speaks Afrikaans and English. Home is contradictory. It is his and his mother's, yet it is not. Lunga thinks aloud: "Home. Strange thing that. Home was not home although it was the only one he knew. The only one he had. His mother called it that and so he called it that. They had no other. Except it wasn't theirs. Not really. Never had been. And never would be."[27]

These representations are also based on class. The Walkers provide for all of Lunga and his mother's needs. They even advise them on how to react against apartheid's indignities. They are their parents. In their parental role, the Walkers urge Lunga to be patient about change in South Africa. These relations are also based on power. The Walkers have the money. As whites, they have power over Lunga and Selina. Not only do they have power over the present, for example, by deciding on what schools Lunga will attend but they also have power over the future since they will buy a house for them.

The home that Lunga has grown to love is shattered as political reality sets in: "He was not only growing into man-hood but into *black young man-hood*."[20] Life changed when Lunga joined a township youth movement. His friends teased him about his white father. In an effort to prove himself to them, Lunga kills Mr. Walker. He wishes he could take the act back. For him and his mother, home is shattered as he faces a death sentence and the prospect of his mother's unemployment.

As the male figure of the family, Mr. Walker takes care of his family. After Mrs. Walkers' death, he depends on Lunga for companionship. This dependence also signifies the complex relations between the two races. His death makes it more explicit. Lunga is in shock: "Fear swiftly gave way to a sinking feeling as millions of little worms gnawed frenziedly at the walls of his stomach. Cradling Mr. Walker, Lunga had slumped onto the cold unyielding floor, unseeing eyes staring into nothingness, mouth wide and dry as the desert, body bereft of feeling. And that is how, hours later, his mother had found the two."[29]

POST-APARTHEID LITERATURE

"The Naked Song," by Mandla Langa, is about a man named Richard who has returned from exile. Richard is alone; he has neither country, nor family or friends to return to. Richard was a dedicated member of the ANC, but this fact does not help him. Richard is also a talented musician. Without any support in post-apartheid South Africa, Richard relies on his talent for healing. Richard leaves South Africa in 1976 to join *Umkhonto We Sizwe* (ANC military wing) and meets Nozi, another cadre in *Umkhonto We Sizwe*. They get married, but shortly thereafter Nozi disappears during one of her missions. In 1990, Richard returns to South Africa, where he searches each township but is unable to find Nozi. In 1994, just when the country is celebrating its first general elections, two comrades knock on Richard's door to inform him that Nozi died in 1990 under suspicious circumstances. Afterward, "Richard was in a daze all day. In the afternoon, he ventured out of his Berea flat into scenes of jubilation. Thousands of people on the street, even foreigners, all exulting in one of the greatest victories of the century."[30]

When Richard returns to his flat, he reads Nozi's letter, which the visitors left. It affirms her love for him. He starts howling until a neighbor breaks the door down. Richard is rushed to the hospital where doctors cannot find any medical reason for his ailment. But Richard has lost his power of speech. We learn about Richard through Gama, his psychiatrist, who cautions him that the sessions will be painful but helpful.

The new South Africa is involved in a painful journey of coming to terms with its past, just as Richard must do. There are no dramatic changes from the past. Richard is upset because the ANC did not inform him that Nozi had gone missing. He also wonders why the ANC waited until the day of the celebrations to tell him the tragic news. No one answers his questions. Upon his return to South Africa, Richard discovers that people who were used to war must now find other means of making a living. Some people join schools as students, "knowing that the future dispensation would have no role for them, Richard was sent home in the same contingent as Oliver Tambo."[31] Former liberation fighters must learn to live in a South Africa that they do not know. There are no rewards for their hard work liberating South Africa. These former fighters must also learn that "there was no such thing as returning from exile. Exile was not so much a geographical dislocation as a state of mind, something that consumed and branded and left one marked for life. Many, like animals whose limbs were left in a snare, walked through life crippled, their minds locked on that fateful moment of rupture."[32]

In the new South Africa, the change of the rulers' skin color is the only transformation. Home continues to be plagued by uncertainty, as the new government inherits the problems of apartheid such as transportation and crime. The language question is also a problem. Can there be a single nation without a national language? "How would the new South African National Defence Force deal with commands such as 'Attention!' or 'Fall In!' in eleven languages?"[33] Similar to other artists who gave their lives to the struggle, Richard feels that he has been betrayed by the new nation. Gama asks, "What have we done for the artists? For the Richards of the world who come and expose the more unpalatable features of our society and are then left alone to groan under the weight of discovery?"[34] The only way that South Africans can help themselves and people like Richard is by re-living the traumatic past so that they can survive the present. In Richard's case, Gama would use music "to evoke memory and stimulate imagination."[35] He would tell Richard the following:

> Yes, all the women involved in the struggle are Nozi. They are there, these women in the shacks of our country, trying to maintain their dignity in the face of abuses; they are there in hospitals, looking upon the eyes of men, women and children who have been ruined by disease and poverty. They are there these women, singing their sad songs as they bury their loved ones cut down at a tender age by our collective cowardice. They will be there at the victory hour, when poverty and strife, pestilence and death are finally eradicated from our soil-and it is not a blasphemy to love them, but the highest tribute to Nozi's memory.[36]

Home can only be redeemed through a collective healing process. Such a process not only addresses past problems but also finds ways of dealing with present ones. However, collective healing is a long and difficult process. Although the problems in post-apartheid South Africa are complex, they can be solved. Richard must go through the therapy sessions and reclaim his music in order to use it in the new nation. Art then becomes an expression in the context of liberation. In this work, art is not marginalized, nor is it reduced to national reconstruction; rather, it has an important role to play in the new South Africa.[37]

Life's contradictions in the new South Africa is also the subject of Marlene van Niekerk's, *Triomf*. What happens to failed dreams? Who are the victims of nationalism and liberal democracy? Is nationalism really what it says it is? *Triomf* is meant to be about the success of Afrikaner nationalism, but, in reality, it is about the failure of nationalism to transform the plight of poor Afrikaners. The National Party (which came to power as these peoples' savior) only takes note of Afrikaners during elections. The NP helped these Afrikaners settle in cities and find work with the railways; however, their dreams were never filled. Other white minority political parties also use poor Afrikaners as their pawns. In the new South Africa, the far right tries to recruit Afrikaners to fight for their rights while the NP aims at their votes.

Triomf is a powerful story based on the events that led to the transition from apartheid to majority rule. Triomf is about failed dreams and the contradictions of nationalism. It concludes with the 1994 general elections. *Triomf* revolves around the Benade family: the father, Johannes Lambertus Benade; the mother, old Mol; two sons, Treppie

(Martinus) and Lambertus, Jr. (little pop); and a daughter, little Mol. The Benades are poor and illiterate and have moved to Johannesburg from the countryside. Mr. Benade works for the railway while old Mol works at a garment factory. Little Mol joins her mother at the garment factory when she turns fifteen years old. Mr. Benade is a nationalist: he votes for the NP, believes that even poor whites are superior to Africans, and rules his family with an iron fist. He is also a drunkard who beats his wife into submission.

Triomf is also about incest. Mr. Benade beats Treppie for having intercourse with his sister, little Mol and warns his wife to keep the children apart as he believes only a monster could result from their union. After the beating, Treppie refuses to speak to his father. Soon afterwards, Mr. Benade hangs himself. He loves Treppie, whom he entrusts with the nationalist dream. But, on the day that Benade dies, Treppie resumes his sexual relations with little Mol. As far as the family is concerned, the most important thing is for them to stay together, take care of one another, and to have a roof over their heads. Old Mol cannot keep the children apart. She dies of tuberculosis.

The Benade children are left to fend for themselves. They do not have any friends. Mol continues to work in the garment factory. Treppie and little Pop start a refrigerator business, which fails. Out of their union, the two brothers and sister conceive a son whom they name Lambert. They move from Vrededorp to Triomf, a town built on the ashes of Sophiatown (destroyed by the NP in 1955). NP nationalists claim that these whites have good lives in the suburb. However, in reality, they live in city slums where the only security they have is their skin color. The NP also claimed that poor whites were employed and successful, but, in fact, most were unemployed and dependent on government handouts. Thus, the NP's claims about poor whites and their lives were in stark contradiction with the reality they faced.

Marlene van Niekerk's novel is a scathing criticism of the NP and ANC as well as the far right.[38] As depicted by the characters in this story, the NP has failed its rank and file members. The ANC takes over the new South Africa with all its past problems while the far right mobilizes people based on fear. Through the characters, the reader understands how the NP represents itself as the savior of Afrikaner people. Home is understood as complex and violent, dirty, and uncertain. *Triomf* also demonstrates the contradictions of this representation. The NP forced Africans out of Sophiatown where there were jazz clubs, art, and other cultural events that brought Africans and Afrikaners together. Sophiatown is replaced by *Triomf*, which is an upgraded trailer park. At one stage, Treppie speaks of the dogs that keep howling at night as though they were the ghosts of Sophiatown. NP representatives in the area regard poor whites as cultural rejects and trash. Nevertheless, representatives continue to visit to persuade the poor whites to vote for them, as they will protect their minority rights.

The concept of home is also shaped by gender and class. A poor woman's conception of home is different from that of a member of the middle-class. Afrikaner working class women are oppressed, both at home and at work. This oppression has its own contradictions. Women are the core of the nationalist dream and family yet, they are also the most oppressed. Old Mol supported and voted for the NP throughout her life, but the NP did not help transform her standard of living. Little Mol followed in the footsteps of her mother, but the NP did not help her either. Old Mol works at the garment factory to support the railway salary of her husband. She is not interested in politics. She is simply interested in feeding her family and living a decent life. It is difficult to remain white and superior when one is poor and illiterate. At a moment of desperation, she wishes that she were a Kaffir so that she could feed her family with porridge without embarrassment. Mr. Benade beats her because he believes that the white race is entitled to certain rights, most specifically, good food. Over time, the physical and emotional abuse wear Mol down. Two fears confront Mr. Benade: that the Kaffirs will take over his way of life and incest among his children (which is popular among poor Afrikaners). In his suicide note, he writes,

> I know you're sick in your lungs, Mol. Look after yourself. Don't let the Kaffirs take over your job. Be careful, the Jew Communists will undermine you. They're heathens, the whole lot of them. A person has only one life and one soul but mine is finished. . . . Give Treppie my mouth organ. Lambertus plays better but Treppie needs it more. Try to keep them off each other's bodies, Mol, in God's name send them away to different places if you can. So an end can come to you know what. Only a monster will be born from this sort of thing. I've heard from the others, more and more such cases are happening among us railway people.[39]

Old Mol loses control over her home upon her husband's death. Treppie "began to act like he was boss of the house. It was also then that Treppie started running [raping] her [little Mol] into the ground. She tried to complain to old Mol, but by then old Mol was a broken woman."[40] The running continues until Mol gives birth to her epileptic monster son, Lambert. Treppie, Lambert and Pop share Mol. "Three in one!" Treppie said, talking at the top of his voice. "Services them all! Father, son and Holy Ghost, into their glory!" "Three in one," his mother said.[41] Mol is represented as an idiot who never thinks for herself. She is emotionally, physically, and sexually abused by her son and by her brother (she is married to the quiet brother). During one of Lambert's wild fits, he stuffs her in a refrigerator for hours until Treppie and Pop find her frozen to the bone. After that ordeal, she loses some of her marbles (her thinking ability), which explains her forgetfulness and the cough. Similar to her mother, Mol never fights back. She has been beaten into passivity. Even Lambert, her mentally challenged son, notices that his mother is neither clever nor aggressive: "Treppie's his mother's brother, but even he's given up on her. No matter how much he carries on with her, she just takes it lying down, like a scared little dog. Never backchats. And the day she does open her mouth, then it's to say the same thing he's just said to her. Like a blarry echo machine."[42]

Mol is scared all the time. All she knows of the world is what Treppie tells her but she is loyal to her family no matter what. When Lambert goes wild, it is Mol who calms him down. When Treppie wants to share family secrets he does it with Mol. She also comforts Pop. Mol acts as the cement that holds the family together. But she is also the most powerless of all the Benades. Mol is not a victim. She can leave but she chooses to stay with her family. Lambert forces Mol to cut the lawn at midnight, which she does without any complaints. Instead of fighting for her rights, Mol wishes that the government would build a big whore house so that the men could leave her alone.

Class discrimination is based on power relations. The Benades are outcasts as far as the white middle-class is concerned. But when confronted by Africans or mixed-people, they *know* their rights as white people who must be respected by Kaffirs. Lambert is grateful to the African who saves his life at the garbage dump. But he is also very keen that the latter knows how to behave in the presence of a white man. In all their encounters with Africans, they are referred to as sirs and madam. Treppie does not mind going to African jazz clubs. Treppie believes that Sophiatown had "a better class of Kaffir."[43] He works for a Chinese family with whom he gets along well. Treppie does not speak as negatively of Africans as Lambert does. In fact, he thinks that it is a good thing that Africans moved to the house across the street from them because they are planting maize on the pavement, a "new development." On Lambert's fortieth birthday, Treppie and Pop pay a hundred Rand to a mixed-race call girl for him. Lambert first thinks the call girl is white. When he discovers that she is a Kaffir, he decides that she can pass for white if she treats him right. But she insults Lambert by calling him white trash, upsetting him. No Kaffir should insult a white man, he vows, and decides to rape her but she escapes.

Throughout this story women are represented as sex objects. There are constant references to Marika's (F. W. de Klerk's wife) cosmetic surgery to remove a frown. Her only concern is her looks. The lesbians who live across the street from the Benades are also depicted as sex objects and the bikinis (two scantily dressed female neighbors) live next door. Women are also represented as staunch enemies. The women next door join their husbands to attack Mol, her son, and brothers/husbands. In rebuttal, Mol joins her family against these women. It is only after Lambert's leg is amputated and Treppie is too old to "share family secrets" with her that Mol finally gets some rest.

The Benades know that the NP has *failed* them but they still support the party. They vote for it out of tradition rather than loyalty. Though it claims to be the new NP, it is still the same party. It is simply in search of new recruits. It changes its flag's colors to reflect the new South Africa. Of the new flag, Treppie remarks, "Hell, after all this time, the NP still thought it was God, with the sun shining out of its backside. God or no God, pop said, he was going to miss orange-blanje-blou a lot. How was a person supposed to rhyme the new flag? But the NP-man's girl who always comes with him on his rounds, suddenly said, 'the more colours, the more brothers!'"[44]

The Benades respect the NP. The only time that Mol removes her house coat is when the representatives of the NP visit her home. The past, present, as well as the future are all presented as uncertain. The only visitors to the Benades' home are Jehovah Witnesses and NP representatives. The Benades have kept to their kind throughout their history. They are not sure of the kind of home they will have after the election. So they prepare to leave for the north. Treppie (who is the family genius), advises them that with "the shit flying after the election, Lambert should get ready for a shitstorm, or, as it was written, the fulfillment of the law and the prophets." They have stored petrol in large cans in their backyard in case of an emergency.

The limitations of the changes carried out in the new South Africa are exposed by the occurrences of election day. The Benade's home is painted white by Wonder Wall, a painting company, and are promised that the services would be free (they had won a prize). Like the new government, the company does not make repairs on the house. Instead, they simply paint it with its leaking roof. The floor boards and the windows are broken, the toilet and the garbage sit outside, and the smell of excrement covers the whole house. The painters move the few possessions of the family into the center of each room. All the furniture is covered in white sheets. Pop, the only calm member of the family, observes,

> Three more panfuls of loose floor-blocks from the dark passage. Everything into the bag to make sure that nothing will be lost. Not him either. Now they're throwing sheets over everything. All is white. White for the crossing over. High above the roofs of Triomf, the roads and the towers and the flat, yellow mine dumps. The chimneys that smoke and blow fire to one side, as if in a salute, beyond the earthly city's limits. Higher and higher, a seed in a white husk. Cries and psalms from other windborne souls. And then again, from far off, the ground approaching at long last, rocking to and fro, the horizons tilting from side to side. To one side, a small, white house, its doors and windows tightly shut, where he can finally come to rest against the clean, sun-warmed walls, nothing but the whisperings inside as if his ear were pressed to a shell, throughout the bright and endless winter.

The house across the street, in which an Afrikaner and English lesbian couple live, is also painted white. An African family moves into the neighborhood. But life in the new South Africa has its own problems. For example, there are more political parties from which to choose, confusing the Benades. There is greater pressure for the Benades to work: they have more bills to pay and are trying not to appear as cultural trash. The Benades discover that the prize they had won was a bill for only half the cost of the painting. They must obtain a loan to pay the 26,000 Rands, which will, with interest, add up to 90,000 Rands. Old South Africa's problems continue in the new. The only difference is that they are more complicated than before.

Lambert discovers his family roots on election day. A painter gives him a set of keys, keys he has never seen before. Lambert, who is now forty years old, decides to find out what is held in the family drawer. He finds a photo with Vrededorp 1938 (the year of the ox wagons) written on it. Also written is the following: "mum and dad and Treppie-10, little Mol-14, Lambertus jnr., in front of our little house. Given for safe-keeping to Treppie (Martinus), the apple of my eye, so he'll never forget from whence he comes."

Lambert looks on, "Treppie! That's him standing there with the pinched mouth! *One* old pop, two sons!. . . . If Pop's his mother's brother and he can sleep with her, and if Treppie's also mother's brother . . . who the fuck's his father, then? Whose fucken child is he?" Lambert breaks the drawer on Pop's head, killing Pop on the spot. He finds Treppie on the toilet seat, chases him out and around the yard until he pins him down and breaks all his fingers. He finds Treppie's pocket-knife and uses it to stab Mol in the ribs. Then he kicks the prefab wall between their house and the neighbors and breaks his ankle.

At the hospital, "they were all bandaged and plastered up and at last they stood there, next to the doctor, who had to write out the death certificate for Pop on the trolley."

When the doctor pronounced the cause of death as a heart attack and multiple fractures to the skull, the family insisted that Pop fell off the ladder while painting. "'Were there any other relatives?' the doctor asked. They said no, and the doctor said, well, in their case he thought a police statement was perhaps unnecessary. 'Superfluous!' he said, and that's what they all three said, as if they'd practised it all their lives, just for this moment."

Similar to the Benade's shack that is painted white on election day and the Benade family that is plastered and bandaged, the new South Africa inherits the problems of the old. The lies continue as they did under apartheid, and the ANC plays along as it urges the people to forget the past. According to this story, the transition is not a break from the past. Old South Africa lives on as whites learn to stop calling Africans Kaffirs. People are celebrating everywhere. For Mol, if she had "a cannon she would also have shot off a cannonball here out of the heart of Triomf for old Mandela, cause he walks so upright and he shook everyone's hands and he said, what was past was past, everyone must roll up their sleeves and look to the future now."[51] The African and Afrikaner elite all benefit from the transition from apartheid to liberal democracy. Thus, they get better jobs, move to new neighborhoods, and travel abroad. The African ice cream seller continues with his business as usual, except in the new South Africa he carries flags from diverse political parties.

Conclusion

The works discussed here, which include short stories and novels, provide another perspective of the imagined community. Unlike the official representation by the NP, ANC, BCM or PAC, these works demonstrate the contested nature of both "home" and the imagined community in South Africa. Each group defines the concept of home in a particular way; the definitions are influenced by class, race, and gender. These definitions have their own contradictions. The ANC and NP have failed to meet the needs of poor people. These people are marginalized in the new South Africa where they are not participants in the transition but powerless observers of the process. The ANC, as the party in power, does not make any repairs to the new home. Instead, it simply paints over the house, leaving the foundation untouched. Life in the new South Africa is also full of contradictions as people learn to live within more complex relationships such as economic hardships and crime. Home is not perfect, it is full of painful memories that one must learn to overcome. This condition is well demonstrated by Mandla Langa's "The Naked Song."

In Triomf, the characters are not victims. They have choices. Thus, Mol can leave her family. The Benades can vote for another party but they choose not to. These characters have decided to live the way they do. Mol can refuse to mow the grass at midnight, but she does not. The same theme of lies, sacrifice, and hypocrisy informs the characters depicted in *The Smell of Apples*. Frikkie decides not to reveal his ordeal just like the characters in *Ancestral Voices* decide to lie about crazy Tilly's biracial child. Again nationalism's contradictions are laid bare as the reader notices the discrepancies between reality and rhetoric.

FURTHER READINGS

Athol Fugard, *Tsotsi*. Johannesburg: AD. Donker LTD, 1980.
J. M. Coetzee, *Disgrace*. London: Random House, 2000.
Karonda, Farida. *Against the African Sky and other Stories*. Cape Town: David Phillip, 1995.
Melamu, Moteane. *Children of the Twilight*. Cape Town: CTP Book Printers, 1996

CHAPTER 5

CHANGES IN SOUTH AFRICA'S ECONOMY, 1976–1994

> Most countries strive to raise the quality of their human resources; only South Africa made it an express purpose of official policy to lower standards and frustrate the aspirations of those who wished to improve their contributions to the economy.
> —Charles H. Feinstein, *An Economic History of South Africa*

IN THIS CHAPTER, WE WILL DISCUSS THE MAJOR CHANGES EXPERIENCED BY the South African economy between 1976 and 1994. We will analyze how these developments transformed the ruling elite. We will trace the economic developments that forced the National Party to change its policies. This analyses will be followed by an examination of the changing Afrikaner class base as a result of economic prosperity. The rest of the discussion in this chapter will focus on answering the following questions: how did African militancy affect the economy? What reforms were introduced as a result of the Soweto rebellion? Did the involvement of South Africa in destabilization wars in Angola and Mozambique affect the economy? Finally, what was the impact of international sanctions and the fall of the Soviet Union on the economy?

According to Robert Price, several developments resulted in the Soweto revolt. These were: regional transformation, economic stagnation, external threat, military buildup that also resulted in political repression, and the "psychological stimulus" to revolt by the ANC, which resulted in material support from opposition supporters.

In the mid 1970s, the apartheid regime faced four challenges. The first challenge, African resistance, which climaxed with the Soweto revolt of 1976, continued throughout the decade. The apartheid state sent its military to occupy townships, which resulted in more resistance. State repression, arrests, and emergency curfews did not result in stability. After 1976, these townships became ungovernable as violence escalated in the mid 1980s. Secondly, African resistance was compounded by economic stagnation, as workers took to the streets and international sanctions increased. Third, state access to some foreign funds and technology was blocked, causing the white minority's standard of living to fall. As a result, some transnational corporations began divesting from the country. Fourth, the independence of Angola and Mozambique left South Africa without a buffer on its northwestern and northeastern borders.[1]

APARTHEID AND ECONOMIC CHANGE

The success of apartheid resulted from class alliances between Afrikaner and other whites; alliances were built amongst white workers, commercial farmers, industrial entrepreneurs, and the emerging Afrikaner petty bourgeoisie. This alliance was based on the social, economic, and political rewards of apartheid. Since 1948, in successive "whites-only" elections, the NP promised to advance the interests of its supporters by restructuring the economy in their favor. By 1960, apartheid provided 40 percent of the Afrikaner population with blue-collar jobs.[2] As a result, a political alliance developed between industrial capital and white labor, which protected each party's interests against those of the Africans. Africans were denied access to the major central business districts through influx controls and various other laws. This also meant that Africans could not operate their own businesses in the informal sector. As Africans were forced to spend their savings on white-owned businesses, the accumulation of capital for Africans was nearly impossible. Members of mixed-race, Indian, and Malay ethnic groups were allowed some economic mobility, which contributed to the development of a small middle-class comprised of businessmen and professionals (that is, lawyers, doctors, and educators). Henceforth, race became the most important criterion for determining one's privileged position in the economy. However, race was only important during the early period of apartheid. As Seekings and Nattrass have demonstrated, by the late 1970s class had replaced race as the major criteria for economic success.

The insider/outsider division was also expressed within the Homeland system, where African laborers were forced to reside. The massive removals and displacement of Africans by the state replaced tenant labor with a contract system. As long as the state kept African political, economic, and social demands in check, the white minority rallied behind the National Party, which subsequently rewarded it with well-paying jobs and high standards of living. The state also subsidized white farmers. Afrikaner firms handled government contracts, while Afrikaner banks managed their accounts. Afrikaners also occupied high positions in the military, as well as in the administration and the education system. Afrikaner publishers and publicists handled the community's cultural production. Afrikaner workers were absorbed into state bureaucracy where they benefited from "soft loans, housing bonds, and other benefits."[3] Capital accumulation coincided with race, which Stephen Gelb describes as "racial fordism." Gelb further notes that the foundation of this model was "the expansion of exports of gold and precious metals, and their stable prices on world markets."[4]

State capitalism under apartheid was so profitable that by the mid-1970s it had transformed some Afrikaner small farmers into middle-class capitalists. A study showed that the state was more responsive to Afrikaner demands than to lobbying from large English firms or to African demands.[5] Most Afrikaners had also moved from blue collar positions to white collar ones. The population of Afrikaners in white collar jobs as opposed to those in blue collar or agricultural jobs rose from 29 percent in 1946 to 65 percent in 1977.⁶ By the 1980s, Afrikaners controlled 60 percent of overall investment. Sanlam (an Afrikaner company), was the second largest corporation in the Johannesburg Stock Exchange. The company's total assets of 4.9 billion rands in 1972 had soared to 31.65 billion rands in 1982.⁷ Afrikaner capital also worked in corporation with English capital. Thus, Sanlam started working with Anglo-American as early as the 1960s. As the precursor of *verligte* policies, Sanlam also demanded better job training for Africans to ensure adequate economic growth.⁸ The economic boom financed by international capital subsided by 1976, when capital flight became so severe that the government lost a quarter of its foreign exchange reserves. By 1984, Afrikaner capital was competing with foreign capital for control of the mining, manufacturing, and financial sectors of the economy. During this period, Afrikaner investment also increased, but Afrikaner unity came under stress because apartheid was unable to prevent the manufacturing sector from becoming too dependent on African labor.

Indeed, for the first time since 1948, skilled and semi-skilled white workers were seriously threatened by African workers. According to Hermann Giliomee, between 1960 and 1980 the number of white workers in the manufacturing sector rose by 75 percent (from 208,900 to 357,700), while the number of African workers jumped by 140 percent (from 314,000 to 772,000).⁹ Lower-class whites also faced competition from people of mixed descent. Approximately 50 percent of economically active Afrikaners were employed by the public and semi-public sectors, and 80 percent of all jobs in these sectors were held by Afrikaners.¹⁰ Between 1975 and 1977 total investment fell by 1.3 percent.¹¹ The world economic crisis of the mid-1970s, triggered primarily by high oil prices, also affected the economy. Annual GDP growth dropped to "1.9 percent until 1984 and 15 per cent for the rest of that decade."¹² At the macro level, orthodox economists stressed the impractical politics of the apartheid government, which because they attracted international sanctions, were seen as the major obstacle to the proper functioning of a free market economy.

Vast amounts of resources (human, material, and financial) were diverted from development and into maintaining the infrastructure of apartheid. Such wasteful expenditure included building separate facilities for each racial group (including three separate school, technical colleges, and university systems) maintaining a bloated and inefficient bureaucracy (including a separate one in the Bantustans), and an overcrowded and expensive prison system.¹³ Furthermore, Africans in urban areas did not own land; therefore they could not be taxed. According to Vella Pillay, the apartheid economy faced three major problems: African demands, capital flight, and the lack of resources to finance apartheid.¹⁴ Apartheid was also becoming more expensive to administer. For example, the administration of the pass system, which determined the residential, travel, and work space of Africans, cost over US$ 150 million a year. The budget of the Department of Cooperation and Development in the ministry that controlled "Bantu" affairs amounted to US$ 1.15 billion, representing 10 percent of the total state budget.¹⁵

To grow further, the economy needed to expand its market; however, the majority of the South African population did not have enough disposable income, making this expansion impossible. Once the white minority had purchased all the goods it needed, the excess production had no further outlet. Thus, by the late 1970s, the car industry was capable of manufacturing 400,000 cars but the market could only absorb less than 200,000.[16] Like other industries in South Africa, the automobile industry's production capacity was underutilized. As the economy stagnated, Africans provided an untapped market for the manufacturing sector. This predicament could only be resolved through a substantial increase in the salaries of the Africans. Economic growth would also increase the purchasing power of Africans. Such situations demonstrated the irrationality of a capitalism that favored whites. The apartheid economy came under attack during this period as a result of three developments: a shortage of skilled labor, market saturation, and plant underutilization. Eventually, a major contradiction between economic growth and apartheid developed. The economics of apartheid was threatened by economic stagnation, change of policy preferences, and the socioeconomic make up of Afrikaners. Apartheid was in contradiction with free trade. To resolve this contradiction, it was increasingly necessary to replace "the old-style ideology of Divine mission and exclusivism . . . with a more pragmatic, secular style of survival politics."[17] Economic and symbolic conflict developed over state policies, as well as over the objectives of nationalism.[18]

THE MANUFACTURING SECTOR

The South African economy underwent significant changes in the mid-1970s. Most of the economic growth, and the related increase in jobs, took place in the manufacturing sector (rather than in the agricultural sector). While the African population in urban areas increased significantly, apartheid laws prohibited African workers from obtaining skilled and semi-skilled jobs and to the needed related training. Apartheid also resulted in labor scarcity, artificially raising salaries. Yet, when manufacturers sought African workers, they found an undereducated workforce: 40 percent of the African male population lacked any educational qualifications and 82 percent had less than six years of primary education. Between 1972 and 1975, "there was a structural break and a shift to much lower rates of growth of output, employment, and productivity. The average annual rates of growth of real manufacturing output plunged from 7 percent in 1948–1974 to a miserable 1.6 percent over the two following decades."[19] Employers had to bear the cost of job training for Africans and the enforcement of pass laws; they also had to provide separate racial facilities and further training to replace detained workers. Added to this was constant police harassment and searches for "illegal" Africans. Those found without valid passes were deported to the homelands. These security concerns introduced a significant degree of uncertainty and instability among the African workforce. Employers increasingly relied on "a stream of short-term workers" who were expensive to train because of the high turnover rate. By 1970, labor bureaus in the homelands (working with employers) recruited 40 percent of the African male labor force for short-term contracts. Most of these workers were employed in areas that were designated "white."[20]

Hermann Giliomee notes that labor was not an issue in the dispute between Afrikaners who wanted change *(verligte)* and those who preferred to maintain apartheid *(verkrampte)*, or in the dialogue between business and government. Giliomee argues that if African labor had been an issue, it would have been reflected in the debates within the Prime Minister's Economic Advisory Council (EAC), which was not the case. In 1977, a prominent Afrikaner stated, "The English-speaking private sector has been heavily represented in the EAC right from the start in 1960. Right through that decade they never presented a convincing case for the need to train and develop blacks, or for housing and so on, beyond expressing their opposition to certain laws such as physical Planning Act."[21] An English-speaking member of the EAC addressed the concerns by stating, "How convincing a case did they want?" At the very least, this demonstrates a lack of cogent arguments and unity of purpose between the Afrikaner business elite and their English-speaking counterparts.[22]

According to Giliomee, the real battle was over the goals of Afrikaner nationalism and the rationale for the apartheid state. Once the ideal of uniting all Afrikaners was achieved by the mid-1960s, the leadership shifted its attention to state-building and to securing jobs for Afrikaners. As a result, some Afrikaner people became the most ardent and enthusiastic supporters of the state. The agricultural sector underwent significant technological changes in the 1960s, thereby requiring fewer workers. Wages also became a smaller portion of the total cost of farming. The government increased wages to fuel the economy. By the mid-1970s, the South African Agricultural Union (SAAU) demanded higher wages, improved working conditions, and better access to training and education.[23] In 1979, the SAAU demanded that the policy of influx controls be abandoned. However, all Afrikaner farmers were not united on the issue of policy changes. Conservative farmers in the Transvaal did not support the changes. These farmers supported the Conservative Party because "on the one hand the government cut back severely on subsidies and price support for maize farmers, while on the other hand P. W. Botha in the early 1980s alienated delegations from those farmers in a particularly damaging way."[24]

Mining corporations occupied a central place in the South African economy. Their labor requirements determined both economic and public policy, particularly with regard to migrant labor, housing facilities, and taxation. The exceptional stability of the price of gold, which remained constant between 1934 and 1970, meant that this sector was passing the increased cost of production on to other sectors. Because farmers had preferential access to African labor, mining firms were forced to resort to migrant labor from other Southern African countries, particularly Mozambique. Because they were foreign-owned and lacked the power to influence public policy, mining ventures were heavily taxed. By the mid-1970s, the labor policies of the mining sector turned against job segregation. According to Merle Lipton, these changes resulted from four separate developments. First, an increase in gold prices during this period resulted in higher salaries. Second, beginning in 1973, there was widespread and endemic unrest among African workers, which could only be quelled by improving the workers' conditions. Third, increased foreign criticism and pressure forced this sector to introduce labor policy changes. Finally, mining policies faced pressures from two other sectors in the economy: manufacturing and commerce.[25]

The apartheid state was plagued by severe political and economic crises. For example, beginning in 1979, the state was forced to over pay the mining companies for gold with a continuously devalued rand. Although the mines received their funds, the state was faced with the problem of selling the gold abroad. Between 1981 and 1982, the price of gold fell, triggering capital flight. In 1982, the South African Chamber of Mines recognized African trade unions, thus allowing African workers to demand higher wages. In 1984, African miners went on strike and won a 20 percent wage increase, significantly increasing the cost of mining operations. "In 1984 the state received gold-related tax revenue of about R2.2 billion, amounting to 11.7 percent of total revenue. In 1985, this revenue declined to about R 1.8 billion, or 8.4 percent of total state revenue."[26] In 1987, more than 350,000 African mine workers went on strike, resulting in a 30 percent pay increase.[27]

The increased cost of mining operations required a drastic change in labor policies in order to significantly increase the profitability of the mining sector. Such change involved a substantial relaxation of apartheid laws and regulations (particularly in flux control) and the lessening of strikes, labor-related disputes, and violence, all of which would result in increased profits for mining firms. Investors in this sector became critical of apartheid, as it became increasingly perceived as a major obstacle to their profit-making ventures. The commercial sector also underwent major changes. In particular, the sector was plagued by changing demands and technology, which made it difficult to classify jobs simply as skilled or unskilled. The instability of the work force added unnecessary costs for training, work permits, and employee bailouts. To avoid these costs, the commercial sector demanded a permanent urban workforce and was prepared to pay higher wages so as to motivate the workers and achieve better performace. While the commercial and manufacturing sectors did recognize African trade unions, they still clung to some of the apartheid policies. Like other economic and policy-making sectors, manufacturing and commerce were split between conservatives (who were represented by the Afrikaanse Handelinstuut (AHI) and the Federated Chamber of Industry (FCI)) and the progressives (represented by the Associated Chambers of Commerce (ASSOCOM)). By the late 1970s, ASSOCOM and FCI found apartheid uneconomical, unwieldy, and excessively costly. Pressure for change led to the adoption of the Business Charter in 1985, a result of a joint AHI-Chamber of Mines initiative. This pressure continued until 1990–1991, when the NP finally repealed major apartheid laws such as the 1950 Group Areas Act, the 1913 and 1936 Land Acts, and the 1950 Population Registration Act. The NP also revoked the state of emergency.[28]

THE CHANGING AFRIKANER CLASS BASE

Apartheid was originally rooted in an Afrikaner ethnic identity forged through the poor economic conditions and insecurity forced upon Afrikaners by British imperialism. By the mid-1970s, most Afrikaners were economically competing with English capital. They were bona fide capitalists whose businesses were competitive in both domestic and international markets. The Afrikaner elite progressively came to view some of the most repressive apartheid policies, such as job discrimination and pass laws, as a threat to white supremacy. This elite also started to expand Afrikaner identity by distancing itself from the apartheid state. Since Afrikaners were economically well off as a result of the NP's economic policies of favoritism and entitlements, the elite was able to make a distinction between "apartheid and white supremacy and to attend to the latter by abandoning significant aspects of the former."[29] To the extent that they retained economic power, whites could still control the country without dominating it politically. Furthermore, whites increasingly preferred to end apartheid while preserving white supremacy. To that end, it was important to open up the political arena to other racial groups while maintaining control of the economic sphere. Such a strategy had the advantage of maintaining the essence of white supremacy while appearing to relinquish political control.

Economic transformation resulted in changes in the electorate. The business sector and the NP alienated civil servants and farmers. Civil service salaries were frozen in "September 1984 despite an annual inflation rate of nearly 20 percent."[30] Fearing unemployment, most workers defected from the NP. As the economic slump worsened, white unemployment tripled to an estimated 5 percent.[31] White trade unions mobilized workers under the banner of the Conservative Party. These parties used workers' discontent to woo them away from the NP. A right wing candidate explains this process, "The appeal for reform does not strike emotional cords in the Afrikaner.... You must tell him in the midst of inflation and the falling value of the rand, how much money the government is spending on black education and development, and he will go crazy."[32]

White farmers also defected from the NP due to high interest rates and unfavorable government pricing policies. In 1982, white farmers experienced various problems. In 1983, as a result of low prices for agricultural commodities and food products and decreasing government subsidies in the agricultural sector, white farmers' income decreased by 42 percent compared to the previous year.[33] By 1985, the total debt of white farmers increased to 1 billion rand, with half the country's farmers teetering on the edge of bankruptcy. To make matters worse, in April 1985 the Ministry of Agriculture refused to increase maize prices.[34] Capital flight increased to US$2.09 million [about R 5.5 million] in 1984. By 1985, it was estimated at $1.2 billion. Without international loans, resources to finance the apartheid system could only come from business profits and from the white minority "through cutbacks in their privileged living standards."[35]

In general, poor Afrikaners in the manufacturing sector (especially those from the working class) strongly favored apartheid labor laws while Afrikaner industrialists opposed them. However, the division between these two classes was not so clear-cut: poor Afrikaners and Afrikaner industrialists agreed on key issues at times, such as the maintenance of white supremacy. The disagreement, however, stemmed from the means by which to achieve this supremacy. The disagreement was essentially over strategies for political change, as reflected in the perennial *verligte-verkrampte* conflict. *Verligte* were Afrikaners who favored change yet desired to control the process. This group was comprised of intellectuals, politicians, and members of the business community. *Verkrampte* were conservatives (made up of people from different social classes and professional categories) who wanted to maintain traditional Afrikaner power. Additionally, there were Afrikaner intellectual dissenters (such as Andre Brink, Braam Fisher, Leo Marquard, and Uys Krige) who did not fit neatly into any of these categories. The goal of these Afrikaner intellectuals was to do away with apartheid. The terms *Verkrampte* and *Verligte* were first used by journalists, and were subsequently incorporated in their respective studies by key experts of Afrikaner nationalism, such as Hermann Giliomee, Andre du Toit, Heribert Adam, Dan O'Meara, and Sam Nolutshungu. By late 1970s, the Afrikaner imagined community was no longer as united as it had been between 1948 and the early 1960s. The *Verligtes* attacked apartheid's idea of a "white nation." This brought it into sharp conflict with the *Verkramptes* forcing the NP to seek new alliances with English capital (which favored a reform of apartheid in order to improve the economy).

From its inception, a white minority controlled the apartheid state. As Giliomee shows, the essence of the apartheid state was Afrikaner control "its *Boereplaas* (literally the Afrikaners' farm)." But the state's extensions, such as the homelands, the police, and the bureaucracy, included other racial groups. The pressure to expand access to the other racial groups increased in the 1980s. In order to mitigate conflict and to attract international capital, the Afrikaners began opening the state up to other racial groups. This expansion had its own contradictions. For example, Afrikaners still controlled the core state while the "extended state" that is, the homelands, was under African "puppet" government leaders. The multiracial nature of the extended state was invoked in order to mute the criticism of the regime. In the 1980s, the NP came to believe that it "should seek freedom from domination by non-members" rather than try to dominate the black groups.[36]

To survive in a rapidly changing environment, Afrikaner nationalism had to create alliances across class and race. In a key speech, H. B. Thom, chairman of a Brooderbond front called the *Federaise van Afrikaanse Kultuurverenings* (FAK), urged Afrikaners to make contacts across language and color because "the gates of the Laager have to be thrown open; our Afrikanerbond must be extended fearlessly."[37] As a result, the claims that people of mixed race and Indians made on the state were accepted, although whites remained in charge. The new, all-inclusive discourse of the NP ignored class, gender, and racial divisions. According to this discourse, every social and racial group would benefit from changes in the economy. As a result of this strategy, the NP lost its traditional political base without obtaining a new one. Its support among Afrikaners fell from over 80 percent in the 1981 election to under 60 percent in the 1987 election. Between 1982 and 1983, the financial base of the NP changed as a result of its alliance with English capital. For the most part, English capital did not support apartheid. Instead, it sought to build a class alliance with Afrikaner capital in the hope that the NP would eventually dismantle the apartheid regime for capitalism to function more efficiently. This relationship was problematic and was often marked by conflict. For instance, when English capital sensed that the NP was not moving fast enough to dismantle apartheid laws, English capital would distance itself from the state. The NP made more attempts to unite the Afrikaner bourgeoisie. Conflict over the state and the goals of Afrikaner nationalism within the NP led to a split in 1982. This split was complex, with some trying to maintain an unreformed apartheid without leaving the NP. Meanwhile, right-wing opponents of the NP created the Conservative Party. Others joined the far right in the *Afrikaner Eenheids Beweging*. Some "liberals" within the Afrikaner nationalist movement left politics altogether for the business sector.

As it faced the African challenge, the differences within the National Party on how to address this challenge resulted in a severe ideological crisis. Differences within each cultural/linguistic group were larger than those between Afrikaners and Anglos. The NP had undergone significant changes. As a leading nationalist observed, "Now, the NP has become bourgeois itself, espousing middle-class values and finding bridges across language and racial barriers."[38] P. W. Botha's government tried to meet bourgeois demands by implementing new labor laws and addressing the threats posed by the African working class. The NP also aimed at creating an alliance between Indians, Malays, whites, and people of mixed descent against Africans.

The Broederbond underwent major changes during this period, as well. In 1983, it was taken over by reformists, who transformed its informal institutions into overtly political ones. Reformists no longer conformed to earlier nationalist objectives, nor were they capable of "playing the opinion-leading role on behalf of the NP in Afrikaner communities that the united network of the Broederbond institutions had fulfilled in the past."[39] From then on, the *Verligte* wing of the Broederbond shaped the direction of reforms. Another core institutional supporter of apartheid, the Dutch Reformed Church (DRC), also changed during this period. Contrary to previous assertions, the DRC now declared that apartheid was not ordained by God.

The economy reflected the changes occurring in the society. Sanlam, a *verligte* company, controlled *National Pers*. The *verkrampte* camp controlled the Volkskaas bank and the Perskor newspaper group. The civil service hired more *verligte* managers. Universities joined in the conflict between conservatives and liberals, with the University of Pretoria becoming the main base for the conservatives. As opposition against apartheid mounted, business began distancing itself from the state. The business sector was afraid that its relationship with apartheid threatened its profits. To counter apartheid, this sector developed a free market ideology that encouraged free enterprise by legalizing the free movement of persons, goods, and capital, the establishment of trade unions and by disengaging the state from the economy.

Endemic political internal instability made it necessary for business leaders to initiate talks with the ANC. A number of prominent businessmen who operated in South Africa, including Afrikaners, Anglos, and foreigners, took the initiative by visiting the ANC leadership in Zambia in 1986. These businessmen focused on finding an alternative to apartheid. The NP endorsed the idea of a democratic South Africa, but was against the nationalization of the economy. In spite of its being officially banned, a meeting between the ANC leadership and some key NP politicians was arranged during the same year. During the meeting, both sides agreed that a political settlement was possible and could be achieved. Another meeting followed in November 1986 between ANC Secretary General Oliver Tambo and Mikhail Gorbachev in the Kremlin, which enumerated three conditions: "an end to Pretoria's acts of aggression against independent African states; the granting of independence to Namibia in accordance with UN resolutions; and the removal of the apartheid regime in South Africa as the 'primary cause of conflict in the region.'"[40] Some members of the judicial system also distanced themselves from the apartheid regime. Only the security institutions continued to support it.

In a document written in July 1989 entitled "Political values for the Survival of the Afrikaner," the Broederbond urged the NP to rethink the logic of apartheid. It argued that the exclusion of effective black sharing in the political process at the highest level had become "a threat to the survival of the white man."[41] In its conclusion, the document urged "Afrikaners to take risks in case they found themselves in the opposition seat. There could no longer be a white government and the head of government did not necessarily have to be white."[42] During this period, Afrikaner identity also changed. For example, before De Klerk's speech in 1990, the FAK journal, *Handhaaf*, a Broederbond mouth-piece, presented sensible Afrikaners as those who, on the one hand, rejected the right wing's violent tendencies, and on the other had a clean break with the past and "wanted to consider themselves not as Afrikaners but Afrikaans."[43] As a cultural concept, Afrikaans embraced all Afrikaans speaking people, thus broadening the imagined community's boundaries.

AFRICAN MILITANCY

During this period, Africans were not passive. From 1948 to 1960, they used legal, non-violent forms of mass resistance. Between 1861 and 1973, armed struggle and guerilla warfare became the main form of struggle. After 1973, the liberation struggle was based on a synthesis of non-violent, passive resistance and armed struggle. Armed struggle in the form of violent confrontations with the apartheid state became a common feature. The end of Portuguese colonialism in Angola and Mozambique in 1975 encouraged guerilla warfare that targeted key leaders and institutional symbols of the apartheid regime. Throughout these struggles, the nature of the apartheid state remained constant: after 1961, any form of opposition or resistance was perceived as a threat to the regime. Four developments triggered the resurgence of popular resistance in the 1970s. The first was the economic crisis, which resulted in job loss, low wages, and high rates of unemployment. Secondly, the independence of the former Portuguese colonies in Southern Africa (Angola and Mozambique) inspired many Africans. Thirdly, the BCM introduced radical ideas based on "psychologism," namely "the conviction that the key to African liberation lay in psychological liberation."[44] The fourth development was the tendency of the opposition to associate every deprivation of their lived experience (be it racial discrimination, lack of housing and universal education, and/or poverty) with the apartheid regime, thus sharpening the political consciousness of the oppressed.

By the mid-1970s, the first "apartheid generation" without any links to the homelands had come of age. This generation was street wise, bold, and familiar with apartheid, having grown up in some of the most vibrant townships in the country such as Sophiatown and Soweto. While this generation had grown up within the confines set by apartheid and, as such, experienced harassment, pass laws, and humiliation, it was, unlike previous generations, *not* intimidated by apartheid. It was also a much younger generation with most members between the ages of fifteen and twenty. This youth was also greatly influenced by the Black Consciousness Movement. It was this fearless generation that was crucial in shaping the events that transformed the country. As a result of urbanization, African high school enrollment increased from 123,000 in 1970 to over 300,000 in 1975.[45] In April 1976, the prices of maize, cooking oil, and other African food staples went up by 18 percent. Meanwhile, unlike whites, Africans were obliged to pay "school fees, which could easily come to a month's income to send two children for a year."[46]

Three factors caused the Soweto revolt of June 1976. The first set of factors situational variables, included the housing crisis, rent increases, inflation, and recession. The second set of causes was based on ideological variables such as Black Consciousness and the regional transformation that followed the independence of Angola and Mozambique. The final set of factors were based on organizational variables provided by student organizations arising out of the Black Consciousness Movement.[47]

The Soweto revolt was not a coherent, carefully planned and executed insurrection. Rather, it was a spontaneous and leaderless uprising of the marginalized and excluded poor urban youth. Initially, the rebellion started as a reaction against the imposition of Afrikaans in African schools. Unlike their parents, the younger generation of Africans had better access to the media, which exposed them to the limitations of apartheid education. These young Africans despised an educational system that relegated them to the status of servants in the land of their birth. Instead of learning mathematics and science, African children were taught arithmetic and agriculture to prepare them to be laborers. The rebellion also aimed at eliminating white supremacy. Workers joined the students in organized boycotts. This class alliance was significant, given the critical role of the African working class in the economy.

The large African urban population increase was not matched by improved housing conditions. Between 1967 and 1976, not a single house was built for Africans in Pretoria. Between 1972 and 1975 the government spent R 138 million for housing in the homelands compared to R 27 million in urban areas. This was a deliberate state policy designed to discourage Africans from living in urban areas. In the whole country, "only 9,808 family houses were built for Africans during 1975."[48] The state also destroyed African townships and forced other Africans into Bantustans. While the government was cutting back on housing for Africans, older townships that were deemed to be "too close" to white areas were demolished, further limiting the availability of housing for Africans in urban areas. Housing availability was frozen at a time of high demand. As a result, there was an increase in squatter dwellings and high rents for the few houses available. Between 1986 and 1991, whites occupied 33.2 square meters compared with 12.0 square meters for people of mixed descent, 18.0 square meters for Asians and 8.9 square meters for formal housing for Africans (4.8 backyard shacks and 4.2 squatter housing).[49] In 1991, 34 percent of Africans in urban areas in Bloemfontein lived in informal dwellings (backyard shacks or squatter settlements) compared to 58 percent in Cape Town. Durban had the highest number of Africans in informal dwellings at 69 percent while Port Elizabeth had 55 percent. In the same year, the percentage of rural population with access to health protection (four walls) was as follows: Eastern Cape at 27 percent; Northern Cape at 33 percent; Natal at 39 percent; Orange Free State at 45 percent; Northern Transvaal at 41 percent; and Southern Transvaal at 16 percent. The wealthier the province the better the housing, for example

Western Cape, which is very wealthy compared to Southern Transvaal, a poor region.

By the mid-1970s, unemployment also increased. In construction, 60,000 semi-skilled and unskilled African workers lost their jobs in the first three quarters of 1976. To compound these problems, African wages were very low. Out of the total African population of 27 million, only 9.5 million were economically "active."[50] An IMF report in 1984 put the number of unemployed Africans between 2.5 and 3 million. By 1984, the South African Research Service (SARS) estimated unemployment in the Bantustans (and especially in the Ciskei, Bophuthatswana, KwaZulu, and Gazakulu) to have risen to more than 50 percent. According to an economist with the Johannesburg Consolidated Investment Company, in 1987 African unemployment stood at 4.5 million and could reach 7.8 million by the year 2000, given growth of one percent a year. Those Africans who were employed had to travel long distances to their jobs. As a result, most of the wages they earned was spent on transportation. The average distance that workers traveled to their job sites increased over the years. For example, in Cape Town, workers traveled an average of 16.7 km in 1990 compared to 14.9 kilometers in 1975.[51]

The Soweto uprising was the most successful political revolt in South Africa's history. It shook white dependence on African labor. State symbols were burned and its representatives in the townships, such as councilors, police, and tax collectors, were attacked. It shook the Afrikaner elite, who began to question the viability of apartheid. The revolt also undermined the ideological coherence of the NP by creating new political space (through the disruption of state control), which the ANC then used to distribute leaflets. The open revolt of Africans against the system further compounded the government's problems and ability to govern. After the uprising was quelled in 1977, political unrest continued throughout the country in spite of the military occupation of the townships.

Student demonstrations, which began with the revolt, continued into the 1980s. These were followed by ANC sabotage attacks that disrupted the economy. The ANC's attack on SASOL (South Africa's coal to oil conversion plant) cost the state $8 million in damages. School and college boycotts in 1980–81 exposed the generational tensions that first exploded during the Soweto uprising. These tensions arose over the best way to fight the state. The young generation preferred confrontational tactics, such as demonstrations, boycotts, and mass disobedience. Members of the older generation and some from the younger generation preferred milder tactics, such as asking leaders to address their problems while still keeping their jobs. There was also tension over whether or not African children were to attend apartheid schools or boycott them altogether. This tension was also noticed within the ANC. Winnie Mandela, who was popular among the youth, warned the leadership that there was growing discontent among the youth. She also urged the ANC leadership to tap into the youth's anger by mobilizing them. The older generation within the ANC did not heed the warning.

As a result of the economic recession that followed, 84,000 jobs were lost between 1982 and 1984.[52] Africans organized at various levels to address their conditions. The women's movement was reinvented with the formation of the Federation of South

African Women (FEDSAW) in the Transvaal. In the Cape Province, the United Women's Organization (UWO) was founded. African professionals joined various progressive organizations such as civic township organizations and women and youth congresses. These congresses were comprised of children of the working class in urban areas. Unlike earlier generations, these children had grown up in urban centers, bearing the humiliations that the apartheid system imposed on them. They were courageous and willing to take risks their parents never dreamed to take. These "children of Soweto" were also "the least inclined to accept the limits and restrictions of the apartheid system."[53]

In 1983, the above-mentioned organizations formed a coalition under the umbrella of the United Democratic Front (UDF). The UDF had a weak link with workers' organizations, but churches and non-governmental organizations were active. The UDF's influence was strongest in the Eastern Cape and Transvaal and weakest in Natal and the Western Cape. Generally speaking, its leadership was drawn from a radical set of middle-class Africans. Defiance against the regime became more assertive in various mass demonstrations and strikes that led to the banning of the UDF in 1988. During the same year, various popular movements regrouped to form the Mass Democratic Movement (MDM) under the leadership of the church and of labor. It launched a campaign of civil disobedience that further challenged the regime's legitimacy. The MDM disbanded in 1990, when all liberation movements in the country were legalized.

WARS OF DESTABILIZATION

In 1975, the buffer zone around South Africa, namely Mozambique and Angola, fell with the independence of these countries from Portugal (June 25, 1975 and November 11, 1975, respectively). These Marxist-Leninist regimes were hostile to apartheid. They had fraternal relations with the ANC and all received military and financial assistance from the Soviet Union. In August 1987, despite Angola's offer for negotiations, Pretoria escalated its war against the Popular Movement for the Liberation of Angola (MPLA). This intervention added to its cost of occupying Namibia (although it was exploiting its minerals). By that time, the state's annual military expenditure was amounting to R 41 billion.

In Angola, the apartheid regime was supporting two rival parties: the National Front for the Liberation of Angola (FNLA) and the National Front for the Total Independence of Angola (UNITA). South Africa increased its military build-up as a result of the war in Angola. In 1975, it spent 650 million rands but by 1979 it was using 2,189 million rands for defense. This amount increased to nearly 4,000 million rands in 1984 and to 5,123 in 1986–87.[54] Because of poor economic conditions and political unrest, this intervention was unpopular at home. The regime had to pay for extra security for farmers to farm along the Transvaal border. In January 1976, South Africa pulled its forces away from Angola. South African military forces were moved to the Namibian border, from where it continued to carry out sporadic attacks on both Angola and Mozambique to root out "ANC terrorists." After Mozambique became independent on June 25, 1975, it made its territory available to the Zimbabwe African National Union (ZANU) which was fighting its own war of liberation against Ian

Smith's white minority regime. South Africa's northern borders were now no longer safe. The apartheid state was also spending enormous amounts of funds for propaganda purposes. It set up bogus companies and newspapers like *The Citizen* as propaganda outlets. The regime was also busily engaged in lobbying activities abroad, particularly in the United States where it contributed funds to campaigns of prominent senators in order to win friends abroad. The process of using various front organizations to further state goals culminated in the "Muldergate affair" which resulted in the resignation of Prime Minister John Vorster.

Prime Minister Botha's 1978–1979 "Total Strategy" aimed at creating a constellation of Southern African states under South Africa's hegemony. Such a system would have made it possible for South Africa to rely on economic and political control of these states, reducing military reliance. Robert Mugabe's landslide victory in Zimbabwe on March 4, 1980 shattered South Africa's dream of centralizing power in the region. In April 1980, nine independent states in the region created the Southern African Development Coordination Conference (SADCC) aimed at reducing the member state's economic dependence on South Africa through cooperation on specific projects in priority areas. As a result, South Africa's war of aggression accelerated. By 1981, it had a force of 11,000 soldiers in Angola's Cunene province. It also embarked on a military build-up to prevent a communist take-over of the region. According to Robert Price, over the period 1973 through 1980, "defense expenditure recorded a jump of 454 percent; the share for defense in total government spending expanded from 12 to 20 percent; and as a proportion of GNP, military expenditure rose from 2.3 percent to 5.2 percent."[55] To meet these expenses, the state imposed severe cuts on the white minority's standard of living. The military also severely strained the state, which, as a result, suffered severe personnel shortages as only white men were permitted to serve. In order to allow more 18–35 year old white males to be free to work in other sectors, the military needed to recruit African soldiers. Although the regime allowed Africans into the army in the late 1970s, apartheid was an obstacle to dedicated fighters. Africans could not defend a system that discriminated against them. Military demands pressured the NP to rethink its policies.

Post-Soweto Reforms

For the first time in its history, the NP government faced too many challenges at the same time. Military power and repression alone could no longer ensure its security. This resulted in a crisis of the hegemony of racial rule. Throughout its history, apartheid was based on two pillars. The first was that racial separation based on group identity was the best way to avoid conflict. The second pillar was based on the notion that apartheid was a morally superior system, was the best means for creating peace. The Soweto revolt shocked the Afrikaner elite and shook apartheid's foundation. The open defiance aimed at eliminating all signs of white supremacy undermined the ideological foundation of apartheid and destroyed the self-confidence of the Afrikaner elite. A comment appearing in *Rapport* (an Afrikaans newspaper) in January 1977 demonstrates this ideological trauma. It called for a vision that would move the country out of its difficult times. In essence, Afikanerdom could only survive as it had done in the past by seeking a vision that would provide a trajectory for its future.[56] The business community's surprise at the rebellion prompted the Anglo-American Corporation and the Rembrandt Group to create the Urban Foundation, a foundation dedicated to urbanization and housing strategies. The Urban Foundation aimed at creating an African middle-class with Western-style materialistic needs and ambitions. This middle-class would help defend the system in order to protect its interests. The white minority would also have an ally in an African middle-class that could act as a buffer between poor Africans and the white minority. As the members of this middle-class would run for political office, "irresponsible" Africans would be discouraged from engaging in politics.[57]

There was an emphasis on replacing racial discrimination with economic discrimination. Jan Lombard, a leading *verligte* ideologue, declared that "if . . . the maintenance of order requires discriminatory provisions in our legal system, these provisions must be defined in terms of other characteristic [than race]."[58] If apartheid was a threat to white security and prosperity, then it had to be abandoned. P. W. Botha used the ANC threat to build up support for his so called total strategy. This meant mobilizing all of South Africa's resources against the revolution. An official admitted the following privately, "there is a threat as perceived by government, but the concept of this threat is used for other reasons than the real threat; to bring people together whom government thinks should be together."[59] *Verligte* policy-making was controlled by a small group made up of NP leaders, military personnel, and the Broederbond.

In 1979, the Riekert Commission on urbanization made it a criminal offense for employers to hire Africans who did not possess residential rights in the cities. Set up the same year, the Wiehahn Commission on industrial relations recommended the abolition of job reservation, the registration of all trade unions (including African), and that each union should be free to prescribe its own membership qualifications.[60] The main thrust of these reforms was to ensure "that as many people as possible share in prosperity and find their interests best served by an alliance with capitalism."[61] In this perspective, the objective of the Riekert Report was to divide urban Africans into two categories: "qualified" and "disqualified" urban dwellers. The qualified dwellers constituted an urban middle-class that was entitled to certain privileges. According to *The Financial Mail*, "the small group of privileged urban blacks whose quality of life will undoubtedly improve may well become less urgent in their demands for political power and serve as the lid on the kettle of revolution for some years to come."[62] In the process of creating this urban middle-class, the regime appeared to withdraw from the Africans' daily lives as it privatized the economy.

After the Soweto revolt was quelled, the government set up a commission in 1980 under Supreme Court Justice Petrus Malan Cillie to investigate its causes. The Commission heard testimony from 563 witnesses in every part of the country. The major grievances included the following: influx-control that limited the movement of Africans; residential rights; administration boards in African townships that charged excessive fees for sewage and roads; and the general upkeep of townships. Because it fell under the responsibility of the administration boards, the state did not have to spend funds to develop African townships. Discrimination against Africans "engendered not only dissatisfaction but also a great hatred in many that produced a spirit of revolt."[63] Africans had to endure immense economic hardship and discrimination just to survive in South Africa. Their low salaries were spent entirely on school fees, rents, bus fares, and basic needs. Designed as the best safeguard of white supremacy, apartheid had now become its greatest threat.

Prime Minister P. W. Botha embarked on various reforms to ensure white security. To resolve the contradiction between capitalist accumulation and popular demands, two innovations were required. First, a new base of consensus had to be created. This implied restructuring the apartheid political and ideological bases and ultimately overturning them. Secondly, the post-war (1945) accumulation process had to be restructured, which effectively meant adjustments in economic policies, state and civil society relations, and in political and popular organizations. The reforms were aimed at institutionalizing consent and coercion by reshaping the structure of production, distribution, and consumption so as to revive the failing economy. This involved attempts to restructure political institutions in order to strengthen capital and labor relations.

These reforms did not include one of the cornerstones of the apartheid system, namely the schools. Additionally, these reforms revealed that the system, which presented itself as omnipotent, had weaknesses that could be used to overthrow it. In spite of presumed government-sponsored efforts to open up skilled jobs to African labor, there was no major transformation in the racial and occupational composition of employment between 1970 and 1980. While skilled jobs were nominally opened to Africans, built-in barriers that prevented their employment remained in tact. According to A. Stadler:

> It has been suggested that with the general elevation of the white worker into the managerial classes and into the burgeoning bureaucracies of the apartheid system, the resulting shortage of skilled workers opens new opportunities for black workers to rise up the ladder of skilled jobs. However, what in fact appears to be happening in the manufacturing industry is the diminishing need for skilled workers in the labor process, thus producing built-in barriers of black advancement.[64]

Throughout the late 1970s and into the 1980s, trade unions challenged the viability of apartheid. Trade unions secured major wage increases for their workers and also provided a strong institutional foundation for the workers' liberation struggle. Faced with strong and multifaceted resistance from civil society, P. W. Botha told white South Africans to adopt or die. With that, he earnestly embarked on a policy of deracialization of apartheid. In reality, his reform program was merely buying time, as political instability swept through the country and the broader southern African region. The first phase of the reforms aimed at restructuring labor and urbanization policies. Some political changes did occur within the state, but the problem was presented as one of security, which required a "total strategy" to defend the state against a "total onslaught." This strategy called for the widespread militarization of white society, "closer cooperation between state and capital, and new initiatives geared at taking into account the aspirations of our different population groups in order to gain and keep their trust."[65] P. W. Botha worked with the business community to promote his reforms. By 1979, mining magnate Harry Oppenheimer of the Anglo-American Corporation had become "the most credible spokesman for Mr. Botha's new initiatives [overseas]."[66] These reforms, however, were purely cosmetic as they were based on the false assumption that Africans had political rights in the homelands. Forced removals of Africans from areas designated as white continued. To assuage middle-class Africans, freehold property rights and local councils opened to African membership were introduced in the townships.

By 1979, some members of the Afrikaner elite had come to realize that the NP would have to negotiate with the ANC. Willem de Klerk, editor of the NP newspaper *Die Transvaler* and a member of the Broederbond executive, noted that negotiations over a new dispensation were on the agenda. However, negotiations did not mean dealing directly with the ANC, which was still outlawed and viewed as a terrorist organization. According to Willem de Klerk, "the whites want to give their meaningful compromise for a political settlement that will link us as partners."[67] The NP had a three-pronged strategy for social and political change. First, overt racism was abandoned and a liberal capitalist ideology was introduced to counter apartheid. In the new discourse, capital accumulation was presented as a phenomenon in everyone's interest. Whites would continue to enjoy their high living standard, while economic growth would also improve Africans' standard of living. Whites, seen as the modernizing elite, would control the process. Whites would also initiate job creation, training, and food production; they would also maintain political stability to ensure their security. In the mind of Afrikaner political leaders, such an outcome could only be guaranteed under NP rule.

In the new vocabulary of transformation, the term populist was replaced with scientific. What was important was not how popular an idea was, but whether it was based on reason. Capitalism was also presented as impersonal. South African businessmen who met with the ANC in 1985 represented this perspective. They argued that economic growth and wealth creation were necessary for improving the economic conditions of Africans. Such economic changes were only possible "through the proclaimed 'rationalizing' process of the market economy. [The businessmen] saw that process as both a necessary and sufficient condition for making the institutions and structures of apartheid increasingly irrelevant."[68] In 1983, the NP initiated "power-sharing" policies with Indians and people of mixed race, who were given representation in parliament. While the state presented itself as "multinational," emphasizing similarities across color lines, it continued to exclude Africans. Within this representation, Afrikaners were in control. A survey taken at Stellenbosch University during this period revealed that although Afrikaners had come to accept a multiracial and politically inclusive state, they still assumed that it was their "divine right" to govern South Africa.

During the second phase of reforms (1982–87), the state focused on institutional change, however, its political efforts were blocked by apartheid policies. As long as state reforms were cast within a racially divided South Africa, they remained ineffective. In 1986, the state ended influx control. This constituted a major shift in the policies of apartheid, as the regime accepted the "interdependent and interconnected nature of South African political economy."[69] As part of the deracialization of social life in 1985, the government allowed the formation of nonracial trade unions. By 1986,

African trade unions had a total membership of over one million spread between two national federations: the large and all-inclusive Congress of South African Trade Unions (COSATU) and the Black Consciousness inspired Council of Unions of South Africa-Azanian Confederation of Trade Unions (CUSA-AZACTU). Between 1982 and 1984 there were 1,199 strikes and work stoppages. As open defiance against the regime increased, the economic and political rights of Africans further deteriorated. In 1985 alone, there were 389 strikes involving 240,000 African workers. Others followed in 1987 "in the railways, and gold mines, which involved over 500,000 workers."[70] Between 1985 and 1987, the business sector also supported lockouts.

Among Africans, women had the worst paying jobs. According to the 1993 Microeconomic Research Group (MERG) report, between 1965 and 1987, "while the proportion of African working-class enumerated employees in 'unskilled' and 'menial' occupational categories decreased, the proportion of females in these categories increased."[71] Women were over represented in menial jobs because they were the least educated. Wage differentials were greatest between males and females in the lowest jobs. Between 1970 and 1980, the majority of blacks held unskilled jobs. In 1970, 94.1 percent of whites were in managerial positions compared to 1.7 percent of blacks. In 1980, 91.7 percent of whites were in managerial positions compared to 2.9 percent of the black population.[72]

During the third phase of reforms (1987–1994), the state abandoned the reform progress and allowed the National Security Management System (NSMS) to co-ordinate the redistribution process. The NSMS operated like a parallel state bureaucracy, with its own powers and privileged connections with the state police and military apparatus. Thirty-four of the most politically volatile townships were targeted for upgrading while 1,800 renewal projects were introduced in two hundred others. The thinking behind this initiative was that the lack of classroom space was not a security threat at present but, if the number of insufficient class space rose, it would become one. It was important, therefore, to correct the problem before it threatened the white minority. The NSMS expedited the reform process by recasting it as a security threat. The hope was that it would provide the measures that would stabilize rebellious townships. The NSMS remained consistent with the state's ideological base even in the face of strong resistance. It isolated certain townships while militarily occupying others. Thus, resistance weakened the regime without threatening its military establishment. The NSMS succeeded in creating a split within the ruling elite, that is, amongst the capitalists, the state bureaucrats, and the NP government, over the best way to maintain the system. The state itself was torn apart by inter-departmental struggles between conservatives and reformists. Internationally, the state was weakened by economic sanctions and slow economic growth. The democratic movement of the 1980s, especially the UDF, was instrumental in "deepening and extending the complex difficulties encountered by the ruling block and forcing it to try and fashion a response that would transcend the exclusionary political framework."[73]

On August 14, 1989, F. W. De Klerk replaced President P. W. Botha as acting President until September 14, 1989 when he was officially elected president by the National Party. However, De Klerk kept P. W. Botha's top advisers, bureaucrats, politicians, and securocrats (P. W. Botha's advisers who worked within security departments).

According to David Ottaway, some of the people who had served under Botha also worked for De Klerk who "proved to be no reformer or promoter of affirmative action when it came to the South African Police (SAP) and the South African Defence Force (SADF)."[74] By mid-1992, the same people who had led the struggle against the liberation movement controlled the SADF. Some of these individuals were rewarded with promotions. For example, General A. J. "Kat" Liebenberg, who had the worst reputation for "eliminating ANC activists," was promoted to chief of staff of the SADF, while "Christoffel van der Westhuizen took over the Military Intelligence Department."[75] Under De Klerk, the National Intelligence Service became one of the most prominent departments within the SADF. Within the police force, De Klerk focused on finding better ways of fighting crime and racially integrating the force. In 1992, police colleges were mandated to integrate but colleges that rejected integration were not forced. For example, whites held 95 percent of the positions at the command level, even though Africans and people of mixed descent made up 60 percent of the rank and file. By mid-1992, the entire South African Police force had only four black brigadiers and no black generals. Systematic and widespread police brutality against Africans continued in spite of the reforms.

The economy continued to stagnate, as its share of exports fell from 1.3 percent in 1980 to 0.7 percent in 1989.[76] Within Africa, foreign direct investment favored oil-producing countries like Nigeria. Between 1990 and 1994, Nigeria attracted 45 percent of FDI while South Africa experienced a net outflow. Most foreign companies used South Africa as a springboard to invest in the rest of Africa instead of investing in South Africa itself. According to an export promoter, "investors coming to South Africa want to use [South Africa] as a springboard to trade in Africa, not necessarily for new investments; they are eyeing the huge tracts of land and stocks of minerals [there]."[77] Most of the capital invested was in stocks and bonds, with foreign companies buying off South African companies or establishing joint ventures with them. Apartheid protected and heavily subsidized certain industries, thereby reducing their competitiveness. The regime did not have any "strategy for promoting new infant industries, and [failed] to offset the effects of protection by forcing firms to invest in building export markets."[78]

The resistance movement and the state were both faced with a stalemate. African resistance made it impossible for the state to govern without resorting to violence. Yet, such resistance was militarily too weak to constitute a serious threat to the regime. Apartheid leaders were concerned not so much with the prospect of a revolution, but with the likelihood that "the state and opposition would become entangled in a death embrace that could destroy South Africa's integrity as a nation-state and a viable zone for capital accumulation and, with that, [destroy] white privilege."[79] The ruling class also realized that economic recovery was impossible without political stability. Negotiations could only be legitimate if they involved the ANC, which had emerged as the leading liberation movement during this period. Winnie Mandela's chance encounter with Justice Minister Kobie Coetzee on a flight to Cape Town in 1985 was instrumental in changing the government's position about negotiations with the ANC. The government realized if Nelson Mandela died in prison, South Africa would become ungovernable. Coetzee visited Mandela in the hospital, thereby initiating the long negotiation process. Shortly thereafter (in 1988), the middle-class within the NP created a five-member committee headed by Hendrik "Kobie" Coetzee and National Intelligence Service Chief (NIS) Neil Barnard. This committee met with Nelson Mandela no less than forty-seven times from 1988 to 1990. Coetzee first met Mandela in secret in July of 1986. The NP eventually released Nelson Mandela from jail on February 11, 1990 as a result of these secret meetings and various other factors, including shifting Afrikaner class alliances, international political pressure and economic sanctions, and resistance at home. In anticipation of the negotiations for a new political dispensation, the ban on all thirty-two political parties and movements was lifted. In spite of this official unbanning, returning exiles and members of opposition parties still faced harassment by state officials.

INTERNATIONAL PRESSURE AND ECONOMIC RECESSION

International pressure also influenced events within South Africa. Three days into the Soweto revolt, the United Nations Security Council passed a resolution "strongly condemning the South African government for its resort to massive violence against and killing of the African people," and calling on the government to "eliminate apartheid."[80] In November 1977, an arms embargo was imposed on South Africa with the support of key Western nations. It was difficult for the regime to access military as well as civilian equipment "with a potential military use, such as certain computers, light aircraft and helicopters."[81] International isolation exposed the regime's vulnerability. However, it would not have been as significant as it was had it not coincided with an economic slump and transformed the regional political landscape. Since South Africa had a small domestic market, foreign markets were crucial to the expansion of capitalism. Access to these markets was blocked by international pressure, thereby worsening the economic recession. Capital flight greatly exceeded capital inflow. For example, capital swung from a net inflow of US$677 million in 1977, to an even more massive outflow of US$1,073 million in 1978.

Foreign investment in South Africa in 1982 amounted to US$20 billion, of which 54 percent came from Britain and other European Economic Community countries. In the first half of 1983, disinvestment attempts in South Africa amounted to US$4,650 million. Following the disinvestment movement, five U.S. multinationals withdrew from South Africa after reassessing apartheid and its costs. In 1977, the U.S. ambassador to the UN stated that "at some point we've got to come to the conclusion that we no longer are going to finance apartheid."[82] Increasingly militant civil society anti-apartheid movements in Europe and the United States put pressure on their governments to isolate South Africa. By 1978, new loans to the regime were frozen, forcing the government to impose a 15 percent surcharge on all imports. It also cut back on imports to alleviate the balance of payments problem. Finance minister Owen Horwood admitted that domestic political conditions had resulted in a decline in foreign loans, which had received "biased and exaggerated reports in overseas news media."[83] State expenditure doubled between "1980 and 1984 . . . reaching almost 18 percent of the nominal GDP. The state budget, incurring deficits rising to R 4.3 billion in 1984, has been financed in large part from domestic and foreign borrowings."[84]

By 1980, there were one thousand UK companies operating in South Africa compared to three hundred and fifty in France and three hundred and forty in the United States. In 1982, private investment in U. S. dollars (millions) was estimated at $6,342 (United Kingdom); $2,800 (United States) and $260 (France).[85]

Between 1984 and September 1985, major U. S. companies, including Ford, reduced their holdings in South Africa. Other companies left entirely, which led to the fall of the rand by 50 percent. Prior to the Soweto revolt, foreign firms re-invested their profits in the economy. After the revolt, these companies invested abroad. This crisis was part of the global economic recession. In July 1985, international banks led by Chase Manhattan refused to "roll over short-term loans to the private sector in South Africa, representing almost two-thirds of South Africa's foreign debt of over $20 billion."[86] Other banks followed suit after the South African president rejected further reforms. Transnational corporations that remained in South Africa began to lobby more aggressively for the elimination of apartheid laws in the hope of promoting their own-long term interests. Demand for gold decreased, which led to a deficit in the budget. These developments decreased the regime's control over the economy. Though they were not meant to dismantle apartheid, they did "increase the potential risks of continuing commitment to apartheid."[87] The business community was increasingly concerned about South Africa's relationship with the West.

This economic crisis was also a regime crisis. The discourse of the National Party changed from aggressive to conciliatory. In 1985, P. W. Botha noted that the government was committed to a united South Africa based on a model chosen by its citizens. Toward this goal, the regime began opening up its political institutions. Thus, government positions were opened to blacks. Meanwhile, the economy was steadily deteriorating: by 1988, the economic deficit was running at over 4 percent of the GDP, compared to around 2 percent in 1980.

Political developments in the Soviet Union also influenced the pace of political change in South Africa. From the mid-1980s onwards, Mikhail Gorbachev embarked on a series of reforms aimed at transforming the communist regime. In order to maintain good relations with the United States, the Soviet Union preferred a political settlement in South Africa. In 1987, Gorbachev noted that racist rule in South Africa was unacceptable. It was important that both Pretoria and the ANC came to an agreement over a new dispensation. This could only be achieved by a political settlement. Given the experience of Zimbabwe's independence (which ignored the people's claim to the land), Oliver Tambo wanted to negotiate a political settlement that would benefit the majority of South Africa's population. Speaking in his personal capacity, Professor Starushenko Gleb, deputy director of the Soviet Africa Institute, called for "comprehensive guarantees for the white population" in South Africa.[88] Starushenko's remarks were in accordance with the changing political and economic environment of the Soviet Union. In September 1987, the ANC executive reaffirmed that the movement and its supporters were willing to engage in genuine negotiations so long as these aimed at transforming the system into a nonracial democracy. *This and only this should be the objective of any negotiating process.*[89] According to the ANC executive, the timing was good because the international community was focused on the political settlement of various conflicts, particularly the settlement of those in

Angola and Namibia. Cuba, which was also militarily involved in Angola, supported a political settlement in South Africa. After meeting with a U. S. representative, ANC president Oliver Tambo expressed the need for tripartite talks between the Soviet Union, the ANC, and Pretoria. As the main sponsor of the ANC, the Soviet Union also put pressure on them to negotiate. The fall of the Soviet Union in 1989 provided a major impetus to this process. The National Party lost control of the African population because the latter ignored apartheid laws. Loss of confidence in the civil service resulted in low morale, thereby exposing the leadership's vulnerability. This was compounded by the capitalists' loss of faith in the economy and strong civil society based popular movements such as the United Democratic Front that undermined apartheid's legitimacy. Whites were also alienated from the state. By 1986, the NP had two choices. The first one was to abandon constitutionalism. This could be done by repressing the far right, enabling the NP to deracialize the state without giving in to workers' demands. Such a process would result in opposition both from the right and left, further complicating the NP's predicament. The second option involved giving in to popular demand and violent protest, that is, deracializing the state through democratic reform and power-sharing as a result of negotiations.

Why did the NP agree to negotiate with the ANC? According to Hermann Giliomee, three issues prompted this decision. First, there was a shift of power within South Africa that gave increased bargaining power to the urban African population in cities. Speaking at a *Nasionale Pers* function, F. W. de Klerk noted that the NP had to take the initiative to control the negotiation process. That way it could also ensure that the process was peaceful. The rise of African militancy made it impossible for the NP to govern peacefully, since it failed to co-opt people of mixed descent and Indians. The NP realized that apartheid threatened the very survival of the Afrikaner. Secondly, resolving the economic crisis required a political solution. Though at first the NP denied that sanctions were affecting the economy, soon after it abandoned apartheid several senior party spokesmen candidly acknowledged that "the economy had been bled white."[90] A 1989 survey of "attitudes of private and public sector white elites in which NP supporters predominated more than 60 percent felt that international pressure and sanctions would force the opposing parties to negotiate."[91]

Major changes in the international system finally encouraged the NP to negotiate. The fall of the Soviet Union allowed the United States to put increased pressure on the regime to negotiate. The NP believed that without Soviet support, the ANC was "manageable" and that the negotiation process would enhance its powerful position. The Soviet Union also called for a peaceful resolution to the South African problem. From its secret talks with Mandela, the NP realized that the ANC did not have the military capability to dismantle apartheid. It also realized that the ANC was more interested in securing political power than economic power. According to Martin Meredith, "Mandela's secret talks with government officials had convinced them that he was a man with whom the white establishment could do business. Like other white communities in Africa, they had come to accept the old adage: give them parliament and keep the banks."[92]

CONCLUSION

Taken individually, African militancy, economic stagnation, destabilization wars, changes within the ruling block, and changes in the international community could not have resulted in the downfall of apartheid. Together, however, these developments were lethal. Each opened cracks in the system. The Soweto revolt exposed the vulnerability of the ruling elite. It also exacerbated differences within the elite, culminating in the formation of the Conservative party. Prime Minister John Vorster's reforms also opened another crack in the system: Africans realized that apartheid could be overthrown. The "reform" process continued under P. W. Botha. The fall of the Portuguese buffer zone in 1975 left South Africa's borders vulnerable. It also encouraged armed resistance, thus further complicating the state's predicament. International economic sanctions and a slow and declining economy further weakened the regime. Faced with these challenges, the Afrikaner elite expanded its imagined community to include people of mixed descent, who happened to share the Afrikaners' language and culture. It also began negotiations with various political parties for a new dispensation. Both the African National Congress and the National Party played significant roles during this process. The fact that the ANC gave up all claims to control the economy and the military/security apparatus and focused instead on achieving political power and on control of the state machinery greatly facilitated the negotiations for a new dispensation, to which we will now turn.

FURTHER READINGS

Feinstein, Charles H. *An Economic History of South Africa*. Cambridge, UK: Cambridge University Press, 2005,

Meredith, Martin. The Fate of Africa: *A History of Fifty Years of Independence*. New York: Public Affairs, 2005.

Price, Robert M. *The Apartheid State in Crisis: Political Transformation in South Africa 1975–1990*. New York: Oxford University Press, 1991.

CHAPTER 6

THE NEGOTIATIONS FOR A DEMOCRATIC SOUTH AFRICA, 1990–1994

> Exactly how delinquent the ANC was can be seen from the fact that, after almost eighty years as a liberation movement, the organisation first formed a dedicated department of economic policy in 1990, with Trevor Manuel as the head. Consequently, the ANC entered the multiparty negotiations at a severe disadvantage against the ruling National Party's massive economic capacity, which included both the business community and all the state's resources.
>
> —William Mervin Gumede,
> *Thabo Mbeki and the Battle for the Soul of the ANC*

THIS CHAPTER EXAMINES THE NEGOTIATION PROCESS, WHICH INITIATED the transition from apartheid to multiracial democracy. This chapter is divided into seven sections, dealing respectively with the main actors, the issues, pre-negotiation talks, the actual negotiations, the final talks, the obstacles encountered during the negotiations, and the outcome.

THE MAIN ACTORS

To understand the negotiation process, an understanding and knowlegde of the main actors is needed. In particular, we need to analyze the philosophy, leadership, organizational structure, and internal factionalism of the main political parties and movements involved. The ANC, as one of the key actors, is of particular interest. According to William Gumede, as the ANC emerged from exile it was divided into four distinct factions. ANC members who were in exile controlled its finances, as well as the intelligence and military networks. The elders (older members of the ANC) were Nelson Mandela, Walter Sisulu, and Govan Mbeki (Thabo Mbeki's father). The internal wing, or "inziles"—those who remained home—were represented by the United Democratic Front (UDF). *Umkhonto we Sizwe* soldiers (the military wing of the ANC), who supported the exiles, constituted the fourth faction. There was disagreement as to who and, specifically, which faction should head the negotiations for the new political dispensation. Some people supported Thabo Mbeki and the exiles who wanted to continue with the talks at all costs. However, the "militants" who backed Cyril Ramaphosa won the day.

According to David Ottaway, the ANC resembled a "holding company, or a gigantic conglomerate" made up of many subsidiaries, for example, the returning National Executive Council (NEC) old guard, COSATU, SACP and the various township civic organizations each with a turf to defend "ANC Inc., if you like."[1] The ANC leadership was divided between local, national, and regional leaders. Sometimes, the former made decisions without consulting the national leadership, which often resulted in conflict. Differences between "militants," such as Harry Ngwala, Winnie Mandela, and Chris Hani and the moderates, who included Nelson Mandela and Thabo Mbeki, also plagued the ANC. Although Hani and Mbeki were both in exile, the latter identified with the old guard based in Lusaka. Most ANC supporters viewed this group as distant from the daily struggle, unchallenged, closed, and secretive. The ANC National Executive Council had nine members in 1969, thirty in 1985 and thirty-five in 1990. This authority was challenged by the United Democratic Front, which was in direct competition with the old guard. The ANC alliance did not even agree on the economic policies to be pursued after apartheid. It had initially opted for socialism. However, under pressure from the business community and the World Bank, and as a result of the fall of communism, a liberal capitalist economy remained the only option. Nelson Mandela said that the ANC would reconsider nationalization. The fall of communism also weakened the ANC because the abandonment of socialism left it without a coherent ideology. Thus, the ANC became ideologically rudderless, with only political power and "electoral democracy" (in other words, free and fair elections) to offer as a liberation platform to its African constituents.

According to Mandela, the ANC was made up of conservatives and liberals who were united in their common desire for African freedom. As a result, "there could be no question of ideology because any question approaching ideology would split the organization from top to bottom."[2] Ideological confusion and a crisis of identity were compounded by disagreement over future leadership. This was not unusual, given the fact that the ANC was a broad-based movement rather than a political party. In spite of these challenges, the ANC was able to assume political control over the state. However, the ANC could not provide a coherent post-sanctions policy. ANC Secretary-General Alfred Nzo suggested coordinating a strategy that would control how and when sanctions would be removed. Nzo also called on the ANC to provide a clear economic plan.[3] After 1990, the ANC, COSATU, and the SACP formed a "tripartite alliance" to coordinate a common policy against the NP.

What was the state of the NP on the eve of the negotiations? Since its break with conservatives in 1982, the NP was no longer torn between conservatives and liberals. Although most of its conservative members had left either for the Conservative Party or for the far right Afrikaner political parties, such as the *Afrikaner Weerstand Beweging* (Afrikaner Resistance Movement), it was not liberal. The NP was structured as a federal party with four autonomous branches in each of four provinces, which held four separate annual congresses and were governed by four regional leaders. As a federal organization, the NP also had branches in the other provinces of the country. Under F. W. De Klerk, the state cabinet, which was made up of sixteen members, became the central policy-making body. Most decisions were made in *bosberaad* or, in other words, in informal meetings at vacation resorts. The negotiating parties eventually adopted this method. Once this cabinet reached a consensus, it informed Parliament, which was made up of ninety-three members. The Afrikaner broederbond closely advised the cabinet in its decision-making. According to David Ottaway, De Klerk was advised by an "inner circle" that was made up of:[4]

- "blue-blood" Afrikaners dedicated to survival

- several ministers or deputy ministers in P. W. Botha's cabinet who stayed on in different portfolios under de Klerk

- All the members were *verligtes* except Coetzee; they believed in the prominence of the party (not the security establishment). The only securocrat (people who worked in the security establishment) in the team was Roelf Meyer who later became a "liberal." (By the standards of Afrikaner nationalism, Roelf Meyer was considered a "liberal" because of his progressive ideas, such as his willingness to negotiate with the ANC but in a broader liberal setting he would be considered a conservative.

The NP was essentially an elitist, undemocratic, and centralized organization that consistently failed to consult with its rank-and-file. For example, it won the 1989 September elections on a campaign platform opposing negotiations with "terrorists." In 1990, the NP changed its tone and began negotiating with the ANC. The rank-and-file did not question the shift in policy, nor did party members demand that a special meeting be convened to discuss the issue. The Conservative Party criticized the actions of the NP. Poor Afrikaners still believed in an Afrikaner imagined community that shielded them from African economic competition. Most of these Afrikaners were either members of the Conservative Party or the far right, such as the AWB. An affluent and economically secure elite controlled the NP. According to Heribert Adam *et. al.* this affluent elite sold out poorer Afrikaners because it felt more confident about its ability to either survive in or leave the new South Africa.

The Issues

What demands were made by the major political parties? The ANC aimed at ending minority rule by replacing the National Party. For the ANC, the main objective of the negotiations was to transform the regime from a totalitarian to a democratic one. Its view of the decolonization process involved an interim government and a constituent assembly that would oversee the transformation process. According to Ivor Sarakinsky:

> The ANC position would ensure that it would gain a share of power before the elections, preventing the NP from using the levers of government to influence the result. Its

view, and that of the PAC, that elected representatives should write the constitution ensured that the majority could do so alone. The NP, IFP and CP had a stake in preventing this. It was important to the NP to remain the government; vital to the IFP, whose support was concentrated in Natal, both to continue administering KwaZulu until an election and to guarantee white right not to leave the fate of a *volkstaat* in the hands of a hostile majority.[5]

The Inkatha Freedom Party (IFP) in KwaZulu/Natal did not share the ANC ideals. The IFP would only agree to participate in the negotiations after a constitution that ensured a federal system was in place. Bopthatswana wanted grassroots organizations as well as traditional leaders to be involved in the process. For the PAC, genuine negotiations would lead to a free South Africa in which the land issue would be resolved. According to this view, a constituent assembly had to be in place to oversee the negotiating process. The NP advocated a transition "from above" in which it would determine the length of the negotiations, control their outcome, and remain in power for as long as possible. The NP believed that since the ANC lacked governance experience, it would be incapable of functioning effectively and efficiently once in power. Hence, the ANC would be forced to work with the NP. Based on this belief, the transition would be introduced in broad terms, for example, the liberalization of the economy, democratization, and finally the consolidation of democracy. By prolonging the process, not only would the NP weaken the ANC, it would also gather new supporters. The NP would do so by ensuring that there was a constant flow of "low-intensity warfare" which in turn would produce "low-intensity democracy," therefore strengthening the minority position.[6] The NP also believed it had the power to shape the type of democracy that would eventually emerge by limiting the material, financial, and human resources to which the new government would have access. It agreed to negotiate a new constitution with these goals in mind.

The Conservative Party opposed the negotiations until the issue of an Afrikaner *Volkstaat* (homeland) was discussed. Major differences developed between the parties that favored a two-stage transition (ANC, PAC), with an interim body to oversee the process followed by an election and those who wanted a one-stage transition, like the NP, CP, and IFP. The latter parties wanted a one-stage transition because they believed homelands would be maintained during the extended process. The Conservative Party rejected an interim constitution because it did not want to leave the fate of an Afrikaner *volkstaat* to the majority. The Afrikaner Volksunie was dominated by CP positions. The Democratic Party opposed the ANC's two-stage transition. It wanted the minority government to stay in power until a new dispensation was agreed upon. All these parties had one thing in common, however: they would present their interests to shape a new dispensation.[7]

The IFP, the NP, and the CP demanded a constitution as a prerequisite to elections. Of all the parties involved in the process, the ANC was the one that shifted its position the most. For example, the ANC did not insist on the need for state institutions to be controlled by a multi-party body and it accepted that the NP stay in power during the transition period, though with reduced authority. To the extent that this compromise was based on the NP's negotiating paradigm, it was an important concession on the part of the ANC.

Pre-negotiation Talks

One of the hallmarks of apartheid was its ability to adapt to a changing political environment, including to pressure from civil society. Such strategic flexibility is exemplified by the initiation of the Bantustan policy in the 1960s by the Afrikaner ruling elite—precisely when the wave of political independence swept across the continent—represented by its proponents as "self-determination" for the Africans. The Sharpeville massacre of March 1960 led to an intensive period of state repression, which was broken in 1976 by the Soweto revolt. This uprising shocked the Afrikaner ruling elite, plunging it into a severe crisis of legitimacy. The Afrikaner elite finally came to realize that it could not rule over the majority by force alone. Soweto paved the way for political, economic, and social changes, which culminated with the unbanning of political parties and the release of political prisoners in 1990.

Other measures had to be introduced in order to enable the NP to govern while maintaining the minority's security. After the Soweto revolt, Prime Minister Vorster introduced reforms that quickly reached their limit in 1978, when P. W. Botha took over power. Far from ensuring peace for the minority, these reforms led to more uprisings. The economic interdependence between Africans and the white minority meant that the NP could never have an exclusively white South Africa. The only option left for the two groups was to negotiate. Nelson Mandela began secret talks with the Minister of Justice, Kobie Coetzee, in 1985. In 1986, Thabo Mbeki secretly met the Broederbond's chairman, Peter de Lange, in New York. This meeting was a "get to know you" session amongst former enemies. The willingness of the ANC to negotiate was expressed in its *Constitutional Guidelines for a Democratic South Africa*, published in August 1988.

On July 5, 1989, Mandela was escorted to P. W. Botha's residence for tea, with the anticipation for talks about a new dispensation. Botha was not very forthcoming. His reforms had reached their limit, so a new personality was needed to move the reform process forward. The opportunity for negotiations for a new political dispensation occurred after P. W. Botha suffered a stroke and was replaced by F. W. De Klerk, who released Mandela on February 11, 1990. De Klerk and leading members of the *verligte* camp within the NP convinced the party that negotiations were its best option. With this in mind, De Klerk embarked on further reforms. Thus, in 1990, the NP eliminated the death penalty, political refugees were allowed to return, civil rights were restored, free political activity was also allowed, and the state of emergency that had been in effect since 1986 was lifted.

Pre-negotiation talks between the ANC and NP began on May 2, 1990, when delegations of the two parties met at Groote Schuur in Cape Town. The ANC delegation included seven Africans, two whites, one mixed-race person and one Indian. It was meant to make a racial statement. The NP, however, sent nine Afrikaner men. During this meeting, the ANC insisted on the unconditional release of political prisoners and on the unhindered return of political exiles. Both parties signed the *Groote*

Schuur Minute. In August 1990, they met again in Pretoria when the details and misunderstandings of the *Groote Schuur Minute* were clarified in the *Pretoria Minute*. *The Pretoria Minute* also called upon "all those who have not yet committed themselves to peaceful negotiation to do so now."[8] According to the *Minute*, the ANC suspended all its armed resistance activity so as to facilitate the negotiation process. Raymond Suttner justified this decision by stating, "The leadership saw the armed struggle as a blockade in the way of continuing the peace process. Even though it was felt that the government's objections to armed struggle were unreasonable, it was regarded as necessary to make this compromise in order to realise our broader strategic objectives."[9] With all other avenues closed, the ANC realized that "the subjective or objective marginalization of the armed struggle, mass action and sanctions during the period of transition left negotiation as the dominant form of political activity."[10]

The ANC had abandoned armed struggle without consulting either branch members or regional leaders, much to the disappointment of the rank-and-file, which criticized Nelson Mandela for this decision. The interests of its popular base were not taken into account when the decision was made, fueling the growing criticism that the ANC was becoming elitist. Most of the ANC supporters felt that the leadership was sidelining them. Disagreement intensified between ANC leaders and members over the negotiations. Realizing that the ANC leadership was not taking any measure to defend them, the majority of rank-and-file ANC members felt compelled to defend themselves against the escalating violence. Thus, Chris Hani and Ronnie Kasrils called for the creation of self-defense units (SDUs). MK leaders also wanted to defend themselves against state violence. They felt abandoned by the ANC because, in spite of the on-going negotiations, the state continued to harass their cadres and returning exiles. These members also accused the ANC of turning away from the people. According to them, the ANC continued to meet NP demands without getting anything in return. As a result, the ANC was faced with a disillusioned mass base and nothing left with which to bargain. According to Johannes Rantete, the masses were alienated from the ANC because they lost interest in the organization. The dialogue with the leadership dampened negotiations and many followers were turned away from the ANC because of the escalating violence. Lack of communication between the leadership and the masses further weakened this relationship.[11]

On February 12, 1991, the ANC and the NP signed *the D. F Malan Accord* that exempted MK "from the Peace Accord's restrictions on private armies."[12] The ANC agreed not to use MK soldiers to infiltrate South Africa or bring in arms or organize armed resistance. The government granted the ANC the right to express its interests by peaceful public demonstrations and promised the ANC that it would investigate reports of security involvement in political violence. As a precondition to negotiations, the ANC insisted on the removal of apartheid from South Africa's statutes, which were revised accordingly in 1991. In May of the same year, there was a breakdown in the talks amid ANC allegations that the NP was involved in fomenting political violence. Nelson Mandela and other ANC leaders were frustrated by the inability (or unwillingness) of the NP to curb the violence. The NP preferred a long negotiating process that ensured its control by weakening the ANC and distancing it from its supporters. On the other hand, the ANC preferred quick negotiations in which an "elected constituent assembly, not the government's multiparty conference" would oversee the process.[13]

Discussions on the economy were intense during the negotiation process. Issues such as redistribution, control of the South African Reserve Bank, and the nature of the economy were of particular interest. The NP, the South African Reserve Bank, and the business community wanted to privatize the economy. In 1991, when an ANC lawyer introduced the idea of a "capital levy," which proposed that one-third of the wealth of all individuals be spent on addressing the inequities of apartheid, the mainstream press labeled the idea as "loony."[14] The ANC/SACP position was less clear. Once communism fell, the ANC/SACP economic agenda, which included introducing a degree of equity in wealth distribution, was modified. The ANC "promised to lift exchange control, to introduce capital protection measures and anti-trust laws with a view to repatriating profits, and to postpone the nationalisation of the mines and banks."[15] The ANC introduced the idea of "a mixed economy, which would meet high rates of growth. Such an economy would also ensure the removal of poverty and racial inequality."[16] Both COSATU and the SACP were committed to socialist ideals; however, they put these aside for short-term gains and the need to preserve the unity of the tripartite alliance with the ANC.

The *Groote Schuur*, the Pretoria Minute, and the *D. F Malan Accord* were all "dead letters" because both the ANC and NP could not agree on the nature of a constitution. The NP insisted on a "consociational democracy" model based on the belief that South Africa was made up of many nations. In such a democracy, the NP would be able to veto ANC policies. The ANC insisted on the strict majority rule.

By April 30, 1991, in spite of the promises of the NP in this regard, no political exiles had returned to South Africa. The ANC constituency, which had opposed the talks in the first place, was becoming suspicious about the motives and intentions of the moderates. All these events worked to the NP's advantage. According to David Ottaway, "wittingly or not, de Klerk was making matters worse for the ANC moderates led by Mandela, who were at least ready, even anxious, to negotiate a peaceful resolution."[17] Talks broke down amidst mutual accusations between Nelson Mandela and De Klerk and political violence escalated. The business community became increasingly worried about the decline of the economy. Simons Adams noted:

> More importantly, for the white establishment anyway, the violence did little to encourage foreign investment confidence, the economy remained in recession and in some areas workers were absenting themselves from production *en masse* in order to protect their communities from attack. Therefore, having first weakened the ANC by vigilante terror and by propping up Inkatha, the government now moved to undermine and conservatise the ANC by entering into protracted negotiations, beginning with the original CODESA talks of December 1991.[18]

NEGOTIATIONS

The stalemate was broken when Nelson Mandela called for an all-party convention to negotiate the contours of a constituent assembly. Both parties were joined by other political parties in signing the *National Peace Accord* in September 1991; this agreement aimed at combating violence and creating a peaceful environment for talks. The signatories agreed that they would hold a national Convention for a Democratic South Africa (CODESA) on December 21, 1991. When CODESA met in Johannesburg, a total of nineteen organizations were represented and about two-hundred and thirty delegates attended the Convention, with the ANC and the NP as the key players. CODESA starkly exposed the conflicting views of the major parties over the nature of the new South African state. For example, while the ANC aimed at controlling political power through majority rule, the Inkatha Freedom Party preferred a federal system that would recognize its ethno-regional power-base. Smaller political parties did not want to be marginalized. The NP aimed at continued control over the state while progressively opening it up to Africans.

For the first time in the history of the negotiating process, delegations from a variety of parties listened to each other, and shared motives, fears, and concerns. CODESA did not produce any agreements, but it planted the seeds for compromise between the major parties involved. It also provided a declaration that facilitated the process by emphasizing the need for a united South Africa, a peaceful transition, a bill of rights, and universal suffrage. Based on a minimal consensus between the ANC and the NP, this declaration constituted a framework within which the key negotiators could reach a final agreement. CODESA I allocated items for negotiation to different working groups in order to make the negotiating process more efficient. One working group focused on equal political conditions while another dealt with constitutional principles. A third working group addressed the transition from apartheid to democracy and a fourth focused on the creation of a united South Africa (particularly on how to incorporate former Bantustans). The final working group, added as an after thought, focused on the issue of gender. CODESA did not directly address the competing visions or contrasting views of "imagined community" that the ANC and the NP held of a post-apartheid South Africa. The NP still believed that South Africa was made up of diverse nations, while the ANC envisaged a racially and ethnically united country. There was no basic agreement over the nature of the state. Another fundamental disagreement was over which group/political party would be in power during the transition period.

A number of political obstacles were removed during CODESA I. For example, an agreement in Working Group II (the creation of a climate for free political activity) on speeding up the release of political prisoners and the return home of exiles and their families was reached. Working Group II also agreed that:

- The interim government could impose emergency regulations and detention without trial on the advice of the multi-party executive council.

- Discriminatory laws should be repealed.

- The use of military means to pursue political objectives would end.

- The political neutrality of free and fair access to state-controlled media, including the SABC and television, as well as those in the TBVC states, would be established.

- An independent Peace Accord would be implemented-CODESA committed itself to a peaceful settlement.

- The security forces would be placed under the control of an interim government and mechanisms be established to ensure their accountability.

- The funding of political organizations and parties up to six years after the general elections should cease.

- A spirit of tolerance would be fostered among political parties and an intensive educational campaign would be embarked on in respect to political tolerance.[19]

Working Group III agreed to a two-phase transition. During the first phase, the Transitional Executive Council (TEC) would oversee the process. CODESA I collapsed in May 1992 because the major parties could not reach common ground. In particular, the NP did not want to give up on its insistence of protecting minority rights, while the ANC stuck to its demand of majority rule. The different working groups, which sometimes had as many as eighty representatives, were too large to reach any agreement. By the time CODESA I broke up, the ANC was already under pressure from its militants and the labor movement. Both wanted to organize mass demonstrations to force the government to curb the violence. The infamous Boipatong massacre of July 17, 1992, in which forty-five ANC supporters (mainly women and children) were killed, exposed the government's role in fomenting political violence. The government was now under pressure from the international community and the ANC to return to the negotiation table and to curb the violence. Some ANC leaders also felt that the organization was giving in too much without getting much in return. The ANC's rank-and-file was highly critical of the secretive nature of the CODESA proceedings. They blamed Mandela for leaving them at the mercy of a shadowy "Third Force," namely members of the apartheid security forces who aimed at destabilizing the country. The Third Force terrorized South Africans and the mainstream media presented the terror as "black-on-black" violence. There is substantial evidence that supports the ANC's claim that the NP government trained Inkatha Freedom Fighters for this purpose.[20] The ANC threatened to withdraw from the negotiations unless the government halted the violence.

Final Talks

Mandela presented three demands to the NP as a precondition to return to the negotiation table: the release of all political prisoners, the installation of fences around workers' hostels, and the banning of the use of dangerous traditional weapons. The NP was itself moving toward a middle ground. It abandoned its insistence on power-sharing as well as its demand for a rotating presidency. A major consensus was reached between the two parties after June 1992, when the NP argued for the inclusion of elements in the constituent assembly similar to those advocated by the ANC. The NP accepted the idea that both parties should find the means of ensuring that the nonracial dispensation would not be delayed by prolonged negotiations. While it dropped its demand for automatic minority vetoes, the NP needed guarantees against the tyranny of the majority, such as a constituent assembly based on mutually agreeable principles. The NP also called for constitutional continuity during the transition period. In return, the ANC agreed to a two-phase transition period. A nonelected negotiating forum would draft an interim constitution during the first phase; "it would also make law until it drafted the permanent constitution."[21] Thus, there would be no constitutional void during the transition.

Both the ANC and the NP made major compromises. The ANC came to realize that a majority party needed checks and balances. This common ground was further exposed when the two parties signed *The Record of Understanding* in September 1992, whereby it was agreed that a government of national unity (GNU) would govern during the transition on the basis of an interim constitution. The GNU would be governed by a single presidency from the majority party and would work with a multiparty cabinet. A party other than the majority would occupy the deputy presidency position. There was disagreement over the powers of the Senate. For example, the NP and DP wanted a strong Senate while the ANC preferred a weak one. Both parties agreed that a 60 percent vote was needed to ratify the constitution. They also agreed that the constitution should be written in "two years provided that the interim government lasted for five years."[22] The ANC hoped to reduce the level of violence by controlling the security forces through an interim government. Such a government would place the ANC in a powerful position vis-à-vis the nationalist government by limiting the actions of the latter. As the key players in the negotiation, both the ANC and NP made various attempts to bring in other parties like the IFP, the PAC, and the Conservative Party. As a result of these efforts, negotiations resumed on March 5, 1993 at Kempton Park.

On opening day (April 5, 1993), the CODESA II Multiparty Negotiating Forum (MNF) was attended by twenty-six parties that agreed to formal negotiations. This new Forum had a different structure than CODESA I. For example, it had a ten-member planning committee that debated and provided recommendations to the negotiating forum. The planning committee was comprised of administrative and technical committees that took over the work of the Working Groups of CODESA I. The most extensive negotiations took place in the negotiating council and each party had two delegates and two advisers present. The MNF, which was made up of four delegates and two advisers, was later abandoned. The Plenary was made up of ten delegates per party. Unlike CODESA I, which did not have women representatives, all party delegates in CODESA II had to include a woman.

There was also pressure from the IFP and CP as both felt that the Forum was not meeting their demands. A right-wing Afrikaner organization, the Afrikaner Volksunie (AVU), organized demonstrations outside the negotiating venue. There were also teacher demonstrations demanding higher pay. On June 1st, the Negotiating Forum agreed on a two-phase transition, an elected constitution-making body, an interim constitution, and a technical committee that would make "recommendations of the powers, structures and functions of regions during the transition."[23]

Joe Slovo, a prominent member of the ANC executive, introduced a resolution that committed delegates "to ensure that the negotiating process moves forward over the next five weeks to set the exact date for an election that should take place not later than the end of April 1994."[24] As the future governmental authority to redress past economic inequalities, Slovo urged the ANC to make its position clear on issues such as minority veto, power-sharing, and regional government power. These were all issues upon which the ANC could not compromise. On Slovo's advice, the ANC agreed to "sun-set clauses" which guaranteed job security and generous compensation and retirement packages to the overwhelmingly white and Afrikaner civil service. According to Slovo, these clauses guaranteed power-sharing for a predetermined number of years. The ANC and the government agreed in advance about regional borders, general amnesty, the civil service, and security forces. Agreement on these key issues constituted a major breakthrough in the negotiating process.

The ANC alliance was plagued by severe tensions between two main factions. Moderates, such as Nelson Mandela and Walter Sisulu, were pulling the organization to the center. On the other hand, the radicals, such as Winnie Mandela, Harry Gwala, Chris Hani, and Blade Nzimande, sought to substantially change the system in favor of the African majority. Some leaders and members of the South African Communist Party (SACP) were extremely critical of the sunset-clauses. Blade Nzimande noted that these provisions were fully one-sided and lacked any broad support from the masses. Harry Gwala wondered why Slovo went to such great pains to reassure the regime without addressing the concerns and needs of the majority. As he remarked, "It is not the good intentions of the negotiators and their ability to talk that will determine the fate of this country, important as this part of the struggle may be. But it will be the strength and ability of the contenders in the struggle that, in the final analysis, will determine the fate of this country. Any political expediency will be a disaster."[25]

The suggestions put forward by Slovo were adopted, with regard to his detractors' criticism. As the undisputed leader of the moderate camp, Nelson Mandela played a key role in silencing critics. According to Barnabas Wondo (a SACP activist), in Boksburg the workers wanted to revolt, but out of respect for "Comrade Mandela" as a person they abandoned the revolution.[26] These debates were reflected in a document from the ANC's National Executive Council (NEC) entitled *Negotiations: a strategic perspective*, which was adopted in Durban on November 23–25, 1992. The document set out an ANC strategy that combined mass demonstrations and international pressure. According to this strategy, each phase of the transition would be used to effect major changes in the system, culminating ultimately in a complete democratic transformation. *Negotiations* outlined five phases in the transition to democracy. The first phase was the preparation period: the ANC would use this period to secure an agreement from the National Party on free and fair elections. Phase two would be the period from the establishment of the Transition Executive Council to the election of a Constituent Assembly. In phase three, the Constituent Assembly would draft the new constitution. During this period, the main objective would be to secure a joint agreement over the control of the armed forces and a peaceful transition. In phase four, the new constitution would be introduced, followed by the dismantling of the apartheid system. The democratic transformation would be consolidated in phase five.

According to the NEC document, the transformation process was to be people-based and driven by the masses. In order to advance this process, the ANC had to make certain compromises. Slovo's compromises were accepted, subject to negotiations with the NP. Although the ANC had initially adhered to the principle of majority rule, the NEC document introduced the idea of a government of national unity regardless of the results of the elections. It also provided the blueprint for the political strategy of the ANC between 1992 and 1993. Following the adoption of the NEC document, the ANC held several bilateral meetings with the NP.

In December 1992, both parties established committees to examine the possibility of a two-phase transition. The assassination of Chris Hani on April 10, 1993 and the sudden death of Oliver Tambo, the ANC National Chairman, two weeks later (April 23, 1993) introduced new tensions into the negotiations and brought South Africa to the brink of civil war. Chris Hani was an upright, selfless, and dedicated ANC leader, extremely popular with the party's base, uninterested in political power, and genuinely concerned about a political settlement that would positively transform the socioeconomic conditions of the African majority. Oliver Tambo, who was ideologically and politically very close to Chris Hani, died two weeks after the latter. Chris Hani "fought for negotiations that deliver. He fought for a settlement that [would] produce not just nice words, not just a flag and anthem, not just new faces in the cabinet. He fought for a settlement that [would] open way for a process of profound change of our country."[27]

As a result, political violence escalated in the townships, thereby throwing the negotiating process in disarray. In Natal, the death rate increased from an "estimated 800 in 1989 to more than 1500 in 1990, dropping slightly in 1991 and 1992 climbing to a high of 2009 in 1993."[28] Some observers linked the rash of political violence to the negotiations. On the Reef (Johannesburg area) "there were 1000 fatalities in 1990 and more than 2000 in 1993."[29] The level of violence rose as the negotiations began and accelerated throughout the process. In addition to Hani's death, many Africans were also frustrated by the slow pace of the negotiations. Others felt that the ANC was negotiating their future away. Most people felt left out by "a [probably inherently elite] negotiation process."[30]

The close relations that existed between the NP and the IFP did not improve matters. While the NP publicly denied having supported the IFP, damaging evidence linked the NP to its clandestine activities. Some critics also noted that both the IFP and the NP were using violence as a strategy to delay the negotiations. Following Hani's assassination, the NP worsened matters by deploying more than twenty thousand SADF (military) and SAP (police) personnel to "protect what was seen by many as white interests."[31] In the Transkei, where it was rumored that APLA guerillas found refuge, white children were escorted to school in military vehicles. Furthermore, the NP pointed to the few incidences of violence as proof that the ANC could not control its supporters. A sense of urgency developed among the negotiators. They felt that they had to set an election date to curb the violence. ANC supporters criticized negotiations "that lead to hell" and "the organization that has become an undertaker," prompting its leaders to demand an election date.[32]

Another meeting held in January 1993 between the ANC and the NP focused on security issues. These talks centered on the future of the NP-controlled military. On April 22–23, 1993, the first meeting between SADF and MK representatives took place in Simons Town. It addressed the problem of military control during the transition. There was also growing concern over the racial make up of the military. For example, in "1986, 76 percent of its members were white; in [1993] blacks outnumbered whites, although the command of all its arms remained almost exclusively white and Afrikaans-speaking."[33] The South African Defence Force agreed to address the issue of the integration of other armies. The second issue was an agreement in principle for the need of a National Peacekeeping Force to combat violence. Finally, the members resolved to integrate all the armed forces into a national defense force. *Umkhonto we Sizwe* agreed to disband, as its members received "training" in preparation for integration. As a result, 8,000 to 10,000 MK soldiers were trained, "bringing the estimated number of troops available for integration to around 14,000 to 16,000."[34] Some MK members took up political offices, while others remained in the "new" South African National Defence Force (SANDF). The ANC formed a Military Research Group (MRG) made up of scholars and analysts with practical experience; the MRG played a limited advisory role in security/military policy-making.

In contrast to the NP that provided seasoned analysts, the suggestions of the ANC's MRG were accepted mainly because there were no alternatives. Thus, according to Mark Shaw, "this is possibly an understatement; MRG ideas were often accepted simply because there were no counterproposals. Advisers became policy-makers; this soon became a source of tension, worsened, say insiders, by the fact that most advisers were civilians, and to a lesser degree because they were mostly white. More importantly, key MRG members Nathan in particular, were distinctly anti-militarist. While this irritated the soldiers, it influenced ANC proposals, which stressed that defence force should be subordinated to civil authority."[35]

The armed forces of the Homelands, such as the Transkei armed forces, were active in the negotiations and scheduled to be integrated in the new defense force. No efforts were made to integrate the military wings of extreme-right Afrikaner movements such as the Afrikaner *Weerstand Beweging* (AWB). At first, the PAC remained out of the talks, but it later joined in. The Azanian peoples' Liberation Army (APLA), which was made of BC sympathizers, did not participate in the talks. MK soldiers were effectively "incorporated" rather than "absorbed" in the SADF (which became the South African National Defence Force, or SANDF). MK's integration into the SANDF did not disrupt its organization. There was disagreement over who would control the integration process. The SANDF wanted complete control, which the ANC objected to.

Negotiations on the nature and composition of the defense forces continued. All parties agreed on the creation of a single military force placed under civilian control. The ANC wanted SANDF to be made up of a merger of each of the individual armies (SADF, MK, and Homeland forces). For its part, the NP simply wanted to integrate the other armies (MK and Homeland forces). The NP also demanded that the "nature and character of the defence force should be apolitical."[36] It also laid down four goals: "the SADF was to form the core of the national defence force; its structures should be retained; the future of all SADF members should be assured; and other forces should be integrated into existing SADF structures."[37] The ANC called for an end to universal conscription save under exceptional circumstances and with the authorization of parliament. Invoking the need to have a constant flow of volunteers, the SANDF disagreed. After the other parties agreed that the issue did not need to be addressed at this point in time, the ANC dropped its demands. The parties agreed that soldiers could disobey orders that contravened both national and international law. All the SADF/NP conditions were met while the ANC demands were not addressed. In addition, the ANC agreed to dismantle South Africa's nuclear military capability. In practice, there were so many built-in restrictive clauses in the constitution that the ANC lost any political control over the military. This was no accident. By ensuring continued white minority control over the military, the ANC would be in no position to "misbehave." As Vishwas Satgar has argued elsewhere, by protecting white military personnel, the SADF/NP also constrained the future of MK and other armies that were *de facto* integrated into an apartheid structure that exclusively served minority needs (the complete opposite of ANC/MK's ideals and demands).

By August 1992, the ANC was under increasing pressure to set an election date. In November, COSATU and South African National Civic Organization (SANCO) announced demonstrations to "demand an interim government and the elections of a constituent assembly."[38] A colleague of Joe Slovo, Essop Pahad, noted later that "it put a lot of pressure on the process. We felt very strongly that unless we set a target date, one could continue to prevaricate, and only end up Codesa-ing."[39] Mandela warned that unless an election date was set during the next meeting between the ANC and NP, the talks would cease. The ANC demanded that an interim government be set up by March 1994. The negotiations were also threatened by the withdrawal of the IFP. The Zulu King also demanded that the negotiations include small parties, traditional leaders, and women. Both the ANC and the NP attempted to meet these demands. On June 3, 1993, the Negotiating Council formally announced April 27, 1994 as the date for the country's first general elections.

Obstacles

In opposition to the ANC-NP *entente cordiale* (friendly agreement), various homeland leaders joined the Chief Mangosuthu Gatsha Buthelezi (IFP) and the white right (such as Conservative Party leader, Andries Treurnicht), who promised joint action "by those who refuse to live under ANC / SACP tyranny and betrayal by the government."[40] The IFP noted that it could only be involved in the negotiations if the constitution was written before the elections. It also demanded that South Africa adopt a federal system of government before the talks. According to this perspective, the homelands had to be maintained until the new constitution was introduced. The IFP steadfastly refused to participate in the general elections until the very last minute when it realized it had no other options left.

The PAC demanded that the Constituent Assembly should be responsible for writing the constitution. It also preferred negotiations in foreign locations overseen by neutral parties. As a result of the intense pressure from foreign sympathizers (such as China) to negotiate, the PAC eventually abandoned its demand for external talks. The PAC, however, would not renounce armed struggle as a precondition for joining the talks, although it agreed to rein in its military wing (*poqo*), a position supported by the ANC but strongly opposed by the NP. The PAC eventually agreed to renounce armed struggle and was thus allowed back to the negotiation table by the NP. As it returned to the talks, the PAC continued to insist that the main purpose of the negotiations was to plan the election of a Constituent Assembly, a demand that it gradually dropped. In spite of this, the PAC remained popular among the African masses throughout the negotiating process.

The Conservative Party (CP) made the guarantee of Afrikaner freedom a precondition for joining the negotiations. Only an Afrikaner homeland would ensure that Afrikaners would be able to maintain their language and culture. The CP insisted that it would not negotiate with the ANC and the SACP. It was assured that the issue would be discussed if it had a popular mandate. The white right threatened civil war unless an Afrikaner state was on the agenda. Eventually, however, both conservative fronts were convinced to be involved in the negotiations after they realized that this is what their leaders wanted.

The IFP and other political parties rejected the idea of a national Electoral Commission while both the ANC and the NP disagreed on the role and powers of the Transitional Executive Council (TEC). The NP wanted the TEC to be under the authority of Parliament while the ANC preferred it to have executive powers. Both parties agreed to create sub-committees to address the issue. They also realized that the rejection of the TEC by some parties would limit its role in the electoral process. After five hours of intense debate, a majority of the Council agreed to a two-stage transition that involved "an elected constitution-making body bound by agreed principles; interim regional governments; and an interim constitution."[41] The IFP agreed to soften its demands on regional powers in order to be assured that regional boundaries and structures would be determined beforehand. It also wanted a Constitutional Court to be put in place in order to address issues related to the interpretation of the constitution.

The ANC's acceptance of the fact that the TEC should be bound by agreed principles was a triumph for the IFP. The powers of the TEC were never clearly defined, resulting in constant tension between the NP and ANC. A particular point of disagreement between the TEC and the NP had to do with the best way to deal with the KwaZulu/Natal conflict. The TEC intervened to create a favorable environment for elections. The NP government, on the other hand, rejected the TEC's declaration of a state of emergency. Sometimes, bargaining between the TEC, the ANC, and the NP involved other agencies, such as the National Housing Forum. The TEC prepared the ground for a Government of National Unity by developing a culture of negotiation and compromise among various political leaders. The relationships between the leaders of the various parties that developed out of this process were important in providing the foundation for a new dispensation. The ANC and the NP had opposite conceptions of the transition. For the NP, the transition was a democratization period similar to those experienced by authoritarian regimes in Latin America such as Argentina and Chile. Such a process involved the liberalization of the economy, the inclusion of Africans in state structures, and the dismantling of apartheid. For the ANC, the political transition was similar to the decolonization process experienced by other African countries. This is why the ANC insisted on "the formation of an interim government and the holding of national elections for a Constituent Assembly that would ultimately facilitate the transfer of power to an elected government."[42]

Disagreements also emerged over who would oversee the election process. Liberation movements (such as PAC and the ANC) demanded the participation of international observers in order to guarantee the fairness of the process. The NP did not want any observers present. Both parties finally agreed on setting up an Independent Election Commission (IEC) to oversee the electoral process. The other obstacle concerned the definition of citizen. The NP considered permanent residents in South Africa to be citizens. When it came to the question of prisoners, there was disagreement over who could vote. Workers were required to travel to their home base to vote. The ANC wanted both workers and prisoners to be allowed to vote. After several meetings, these differences were finally ironed out. At the World Trade Center negotiations in September 1993, four bills were passed: the Transitional Executive Council (TEC) Bill, the Independent Electoral Commission Bill, the Independent Media Commission Bill, and the Independent Broadcasting Authority Bill. The task of the TEC was to ensure that political parties and individuals were able to campaign and vote without hindrance or intimidation. In essence, every South African who had registered to vote should be able to do so.

Outcome

Several individuals, countries, and organizations shaped the development and influenced the outcome of the negotiations. In particular, the United States and the former Soviet Union played a critical role during this period. Both held talks with the negotiating parties to inform them of their desires, particularly of their preference for a negotiated political settlement. The major personalities involved were F. W. De Klerk (NP), Nelson Mandela (ANC), Joe Slovo (SACP), and the informal communication "channel," which was made up of Cyril Ramaphosa (ANC) and Rolf Meyer (NP). These two representatives were able to solve critical issues during their many informal outings. As a result, they found common ground where previously none was seen. At first, De Klerk framed the parameters of the talks, blocking the talks when the parameters were not in his party's interest and supporting the talks when they were. This method of negotiations is best amplified by the success of the "sunset clauses."

In the context of international euphoria that surrounded the negotiations, the world media represented Nelson Mandela as a martyr and as a saintly figure (somehow floating above humanity), whose urgent calls for moderation, forgiveness, and reconciliation completely silenced his critics. According to Dinesh Prashad, after Steve Biko was murdered in 1977 both the apartheid regime and the United States government needed a martyr to replace him. For this reason, Mandela was kept alive because he no longer posed a threat to the system, hence, the Free Mandela campaigns that represented him as the true savior of the African majority. According to Prashad, Mandela's isolation from world events during his imprisonment (which alienated him from the true rhythm of South African politics), his desire to please the white minority at the expense of the majority, and the way western media presented him, were all conflicting with the interests, priorities, and needs of the African majority. By late 1969, due to government repression, ANC influence in South Africa was very weak. In addition, government informers played a crucial role in marginalizing the ANC during this period. When the *Washington Post* correspondent Jim Hoagland visited South Africa in 1970, "he found that Luthuli, Mandela, and Sisulu were perceived dimly, as if they belonged to another time, long past and long lost."[43] Had it not been for Winnie Mandela's relentless activism, Nelson Mandela as an individual and the leader of the ANC would have been forgotten. Once the white minority understood that it could 'work' with Nelson Mandela he "carried the show." For example, at the ANC national conference held in July 1991, he wanted the ANC to reconsider its attitude towards the negotiations. According to him, the negotiations had to be viewed as "another theater of struggle" which was a "victory" against the white government. Mandela stated that "it [could] never be in our interests that we prolong the agony of the apartheid system. It does not serve the interests of the masses we represent and the country as a whole that we delay . . . the achievement of the objective of the transfer of power to the people."[44]

The negotiations and debates between the NP and ANC elites totally silenced and marginalized their detractors. Those individuals and organizations critical of the NP and ANC leadership were represented as "irrational," and as the enemies of "free trade" and "democracy" by the international media. This explains why the NP distanced itself from the Conservative Party and from the Afrikaner Volksunie. Both the NP and the ANC tried to present the moderates' views within their respective parties. Winnie Mandela was appalled by Nelson Mandela's moderate position, but especially by his close relationship with the former enemy of the ANC, de Klerk, as well as by Mandela's conservative position on the land question. Within the ANC alliance, discontent continued to simmer over the sun-set clauses. Harry Gwala, leader of the ANC Natal-Midlands region, noted that the organization was ready to surrender even before the negotiations: "We find the agreement unacceptable. It is a drastic departure from what we have always known the ANC to stand for. This is indeed a strange way of appeasement. We are already setting down the rule of surrender before we meet the enemy. If we go out to negotiations with such terms of surrender, where do we draw the line?"[45]

Discontent among the ANC critics further escalated when the party's Natal-Midlands region was joined in its opposition to the ANC mainstream by both South and North Natal areas and Allan Boesak's "Western Cape region, the PWV region and Southern Natal structures of COSATU, the SACP and the Youth League, as well as the Marxist Workers Tendency."[46] All these parties demanded that the ANC reconsider its negotiation demands and believed that the ANC was too accommodating to the demands of the NP without getting much in return. The ANC leadership silenced these critics by presenting them as "militants" or "enemies of peace." It also focused on down playing differences. Thus, an ANC constitutional clause was invoked to remove Harry Gwala from the Natal-Midlands region on the flimsy premise that he was also serving on the NEC. Gwala offered to resign from the NEC thereby defeating this move. Winnie Mandela warned against "a looming disaster from the distortion of the noble goal in favour of a short cut to parliament by a handful of individuals."[47]

Winnie Mandela's warning was dismissed as one individual's opinion and, therefore, without merit. COSATU also felt sidelined by the ANC. Its leaders threatened to demonstrate in defense of their rights. In the negotiation discourse, "individualism" replaced the Afrikaner imagined community. Poor Afrikaners were left to fend for themselves in an increasingly competitive environment. In spite of its populist rhetoric, the ANC elite also left out the African majority by negotiating away their fundamental economic and social rights. In the culture of liberal democracy, such economic and social inequalities would last for a very long time, which explains why the NP was attracted to this type of democracy. In essence, its economic and military positions would remain unchallenged for years to come. Heribert Adam et. al. note that "the affluent Afrikaners led by De Klerk and his negotiators, peacefully negotiated away the position of ethnic dominance on the gamble that these historical discrepancies would be a long time in disappearing and would, in any case, be protected by the rights culture of a liberal democracy."[48] According to Saki Macozoma, former ANC member of Parliament, the ANC assumed that "the economic question would be dealt with once the democratic government was in place."[49] Similarly, William Gumede believed that the NP and its various partners "outfoxed" the ANC in the economy. Nelson Mandela and his cadres settled for political power while abandoning any claim to economic power. This, in essence, made South Africa a neo-colonial country, albeit a very sophisticated one.

Worst still, there was no alternative radical/revolutionary discourse that would have united the people in a coordinated insurrectional effort. As a result, any opposing debate was silenced as moderates from both parties worked together toward a political settlement. Since the ANC and SACP were core actors in this effort, revolutionary impulses gradually dissipated. Interestingly, all "radicals" were eliminated either physically (Hani and various military personalities) or through character assassination (Boesak, Ngwala, Winnie Mandela). In essence, the negotiations were a settlement between the NP and ANC elites. Doreen Atkinson notes that from the very beginning, the two parties knew that they would have to carefully steer the process through multiple obstacles if it was to move forward without been sabotaged by outside elements. This type of settlement is essential if "an elite settlement is to last, and which might be part of the political landscape for many years to come. The new style is an amalgam of opposites. It combines secrecy with openness; chicanery with principle; deals between the two big parties with concessions to others. Most importantly, in a society whose elites must work together or die apart, it shaped a generation of leaders who loved power but were willing to use it to try to steer the country away from sectional conflict, not towards it."[50]

Important details were left out, as both the ANC and NP tried to reach compromises. The negotiating process was also important because it shaped a generation of elites who were willing to work together. Toward this end, they aimed at consensus rather than conflict and confrontation.

In spite of the international euphoria reflected in the world press and Nelson Mandela's charm as an iconic figure, which resulted in the success of the negotiations, there were few concrete gains for the African majority. Johannes Rantete's sober assessment of the outcome is revealing in this regard:

With a power-sharing deal for a fixed number of years, with attempts to secure the jobs of the current civil service, with the existing government disposing of state assets and with constitutional provisions which sanctioned the suppression of workers' strikes, it was questionable what meaningful gains had been negotiated for ordinary people during the interim period, apart from regaining their citizenship and going to the polling stations. Except for marking a historic moment of cheering, ululation and "sloganeering," Freedom Day appeared set to be a long sunset with little hope dawning for the black majority.[51]

Conclusion

Those individuals and organizations critical of the ANC note that the ANC got exactly what it wanted, namely a neo-colonial settlement that left it without control over South Africa's economy and security. The ANC did not control the negotiating process. The agenda was set by the NP and its Western allies, who capitalized on the ANC's eagerness to capture political power. In the course of the negotiations, members of the business community and the World Bank made major economic decisions. The ANC came into the negotiations poorly prepared to deal with economic issues, which explains why the NP's seasoned negotiators won the day. Nelson Mandela and Thabo Mbeki were so eager to be accepted by their Western patrons that they took extremely "moderate" positions on the economy and on military/security matters. The resulting agreement was tantamount to selling the majority of the African population to the lowest bidder. Critics believe that the ANC betrayed the Freedom Charter and hold the ANC responsible for not adequately addressing the national question. Thus, the "negotiations" were ultimately only about political power over the country.

All the participants wanted to protect their interests. The liberation movements shared several common objectives, such as the transition from apartheid to democracy. However, they differed in their strategies. The ANC preferred the negotiations to take place in South Africa while the PAC wanted them to be conducted on foreign territory. These liberation movements wanted to secure human, political, and socioeconomic rights for Africans while the NP was out to protect white minority rights. The PAC, the ANC, and the IFP disagreed on the nature of the post-apartheid state, particularly on whether it should be a unitary, semi-federal, or federal state.

Irreconcilable positions appeared during the negotiations. For example, the Afrikaner extreme-right's demand for a homeland was in conflict with the ANC's call for a united, nonracial South Africa. Within the ANC, the Africanist/Socialist position demanded that negotiations could not take place until apartheid was defeated. Given *Umkhonto we Sizwe*'s limited military effectiveness, and because of changes in the international economy that left the capitalist system as the only option, defeating apartheid militarily would have been impossible. This forced the ANC to make major concessions, such as agreeing to sun-set clauses in order to accommodate key NP demands.

The final outcome of the negotiations was also influenced by the major parties, namely, the ANC and the NP. Once they reached agreement on an issue, they were able to persuade the other parties to join in. Both parties effectively marginalized and silenced their critics. The NP silenced criticism from the civil servants by agreeing to the ANC's sun-set clauses. Major compromises were reached. The ANC left the South African National Defense Force intact, but it simply integrated the other armies within its own structure. The ANC also agreed to dismantle South Africa's nuclear military capability. By agreeing to the sun-set clauses, the ANC effectively ensured that socioeconomic progress and equality for the African masses would become a distant goal. The final settlement reached by the negotiating parties resulted in three major contradictions. First, since the white minority still occupied key positions within the administration, transformation would be more difficult to achieve. Furthermore, since that same white minority remained firmly and exclusively in control of the economy, socioeconomic inequality between (and within) the various racial groups in South Africa would be maintained and would probably increase. Second, lacking control over the key sectors of the economy and military/security, the new South African government would simply become another African neo-colonial state, a quasi-state lacking the attributes of substantive power. In terms of Africa's status and role in the world, it would be "business as usual." The only new development would be that Western capitalism (particularly transnational corporations) would now be in a position to use South Africa as a springboard to penetrate the rest of the continent, including for the sale of weapons to fuel African conflicts. In reality, South Africa's "freedom" became the last nail on the independence coffin of the continent. Third, without these major compromises, the white minority would never have agreed to relinquish political power. These contradictions continue to plague the attempts of the ANC at socioeconomic transformation. We will address this in the next chapter.

FURTHER READINGS

Gumede, William Mervin. *Thabo Mbeki and the Battle for the Soul of the ANC*. Cape Town: Zebra Press, 2005.

Shubin, Vladimir. *ANC: A View From Moscow*. Cape Town: Mayibuye Books, 1990.

Sparks, Allistar. *Tomorrow is Another Country: The Inside Story of South Africa's Negotiated Revolution*. Johannesburg: Struik Book Distributors, 1994.

CHAPTER 7

A WORK IN PROGRESS

SOCIAL AND ECONOMIC POLICY CHANGES BY THE ANC, 1994–2006

> The National wealth of our country, the heritage of South Africans, shall be restored to the people; the mineral wealth beneath the soil, the banks and monopoly industry shall be transferred to the ownership of the people as a whole; all other industry and trade shall be controlled to assist the well-being of the people.
> —*The Freedom Charter*, June 1955

> What is an African leader anyway? . . . If the African people don't begin to more closely examine the characters of the people they call leaders—and stop mistaking demagogues and orators for leaders—their problems will be endless.
> —Thula Bopela and Daluxolo Luthuli. *Umkhonto we Sizwe: Fighting for a divided People*

THIS CHAPTER EXAMINES HOW LIBERAL, MULTIRACIAL DEMOCRACY translated into the delivery of economic and social goods and services for various racial, social, and gender groups in post-apartheid South Africa. Specifically, we will ask the following question: Who got what, when, and how? In the process, the contradictions that plaque the political and economic systems will be identified. Using statistical data, this chapter will test the hypothesis that the South African middle-class, regardless of race or ethnicity, is threatened from above and below. In particular, this chapter will show that popular demands from below will sometimes lead the middle-class to partially satisfy the demands of the African majority. However, the middle-class's room to maneuver is limited by the interests of its own class base, as well as by those of the national and international business community. As we shall see, these constraints will force the middle-class to make compromises that will be detrimental to the economic and social interests, priorities, and needs of the African majority.

In this chapter, I will use Fanon's definition of the middle-class. According to Fanon, as it was set up solely to service the colonial ruling elite, the middle-class in under-developed countries lacks economic power. As a result, the middle-class is not engaged in material or intellectual production, but rather in (conspicuous) consumption. In essence, the middle-class acts as a business agent of Western capitalism the sole concern of this class is to protect his patrons' interests.[1] The only way the middle-class could have been an agent of change is if it had been following a revolutionary path. In South Africa, the middle-class is made up of people from all racial groups, political parties, and various business and community-based organizations. The South African Middle class has access to better educational facilities and enjoys higher salaries and better standards of living than the majority of the country's population. This being said, the middle-class is neither static nor homogeneous; it changes and adapts according to the various pressures from above and below to which it is subjected (be they popular or the exigencies of the national and international business communities).

This chapter is divided into seven sections. The first section looks at the changes in the economy (particularly, liberalization) and how these changes shaped the ability of the ANC to redress inherited poverty and inequality. In section two, I analyze two successive and different development programs: the Reconstruction and Development Programme (RDP) and Growth, Employment, and Redistribution (GEAR). In section three, changes in social services, that is, in education, health, and housing, are examined. Changes in the military, police, and the civil service are the subject of section four. Sections five and six discuss changes in the judicial system and land tenure, respectively. Section seven identifies and explains what social, racial, and gender groups are the actual beneficiaries of multiracial, liberal democracy in South Africa.

ANC:
LIBERALIZATION VS. POPULAR DEMANDS

Drawing on the work of Michel Foucault, Edward Said, and Robert Cox, Rita Abrahmsen shows how development discourse has constructed the third world as underdeveloped, and has subsequntly normalized and legitimized the right of the North to intervene in, control, and develop the South. In her view, the "good governance" discourse is merely the latest reproduction of the "dream of development" and similarly entitles the North to develop and democratize the South in its image. The South becomes the object of the North's development projects and activities. Thus, the development discourse emerges as a crucial element in the understanding of recent transitions to multi-party democracy in Africa.

Abrahamsen further argues that many newly elected governments in Africa face two irreconcilable constituencies: external donors and creditors and the poor domestic majorities. While African governments are crucially dependent on both for their financial survival and reelection, respectively, they cannot satisfy both constituencies at the same time. The first casualty of this dilemma is the democratic process itself.

Abrahamsen argues that the form of democracy demanded by donors and creditors (including the Bretton Woods institutions) offers African incumbents and elites the possibility of holding on to or capturing power, without giving in to any of the demands for social welfare and redistribution at home. In this sense, says Abrahamsen, a de facto alliance occurs between the African elites and the foreign donors and creditors, in that they share a broadly similar conceptualization of democracy that centers on political rights and a continued economic liberalism.[2] In this perspective, the majority of South Africans should be content with and, thus, need not go beyond electoral democracy, that is to say, regular, free, and fair elections. According to Patrick Bond, South Africa's transition from apartheid to democracy was essentially an "elite transition" which entailed the wholesale adoption of neo-liberalism and the total rejection of any populist development strategy by the ANC. Class cleavages sharpened as a result of this process: "95 percent of the poor are black 'African', and 4 percent are 'coloured' [people of mixed descent], with people from the white and Indian race categories comprising less than 1 percent of the poor."[3] The key priorities in the new South Africa include the protection of the economic interests of the white minority and the creation of a climate favorable to free enterprise.[4]

Drawing on the work of O'Donnell and Schmitter on Latin America, Abrahamsen makes some observations that are quite relevant to the South African situation. Discussing "democratic pacts" as a specific feature of transition processes in Latin America (and South Africa), she notes that such pacts were negotiated among established, highly hierarchical elites and aimed at reassuring traditionally dominant classes that their vital interests would not be jeopardized under democracy (including amnesty from prosecution). At the same time, however, such democratic pacts may serve as a vehicle through which elements of the previous authoritarian regime continue to influence the new democracy. In this manner, pacts may entail the marginalization of popular demands for improved living standards or allow fairly minimal and gradual transformation in gross social and economic inequalities. Political pacts also contribute to economic compromises, as the new elite tries to accommodate the old one, and, in the process, exacerbates class inequalities.

Fred Hendricks' *Fault-Lines in South African Democracy: Continuing Crises of Inequality and Injustice* demonstrates the negative impact of the historic compromise between the African National Congress (ANC) and the National Party (NP) during the negotiations on democracy and development in post-apartheid South Africa. Seekings and Nattrass argue that income inequality in South Africa substantially increased in the ten years following the transition from apartheid to liberal democracy. By the late 1970s class (rather than race) was becoming the major cleavage marker in South Africa. As the white minority became economically secure, class became more important than race. According to these authors, the elimination of apartheid's legacy "requires a fundamental reorientation of the growth strategy and of the role of the state in shaping distribution."[5] Apartheid was a "distributional regime, that is, a regime that combined (often uneasily) welfare, labor-market, and growth path policies in ways that shaped and reshaped distribution in South Africa."[6] Generally speaking, studies on South Africa overemphasize the role race played over class. Yet class is equally important especially towards the end of the apartheid regime. According to Seekings and Nattrass, three key features contribute to inequality: "Labour-market and other policies that encourage growth along a path that favours a small group of economic 'insiders' while excluding the poor; spending on public education that fails to improve significantly the educational opportunities open to poor children; and the lack of any welfare provision for people who are poor because they are unemployed . . . a transformed distributional regime would require a social accord between state, capital, and labour, with the goal of expanding employment."[7] Deracialization left the apartheid economic structure intact in South Africa. In post-apartheid South Africa, the prosperous group (bourgeoisie) is multiracial, the middle group (petty bourgeoisie) is mostly African, while the "impoverished" third category (rural and urban poor) is "entirely African."[8] Deracialization aimed at removing racial discrimination from public policy while at the same time opening up economic opportunities to formerly disadvantaged racial groups.

In South Africa, the gradual transition form the initial populist economic and social transformation program (Reconstruction and Development Programme) to the World Bank and IMF-inspired GEAR (Growth, Employment and Redistribution) program in 1996, perfectly illustrates the perpetuation of class inequalities inherited from apartheid. Once pacts have been negotiated, changes occur in power relations between the elite and external forces.[9]

According to Jeremy Cronin, the African elite is powerful only within the political arena; as a result, it side-lines the development agenda. Instead, its energy is focused on competing against other elites, with the backing of one or the other external force.[10] The black bourgeoisie has no options. It cannot form its own secret organizations like *Broederbond*—an economic advisory body—or the Randlords (powerful companies that contribute to economic development) to pursue a strategy of economic self-reliance. The only option left is for the bourgeoisie is to "either choose to be neo-colonial adjunct or fake its place within a development process led by other social forces."[11] Joe Slovo rejects Cronin's assessment of the strategic role of the bourgeoisie when he argues that this class cannot make any progress without entering into an alliance with black workers.

For Pallo Jordan, the ability of the bourgeoisie to act is "a function of both their choices and those of the International Monetary Fund. In the context of a particular configuration of those forces, that ability will either be enhanced or diminished."[12] In essence, the ability of the ANC to transform the economy is limited by IMF and the World Bank imposed conditionalities and by the Post-Cold War world economy in which capitalism is triumphant. According to an ex-activist, the ANC is so constrained by both local and international economic interest that it lacks any ideological commitment. As a result, it uses rhetoric to keep its supporters and to win over new ones. In its efforts to please everyone, the ANC is "frequently paralysed."[13] The ANC has attempted to win over COSATU (Congress of South African Trade Unions) to its side without adopting its agenda. Its efforts at racial mobilization have been undermined by class cleavages as the African middle-class increasingly alienates the rest of the population. These social conflicts evolve depending on the interests at stake. John Pilger notes that the United States, Britain and the World Bank made it clear to South Africa that it would be welcomed to the world economy if it adopted economic policies based on liberal orthodoxy and privatization while creating a climate favorable to foreign investment.[14] Heribert Adam further argues that Anglo-American and Gencor (major business corporations in South Africa) "unbundled because they rightly expected black allies to share their vision in a deracialised capitalism."[15]

South Africa is caught up in the two major trends that are now prevalent in the global economy, namely democratization and competitive markets. Acting as the guardians of these policies, the World Bank and the IMF use liberal democracy and market economy to judge whether countries are moving in the "right" direction.[16] To maintain good relations with key financial institutions, the "ANC has to prove constantly that it is worthy of outside support and that, in the threatening words of a U.S. banker, the lights should not be switched off."[17] Heribert Adams et al. argue that the ultra-left criticism of the ANC ignores these constraints. As a result, the ANC must constantly prove its worthy of these corporations' trust so they can invest in the government.[18] Indeed, under the Government of National Unity (GNU), the ANC made every effort to satisfy its conservative partners by accommodating foreign investors in South Africa. After the National Party withdrew from GNU in 1996, the ANC had to stay "within approved parameters."[19]

The ANC believes it is also the party of the poor since (as is the case in other African countries) the poor make up the majority of the population; they are called upon to help the ANC maintain its political power. As Patrick Bond has cogently argued, the major contradiction and dilemma of the ANC is that it must appear to be (and to talk) radical and populist while at the same time implementing conservative economic and social policies designed to assuage its (national and international) business partners.[20]

According to Heribert Adam et al., four reasons explain the policy orientation of the ANC. The ANC took over power with the support of business; it is the only organization with a large popular following; the ANC can appeal to all parties because of its rhetoric of moral superiority and finally, elites from various racial and ethnic backgrounds no longer worry over race and ethnicity but over how to maintain stability by controlling the poor.[21] The ANC sets the legislative agenda within which these actors can operate. Most trade unions were co-opted to support the interests of the business community, and any compromises reached under those circumstances automatically benefits the strongest of the parties. Small business and the unemployed people are left out of the bargaining process.[22] The common bond that unites all these actors is their support for economic growth upon which their survival rests.

ECONOMIC AND SOCIAL CHANGES

Since the publication of the *Freedom Charter* in 1955, the ANC has not introduced a new document on economic policy, though it reaffirmed its commitment to the *Charter* in 1988. It was only in 1990 that the ANC created a department of economic policy. Since then, most people who were involved in the negotiations agree that the ANC was "outfoxed" when it came to the economy.[23] The ANC's lack of a concrete economic program left it vulnerable to outside advice on the "realities of the world."[24] As early as 1993, the ANC stated its economic policy in a letter of intent to the

International Monetary Fund and the World Bank. In that letter, the ANC promised to cut government spending as a precondition for securing an IMF loan. The South African Reserve Bank, which is responsible for determining exchange rates and for the general welfare of the economy, was, as required by the IMF, removed from the control of the government. The ANC even agreed, as a show of good faith, to take responsibility for and pay back the debt incurred by the apartheid regime. The ANC's ability to radically transform the economy was limited not only by the IMF-imposed conditionalities, but also by the spirit of moderation and conciliation that prevailed during the negotiations for the new dispensation. Thus, the ANC assured the NP that it would not alienate white farmers. Land reform was based on a willing seller, willing buyer principle and on market values. The ANC also agreed to the NP's demand to leave the South African Defense Force intact while other armies were forced to integrate into the SADF. Furthermore, the ANC promised to carry out the process of privatization of the economy initiated by the previous government. Finally, because of the sun-set clauses, which guaranteed limited job security and provided generous retirement packages to apartheid-era civil servants, the ANC basically had to work with a bureaucracy that was not sympathetic to its policies. This reconciliation process reached its climax on November 27, 2001 when the ANC agreed to share power at all levels of government with the new National Party. As a result, the ANC now controls the Western Cape provincial administration. In return, the new NP participates in all major decisions, a situation that further contributes to slowing down the transformation process. Far from being sidelined and marginalized, the NP continues to play a key role in the new South Africa, notably by making sure that the economy, the military/security sector, and the land all remain firmly and securely under white minority control. [25]

Besides the fact that the ANC inherited an unreformed apartheid economy, the main problem that it confronted when it took power in 1994 was that it did not have the basic departments to plan and implement its policies.[26] Nevertheless, the ANC attempted to overcome these shortcomings by adopting the *Reconstruction and Development Programme* (RDP), which tried to address a number of unresolved issues, notably land, economic redistribution, and the rural/urban bias. The ANC's long-term development goals incorporated in the RDP included a redistribution of wealth designed to redress and reverse the apartheid legacy in the key sectors of education, housing, health, and development, with a particular focus on the rural poor.[27] The RDP was the brainchild of the radical elements within the ANC, particularly COSATU and the SACP (South African Communist Party). It was adopted after intensive debate and discussions and after going through seven drafts.[28] COSATU viewed the RDP as the agency through which the ANC would initiate and implement a comprehensive program of economic and social transformation designed to improve the standards of living of the African majority, specifically of the lowest sixty percent of the population.[29] The RDP set ambitious objectives, "but it inlcuded statements requiring macro-economic prudence that severly limited the ability to achieve those objectives."[30] By 1995, the economy was coming out of the recession but there were policy problems with service delivery as a result of luck of funds and of the obstructionist attitude of the old bureaucracy that was hostile to change. The RDP was faced with budgetary as well as political constraints. Political resistance slowed down both education and immigration reform.[31] There was also increasing pressure from the (national and international) business community, which was also against the RDP. As a result of these constraints and pressures, the RDP failed to meet its goals during its initial period, thereby forcing the ANC to abandon the program and to switch to the ultra-liberal GEAR program instead. Both COSATU and SACP were extremly disappointed by the ANC's switch to GEAR. Indeed, from then on, this single issue severely strained the ANC/COSATU/SACP alliance.[32] COSATU'S threats to strike against privatization were further course of concern. COSATU was also highly critical of the ANC's propensity for secrecy and for making unilateral decisions without adequate prior consultation with its alliance partners.[33]

Sampie Tereblanche reveals the obstacles that face South Africa's incomplete transition from apartheid to liberal democracy by noting that the ANC made a compromise with the corporate sector to act as the engine for ending economic inequalities that were inherited from the apartheid regime. Several disadvantages emerge from this policy orientation:

1. Given South Africa's history, a 'trickle down" approach cannot work because economic inequalities require an active state that drives policy.

2. The corporate sector is not elected. Its goal is to make a profit. By allowing it to impact economic and social policy and to address accountable to the corporate sector than to the people.

3. A cleavage develops within the society whereby groups that are connected to the corporate sector prosper while the majority of the population wallows in poverty. As a result, the political and economic elite becomes richer, accelerating apartheid economic inequalities.

4. According to Terreblanche, "free market" encourages the destruction of traditional values on which constituted the foundation of society. Traditional values discouraged individual competition at the expense of everyone's welfare. Free market profits the richest and strongest in the community at the expense of the poor.

5. When the National Party came to power in 1948, Terreblanche notes that it implemented "its policy of affirmative action, or social upliftment" by using "its fiscal powers to tax wealthier English-speakers and increase social spending of Afrikaners." Instead of using its political power to effect change by taxing the wealthiest sectors of the population, the ANC decided to collect less taxes from the rich. It also encourages the corporate sector to open offshore accounts that further drain necessary funds from the economy.[34]

Growth, Employment, and Redistribution (GEAR)

When the ANC adopted GEAR in 1996, it was falsely represented as a mere extension of the RDP. The argument was that GEAR would create jobs, which would lead to economic growth through redistribution. What was the rationale and thinking behind the adoption of GEAR? The first observation is that this strategy was adopted as a result of pressure from the business community, the South African Reserve Bank, the Development Bank, and key officials within the departments of finance, trade, and industry. Second, pressure was placed from the emergent black elite eager to consolidate its foothold in the economy. Other important sources of pressure included changes in the global economy and the "Washington Consensus," which includes the IMF, the World Bank, and the United States Treasury.[35]

GEAR was introduced to address structural weaknesses in the economy that inhibited growth by increasing investment, labor demand, job creation, and by carrying out a structural transformation. According to Renosi Mokate, GEAR focused particularly on increasing social spending, fiscal reform, and the relaxation of exchange rates.[36] The ANC adopted GEAR without consulting its two main alliance partners, namely the Congress of South African Trade Unions (COSATU) and the South African Communist Party (SACP). Unlike what happened during the RDP process, GEAR was not the object of any debate or discussions. GEAR was in fact based on a set of guidelines drafted by the South Africa Reserve Bank (SARB) and the World Bank. Its basic premise was that "macroeconomic policy should be entirely devoted to stability, and that growth and transformation will come from elsewhere."[37]

GEAR set off a privatization frenzy with state firms such as Telkom selling 30 percent of its stock to SBC Communications and Telekom Malaysia in 1997. GEAR was intended to lead to job creation through private investment. In reality it led to unemployment. Not only was its over-ambitious goal of creating 100,000 new jobs in 1997 and 84,000 in 1998 not achieved, the exact opposite happened: more than 100,000 jobs were *lost*. Since 1994, almost a million jobs have been lost in the manufacturing, agriculture, and mining sectors. According to William Gumede, between 1993 and 2000, the GNP rose at an average annual rate of 2.5 percent while unemployment fell each year (except in 1995) by 1.7 per cent. In 2003, soon after the Growth and Development Summit held in Johannesburg, President Thabo Mbeki outlined a public works program that would create a million job opportunities over the following five years. While unemployment increased between 1980 and the late 1990s, by 2004 job loss was coming to an end, much to the ANC's relief. The service sector was also affected by the economic slump that followed the terrorist attacks on New York and Washington D.C. on September 11, 2001. GDP was estimated at 3.1 percent while capital formation grew by almost 8 percent.[38] According to Mokate, "the problem with the South African economy is not only that investment has fallen as a proportion of GDP, but that the number of jobs created per rand of investment has also fallen dramatically."[39] GEAR did not have a clear vision of either an industrial policy or an effective job-creation strategy. Its goal was mainly to win international credibility, which depends "not only [on] . . . the substance of investor-friendly policy, but also on the degree of certainty that these policies can be maintained."[40]

GEAR also aimed at attracting foreign currency by reducing spending. As a strategy aimed at soliciting international capital, GEAR was not able to empower the people. GEAR exposed South Africa's economic vulnerability, as diverse actors became more involved in the economy.

According to GEAR, government and private initiatives were supposed to lead to the creation of roughly 400,000 jobs per year. Only 160,000 jobs were created, however. The government also lowered interest and inflation rates to attract foreign investment. As a result, it embarked on strict monetary and fiscal policies. It also restructured state assets through further privatization and liberalization. According to William Gumede, by 1995, the four top South African State corporations (Denel, Telkom, Eskom, and Transnet), which together were valued at R150 billion, made up 91 percent of state assets, 94 percent of its net income and represented 77 percent of public sector employment, were scheduled to be privatized. Between March 1997 and 2004, eighteen state-owned enterprises, ranging from radio stations to South African Airways, were privatized for a total value of R26.8 billion, of which 12 billion were used to service South Africa's foreign debt. The government's privatization strategy is four-pronged: full privatization of non-core sectors; partial privatization of core sectors; concessions; and public-private partnership. The government plans to privatize 30 percent of Eskom by the end of 2008. Privatization reduces the state's ability to redress economic inequality. Without adequate financial resources, how will the government address the needs of the African poor? GEAR also calls for reduced state intervention; yet South Africa needs a strong state to eliminate the social and economic inequalities inherited from apartheid.

Because the private sector is only interested in maximizing its profits, it cannot be expected to pursue policies that would benefit the majority. Privatization will result in the maintenance of the status quo. As a result, the only way that the ANC can reduce poverty is through job creation. Privatization also entrenches white privilege under the Bill of Rights. The white elite and international actors present redistribution as a threat to the country's security. Constrained by a liberal economy, the challenge for the ANC is to create an environment in which there is international competitiveness and poverty reduction at the same time. The industrial reforms advocated by GEAR focused on replacing labor with technology and on resource reallocation. As a result of liberalization, labor-intensive industries were forced to shed jobs. GEAR advocates argue that the strategy moderates wages, accelerates investment, and provides employment while increasing public service delivery.

Radical critics of GEAR point out that the implementation of this strategy has led to increased poverty for the African masses. At the same time, the white minority has criticized the ANC for adopting affirmative action programs, which favor formerly disadvantaged groups, thus exacerbating racial tensions. The government has failed to do "what the DP accuses it of doing-that is, redistributing the wealth and productive resources." As a result of this situation, the white minority has tightened its control over the economy.[41] Post-apartheid South Africa differs from the previous regime in that now there are Africans in the economic sector, albeit in small numbers. According to Ashwin Desai, the ANC does not go far enough to ensure a better life for all.

If a company fails to comply with affirmative action requirements, the ANC is not able to apply sanctions; it simply is able to refuse to give state contracts to such companies. This puts the ANC in an uncomfortable position because half-measures, as this response is, do not satisfy the African poor yet alienate the ANC from the white minority. By adopting half-measures, the ANC marginalizes labor and the radical elements within the party. Since it is now a party to the power-sharing arrangement, the labor movement in general, and COSATU in particular, has lost some of its legitimacy as an honest power-broker in the eyes of the people. Indeed, some of its members have been co-opted into prominent government positions while others, such as Cyril Ramaphosa—head of the National Empowerment Consortium (NEC)—have joined the business sector. Desai further argues that government policy allows a small fraction of the elite to benefit from the new economic dispensation while the others are left to fend for themselves. Those who fail to make it are accused of "hav[ing] an entitlement mentality."[42]

SERVICES:
EDUCATION, HEALTH, HOUSING, AND WATER

The new political dispensation had a positive psychological impact on the African majority in South Africa, who now view the government as being truly "theirs." African people also experience a sense of pride and walk with their heads held high because they have won the struggle for citizenship rights and political equality. In hospitals, white clerks no longer refer to African women as "Jane" or "Kaffermeid,"; they call them "Maa'm."[43] However, these symbolic positive changes, important as they may be, are unfortunately not matched with equivalent material benefits in terms of improved standards of living. A key bottleneck in this regard is the educational sector.

The ANC inherited an unequal educational system that was geared to maintaining the privileged position of the white minority throughout the apartheid period. According to Jeremy Seekings and Nicoli Nattrass, "education was important because it ensured that white South Africans were given huge advantages in the labour market, which in turn meant higher incomes and enhanced capacity to pay privately for health care and to save for retirement. Insofar as white South Africans were already privileged, differential education served to reproduce this privilege. Insofar as some white South Africans had few skills in the 1950s, the disadvantage of one generation was not passed onto the next."[44] By 1953, government spending on African education was tied to the tax that was collected from Africans. Progressively, government spending per child on African education fell from 14 percent of that spent on a white child in 1953 to 6 percent by 1968. Africans had to pay for their own education, which negatively affected the number of graduating students. By 1960, "the number of white students passing matric [high school final exam] was sixteen times the total of coloured, Indian and African students who passed. By 1970, the secondary school enrollment rate reached 90 percent among white children; among African children, it had risen to only 16 percent despite growing fourfold in the previous decade."[45] As the level of education determined access to jobs and high salaries, most (poorly educated) Africans were confined to unskilled jobs and low salaries. There were also marked differences in the quality of education received by various racial groups. For example, most African students were taught by untrained teachers. In 1994, 36 percent of teachers and 40 percent of women teachers did not have the officially required three-year post-matriculation qualification.[46] The drop-out rates among African children was much higher than other groups. The curriculum in these schools was skewed to favor the social sciences (particularly bible study) rather than the exact sciences.

The teacher/student ratio was also much higher in African schools than in others. In the Eastern Cape it was one to fifty one, which was higher than the national norm at one to thirty seven. The school attendance of African children was lower than that of white children. For example, twenty one percent of African children attended pre school compared to thirty eight percent of the white childen.[47] There were also marked gender inequities. Women stayed longer than men in nursing and teacher training institutions, traditionally perceived as female careers. The level of poverty and quality of the schools also differed according to provinces. In the Eastern Cape, 77 percent of the children lived in poverty compared with 20 percent in Gauteng.[48] The restructuring of higher education undertaken by the ANC government has resulted in the closing and merger of many African universities and technikons with institutions that catered to the white minority, which have remained essentially intact. As a result of this process, a new cleavage has developed between white minority institutions and African ones. As William Gumede notes, "Instead, a new apartheid is created: capable, effective white universities, and poor, low-quality black universities. . . . How can it possibly make sense to shut down or cut back on a university or technikon in rural Transkei or Zululand, for example, when entire communities depend on the jobs they offer? Would it not make more sense to refocus institutions to become relevant to the communities they serve by educating a new generation of technicians, entrepreneurs and farmers?"[49]

The ANC continues to face a number of daunting challenges in the educational sector, notably the challenge of improving education by reducing drop-out rates, making education affordable to a majority of the people, and reducing the number of African students repeating classes. The government's provision of milk and sandwiches to school-children has helped reduce hunger and absenteeism.[50] Fewer Africans than whites make it to the top grades. Most Africans who are older than twenty have no formal education. The poorest provinces have poor educational institutions. For example, the Northern Province has the worst education backlog at 36.9 percent. Mpumalanga has an education backlog of 29.4 percent while Kwa Zulu Natal is at 22.9 percent. Access to education also determines employment opportunities with women having less paying jobs than men.[51]

As part of the overhaul of apartheid education, the ANC introduced curriculum 2005 in 1997. The new curriculum replaced rote learning with critical thinking. It focuses on outcomes that will produce "competent future citizens."[52] Curriculum 2005, which required retraining 360,000 teachers, was difficult to implement due to lack of funds. These problems were compounded by teacher retrenchment mandated by the GEAR strategy. Rural areas and poor provinces benefitted the least from changes in education. A School Register of Needs Survey (SRNS) survey, first carried out in 1996 and again in 2000, gathers physical facility, location, and state of school buildings information on South Africa's schools. In 2000, the SRNS survey noted some improvements such as less overcrowding in class rooms, improved teacher/student ratio, as well the increase in the number of physically challenged students. The wealth of the province also determines whether a school facility is well maintained and the teachers were qualified. According to Linda Chisholm:

> There are major changes in the state of South Africa's schools, but there are also deep continuities with the past. It is no accident that the poorest schools are those that incorporate former homelands: the current state of schools in these provinces is closely intertwined with the twists and turns of a history more than two centuries old. But it is also linked to present dynamics and social forces unleashed by the democratization of South African society, as well as the nature of education itself, a system that is slow to change and so embedded in the tensions, stresses and strains of society itself that there is a continuous contradiction between its intentions and outcomes.[53]

Public spending on education makes up most of the budgets of the provinces. The introduction of user-fees has made access to education for poor families very difficult. Instead of integrating formerly all white schools, these schools have used fees to keep poor families out. Furthermore, in formerly all white schools, administrators prefer to assimilate students into minority culture. According to Linda Chilsholm, some schools "exercise a more benign form of assimilation but nonetheless expect children to adapt to the cultural norms and practices of the schools-established under apartheid. The assumption here is that if children want to come to these schools, they must abide by their rules and regulations. These rules and regulations often include hidden forms of discrimination against children who do not share the school's linguistic, class and/or cultural norms."[54] In Gauteng province, most African students are enrolled in formerly Indian and mixed schools while Indians and people of mixed descent have enrolled in white schools. A number of white students have moved to independent or private schools. In post-apartheid South Africa, class rather than race determines what school a child attends. At the university level students are turned away because they cannot afford to pay fees. So far, black students account for only 30 percent of both Masters and doctorate degrees. Poor families are forced to buy school uniforms and books, which, in most cases, they cannot afford. According to Hunter, May, and Padayachee, the new government's education policy is *not*:

> Pro-poor, since the share going to the poor and the ultra-poor is substantially smaller than their share of the population. In South Africa education should be free, but in practice schools require school fees and other costs (such as uniforms, school books and stationery, transport to school) are making it increasingly more difficult for the poorest to access basic education. A clear strategy from government is required in this regard, as it is increasingly evident from the delivery of other services, particularly health care, that user fees and transport costs are hampering the access to these services of those most in need.[55]

Health

While the apartheid state invested heavily in education for the white minority, it did not invest as much in health for this same minority. The (correct) assumption was that by heavily subsidizing white education, the state enabled the white minority to get high-paying jobs giving them automatic access to (expensive) private health care. The state did provide subsidized care for poor white families and for some Africans. "But the state never assumed the kind of role in health it did in education. The state's share of total health care expenditure does not seem to have risen above about 60 percent during the apartheid era."[56] According to Seekings and Nattrass, by 1972 two out of three doctors were employed in the private sector. Since most whites were well paid, they were able to afford private health care. The provision of private health care accelerated inter-racial health inequalities. As a result of unequal access to health services, whites live longer than Africans, a pattern that has continued in the new South Africa. As a result of apartheid, whites-only hospitals were empty while hospitals that catered for Africans were poorly staffed, poorly equipped, and overcrowded. Apartheid health services ensured full provision for the minority but only for some of the majority.[57] These services did not emphasize preventive medicine, such as immunization, nutrition, and sanitation. Instead, they focused on curative medicine. The ANC has introduced comprehensive immunization programs in which three out of four children between twelve and twenty-three months are immunized.[58] As a result of implementing the GEAR strategy, the ANC has privatized health care, thereby exacerbating inequalities. A survey of 294 clinics revealed that only 35 percent had a full-time primary care giver. It also revealed that "fewer than four in five hospitals in rural areas had electricity and 69 per cent had potable water."[59] "The first round of healthcare rationalizations were debilitating to the big hospitals and to their lower-income wards who, because of weaknesses elsewhere in the health system, relied on the facilities as basic suppliers of primary clinic healthcare."[60]

Most people who could not afford to pay for health services were forced to depend on over-the-counter medicine, which, in most cases, worsened their situation. According to a MERG report, "privatisation reinforces those distortions towards curative medicine, since it is primarily concerned with the paying patient (who by definition will be ill)."[61] In general, curative care is much more expensive than preventive medicine.

Privatization of health services also serves an economic need for the wealthy because it reinforces interest groups that influence government medical policy. These interest groups exert excessive influence over the government, which often implements policy in their favor.[62] Privatization also benefits the white minority since half of the doctors, 20 per cent of the nurses, and 80 to 90 per cent of dentists available in the country cater to the private sector.[63]

The South African health system is under stress because of the AIDS pandemic. Every day, more than 1,500 people in South Africa are infected with HIV, the virus that causes AIDS and some 950 die as a result of the disease. The AIDS pandemic also forces families to take care of ill relatives, while children are left in orphanages.[64] According to Patrick Bond, there are three structural reasons that explain why the local fight against AIDS has been lost.[65] First, is the insistence of bilateral institutions that South Africa's budget deficit be maintained at 3 per cent, resulting in lack of funds both for treatment and for taking care of AIDS orphans. Furthermore, combating the AIDS epidemic is not a top priority in the budget of the Mbeki administration; which focuses on very expensive arms deals, repaying apartheid era's debt (R30 billion about 4.5 billion US dollars) and eliminating corporate taxes. Second, pharmaceutical companies have played a key role in blocking access to needed medication. These companies use intellectual property to prevent South Africa from producing generic medicine that would be cheaper than their products. Finally, because of the large size of the South African labor force, companies had no incentive to invest in AIDS' care. Sick or dead workers can always be replaced, sometimes for far less wages. As a result, "corporate South Africa's preferred approach has been, in essence, mass murder by denial of medical benefits."[66] Some companies like Anglo American agree to provide benefits to AIDS/HIV workers on condition that they accept early retirement. Provision of benefits depends on one's medical insurance. In 2001, 14,000 of Anglo American's senior management personnel had access to medical benefits. As the corporation views it, the cost of saving lower-ranked workers far outweighed the benefits:"In a controversial move that could have wide ramifications for how companies in poor countries handle AIDS, mining giant Anglo American PLC has put on hold a feasible study to provide AIDS drugs to its African work force, according to people familiar with the situation. When it disclosed its plans for the study a year ago, Anglo garnered wide praise because it was one of the first major corporations to reveal measures aimed at treating AIDS cases among its rank-and-file African employees."[67]

Anglo American was not the only company that refused to insure rank-and-file African workers. Coca-Cola also refused to insure two-thirds of its 4,000 workers sufficiently to access antiretroviral medicine. Early death payout costs did not encourage companies to provide access to their HIV-positive workers, even when costs reached 25 percent of payroll by 2003. According to the *Financial Times*, "untreated, HIV typically takes four to five years to manifest itself as full-blown AIDS, and companies are reluctant to pay for a risk that they cannot see. . . . Persuading managers to part with fees [AIDS treatment programmes] today for costs that will hit company earnings years down the line has been a hard-sell."[68]

As a result of the rise of AIDS-related disability claims (18 percent in 2001 to 31 percent in 2002), some companies have started taking measures to cut these costs. To address the AIDS crisis, the ANC government finally approved the sale of generic AIDS/HIV medicine in South Africa after July 2003. In November 2003, it promised "that within a year, there will be at least one service point in every health district across the country and, within five years, one service point in every local municipality."[69] By February 2004, the finance ministry drastically cut the budget required for buying medicine. The government's comprehensive plan aims at providing over 250,000 people with ARVS. However, given the high number of AIDS victims, the program is not very effective. About "800 people die of AIDS every day; life expectancy is down from 63 in 1991 to under 50 today."[70] It should be noted that South Africa's AIDS figures have been controversial for quite some time now. In 2003, the World Bank warned in a report that South Africa faced economic collapse because of AIDS/HIV. According to Standard Bank's chief economist, Iraj Abedian, the report was inaccurate and unreliable. In Kwa-Zulu Natal, life expectancy dropped to as low as 43. What is more troubling is that the majority of AIDS victims are Africans. On December 10, 2006, the ANC government announced its five-year plan to fight AIDS/HIV by cutting the infection rate by half.[71] According to a report by Actuarial Society of South Africa and the Medical Research Council, in 2006 an estimated 950 people died each day of AIDS-related diseases, while a further 1,400 were infected with HIV. To combat the rise of the AIDS/HIV pandemic, the government is involved in private-public initiatives that include mining companies and trade unions. Three government departments that intervene in the AIDS/HIV pandemic are Health, Social Development, and Education. According to Tim Quinlan and Samantha Willan, the allocation of funds by the Department of Health for AIDS victims has increased over the years. For example, for the years 2001–2002 it was estimated at 265.84 million rands but by the 2006–2007 period, it had increased to 2008.37 million rands. These amounts included conditional grants and ARV funds. The funds allocated to AIDS and HIV victims by the Department of Social Development (including conditional grants) have also increased over the years: 2001–2002 (14.954 million rands); 2002–2003 (51.153 million rands); 2003–2004 (70.388 million rands); 2004–2005 (78.29 million rands); 2005–2006 (85.153 million rands); 2006–2007 (89.402 million rands).

HOUSING

Unequal access to housing is another major social problem that the ANC inherited from the apartheid state. Several factors account for inequality in access to housing. First, building new houses requires access to land. Unfortunately, because most of the land in post-apartheid South Africa continues to be owned almost exclusively by the white minority, this land is not available for sale. As a result, most of the new housing developments were built in African townships. Second, services were duplicated because diverse administrative departments catered to different racial groups. Third, no ministry specifically dealt with urbanization or housing. Fourth, the government lacked a clear, coherent, and uniform policy on housing, leading to inter-governmental duplications and inconsistencies. Finally, the respective roles of the government, the private sector, and the community in this area were not clearly defined. Mortgage loan lending patterns were biased in favor of white homeowners. Africans were either denied loans or granted loans at higher interest rates than whites. According to a survey carried out by the Institute of Race Relations, compared with other countries at the same level of development, South Africa had almost 40 percent of its assets consolidated in residential mortgage lending, but only 12 to 15 percent of these funds were allocated to township borrowers.[72] By 1993, the NP government did not have a clear policy on urbanization. As a result, the new government did not specifically tackle the land question, the root of the urbanization crisis. According to the National Housing Forum, this failure to address the land issue resulted from duplication of services and from the inability of the government to be accountable for housing. There were no clearly set goals, guidelines, or policy positions for government departments to follow.[73]

For the eight million people who are homeless, economic and social change is the real meaning of transformation. Most people within this group say that not much has changed since they have neither homes nor jobs. This concern prompted Winnie Mandela to suggest that "instead of the liberation movement taking over South Africa the opposite happened."[74] Renters charge exorbitant fees for sub-standard housing (shacks). Squatters continueto occupy land illegally.[75] The initial goal of the government was to build one million new housing units within five years (1994–1999). The ministry in charge of housing (headed by Joe Slovo) put in place a comprehensive low-income housing program, which provided for government subsidies and private-sector low-cost financing. To qualify for the subsidies, residents had to earn 3,500 Rands. Government subsidies ranged between R 5,000 and R 17,500. In 1995, the government aimed at giving 50,000 subisdies but only 6,800 were approved. In 1996, 30,000 subsidies were approved against 150,000 requests further slowing the delivery of houses. This failure resulted from the refusal of the banks to give loans. In 1996, 5,834,819 houses and flats were build, this number increased to 7,680,421 in 2001 then to 9,059,874 in 2004. By 1998, fewer than 200,000 low-cost homes were built because of inadequate financing. Only 14 perccent of the houses built between 1994 and 1999 were financed by banks. The projected number of houses and flats for 2008 is 11,289,299. Between 1996 and 2004 the number of slum housing had increased from 1,580,364 (1996) to 2,066,911 (2004). The number of slums is projected to increase to 2,363,764 in 2008. Since 1994, the ANC government has spent R10 billion on housing. The government subsidies were insufficient to build more and better houses. Furthermore, some developers signed bids but failed to follow with actual construction. The ANC's adoption of a market-friendly approach to housing also resulted in less than 2 percent of the budget been set aside for housing (instead of the promised 5 percent). It is interesting to note in this regard that the banks finaniced less construction of new houses after 1994 than they had done in the 1980s.[76] The long-term goal of the ANC was to have shelter for all by 2003. According to David Hemson and Michael O'Donovan, the one millionth house was delivered in 2003. However, the number of families living in shacks "doubled between 1994 and 2002 to reach 1.8 million."[77]

In order to shorten the distance between the residence of maids and their work site and to transform housing patterns, the ANC government built houses where maids and their employers lived in close proximity. This type of construction (with match box-like houses) has been criticized for reproducing apartheid-era housing patterns. Since 2000, the ANC has had the houses painted to make them more attractive as is the case in Alexandra. William Gumede notes that while the government complains about the high cost of construction, it has ignored offers from local entrepreneurs— as well as examples of mass housing projects from China and India-to build better houses cheaply. The ANC government has also been criticized for failing to build new houses in formerly all-white suburbs, which remain unchanged, save for a trickle of the African middle-class residents. This policy haas resulted in the building of 600,000 new housing units close to African townships. "Consequently, apartheid planning lives on into the next millennium in much of South Africa."[78]

ANC housing policy emphasizes ownership. It does not cater for renters, people who are too poor to rent, or the homeless. It does not take into account squatters who cannot afford houses. These squatters who take over some city parks and graveyards get services faster than people who are on the waiting list for housing. Once some squatters are given housing sites, they sell them for R 1,000 and return to camp in a park.[79] The most effective housing policy in terms of meeting the needs of every category of people would combine rental and ownership. Politically, the ANC is afraid that long waiting lists and spectacular evictions will make it lose its support base. On the other hand, the government is under pressure to show investors that it is capable of dealing with illegal land invasions.

Because of the privatization imposed by the international financial institutions the delivery of essential services by the ANC government-health, education, housing, water and electricity-depend on the ability of people to pay. Not all people can afford to pay for these services. In post-apartheid South Africa, the most pressing problem facing poor families is electricity and water disconnections. In 2001, when the electric service was disconnected for non payment by Eskom in Soweto, its former workers who were laid off offered to reconnect the service for free. The Soweto Electricity Crisis Committee (SECC) currently trains people to reconnect service. A Soweto resident who used SECC says that in an insecure job market, her greatest fear is when the electric company disconnects her service for non-payment; apartheid did not do that to her, "privatization did."[80] Some disconnections last for more than forty five days. According to Mike Muller (the ANC's chief water bureaucrat) 275,000 of all households "attributed interruptions to cut-offs for non-payment" in 2003.[81] As a result, an estimated 1.5 million households were affected by the cut-offs in 2003 alone. Since the mid-1990s, Eskom and other government agencies have raised electricity and water prices dramatically. Reduction of government subsidies also contributed to the high prices. Of the 13 million people who had telephone service for the first time, "ten million were disconnected."[82] During the 2003 State of the Nation address, Thabo Mbeki promised that the ANC government would provide more subsidies to address housing and service needs. In 2004, Thabo Mbeki committed R 14.2 million for the next three years to "basic housing."[83] Most projects need regular funds, which the government is unable to provide because of its priorities (such as spending more on arms) and the inability of some households to pay for services. Government figures show that 30 percent of services are not paid for.[84]

In spite of the apartheid legacy, the lives of ordinary people have changed. Some people who did not previously have access to water do now. Since 1994, 650,000 new water connections have been made, reaching 6.4 million people. Overt racism has been reduced.[85] Availability of water has a domino effect, such as better health, and less work for women. Since 1994, 1.3 million houses have been wired for telephones, and 5 million more people have access to primary health care. As the preceding discussion shows, most of these services have been disconnected due to non-payment.[86]

CHANGE IN THE CIVIL SERVICE, THE MILITARY AND THE POLICE

The Civil Service

The culture of compromise and reconciliation, which characterized the negotiation process, negatively affected the ability of the ANC to transform the economy. Power-sharing meant reaching consensus on all major decisions. Regarding the civil service, the ANC agreed to keep apartheid-era civil servants after the transition. Those who left were assured generous retirement packages. The ANC was unable to overhaul the civil service because of the sun-set clauses. This agreement imposed an excessive financial burden on the ANC. According to William Gumede, "the sunset clause that protected apartheid–era government employees from wholesale retrenchment was designed to prevent disgruntled state employees from destabilizing the transition from apartheid to democracy, but its cost would be exorbitant. One of the most-far reaching compromises agreed to by the ANC guaranteed the full benefits of all public servants who left voluntarily, imposing a huge financial burden on the incoming government of national unity (GNU)."[87]

The father of the sun-set clauses, Joe Slovo, reckoned that it would be some time before the ANC could have full control over the government. His argument was that the bureaucrats of the apartheid-era had to be retained for a smooth and efficient running of the government and the administration. The same reasoning led Nelson Mandela to maintain National Party advisers and economic policies, particularly in the areas of energy, mining, and finance. The emphasis on reconciliation affected affirmative action programs, which could have been used to address the needs of the African majority. Serious policies must be in place "if the initial vision is not to be seen to be too optimistic."[88]

With regard to the public service, the ANC aimed at creating a "people-centered" public service characterized by equality, service, and delivery.[89] Some changes were carried out in spite of the sun-set clauses. But there are still wage disparities based on gender. In the late 1990s, the number of jobs available for women increased but their pay declined "from 78 per cent of male wages in 1995 to just 66 per cent in 1999."[90] According to Patrick Bond, Thabo Mbeki's second cabinet is composed of 40 percent women (eight ministers and eight deputy ministers). The State remains the biggest employer for Africans: 73.10 per cent, Asians 3.70 per cent, Biracial 14.34 percent, and 8.87 per cent for whites.[91]

The Military

Throughout the history of South Africa, the military has been the backbone of the apartheid regime. Outside of the Bantustans, African participation was limited. The South African navy only began actively recruiting Africans in 1990, when its uniformed permanent force increased from 1 percent to 16 percent. The excuse given for not recruiting Africans prior to 1990 was that they did not want to go to sea.[92] The South African National Defence Force (SANDF) is the most sophisticated and powerful military force on the continent. While during the transition from the apartheid to the post-apartheid state, both the ANC and NP represented the military as undergoing major budgetary cuts, it was in fact increasing its spending on different units. In 1995, the budget of the intelligence services (which makes up one of the five units of the SANDF), was to be reduced by 20 percent. Instead there was a "66 percent increase from R427.5 million to R710 million-by far the biggest increase for any government department, and this at a time when health and teaching jobs were cut in the economy."[93] The increase resulted from the integration of 900 former MK, homeland, and PAC agents into the intelligence department. As a result, the "National Intelligence Agency (NIA) has almost three times as many staff as the old security apparatus at the height of Afrikaner paranoia."[94] According to The Suzman Foundation, if it cost that much to ensure a spirit of reconciliation it was worth it.[95] This incorporation ensured the new regime with crucial military support in its early years. Heribert Adam et al. argue, "In many ways, the so-called South African miracle is better dubbed the 'purchased revolution.' The members of the liberation armies who were not incorporated into official defence force received a small pension. Many other potential trouble-makers were bought off by being put on the payroll of the public service or the even more lucrative private sector."[96]

The integration of former MK (*Umkhonto we Sizwe*), PAC (Poqo), and homeland soldiers in the SADF introduced new tensions. One's race was still used as the criterion for promotion and posting and rank. For some MK soldiers who spent many years fighting for freedom, this was a step backwards. According to captain Moses Maisela, Mandela gave in too much to the Afrikaners because he left them to restructure the military as they pleased.[97] MK soldiers were systematically assigned to inferior ranks. MK officers who had the rank of colonel became sergeants under the pretense that they did not know how to use a computer.[98] Soldiers who resisted this treatment were fired for "failing to follow orders." The military was plagued by low morale as well as racial tensions, the massacre at the Tempe military base, where Africans killed fellow white-counterparts, illustrating this precisely. Some former fighters have left the army. The military is increasingly viewed as the white minority's insurance against excessive radicalism on the part of the ANC alliance. According to Len Roux and Henri Boshoff, between 1994 and 2003, Africans made up 38 percent (1994), 57 percent (1998), and 62 percent (2003) of the military personnel. Asians made up 1 per cent (1994), 1 percent (1998), and 1 per cent (2003), while biracial people made up 16 percent in 1994, 12 percent in 1998 and 12 percent in 2003. Whites made up 45 percent in 1994, 30 percent in 1998, and 25 percent in 2003. Women made up 20 percent of the military personnel in 1994, 19 percent in 1998 and 21 percent in 2003.

THE POLICE

In apartheid South Africa, the police were the "people's enemy."; they symbolized oppression in every sector of the society. All police actions were informed by inhumanity and violence toward blacks. The race of the commissioner/officer did not matter: the police only respected the white minority's human and civil rights. Blacks suffered more from fellow police officers because the latter were eager to please their masters. Changes have also occurred within the police force. In the new dispensation, the police force has cut down on inefficiency by solving problems locally. In the "new" South Africa, the police also encourage communities to work with it. For example, the police station in Soweto's Moroka district has reduced its staff and keeps a record of murder and crime statistics; in spite of this, most residents still view it negatively.[99] The South African police has changed from a police of oppression to a police of service, but its structure remains the same. Whites still occupy the best positions. While many changes have been carried out at the lower ranks, no change has occurred at the top level of the officer corps, which still remains "lily-white" and where master/servant relations remain intact.[100] By late 2007, blacks occupied more top positions.

JUSTICE

In *Unfinished Business: South Africa, Apartheid and Truth*, Terry Bell and Dumisa Buhle Ntsebeza (2003) provide a unique insight into apartheid and the politics revolving around the Truth and Reconciliation Commission (TRC). It is not often that the victims of apartheid are given such a prominent voice. The book's major contribution is that it is a personal account of a lawyer who was directly involved in the TRC process and an illustration of the human cost of apartheid. By providing a bird's eye view on the "justice" system in South Africa, Bell and Ntsebeza reveal how the past continues to inform the present. Race continues to determine who recieves "justice" and how. Theoretically, South Africa's judicial system promises to protect every citizen's rights; in reality, however, Africans, especially those in rural areas, continue to be treated inhumanely. ANC Justice Minister Dullah Omar was criticized for allowing apartheid judicial officials to continue to wield enormous power within the justice system. He was also under fire for "allowing enormous problems in the criminal justice system to develop; for his uncreative approach to formalizing community-based justice institutions; for failing to reform court procedures in cases of sexual offenses against women; and for not transforming the legal aid system, hence effectively ignoring constitutional guarantees of access to courts, which most South Africans are denied due to lack of affordability."[101] Farm workers are still abused by their employers. Most of them are afraid to denounce their bosses to the authorities. Others have reported the abuse, but the perpetrators have not been punished. Farmers beat up workers for no apparent reason. A worker says, "I was attacked by the farmer's dog when I came to work here. When I complained he would just throw the (dogs) on me."[102] Without an effective system to enforce the laws, farmers ignore most new laws, such as those that require them to pay minimum wages, provide schooling facilities, and treat their workers in a humane manner. Cases of abuse, such as farm owners beating their workers or refusing to pay them, are common. In Calitzdorp, residents also say that nothing has changed as far as their daily lives are concerned. Farm owners continue to evict workers and to intimidate them if they vote for an opposing political party. Apartheid justice, which continues to inform post-apartheid South African law, makes a mockery of the principle of the strict equality of all racial groups under the law.[103]

A white farmer who beat an African worker, dragged him in his pickup truck and then hanged him grinned at the light sentence that he got (R3,000). Women also suffer from domestic abuse as well as labor exploitation.[104] The ANC has embarked on a complete overhaul of the judiciary by introducing constitutional courts in townships. An example of this is the Khayelitsha magistrate's court, which is the second largest in South Africa after the Johannesburg one. The ANC is also attempting to transform the judiciary by making it more representative of the population.[105] In addition the ANC has created specialized courts that operate on Saturdays to address case backlogs.

Land

Land reform has been very difficult to carry out because of intimidation and obstructionist actions on the part of both the farmers and the military. Farmers have refused to release large, uncontaminated tracts of land that was used during apartheid, but that now remains unused. Most large white farms have not been subdivided or returned to their rightful African owners. As Winnie Madikizela-Mandela noted, "What puzzles me most is to see that our government constantly turns a blind eye to the issue of land, the issue which is central to the gross inequalities in all spheres of life."[106] The standing of small farmers in the national economy is made even more precarious by the inavailability of governmental agricultural subsidies. Henry Berinstein observes that because of its urban-based resistance in the 1970s and 1980s, the ANC did not have any agenda for land reform. This marginalization of the land issue results from the influence and pressure exerted by the business community and the World Bank, which are both resolutely against land reform.[107]

Soon after the 1994 general elections, the government announced its land reform program based on three stages: redistribution, tenure reform and restitution.[108] Between 1995 and 1997 the Deaprtment of Land Affairs' land reform programme (LRPP) was in charge of land distribution. The LRPP agenda was to address rural poverty and gender inequality. It ran into problems because of trying to cast its policies in terms of the market oriented policies of the World Bank, which privileged profit over land restitution.[109] Most established landowners were opposed to changes that would have placed them at a disadvantage. Finally, the slow pace of releasing land to the claimants (which placed women at a disadvantage) compounded the problems.

Financial constraints constituted a major obstacle to land reform. The land reform policy was based on the advise of the Development Bank of South Africa (DBSA), the World Bank, and other agencies. The DBSA proposed that 30 percent of white-owned land be redistributed within five years (1994–1999). Most organizations sympathetic to the rural poor (such as the National Land Committee) were overwhelmed by the number of experts and range of expertise involved in advising the ANC. The connection between land and justice is laid out in the Constitution's Restitution of Land Rights Act no. 22 of 1994, which created a Restitution Commission and Land claims Court as its implementing bodies. These bodies are limited to dispossession as a result of the 1913 Land Act. The legal process through which land claimants have to go through further complicates the experience. Added to this problem is the presence of several claimants to the same piece of land. In 2003, the ANC implemented the communal land Bill to encourage small-scale and co-operative agricultural production in order to improve food production. The Bill ensures land ownership to families (as well as formally marginalized groups in rural areas). The ANC promised to respect local and regional indigenous political systems and institutions.

Some authors argue that land restitution would do very little to transform the living conditions that most people face.[110] For landless people land ownership would provide them with a choice, which is a hallmark of democracy. Land restitution would have great symbolic significance by demonstrating that Africans finally own a piece of the land of their birth, which they were denied by both colonialism and apartheid.[111]

In spite of the attempts of the ANC to address the land issue, problems with delivery of subsidies occurred because of communication breakdown, information gaps, and lack of coordination between the various departments. Farm workers (estimated at six million) are demanding new government laws and regulations that would allow them to own the land on which they work. So far, the ANC government has not addressed these concerns. Instead it has favored large farmers and the business community over the interests and rights of farm workers. The land reform policy of the ANC government continues to be influenced by the interests and priorities of white farmers, bilateral foreign donors, and the international financial institutions. This policy has come under severe criticism, not only for ignoring the interests and needs of farm workers, but also for its "land purchase and sub-division" plan, which has failed to create jobs in the rural sector.[112]

Most landless people who are tired of the slow pace of governmental reform are taking the law into their own hands. Farm killings have resulted in the creation of vigilante groups of law and order personnel made up of white farmers designed to curb the attacks. Members of the Landless Movement continue to clash with police in various demonstrations, resulting in many arrests. Police treatment of peasant prisoners contrasts sharply with that of white farmers:

> While our Constitution is celebrated across the world for the rights it promises, the reality for 26-million poor and landless people is that the rural police, magistrates, prosecutors and even private attorneys conspire to protect the interests of the 60,000 white farmers who benefited from apartheid, while in both rural and urban areas the police and intelligence agencies spend more time trying to lock up landless people struggling for change than they do upholding our rights to protest against policies that keep us poor and landless. That's why white farmers are constantly released on small bails and charges like 'culpable homicide' for killing our people, while we face charges like 'attempted murder' just for attending to the complaints of poor and landless farm workers.[113]

According to Patrick Bond, two women staff members of the Landless People's Movement were tortured in April 2004 (Election Day). The Restitution of Land Rights Act of 1994 was supposed to have resolved all restitution cases by 2005. By February 2005, Land Affairs Minister Thoko Didiza admitted that "it will take an additional two years to redeem the injustices of land seized under apartheid."[114] The deadline has now been extended to March 2008. An extra budgetary allocation has allowed the government to quicken the pace of addressing land claims. Of the 80,000 land claims filed, 75 percent were settled by 2005. Since land reform as carried out by the ANC is based on market values, most land is now out of reach of the government because its value has increased tremendously since 1994. Meanwhile anti-privatization and landless peoples' rallies continue throughout the country.

Beneficiaries:
Race, Class, and Gender

South Africa has the most skewed income distribution in the world. The poorest 50 percent of its people receive about 15 percent of total annual household income, and the poorest 19 percent receive only 1.4 percent of such income. The top 10 percent of households, on the other hand, control 42 percent of income. While the poorest 20 percent earn under R 5,700 a year, the richest 20 percent earn more than R76,000 a year.[115] Only 1 percent of whites are poor compared with nearly 61 percent of Africans who live in what could be "the size of a white family tool shed."[116] As a result, "the income share accruing to the poorest 40% of African earners fell by a disquieting 48%, while the share accruing to the richest 10% rose by 43%."[117] Such socioeconomic disparities will not be reduced by appealing to the good heart of the wealthy to share. Nor will transformation occur through the implementation of affirmative action, which is viewed as a race-based program in South Africa.

The ANC has tried to invole blacks in business through black empowerment ventures by giving ten points to black-owned businesses that compete for government contracts. This new elite is mainly black and male. Critics question the extent to which these companies are "black" since they are still controlled by the white minority. Furthermore, these companies co-opt blacks who are already wealthy, so much so that by 1996 most people believed that they were a sham.[118] By 2002, most black empowerment companies were in financial trouble. Smaller companies could not raise enough capital to sustain them and most of their managers were inexperienced. Even companies that were financially secure could not compete in a free market. Such companies include Union Alliance Media (owned by a consortium of Trade Unions and Community Trust), Mathamo, and African Media Entertainment. The political elite is the greatest beneficiary of black empowerment schemes. In 2003, the ANC published its guidelines on black empowerment, which defines it as an inclusive rather than exclusive process designed to address socio-economic disparities. Such empowerment should focus on skills and enterprise development, not just redistribution of existing wealth.

Class

Business contributed heavily to the political campaign of the ANC. For example, Nelson Mandela asked twenty CEOs of large corporations operating in South Africa to contribute a million Rand each for the 1994 elections and nineteen companies eventually did. Nelson Mandela also consulted Harry Oppenheimer about his cabinet appointments. Oppenheimer, who was Botha's best spokesman abroad during the latter's reforms, also entertained Nelson Mandela at his private estate. When he separated from Winnie, Mandela lived in self-made tycoon Douw Steyn's residence. His daughter Zinzi's honeymoon was partly financed by casino and resort king Sol Kerzner. As we have seen in the preceding chapters, apartheid was based on class, gender, and racial inequalities. As a result, apartheid enclaves of economic privilege continue, particularly in residential areas. For example, Sandton (an upscale Johannesburg suburb) remains unchallenged as the most expensive residential area in South Africa where "5% of the population control 88% of the nation's wealth."[119] Between the hopes of the African majority for meaningful and drastic social and economic reforms and the fears of the (national and international) business community, the ANC must maintain a delicate balancing act. The corporate sector continues to pressure the ANC to discipline those who are frustrated by the lack of tangible change in their lives.

Intra-African class inequalities, which acccelerated during the last years of the apartheid regime have persisted since 1994. During the last decade of apartheid (late 1980s), "the richest 20% of black households experienced a 40 per cent growth in income, while the purchasing power of the poorest 40 per cent of black households declined by about 40 per cent."[120] The top 20 percent (upper bourgeoisie) is the class that is cashing on the democratic windfall resulting from the new political dispensation. To its credit, the ANC elite has so far refrained from engaging in conspicous and wide-scale self-enrichment venture on a wide-scale as the previous regime did.

The black middle-class has also benefited enormously from black empowerment projects. These black empowerment companies have not made any progress in terms of controlling manufacturing or operations. They aim at co-opting a minute African elite into the white corporate world, which is controlled by five companies that dominate the Johannesburg Stock Exchange. According to Lawrence Mavudla, president of Micro Business Chamber (representing informal traders), black empowerment only serves "a small group of about 300 black people . . . taking people who are already rich and making them richer."[121] Most South African and international corporations use blacks to get to the ANC establishiment, prompting one executive to say, "I am the black ham in the white sandwich."[122] The white minority controls most of the black empowerment companies with a few black faces for window dressing. "So at the end of the day, it is a handful of black people that are being enriched."[123]

According to critics of black empowerment projects, they give the false impression that an economically viable middle-class is being created, which is not the case. Instead, these projects are used to sell de-racialized capitalism to silence militants.[124] In 2004 Essop Pahad (a Minister in the ANC Presidency) admitted that large conglomerates were the major obstacle to creating a viable black middle-class. Direct ownership of companies in the Johannesburg Stock Exchange is extremly low (less than a quarter have black directors). William Pomeroy argues that black empowerment projects play a negative role in the economy because they entrench blacks into the white-controlled economy instead of building a self-sustaining black capitalist class. A more effective way of transforming the economy would focus on democratizing South African corporations. These corporations also divert the ANC from implementing its goals as stated in the *Freedom Charter*.[125]

Ironically, the ANC and other progressive organizations have been silent on "racism in South Africa as if no one wants to draw attention to the fact that "*baas is still wearing the nicest*" (italics in the original).[126] Within the ANC alliance, both COSATU and the SACP leadership have managed to join the elite while representing themselves as the champions of the poor. This miracle will continue as long as the tripartite alliance "keeps the lid on the disillusioned poor in the name of unity of the progressive forces."[127]

Because the African middle-class is so keen to preserve its material and financial interests, it has almost exonerated the white bourgeoisie from any sense of guilt over apartheid. The political stability created by the African elite since it came to power has benefited the white elite. Now both mingle in exotic parties and celebrity galas. A former ANC supporter was shocked by the speed with which the ANC leadership "adopted bourgeoisie revelry he had hated among white people."[128] Major local and international business coporations have replaced old powers such as Britain as they use South Africa as a base and export platform, in addition to buying land and opening super markets—these corporations are leading the way in the exploration and exploitation of Africa's minerals. Africans on the continent view South Africa with suspicion because they see it as an instrument of minority interests and international capital designed to rob them dry. To some of these Africans, South Africa is an imperial power that does not respect the lives of Africans from the rest of the continent.[129]

GENDER

The apartheid migrant workers' system contributed to the oppression of women on three levels: race, class, and gender. As this system persists in post-apartheid South Africa, so does the triple oppression of women. Recently, more women have moved to urban areas. Women in rural areas do not have access to health insurance or free education for their children. According to Patrick Bond, "given the durability of migrant labour and the overall failure of rural development, it is fair to condemn the post-apartheid government for deepening the inherited, structured super exploitation."[130] Some changes in the status of women have been introduced. The new government set up the National Gender Machinery to address women's issues. The NGM aims at institutionalizing gender equality in all government sectors. It comprised of:

- The Office of the Status of Women (OSW) and provincial offices of the status of women;

- The Joint Monitoring Committee on the Improvement of the Quality of Life and the Status of women (JMC);

- Women's Empowerment Unit;

- Gender focal points (such as gender desks in each national civil service department, which are tasked with gender mainstreaming and monitoring legislation) on national and provincial level; and

- The autonomous Commission on Gender Equality (CGE)[131]

Ironically, the greatest beneficiaries of the new dispensation are white middle-class women, followed by black middle-class women. In general, women have also benefited from the new government's social welfare provisions. In rural areas, women are the driving force behind community development efforts. They organize water projects, small business ventures, and support groups. They also approach government and non-governmental organizations for financial support. In spite of these efforts, poverty among women-headed homes is at 60 percent, higher than that of male-headed homes (31 percent).[132] The reason for this gender gap include women's low education levels and high unemployment rates. In cities, African women are mostly employed in unskilled jobs where wage differentials are high as a result of past discrimination. The majority of the women in white-collar jobs are white; this is the case for 50 percent of management jobs and 56 percent of occupational categories.[133] Most women continue to be affected by wage discrimination. In the late 1990s, women's share in wages declined "from 78 percent of male wages in 1995 to just 66 percent in 1999."[134] There are still separate medical schemes for women and men.

In post-apartheid South Africa, women's lives have also changed. Domestic workers cannot be fired without reason, otherwise the employer has to pay two years' salary. This has significantly improved working conditions for women by opening new opportunities for them. The Termination of Pregnancy Act of 1996 gives women access to abortion if they choose to. Women are also protected by the Domestic Violence Act of 1998. This Act protects all people in relationships regardless of sexual orientation or gender. The Maintenance Act of 1998 has improved the position of mothers who depend on financial support from former partners significantly.[135]

Fully aware of the fact that 52 percent of voters in South Africa are women, the ANC—which is the only party with quotas for women—has pursued an energetic policy promoting women in the political arena. Thus, the ANC has made a special effort to appoint women in high government positions. After the 1994 elections, South Africa ranked seventh in the world in terms of women representation, with one hundred and seventeen women out of four hundred members of Parliament (MPs), and sixteen women out of ninety senators. Women also chaired sixty committees. The ANC had one woman in every three positions on its national lists, and three in every ten candidates on its regional lists.[136] During the 1994 general elections, 27.7 percent of MPs elected were women. By 1999, that percentage had increased to 29.5 percent. This is revolutionary in a country where women were treated as second class citizens. In the same year, there were eighteen women in the top fifty positions (compared to ten in 1994). In 2004, women made up 40 percent of the ANC cabinet, including the post of foreign Minister.[137]

Conclusion

South Africa's transition from apartheid to liberal democracy is not exceptional; indeed, it is similar to earlier processes of decolonization experienced by many African countries formerly under British, French, Belgium, or Portuguese rule from the 1960s to the 1980s. In their eagerness to accommodate the interests of national and international capital and of the business community and to attract foreign investment, the moderates within the ANC, such as Nelson Mandela, Walter Sisulu, and Thabo Mbeki, bent over backwards and accepted major compromises. For example, IMF and World Bank conditionalities were accepted and the economy and security apparatus was left intact and firmly in the hands of the white minority. In spite of this "historic compromise," the business community has failed to show any confidence in or support of the ANC government. The Marshall Plan type of massive economic and financial assistance to which the ANC leadership felt entitled as a compensation for apartheid also failed to materialize. In spite of these major economic constraints, including the need to liberalize and privatize the economy, the ANC government has provided water, basic health care, and housing (notably for some homeless people). It has also provided access to schools and helped reduce drop-out rates by providing milk and sandwiches for needy children.

The ANC has also made remarkable progress in terms of changing women's lives. It has crossed the public/private divide by giving women prominent political positions. Liberal democracy has led to the restoration of the basic human, civil, and political rights of African people, who are now full-fledged citizens of the South African political community. Restoration of rights has had a tremendous psychological impact on the African masses, who now truly consider the government to be theirs. As a result of its historic compromise, the ANC government is now allowed to operate in a friendly international political and economic environment. What are the economic policy options now available to the ANC government? For one thing, it can slowly open its economy while protecting its education and housing. In particular, the ANC government should invest in education in order to enable the African majority to break out of the poverty cycle. Unfortunately, the government is actually cutting spending on this strategic sector.

FURTHER READINGS

Bond, Patrick. *Talk Left Walk Right: South Africa's Frustrated Global Reforms.* (Scottsville, South Africa: University of Kwazulu-Natal Press, 2004)

Marais, Hein. *South Africa: Limits to Change-The Political Economy of Transition.* Cape Town: University of Cape Town, 2001.

Ntsebeza, Lungisile. *Democracy Compromised: Chiefs and the Politics of Land in South Africa.* Amsterdam: Brill Academic Publishers, 2005.

Seekings, Jeremy and Nattrass, Nicoli. *Class, Race and Inequality in South Africa.* New Haven: Yale University Press, 2005.

Conclusion

SOUTH AFRICA

Toward Democracy and Development

> Seek first the kingdom of money and the ownership of the soil and many things will be added unto you.
> —DDT Jabavu, cited in Peter Walshe, *The Rise of African Nationalism*

> The transition was business saying: 'we will keep everything and you [the ANC] will rule in name. . . . You can have political power, you can have the façade of governing, but the real governance will take place somewhere else' . . . new governments are, in effect, given the keys to the house but not the combination to the safe.
> —Yasmin Sooka, South African human rights activist, quoted in Klein, 2007: 203–4

THE BASIC ARGUMENT OF THIS STUDY IS THAT LIBERAL DEMOCRACY IN South Africa accommodated and left unresolved the major contradictions inherent in South African capitalism and the apartheid economy, as well as in the ANC's multiracial nationalist ideology and discourse. In particular, the delivery of equal human, civil, and political rights in the new democratic dispensation was premised on the acceptance of essentially unequal economic and social relations among different social classes, racial, and gender groups. In addition, the NP was forced to negotiate with the ANC by a combinattion of domestic and international political and economic factors, foremost amongst which were divergent political and economic views with Afrikaner nationalism, sustained international pressure for change from the United States and the former Soviet Union, and structural changes in the global economy. The fall of the Soviet Union and the demise of socialism marginalized the Marxist elements within the ANC and facilitated the transition to the liberal democracy capitalist model of political and economic development. By instantly providing the

African majority with basic human, civil, and political rights (including the right to vote), this model offered an acceptable basis and framework for peaceful interracial coexistence. Furthermore, the South African middle-class (or bourgeoisie), irrespective of race and ethnicity, is threatened by a variety of social and economic forces and demands emanating from above and below. Pressures from the national and international business community severely limited the African middle class's room for maneuver and forced it to make major compromises at the expense of the economic and social interests, priorities, and needs of the African majority. The latter's constant demands for improved socioeconomic conditions forced the ANC government to partially satisfy their requests. These basic economic and social realities will continue to inform the ANC's attempts at transformation for the foreseeable future. By and large, the validity of the argument is confirmed by my findings.

I conducted a comparative study of African and Afrikaner nationalisms as represented by the African National Congress and the National Party using a long-term historical perspective. This work focused on all the actors involved by analyzing how each was influenced by British imperialism in different ways. This study also examined the status and role of marginalized people, particularly the African urban and rural poor, through the lens of race, class, and gender. This method enabled us to see how different socioeconomic forces, such as liberalism, capitalism, education, and religion, influenced African nationalism and liberal democracy in post-apartheid South Africa. We observed that far from being static and constant, nationalism changed according to various influences, the issues at stake, and the changing power relations within and between various actors and social groups. Our analytical framework also allowed us to examine power relations within Afrikaner and African nationalisms, between these two ideologies, and between Afrikaner and African nationalisms and other racially or ethnically based nationalisms in South Africa. Finally, our method of analysis revealed some of the major contradictions inherent in nationalism, particularly the gap between representation and reality.

Several factors shaped both the African and Afrikaner imagined communities between 1867 and 1948. First, the way the two communities were known and represented shaped their boundaries. These factors, in turn, influenced missionary education, which further shaped the thinking of the African middle-class. These representations placed the white race at the top of the pyramid, as the ideal against which all other racial groups were measured. Such representations also informed the Afrikaner imagined community, which viewed itself as part of an eminently civilized and superior nation.

Second, African and Afrikaner communities were imagined within racial parameters. Afrikaners imagined themselves as white and, therefore, as inherently superior. Third, these imagined communities were informed by class as well as gender. When confronted by outsiders, all classes within Afrikaner or African nationalism would unite. Afrikaner nationalism used the suffering of Afrikaner women to mobilize the Afrikaner "volk" against British imperialism. The representation of these imagined communities was also shaped by power relations. Representations included women without giving them equal rights with men both at home and at work. While they unanimously rallied behind the ANC, African women's representation was confined to their own organization within the party, namely the ANC's Women's League. Class also determined power relations among women: middle-class women were not oppressed to the same extent and in the same way as poor women were.

Fourth, religion played a significant role in shaping the development of the Afrikaner and African communities. For example, the Afrikaner imagined community viewed itself as a "chosen people" with a "divine calling," a perspective often invoked by the nationalists for mobilization purposes. Among Africans, religion defined boundaries between the *Kholwa* (the Christian, Westernized Africans) and the "red people" (those who remained faithful to indigenous African beliefs and institutions). In both the Afrikaner and African societies, the middle-class was the leader of its respective imagined community, defining its boundaries and deciding on its trajectory.

Finally, both imagined communities were strengthened by better communication, which integrated diverse communities under a central authority. Journals and newspapers added to these imaginings. While Afrikaners imagined their community as separate and distinct from that of the British, the African elite imagined its community to be similar to British culture, tradition, and religion.

Apartheid has had a profound impact on the Afrikaner and African imagined communities, as well as on the type of nationalism developed by these communities. The National Party viewed itself as the savior of both the Afrikaners and the Africans, as the guardian of Western civilization and the protectors and trustees of the latter. To the NP's ideology of racial exclusiveness, the ANC presented its ideology of inclusive, nonracial nationalism that rejected the notion that South Africa was a white man's country. Assuming that South Africa belongs to all those who are born and live in it, the ANC envisage the advent of a multiracial society. Afrikaner nationalism was influenced by power relations within the NP. This nationalism represented the ANC as a radical (and, at times, even terrorist) organization bent on evicting the white minority from its privileged position in the economy. Afrikaner nationalism generally represented the ANC and all other anti-apartheid parties, movements, and organizations as irrational and violent entities without any legitimate political or economic claims.

The ANC genuinely believed that it was morally superior to the NP. In its view, nonviolent protest and action would force the National Party to eventually stop oppressing Africans and to treat them in a humane manner. In its early stages (1912 through 1962), the ANC appealed to the NP's sense of morality in the hope that the latter would abandon apartheid. While the ANC abandoned nonviolence when forced into exile, it still believed in its moral superiority as the voice of the people. From then on, the ANC resorted to violence and used armed struggle to fight the apartheid regime. For the ANC, democracy meant majority rule in a pluralistic society. The NP believed it was the legitimate voice of all whites and the symbol of Western civilization in South Africa. Accordingly, it was the only organization that would save both from destruction.

The Pan Africanist Congress (PAC), which split from the ANC in 1959, relied on the tradition of struggle to represent Africans as the indigenous and rightful owners of South Africa. Whites could become Africans only if they abandoned any claim to white supremacy. For PAC members, the land in South Africa traditionally belonged to Africans. Transformation could only take place once this issue had been addressed.

Democracy in South Africa meant African rule based on African history, culture, and tradition.

The Black Consciousness Movement (BCM or BC), which emerged in 1968 to fill the political vacuum left by the banning of the ANC and the PAC, relied on mental decolonization and psychological independence to mobilize its followers. The PAC represented all non-white individuals as black and called on black people to be proud of their culture and language in order to be able to confront white people on an equal footing. Like the PAC, BC linked the struggle for black liberation in South Africa to the struggle for the freedom and independence of all Africans, wherever they might be. To BC members and its supporters, democracy meant the end of oppression and exploitation and the political and economic empowerment of all Africans in South Africa, in other African countries, and in the diaspora.

Both the ANC and the NP were shaped by power relations informed by race, class, and gender. The NP represented the interests of the Afrikaner people, although it was led by a small politico-bureaucratic, intellectual elite with its own secret think-tank, the Broederbond. This elite mobilized the Afrikaner people through the agencies of language, culture, religion, and race. Unlike the ANC, which was taken by British cultural symbols, the NP understood that it needed a multi-pronged attack to fight against British imperialism, including the total separation between Africans and Afrikaners. Gender relations also informed power relations within the NP and the ANC. For example, Afrikaner women were actively involved in political mobilization, yet were marginalized within the party bureaucracy. The ANC National Executive was exclusively controlled by men, with women confined to women's issues within their specialized organizations. Both the NP and the ANC experienced tensions and conflict within their respective political elites: between conservatives and liberals (NP) and between militants and moderates (ANC).

Artists were also involved in representing African and Afrikaner nationalism. Through their works, we are introduced to the tensions and fears that shaped life under apartheid. These representations are crucial in understanding both nationalisms because they depict the unofficial version of nationalism and its critics. "Fools" reflects the political vacuum of the 1960s. It is a criticism of an African community that has fallen into despair because of apartheid's repressive measures. It is also a scathing attack on apartheid and its supporters. It blames both Africans and Afrikaners for the continuation of the racist regime: the former because they accepted domination and the latter for continuing to rule over Africans.

The plight of African women, homelessness, fear and apartheid's ability to corrupt both the soul and society are exposed in *My Friend the Outcast*. It also demonstrates the powerlessness of African women and men in the face of the apartheid machine. Tension between the races, classes, and genders also marked life under apartheid. In "Fools," the reader is forced to question the dangers of making the suffering of the Africans into a virtue. Artists are crucial in showing how nationalism represents itself as holistic. For example, in *Triomf*, Afrikaner nationalism represents itself as the champion of the poor; yet, it has, in reality, left them out of development. Nationalism is also based on deceit. Nothing is really as it appears to be: upon close scrutiny, the immense suffering of apartheid's victims is revealed. These artists also demonstrate how nationalism represents poor people. As exemplified by such literary works as *The Age of Iron, Triomf,* and *The Smell of Apples*, the poor are either ignored, silenced, or misrepresented by nationalism.

Various factors led to the beginning of apartheid's downfall in the mid-1970s. The end of colonial rule in Mozambique (June 25, 1975) and Angola (November, 11 1975) inspired Africans in South Africa to launch the June 16, 1976 Soweto revolt. The rebellion also resulted from poor education, housing, unemployment, and the oppression associated with apartheid. In addition to the Soweto revolt, economic changes further weakened the regime. International sanctions forced the regime into an economic slump, which finally convinced the NP to negotiate with the liberation movements. School boycotts, strikes, and labor protests worsened the apartheid economy even further. Businesses lost profits, as workers stayed away from work or destroyed property during the demonstrations and investors were scared away. Both parties decided to negotiate a new dispensation as pressure mounted from the Soviet Union and the United States. The major goal of the negotiations was to replace apartheid with a regime that allowed the white minority to control the economy while giving the ANC political power. The crisis of accumulation within capitalism had to be resolved through political change.

Given the constraints it faces, the ANC credits itself for having done remarkably well in a relatively short time. It has followed its ideals as set out in the *Freedom Charter*. According to the critics of the ANC, the ANC achieved its main aims, namely a typical neo-colonial settlement (such as occurred in many African countries) that left it without control over the South African economy. Furthermore, these critics argue, in spite of its rhetoric, the ANC did not control the negotiating process. The ANC's agenda was set by the NP and its Western allies, who took advantage of the ANC's keen desire for political power. Some of its critics point out that the ANC betrayed the *Freedom Charter*. The national question was never addressed. Thus, negotiations were essentially about exerting political power. As a result, the African elite accepted control over the state while the economy and security apparatus remained exclusively under the control of the white minority. As Yasmin Sooka, a prominent South African human rights activist, cogently remarked, "the transition was business saying: 'we will keep everything and you [the ANC] will rule in name . . . You can have political power, you can have the façade of governing, but the real governance will take place somewhere else' . . . new governments are, in effect, given the keys to the house but not the combination to the safe."[1] While the world media's attention was exclusively focused on the political negotiations taking place, much lower-profile, but equally crucial, economic negotiations between the ANC (led by Thabo Mbeki) and the NP were taking place behind closed doors. Lacking highly skilled economists with the requisite technical expertise and negotiating skills, the ANC delegation was bamboozled into accepting the outrageous terms imposed on the new ANC government by the NP, including wholesale adoption of the free-market orthodoxy (a clear betrayal of the principles enshrined in the Freedom Charter and the RDP), control of the economy by economists from the IMF, the World Bank, the WTO, and the NP, removal of the Reserve Bank of South Africa—which is run as an autonomous entity—from government control, and the responsibility for an apartheid debt costing the new government

30 billion rand annually (about $4.5 billion in U.S. currency) in servicing.[2] All parties to the negotiations wanted to protect their interests. The various African liberation movements had some common features. For example, they all wanted the transformation of apartheid into democracy, yet they differed on the means of the transformation and on the issues. To the PAC and some members of the ANC, liberation could not be complete without African control of the land and the economy. For the moderates within the ANC (who included Nelson Mandela and Thabo Mbeki), the organization had to present a "moderate" face on the economy so as not to scare investors away. The ANC preferred the negotiations to take place in South Africa, while the PAC wanted them on foreign territory. These liberation movements wanted some civil and political rights for Africans, while the NP's goal was to protect white minority rights. As Mandela bluntly put it, "What the National Party was trying to do was to maintain white supremacy with our consent."[3] The PAC, the ANC, and the Inkatha Freedom Party disagreed on the nature of the post-apartheid state. Irreconcilable differences appeared during the negotiations. For example, the white right's demand for a homeland was in opposition to the ANC's call for a unitary non-racial South Africa. Within the ANC, the Africanist/Socialist position stated that there could be no negotiations until apartheid was defeated. Given *Umkhonto we Sizwe's* limited military means and changes in the international economy that left the capitalist system as the only viable option, defeating apartheid militarily would have been impossible. The ANC had to make major concessions to meet the demands of the NP. Furthermore, there was conflict between the ANC and the NP, especially over minority rights. However it is incorrect (as Padayachee and Klein argue) to argue that the ANC negotiators "failed to grasp the enormity of what they were bargaining away" and "did not understand at the time that it was the nature of democracy itself that was being altered in those negotiations."[4] Indeed, the ANC should not be described as a victim. It made conscious and deliberate choices based on its own middle-class interests, with the active support of the South African business community, the IMF, and the World Bank, confirming its adherence to the Washington Consensus.

The outcome of the negotiation was also determined by the major parties, that is to say, the ANC and the NP. Once they agreed on an issue, they were able to persuade other parties to join in. Both parties succeeded in marginalizing their critics. For example, the NP silenced criticism from the civil service by accepting the sun-set clauses, which were proposed by the ANC. Major compromises were reached on key issues. For example, the ANC agreed to leave the South African National Defense Force intact since it merely integrated other armies into its own structure. The ANC also agreed to dismantle South Africa's nuclear military capability.

The sun-set-clauses meant that economic and social inequalities would be harder to address. As Naomi Klein rightly observes, "the concession meant that the new ANC government carried the cost of two governments—its own and a shadow white government that was out of power. Forty per cent of the government's annual debt payments go to the country's massive pension fund [costing 300 billion rand in 2004]. The vast majority of the beneficiaries are former apartheid employees."[5] Furthermore, the sun-set clauses settlement resulted in two contradictions. First, transformation would be more difficult to carry out since the minority still occupied key positions in the public service. Second, without the compromises, the minority would not have given up political power. The end of apartheid in South Africa introduced a new scramble for Africa. Under apartheid, South African companies could not trade openly with other African countries. With the demise of apartheid, these companies had a comparative advantage to the rest of the continent, as they claimed to know African markets. The South African economy continues to produce battery-operated television sets and stoves that are obsolete in Western countries. They know how to pamper African rulers in order to corner the market. This knowledge focuses on pampering African presidents, which involves loaning company jets, throwing champagne parties, and, in the case of Mobutu, turn-key chicken farms, all flown in with eggs from Johannesburg.[6] South African companies also compete with local firms for access to African countries' markets. For example, in Kenya, South Africa's *Castle* beer competes against Kenya breweries on the basis of quantity and alcoholic content. As a result, South African Breweries (SAB) owns 46 percent of East African Breweries and has management control. By 1998 SAB owned 25 percent of the national brewery in Ghana, 50 percent in Uganda, 82 percent in Tanzania and 90 percent in both Zambia and Mozambique. South African Breweries was followed by Eskom and Standard Bank (a British bank based in South Africa) which opened branches in most African countries. By 2003, South African firms had invested US$1.4 billion in African countries with impressive profits.[7] South Africa's firms replaced the United States, Britain, and France as the continent's largest source of direct investment. Since 2001, South African national and foreign companies (active in the domestic sector) have increased their exports to the rest of the continent by 59 percent. Outside of southern Africa, Kenya and Nigeria are its greatest profit-makers. This is not surprising, given South Africa's history as a "darling" of Western countries. It can truly be said that without the support of the West and the Bretton Woods Institutions, apartheid could not have survived. To give just one example, in 1982, the IMF and the World Bank gave South Africa a US$1.1 billion loan. The U.S. government extended another US$623 million loan to the apartheid state. These funds were equal to those set aside by the regime for its 1980–1982 military expenditure.[8] Thus, liberal democracy has created a South Africa that acts as the springboard from which Western investors and South African domestic companies establish a foothold in the rest of the continent.

The ANC considered that it had no other alternative than to accept a historic compromise. The transition from apartheid to liberal democracy was based on pacts between the ANC and the NP elites, which called for compromises. However, as we saw earlier, the ANC made the most compromises. These included leaving the economy and the security apparatus intact, liberalizing the economy, and accepting IMF and World Bank conditionalities. Economic and social inequalities, which developed over a period of three hundred years in South Africa, cannot possibly be corrected in thirteen years, explaining the sharp class differences still present in the society.

In spite of these constraints, the ANC has made some significant changes. Since 1994, 650,000 new water connections have been made reaching 6.4 million people. As access to water improves health, this development has had a positive domino effect. It has also reduced the work-load of women since they no longer have to travel long distances to fetch water. It has also encouraged the development of small businesses such as hotels and training schools. The ANC's economic and social policies have resulted in the improvement of the living conditions of many people. For example, 1.3 million homes have received electricity in some rural areas, access to electricity has enabled children to do their home work and clinics to treat people. Such policies have also provided housing for some homeless people as well as primary health care. Since 1994, 1.3 million people have telephones and 5 million more people have access to primary health care. Immunization programs have been introduced throughout the country. In education, these policies improved the learning environment by providing milk and meals for children, subsequently reducing school drop-out rates. The ANC's curriculum 2005 aimed at replacing apartheid education. In higher education, the ANC has made efforts to bring former "bush colleges" up to par with white ones. This has been carried out through better training, introduction of rigorous research, as well as partnerships with foreign governments to improve higher education. It remains to be seen whether education has improved. All-white institutions have remained intact, but high fees keep them out of reach of most black students. The ANC has also effected remarkable changes in women's lives. For example, it has crossed the public/private divide by giving women political positions. On the job-front, the ANC has introduced laws that protect domestic workers. Majority rule has given the African majority its citizenship rights. Psychologically, they now view the government as theirs.

What are the pitfalls of liberal democracy in South Africa? First, given its extreme economic inequalities, South Africa needs a political system based on concrete economic rights. A liberal democracy, with its emphasis in abstract rights and free and fair elections, will exacerbate these inequalities while giving the majority of the people false hope. As a result, South Africa's society will only become more unequal. Second, for the victims of apartheid, democracy must *mean economic transformation*. This is not possible within a liberal setting, as such a setting privileges the corporate sector over popular demands. In such a scenario, the market and the GDP become more important than social welfare programs, which would address economic disparities and the AIDS crisis. Third, liberal democracy is actually an obstacle to popular democracy because it silences its critics. Both the international community and the Bretton Woods Institutions support liberal democracy because of its focus on economic liberalization, which limits the role of the state. Fourth, given its history, liberal democracy can never be successful in South Africa because of its elitism, individualism, and marginalization of the poor. Finally, liberal democracy is irrelevant in an African setting because it privileges institutions over people. Democracy is limited to multiparty competition. What use is a parliament if the majority of the people are dying of AIDS? What is the use of a vote if one does not have shelter? According to Winnie Mandela, "political freedom is meaningless unless it goes hand in hand with economic upliftment, and she believes that the government's policies are perpetuating rather than relieving the lot of the downtrodden."[9] Winnie Mandela's views are confirmed by a brief evaluation of the impact of free-market, trickle-down economics on the South African economy and society over the last twelve years:

- Since 1994, the number of people living on less than $1 a day has doubled, from two million to four million in 2006.

- As of 2004, twenty-two million South Africans still lived in poverty.

- Since 1990, the average life expectancy for South Africans has dropped by thirteen years.

- Between 1991 and 2002, the unemployment rate for black South Africans more than doubled, from 23 percent to 48 percent.

- Of South Africa's thirty-five million black citizens, only five thousand earn more than $60,000 a year. The number of whites in that income bracket is twenty times higher.

- The ANC government has built 1.8 million homes, but in the meantime 2 million people have lost their homes.

- Close to one million people have been evicted from farms in the first decade of democracy.

- The number of shack dwellers has grown by 50 percent. In 2006, more than one in four South Africans lived in shacks located in informal shantytowns, many without running water or electricity.[10]

Because of these huge economic and social inequalities and its unique history, liberal democracy is not a viable alternative for South Africa, as it merely focuses on cosmetic changes that favor the minority. The right democracy for South Africa is "a social democracy with emphasis on concrete rights and concrete equality; it presupposes substantial investment in the upliftment and the empowerment of ordinary people."[11] The ANC has an advantage that the National Party lacks: legitimacy. However, unlike the National Party, the ANC leadership lacks a concrete vision that could act as the driving force for its policies. While the National Party introduced programs to improve the conditions of poor Afrikaners, the ANC policies are unlikely to develop along similar lines because the ANC—like Kwame Nkrumah did in 1957—consciously opted for the political kingdom rather than the economic one. In terms of opening up the economy, one can argue that the ANC has several choices. One strategy would be to open the economy slowly while controlling its capital market, basic services, and education. The greatest challenge facing Thabo Mbeki and any future ANC political leadership will be to maintain the right balance between addressing the African majority's needs, keeping the middle class content, and satisfying the multilateral institutions' demands while retaining the confidence of domestic and foreign investors. In the twenty-first century, the ANC and any future African leadership in South Africa have two options: to choose their place in the neocolonial arrangement as a business agent for imperialism and its playground or to reject its colonial destiny by taking control over the economy and the security apparatus. This reality will continue to inform South Africa's democracy and the economic and social development program of the ANC for the foreseeable future.

FURTHER READINGS

Ake, Claude. *The Feasibility of Democracy in Africa*. Dakar, Senegal: Council for the Development of Social Science Research in Africa (CODESRIA), 2000.

Klein, Naomi. *The Shock Doctrine: The Rise of Disaster Capitalism*. New York: Metropolitan Books/Henry Holt & Co., 2007.

Mallaby, Sebastian. *After Apartheid: The Future of South Africa*. New York: Times Books, 1992.

Notes

INTRODUCTION

1. M. K. Gandhi, *Satyagraha in South Africa* (Madras: Greenleaf Books, 1974).
2. Heribert Adam, *Modernizing Racial Domination: The Dynamics of South African Politics* (Los Angeles: University of California Press, 1971), 111; See also, Edward Feit, *South Africa: The Dynamics of the ANC* (London: Oxford University Press, 1962).
3. Ali A. Mazrui and Michael Tidy, *Nationalism and New States in Africa from about 1935 to the Present* (Nairobi: Heinemann, 1984), 167–68.
4. Heribert Adam, *Modernizing Racial Domination*, 112–13.
5. Ibid., 168
6. Thomas Karis and Gail Gerhart, *From Protest to Challenge 1820–1990: Nadir and Resergence* 1964, in Thomas Karis and Gail Gerhart From Protest to Challenge, vol. 5 (South Africa: Unisa Press, 1997), 16.
7. Marq de Villiers, *White Tribe Dream: Apartheid's Bitter Roots Notes of an Eight Generation Afrikaner* (Toronto, Canada: Macmillan, 1987), 312.
8. Marq de Villiers, *White Tribe Dream: Apartheid's Bitter Roots Notes of an Eight Generation Afrikaner*, 324; see also Calvin, *The Life of Jameson C. Edward* (London: Arnold & Company, 1922); Vindix (pseud. Rev. F. Verscholes), *Cecil Rhodes: His Political Life and Speeches* (London: Chapman & Hall, 1900), 150–65; Brian Bunting, *The Rise of the South African Reich* (London: International Defence Fund & Aid for Southern Africa, 1986), 406.
9. P. Eric Louw, *The Rise, Fall and Legacy of Apartheid* (Westport, Connecticut: Praeger, 2004).
10. Anton M. Lembede, "Some Basic Principles of African Nationalism," *Ilanga Lase Natal* 924 (February, 1945) in *Freedom in Our Lifetime: Collected Writings of Anton Muziwakle Lembede*, 85–86.
11. Thomas Hodgkin, *Nationalism in Colonial Africa* (New York: New York University Press, 1957), 23.
12. Basil Davidson, *Which Way Africa? The Search for A New Society* (England: Middlesex, 1971), 55–58.
13. Frantz Fanon, *The Wretched of the Earth*, trans. Constance Farrington (New York: Grove Press, 1968), 149, 152–54, 173, 174.
14. Ibid., 124.
15. Ibid., 133.

16. Ibid., 129.
17. Ibid., 159.
18. Ibid., 152–53.
19. Amilcar Cabral, *Revolution in Guinea: An African People's Struggle* (London: Love & Malcomson, 1969), 48.
20. Ibid., 110.
21. Africa Information Services, ed., *Return to the Source: Selected Speeches of Amilcar Cabral* (New York: Monthly Review Press, 1973).
22. Amilcar Cabral, *Revolution in Guinea*, 110.
23. Dan O'Meara, *Volkskapitalisme: Class, Capital and Ideology in the Development of Afrikaner Nationalism 1934–1948* (Johannesburg: Ravan press, 1983), 4; G. D. Scholtz, *Dr Nicolass Johannes van der Merwe 1888–1941* (Johannesburg: Voortrekker Pers., 1942); G. D. Scholtz, *Die Ontwikkeling van die Politieke Denke van die Afrikaner Vol. 1.* (Johannesburg: Voortrekker Pers., 1967).
24. Johann Gottlieb Fichte. "Reden die Deutsche Nation," in *Samtliche Werks* (Berlin: Veit, 1846), 381. Quoted in Theodor Herzl, *The Jew's State*, trans. Henk Overberg (Jerusalem: Jason Aronson Inc., 1997), 45–46; see also D. R. Coverlid, *Richard H. Samule: Selected Writings* (Melbourne, Australia: Melbourne University Press, 1963).
25. Dan O'Meara, *Volkskapitalisme: Class, Capital and Ideology in the Development of Afrikaner Nationalism 1934–1948*, 4.
26. L. M. Thompson, "Afrikaner Nationalist Historiography and the Policy of Apartheid," *Journal of African History* 3 (1992): 125, 138; Quoted in Dan O'Meara, *Volkskapitalisme: Class, Capital and Ideology in the Development of Afrikaner Nationalism 1934–1948*, 4–5; See also, Leonard Thompson, *A History of South Africa* (New Haven, CT: Yale University Press, 1985).
27. C. W. de Kiewet, *A History of South Africa: Social and Economic* (London: Oxford University Press, 1972); R. de Villiers, "Afrikaner Nationalism," Monica Wilson & L. Thompson eds., *The Oxford History of South Africa*, 11 (Oxford, England: Clarendon Press, 1971): 365; Leo Marquard, *People and Politics of South Africa* (Cape Town: Oxford University Press, 1960); T. Dunbar Moodie, *The Rise of Afrikanerdom: Power, Apartheid, and the Afrikaner Civil Religion* (Berkeley, California: University of California Press, 1975).
28. P. Eric Louw, *The Rise, Fall, and Legacy of Apartheid* (Westport, Connecticut: Praeger, 2004), viii.
29. Ibid., x
30. Edwin S. Munger, *Afrikaner and African Nationalism: South African Parallels and Parameters* (London: Oxford University press, 1967); Gail Gerhat, *Black Power in South Africa: The Evolution of an Ideology* (Berkeley, California: University of California Press, 1978).
31. Peter Walshe, *The Rise of African Nationalism in South Africa* (Cape Town: A. D. Donker, 1987), 38.
32. Geoff Eley and Ronald Grigor Suny, eds., *Becoming National* 22.
33. Benedict Anderson, *Imagined Communities* (New York: Verso, 1996), 6.
34. Ernest Gellner, *Thought and Change*, 169 (emphasis by Benedict Anderson) cited in Benedict Anderson, *Imagined Communities*, 6.
35. Benedict Anderson, *Imagined Communities*, 7.
36. Ibid.
37. Ibid., 65.
38. Ibid., 84.

39. Ibid.
40. Ibid., 86–87.
41. Ibid., 140.
42. Ibid., 139; Marx described global imperialism as "the need of a constantly expanding market for its products [which] chases the bourgeoisie over the whole face of the globe," *The Communist Manifesto*, 37.
43. William J. Pomeroy, *Apartheid, Imperialism, and African Freedom* (New York: International Publishers, 1986), 11; Nigel Worden, *The Making of Modern South Africa* (Cambridge, MA: Blackwell Publishers, 1994), 110.
44. On how education can cause frustration by raising expectations see: Robert Ted Gurr, *Why Men Rebel?* (Princeton: Princeton University Press, 1970), 90; Eric Molobi, "From Bantu education to People's Education," in William Cobbert and Robin Cohen, eds., *Popular Struggles in South Africa* (New Haven: Yale University Press, 1988).
45. Guillermo O'Donnell and Phillipe C. Schmitter, "Tentative Conclusions about Uncertain Democracies," in Guillermo O' Donnell, Phillipe C. Schmitter, and Laurence Whitehead, eds., *Transitions from Authoritarian Rule: Prospects for Democracy* (Baltimore: John Hopkins University Press, 1986), part 4, 6; Andre du Toit draws on O'Donnell and Schmitter's work to study South Africa's transition, see his "South Africa as Another case of Transition from Authoritarian Rule," IDASA Occasional Papers, May 1987.
46. Guillermo O'Donnell and Phillipe C. Schmitter, "Tentative conclusions about uncertain Democracies" in Guillermo O'Donnell, Phillipe C. Schmitter, and Laurence Whitehead, eds., *Democratic Transitions from Authoritarian Rule: Prospects for Democracy*, part 4, 37–39.
47. Pierre du Toit, *Power Plays Bargaining Tactics for Transforming South Africa* (Natal, S. A.: Southern Book Publishers, 1991), 129; see also Patrick Bond, *Elite Transition: From Apartheid to Neoliberalism in South Africa* (Scottsville, South Africa: University of Kwazulu-Natal Press, 2005).
48. F. Van Zyl Slabbert, *The Quest for Democracy: South Africa in Transition*, 6–8; David R. Howarth, "Paradigms Gained? A Critique of Theories and Explanations of Democratic Transition in South Africa," 187.
49. Van Zyl Slabbert, *The Quest for Democracy: South Africa in Transition*, 90–92.
50. Rita Abrahamsen, *Disciplining Democracy: Development Discourse sand Good Governance in Africa* (New York: Zed Books, 2000), xi–xv, 109.

Chapter 1

1. Alexander Wilmot, *The Story of the Expansion of South Africa*. (London: Juta Co., 1895), 55–56; see also H. M. Robertson, "150 years of Economic contact between Black and White: A Preliminary Survey part 1," *The South African Journal of Economics* (vol.2, 1934), 403–25. These issues have been dealt with elsewhere see Monica Wilson & Leonard Thompson, *A History of South Africa to 1870* (Cape Town: David Phillip, 1982); Nigel Worden & Clifton Crais eds., *Breaking the Chains: Slavery and its Legacy in the Nineteenth-Century Cape Colony* (Johannesburg: Witwatersrand University Press, 1994).
2. John Ruskin at an inaugural lecture at Oxford University, 1870, cited in Anthony Thomas, *Rhodes: The Race for Africa* (England: Penguin Books, 1997), 88; See also Jean and John Comaroff, *Of Revelation and Revolution: Christianity, Colonialism, and Consciousness in South Africa*, vol. one (Chicago: University of Chicago Press, 1991); Bernard Semmel, *Imperialism and Social Reform: English Social Imperial Thought 1895–1914* (New York: Doubleday, 1960); Anthony Trollope, *South Africa: A Report of the 1878 Edition*,

with an introduction and notes by J. H. Davidson (Cape Town: A. A. Balkema, 1878), 454–62: G. R. Kesteven, *The Boer War* (Ghatto & Windus: London, 1970), 18.

3. Jean and John Comaroff, *Of Revelation and Revolution: Christianity, Colonialism, and Consciousness in South Africa* (Chicago: University of Chicago Press,1991), 87; See also Martin Heidegger, *The Question Concerning Technology, and Other Essays*, Translated by W.Levitt (New York: Harper & Row, 1977), 115; Wlad Godzich, Foreword: in *Quest of Modernity, In Ideology of Adventure Studies in Modern Consciousness*,1100–1750 vol. l by Michael Nerlich, Trans. by R.Crowley. (Minneapolis: University of Minnesota Press, 1987), XIV.

4. Bernard Magubane, *The Making of a Racist State: British Imperialism and the Union of South Africa 1875–1910* (Trenton, NJ: Africa World Press, 1996).

5. Chinua Achebe, "An Image of Africa" Research in African Literatures: 9, cited in Jeanand John Comaroff, *Of Revelation and Revolution: Christianity, Colonialism, and Consciousness in South Africa* volume one,

6. John Barrow, *An Account of Travels into the Interior of Southern Africa in the Years 1797 and 1798* 2, vols (London: Cadell & Davies, 1801–1804), 1, 57.

7. Ibid., *1, 148, 275;* see also Jean and John Comaroff, *Of Revelation and Revolution*,100

8. Jean and John Comaroff, *Of Revelation and Revolution: Christianity, Colonialism and Consciousness in South Africa*, 96; see also "Cornell West, Prophesy Deliverance!: An Afro-American Revolutionary Christianity. (Philadelphia: Westminster Press, 1982), 56.

9. Jean and John Comaroff, *Of Revelation and Revolution: Christianity, Colonialism and Consciousness in South Africa*, 100; see also Brian V. Street, *The Savage in Literature: Representation of Primitive' Society in English Fiction, 1858–1920* (London and Boston:Routeledge & Kegan Paul, 1975), 52ff.

10. Jean and John Comaroff, *Of Revelation and Revolution: Christianity, Colonialism and Consciousness in South Africa, 100.*

11. Georges Cuvier, *Animal Kingdom*, 16 vols. (London: Geo. B. Whittaker, 1827–1853), 1, 197; Karl Figlio, "The Metaphor of Organization: An Historiographical Perspective on the Bio-Medical Sciences of the Early Nineteenth Century" History of Science (1976 no.15), 28.

12. Jean and John Comaroff, *Of Revelation and Revolution: Christianity, Colonialism and Consciousness in South Africa*, 99; See also David Livingstone, *Missionary Travels and Reaches in South Africa* (London: Murray, 1857); and his *Livingstone's Private Journals, 1851–1853* (Los Angeles: University of California Press, 1960), 1. Schapera ed., *David Livingstone: South African Papers, 1849–1853* (Cape Town: The Van Riebeeck Society, 1974.

13. Henry Lichtenstein [W. H.C], *Travels in Southern Africa in the Years 1803, 1804, 1805 and 18062, vols.* Translated from the 1812–15 edition by A. Plumptree (Cape Town: The Van Riebeeck Society, 1928–30), 1, 69.

14. John Edwards, *Reminiscences of the Early Life and Missionary Labours of the Rev. John Edwards* (Grahamstown, South Africa: T. H. Grocott, 1886), 66, 174.

15. Henry Lichtenstein [W. H.C], *Travels in Southern Africa in the Years 1803, 1804, 1805 and 18062, vols. Translated from the 1812–15* edition by A. Plumptree (Cape Town: The Van Riebeeck Society, 1928–30), 1, 69

16. Sander L. Gilman, "Black Bodies, White Bodies: Towards an Iconography of Female Sexuality in Late Nineteenth Century Art, Medicine and Literature," *Critical Theory* 12 (1985): 212; see also Jean and John Comaroff, *Of Revelation and Revolution*.

17. Figure 2.2 George Baxter, *The Abandoned Mother* reproduced from Robert Moffat, *Missionary Labours and Scenes in Southern Africa* (London: Snow, Reprinted, 1969: New York: Johnson Reprint Corporation), 135: See also Jean and John Comaroff, *Of Revelation and Revolution: Christianity, Colonialism and Consciousness in South Africa*, 110; The Abandoned Mother'2.3 is reproduced from Jean and John Comaroff, *Of Revelation and Revolution: Christianity, Colonialism and Consciousness in South Africa*, 111.
18. Jean and John Comaroff, Of Revelation and Revolution: Christianity, Colonialism and Consciousness in South Africa, 109.
19. Richard Elphick and Hermann Giliomee, "The Origins and entrenchment of European dominance at the Cape 1652–1840" Richard Elphick and Hermann Giliomee eds., *The Shaping of South African Society 1652–1840* (Middletown, Connecticut: Maskew Miller Longman, 1988), 549.
20. H. F. Heese, 'Die Inwoners Van Kaapstad in 1800," Kronos, 7(1983), 42. Quoted in Richard Elphick and Hermann Giliomee, "The Origins and entrenchment of European dominance at the Cape 1652–1840" Richard Elphick and Hermann Giliomee eds., *The Shaping of South African Society 1652–1840* (Middletown, Connecticut: Maskew Miller Longman, 1988), 549.
21. Richard Elphick and Hermann Giliomee eds., *The Shaping of South African Society 1652–1840*, 549.
22. Richard Elphick and Hermann Giliomee, "The Origins and entrenchment of European dominance at the Cape 1652–1840," Richard Elphick and Hermann Giliomee eds., *The Shaping of South African Society 1652–1840*.
23. Mary Benson, South Africa: *The Struggle for A Birthright* (London: International Defence and Aid Fund For Southern Africa, 1985).
24. Clifton C. Crais, *The Making of the Colonial Order. White Supremacy and Black Resistance in the Eastern Cape*, 1770–1865 (Johannesburg: Witwatersrand University Press, 1992), 125.
25. Anthony Thomas, Rhodes: *The Race for Africa* (Middlesex, England: Penguin Books, 1997), 94
26. Jack Simons & Ray Simons, *Class and Color in South Africa 1850–1950* (London: IDAFSA, 1983), 34
27. Rian Malan, *My Traitor's Heart* (New York: Vintage International, 1990); see also Robert A. Huttenback, *Racism and Empire, White Settlers and Coloured Immigrants in the British Self-Governing Colonies 1830–1910* (Ithaca, New York: Cornell University Press, 1976).
28. 1852-3 Commission, IV.4–6. Cited in David Welsh, *The Roots of Segregation Native Policy in Natal 1845–1910* (Cape Town: Oxford University press, 1971), 30.
29. Ibid., 36.
30. Cited in Thiven Reddy, *Hegemony and Resistance: Contesting Identities in South Africa* (Burlington, VT: Ashgate, 2000), 20
31. Anthony Thomas, *Rhodes: The Race for Africa* (Middlesex, England: Penguin Books, 1997), 94.; Numerous South Africa school text books presented the view that African ethnic groups were always fighting each other until the white man saved them.; See also Alistar Sparks, *The Mind of South Africa* (London: Mandarin, 1990).
32. 1852–3 Commission Report, 26, quoted in David Welsh, *The Roots of Segregation*, 24.
33. Abortive SNA, 1/8/2: Shepstone to Pine, 9 December 1851. Quoted in David Welsh, *The Roots of Segregation*, 34.
34. Thiven Reddy, *Hegemony and Resistance: Contesting Identities in South Africa;* see also Helen Kuzwayo, *Call me Woman* (Randburg, South Africa: Ravan Press, 1985);

Unknown Author, *Who ought to Win? Oom Paul or Queen Victoria: The South African Struggle* (Laid & Lee Publishers, 1900), 94, 95.
35. H. M. Robertson. "150 Years of Economic Contact Between Black and White: Preliminary Survey" *South African Journal of Economics* (vol. 2, 1934), 420.
36. Trevor Huddleston, *Naught for your Comfort.*
37. *African Leader*, December 3 1933, T. D. M. Skota's Weekly.; CPP, G.8–76 Report on Immigration and Labour Supply for 1875, Memorandum by J. X. Merriman, 3 cited in Colin Bundy, *The Rise & Fall of the South African Peasantry* (Cape Town: David Phillip, 1998), 79.
38. *Natal Witness*, 6 February 1863; David Welsh, *The Roots of Segregation*, 50.
39. *Natal Witness*, 27 March 1863; David Welsh, *The Roots of Segregation*, 50.
40. Donovan Williams, "African Nationalism in South Africa: Origins and Problems," *Journal of African History* (3, 1970):375; see also R. Hunt Davis, "School vs. Blanket and Settler: Elijah Makiwane and the Leadership of the Cape School Community" *African Affairs* (vol. 78, #310, January 1979), 12–27.
41. David Welsh, *The Roots of Segregation: Native Policy in Natal 1845–1910*, 50.
42. J. W. Colenso, Ten Weeks, 72–73. Quoted in David Welsh, *The Roots of Segregation: Native Policy in Natal 1845–1910*, 46.
43. Thiven Reddy. *Hegemony and Resistance: Contesting Identities in South Africa*, 47; J. Phillip, *Researches in South Africa* (London: 1828), ii, 227. Quoted by Bertram Hutchinson, "Some Social Consequences of Nineteenth Century Missionary Activity Among the South African Bantu" *Africa* (Vol. XXVII#2, 1957), 161.
44. Bertram Hutchinson, 'Some Social Consequences of Nineteenth Century Missionary Activity Among the South African Bantu" *Africa* (Vol. XXVII#2, 1957), 161.
45. Thiven Reddy, *Hegemony and Resistance: Contesting Identities in South Africa*, 49.
46. ABMC, IV/2/1: James C. Doward, "The Literature Department of the Zulu Mission," June 1903 cited in David Welsh. *The Roots of Segregation: Native Policy in Natal 1845–1910*, 50.
47. Thiven Reddy, *Hegemony and Resistance: Contesting Identities in South Africa*, 50.
48. Patrick Brantlinger, 'Victorians and Africans: The Genealogy of the Myth of the Dark Continent," *Critical Inquiry* (1985), 181 cited in Jean and John Comaroff, *Of Revelation and Revolution: Christianity, Colonialism and Consciousness in South Africa*, 82.
49. O. E. Emmanuelson, "A History of Native Education in Natal Between 1835 and 1927" (Unpublished M. A. Thesis, Natal University College, 1927), 53.
50. *Imvo Zabantsyndu* March 3 1887, March 301887, April 13th 1887 cited in R. Hunt Davis "School vs. Blanket and Settlers: Elijah Makiwane and the Leadership of the Cape School Community,"; see also D. E. Burchell, "African Higher Education and the Establishment of the South African Native College, Fort Hare," *South African Historical Journal* (No. 8, 1976), 60–83.
51. R. Hunt Davis, "School vs Blanket and Settlers," 20; see also Presidential Address, Native Educational Association (NEA), *IMVO* 2Q July, 1886.
52. David Welsh, *The Roots of Segregation: Native Policy in Natal 1845–1910*, 53.
53. Lionel Forman, *Chapters in the History of the Match to Freedom* (Cape Town: New Age, 1959), 9.
54. *Imvo Zabantsundu*, Editorial, cited in D. R. Edgecombe, "The Non-Racial Franchise in Cape Politics, 1855–1910," *Kelio* 10 (1, 2): 23.
55. John Tengo Jabavu,*Imvo*, March 18, 1901.
56. Trinh T. Minh-ha, *Woman, Native, Other: Writing Postcoloniality and Feminism.* (Bloomington, Indiana: Indian University Press, 1989), 53.

57. Leo Kuper, *An African Bourgeoisie: Race, Class, and Politics in South Africa* (New Haven, CT: Yale University Press, 1965), 73.
58. *Inkanyiso* cited in David Welsh, *The Roots of Segregation Policy in Natal 1845–1910*, 297.
59. B. Rose & R. Tunmer eds., *Documents in South African Education* (Cape Town: Ad Donker, 1975), 201.
60. *The Roots of Segregation Policy in Natal 1845–1910*, 295.
61. *Ilanga LaseNatal*, 19 February, 1908; see also *Inkanyiso*, 9 July, 1891.
62. J. Dexterr ed.,*Christianity and the Natives of South Africa: A Yearbook of South African Missions* (Lovedale, N. D.); cited in Donovan Williams, "African Nationalism in South Africa," 381; *New Nation* (February 1968), 17; Andre Odendaal, *Black Protest in South Africa to 1912* (New Jersey: Barnes & Noble, 1984), 24.
63. Andre Odendaal, *Black Protest in South Africa to 1912*, 24; David H. Anthony, Max Yergan in South Africa: From Evangelical Pan Africanism to Revolutionary Socialist" *African Studies Review* (vol.34, no.2, September 1991), 27–55.
64. David H. Anthony, "Max Yergen in South Africa: From Evangelical Pan Africanist to Revolutionary Socialist," 34; (CA) NA 497, Curnick to Resident Magistrate, Butterworth, 1 September, 1902, cited in Clifton Crais, *The Making of a Colonial Order: White Supremacy and Black Resistance in the Eastern Cape*, 1770–1865 (Johannesburg: Witwatersrand University Press, 1992), 220; Donovan Williams, 'African Nationalism in South Africa: Origins and Problems, 381.
65. Sol T. Plaatje, *Mhudi: An Epic of South African Native Life a Hundred Years Ago* (Johannesburg: A.D. Donker, 1989); Stephen Gray, ed., "Introduction," Tim Couzens (London: Heinemann, 1978); see also Elizabeth Gunner, "Literature & Apartheid," *South Africa in Question* John Lonsdale, ed. (London: James Currey, 1988), 217–33.
66. B. W.Vilakazi "Ezinkomponi" in Amazulu (Johannesburg: Witwatersrand University Press, 1945), 41–45; in translation in Jack & Uys Krige eds., *The Penguin Book of South African Verse* (London: Harmondsworth, 1968), 300–305; see also Elizabeth Gunner "Literature & Apartheid"; Pallo Jordan, "The South African Liberation Movement and the Making of a New Nation," in Maria Van Diepen, ed., *The National Question in South Africa* (London; Zed Books, 1988).
67. Eric A. Walker. *A History Of Southern Africa* (London: Longman, 1957), 466, 483, 493.
68. Craig Charney, "Pixley Seme '06: Father of the African National Congress" *Columbia College Today* (Spring/Summer 19), 16; Peter Walshe. *The Rise of African Nationalism in South Africa* (London: c. Hurst, 1970), 38; Shula Marks, *The Ambiguities of Dependence: Class, Nationalism and the State in Twentieth Century Natal* (Baltimore: John Hopkins University, 1986).
69. Ibid.
70. Gwendolyn Carter and Thomas Karis, *From Protest to Challenge* Volume 1 (Pallo Alto, CA: The Hoover Institution, 1971), 118.
71. David Welsh, *The Roots of Segregation*, 310.
72. Dube to John H. Harris, 6 October 1921, S22, G191, APS papers cited in R. Hunt Davies, Jr. "John L. Dube: A South African Exponent of Booker T. Washington," 498; see also Richard D. Ralston "American Episodes in the Making of an African Leader: A Case Study of Alfred B. Xuma (1893–1962)," *International Journal of African Historical Studies* (Vol. 6, 1973, #1), 72–93.
73. R. Hunt Davies, Jr. "John L. Dube: A South African Exponent of Booker T. Washington," 520.
74. Tom Lodge. *Black Politics in South Africa Since 1945*, 4.

75. Martin Legassick, "South Africa: Capital Accumulation and Violence," *Economy and Society* (Vol.3 #3 August 1974), 282.
76. Gwendolyn Carter and Thomas Karis, *From Protest to Challenge* Volume 1. (Palo Alto, CA: The Hoover Institution, 1971), 215.
77. Ibid., 300–1.
78. Gail Gerhart. *Black Power in South Africa: The Evolution of an Ideology.* (Berkeley: University of California, 1978), 58; see also Robert R. Edgar and Luyanda ka Msumza, eds., *Freedom in our Lifetime: The Collected Writings of Anton Muziwakhe Lembede*, Alex Callinicos and John Rogers. *Southern Africa After Soweto* (London: Pluto Press, 1977); *Eastern Province Herald* (Port Elizabeth), 8 February 1945.
79. Jeremy Seekings, *The UDF* (Cape Town: David Phillip; Oxford; James Currey; Athens: Ohio University Press, 2000), 14, 32 cited in P. Eric Louw. *The Rise and Fall of Apartheid*, 109.
80. *Natal Witness*, 16 October, 1863; See also David Welsh, *The Roots of Segregation: Native Policy in Natal*, 169.
81. Chief M. G.Buthelezi, cited in David Welsh, *The Roots of Segregation: Native Policy in Natal*.
82. Ibid., 73.
83. 1852–3 Commission, vi 44. Quoted in David Welsh, *The Roots of Segregation: Native Policy in Natal*, 45; *Inkanyiso*, 14 May 1891.
84. David Welsh, *The Roots of Segregation: Native Policy in Natal*, 268.
85. LCD, vol. 10, 1887, pp: 113, 115, Quoted in *The Roots of Segregation: Native Policy in Natal*, 268.
86. On women see; Cherryl Walker, ed., *Women and Gender in Southern Africa* (Cape Town: David Phillip, 1990); Muriel Horrell. *African Education: Some Origins and Development until 1953* (Johannesburg, 1963); Harold Wolpe, "Capitalism and Cheap Labour-Power in South Africa: from Segregation to Apartheid," *Economic and Society*.
87. Tom Lodge. *Black Politics in South Africa Since 1945*, 14; Cherryl Walker, "We Fight for Food": Women and the Food Crisis of the 1940s" *Work in Progress* (University of Witwatersrand, 3 January 1978); Belinda Bozzoli, "Marxism, Feminism and South African Studies," *Journal of Southern African Studies* (vol. 9, no, 2 April 1983).
88. Peter Walshe, *The Rise of African Nationalism in South Africa.* (London: C. Hurst, 1970), 38; see also P. Eric Louw, *The Rise, Fall Legacy of Apartheid*, 108.

Chapter 2

1. Monica Wilson and Leonard Thompson, *A History of South African to 1870* (Cape Town: David Phillip, 1985), 232.
2. Peter Abrahams, *Wild Conquest* (New York: Doubleday, 1971), 51.
3. Thiven Reddy, *Hegemony and Resistance* (Sydney: Ashgate, 2000), 36; on Afrikaner Calvinism see also Andre Du Toit, "No Chosen people: The Myth of the Calvinist Origins of Afrikaner Nationalism and Racial Ideology," *The American Historical Review* 88, vol. 4 (October 1983): 920–52.
4. Martin Legassick, "The Frontier tradition in South African historiography," in *Economy and Society in Pre-Industrial South*, ed. Shula Marks and Anthony Atmore (London: Longman, 1980), 44–79.
5. Thiven Reddy, *Hegemony and Resistance*, 37.

6. F. A.Van Jaarsverd, *The Awakening of Afrikaner Nationalism, 1868–1881* (Cape Town, 1961), 123; editorial in *Cape Times* (May 5, 1877); cited in Hermann Giliomee, "The Beginnings of Afrikaner Nationalism," *South African Historical Journal 19* (1987): 121.
7. Hermann Giliomee, "The Beginnings of Afrikaner Nationalism, 1870–1915," 121; See also, Irving Hexham, *The Irony of Apartheid* (New York, 1981), 128.; John Fisher, *The Afrikaners* (London: Cassell, 1969), 237–64; M. S. Appelgryn, *Thomas Francois Burghers: Staatspresdient (1872–1877)* (Pretoria, 1979), 48, cited in Hermann Giliomee, "The Beginnings of Afrikaner Nationalism," 121.
8. Ibid.; *Zuid Afrikaan* was the official newspaper of the BBV; Alexander Wilmot, *The History of Our own Times in South Africa 11* (1880–1888) (Cape Town, 1898), 182.
9. W. A. De Klerk, *The Puritans in Africa: A Story of Afrikanerdom* (England: Penguin, 1975), 6; Leonard Thompson, *The Political Mythology of Apartheid* (New Haven: Yale University Press, 1985); See Martin Legassick, "The frontier tradition in South African historiography," in *Economy and Society in pre-industrial South Africa ed.*, Shular Marks and Anthony Atmore (London: Longman, 1980); See also C. W. de Kiewet, *History of South Africa: social and economic* (Oxford: Oxford University Press, 1941); See also T. R. H. Davenport, *South Africa*, as well as Leonard Thompson and Monica Wilson's various books and articles on South Africa; See especially Leonard Thompson's "The Subjection of the African Chiefdoms," in *The Oxford History of South Africa*, ed. Monica Wilson and L.W Thompson (London: Oxford University Press, 1971); L. W. Thompson, *The Political Mythology of Apartheid (*New Haven: Yale University Press, 1985); I. D. MacCrone, "The Frontier tradition and Race Attitudes in South Africa," *Race Relations Journal* 28. 3 (July–September, 1961): 19–30; Joel S. Migdal, *Strong Societies and Weak States: State-Society Capabilities in the Third World* (Princeton: Princeton University Press, 1988).
10. Hermann Giliomee, "Constructing Afrikaner Nationalism," *Journal of Asian and African Studies* 84 (1983): XVII, 1–2; Thiven Reddy, *Hegemony and Resistance*; John Fisher, *The Afrikaners*; Isabel Hofmeyer, "Building a Nation from Words: Afrikaans Language, Literature, and 'Ethnic Identity,' 1902–1924," in *The Politics of Race, Class and Nationalism in Twentieth Century South Africa*, ed. Shula Marks and Stanley Trapido (London: Longman, 1987), 95–123; A. T. Nzula, I. I. Potekhin and A. Z. Zusmanovich, *Forced Labour in Colonial Africa* (London: Zed Press, 1979); David Yudelman, *The Emergence of Modern South Africa: State, Capital, and the Incorporation of Organized Labour on the South African Gold Fields, 1901–1939* (Cape Town: David Phillip, 1984); William Pomeroy, *Apartheid, Imperialism and African Freedom* (New York: International Publishers, 1986); Harold Wolpe, "Capitalism and Cheap Labour-Power in South Africa" *Economy and Society* 1, no. 4: 425–56; See also R. Horowitz, *The Political Economy of South Africa* (London: Oxford University Press, 1967), 355.
11. John Fisher, *The Afrikaners*, 255; T. R.H Davenport, "The South African Rebellion of 1914," *English Historical Review* 78 (1963): 73–94; David Welsh, "Urbanisation and the Solidarity of Afrikaner Nationalism," *The Journal of Modern African Studies* 7, no. 2 (1969): 269, 270
12. P. Eric Louw, *The Rise, Fall, and Legacy of Apartheid*, 13; cited in Mary Benson, *South Africa Struggle for a Birthright*, 52; Leonard Thompson, *The Political Mythology of Apartheid* (New Haven: Yale University Press, 1985), 42.
13. Ivor Wilkins and Hans Strydom, *The Super Afrikaners*, 104–5; Irving Hexham, *The Irony of Apartheid: The Struggle for National Independence of Afrikaner Calvinism against British Imperialism* (New York: 1981),), 37 cited in Leonard Thompson, *The Political Mythology of Apartheid*, 32. 40; Die Burger (November18, 1933), cited in David Welsh, 268.

14. P. Eric Louw, *The Rise, Fall and Legacy of Apartheid* (Westport, Connecticut: Praeger, 2004), 23.
15. W. A. De Klerk, *The Puritans in Africa: A Story of Afrikanerdom* (Harmondsworth: Penguin Books, 1975), 109–10.
16. P. Eric Louw, *The Rise, Fall, and Legacy of Apartheid* (Westport, Connecticut: Praeger, 2004), 26.
17. Rodney Davenport, "African Townsmen? South African Natives (urban areas) legislation through the years," *African Affairs, 68* (1969) 102; Sipho E. Mzimela, *Apartheid: South African Nazism* (New York: Vantage Press, 1983); A. T. Nzula, I. I. Potekhin and A. Z. Zusmanovich, *Forced Labor in Colonial Africa* (London: Zed Press, 1979); Anthony Holiday, "White Nationalism in South Africa as Movement and System," in *The National Question in South Africa*, ed. Maria van Diepen (London: Zed Books, 1988), 77–85.
18. Eugen Vroom, *The Helpless Boers* (New Jersey: Flanders Hall, 1940), 33; John Fisher, *The Afrikaners*, 181; Peter Warwick, *Black People and the South African War 1899–1902*, 145; Jeffrey Butler, "Afrikaner Women and the Creation of Ethnicity in a small South African Town 1902–1950," in *The Creation of Tribalism in Southern Africa*, ed. Leroy Vail (Berkeley: University of California Press, 1989), 64, 184.
19. P. Eric Louw, *The Rise, Fall, and Legacy of Apartheid*, 31; On apartheid as theory see also G. A. Cronje, W. Nicol and E. P. Groenewald, *Regverdige Rasse-Apartheid* (Stellenbosch: Christen-Studentverenigingmaatskappy van Suid Afrika, 1947); *What I Saw in South Africa*, cited in John Fisher, *The Afrikaners*, 204; A. Ruth Fry, *Emily Hobhouse* (Cape Town: Jonathan Ball, 1929); Jeffrey Butler, "Afrikaner women and the creation of Ethnicity in a small South African Town, 1902–1950," in *The Creation of Tribalism in Southern Africa*, ed. Leroy Vail (Berkeley: University of California Press, 1989);   W. A. De Klerk, *The Puritans in Africa: A Story of Afrikanerdom* (England: Penguin, 1975).
20. P. Eric Louw, *The Rise, Fall, and Legacy of Apartheid*, 37–38; Dan O'Meara, *Volkskapitalisme: Class, Capital and Ideology in the Development of Afrikaner Nationalism* (Johannesburg: Ravan, 1983), 152–53.
21. John Fisher, *The Afrikaners*, 181; Peter Warwick *Black People and The South Africa War 1899–1902*, 145;
22. Irving Hexham, *The Irony of Apartheid: The Struggle for National Independence of Afrikaner Calvinism against British Imperialism* (New York:1981), 40; cited in Leonard Thompson, *The Political Mythology of Apartheid*, 35.
23. John Fisher. *The Afrikaners*, 184.
24. Ibid., 204.
25. Ibid., 178.
26. C. Headlam, *The Milner Papers*, Volume II (London: Caswell & Company, 1933), 242–43.
27. Jeffrey Butler, "Afrikaner Women and the Creation of Ethnicity in a Small South African Town, 1902–1950," in *The Creation of Tribalism in Southern Africa*, ed. Leroy Vail (Berkeley: University of California Press, 1989), 56; De Klerk, *The Puritans in Africa: A Story of Afrikanerdom* (England: Penguin, 1975).
28. Dunbar Moodie, "Ideological Change, Afrikaner Nationalism and Pragmatic Racial Domination in South Africa," in *Change in Contemporary South Africa* (Berkeley: University of California Press, 1975), 19–50 cited in Andre Du Toit; Anne Mclintock, "No Longer in a Future Heaven," in *Becoming National, ed.* Geoff Eley and Ronald Grigor Sunny (New York: Oxford University Press, 1996), 274; Jeffrey Butler, "Afrikaner Women and the Creation of Ethnicity in a Small South African Town, 1902–1950," 66–69; Cheryl Walker, *Women and Resistance in South Africa*; Carnegie Commission

Report, Vol. V(b), *The Mother and the Daughter of the Poor Family* (Stellenbosch: 1932), 169–97, 215; Belinda Bozzoli, "Marxism, Feminism and South African Studies," *Journal of Southern African Studies* 9, no. 2 (April 1983): 161; P. J. Meyer, *Die Afrikaner* (Cape Town, 1940), 33 cited in W. A. De Klerk, *The Puritans in Africa*, 214.

29. Dunbar Moodie, cited in Andre Du Toit "Ideological Change, Afrikaner Nationlism and Pragmatic Racial Domination in South Africa," in *Change in Contemporary South Africa* (Berkeley: University of California Press, 1975), 19–50; Anne McLintock, "No Longer a Future Heaven," in *Becoming National, ed.* Geoff Eley and Ronald Grigor Sunny (New York: Oxford University Press, 1996), 274.

CHAPTER 3

1. Thiven Reddy, *Hegemony and Resistance: Contesting Identities in South Africa* (Burlington, USA: Ashgate, 2000), 109; See also W. A. de Klerk, *The Puritans of Africa: A History of Afrikanerdom* (London: Hamondsworth, 1976); B. Bunting, *The Rise of the South African Reich* (London: Harmondsworth, 1969); T. R. Davenport, *South Africa: A Modern History* (Toronto: University of Toronto Press, 1977); A. Hepple, *Verwoerd* (London: Harmondsworth, 1967); Dan O'Meara, *Volkapitalisme* (London: Cambridge University Press, 1983); T. Dunbar Moodie, *The Rise of Afrikanerdom* (Berkeley: University of California Press, 1975); Deborah Posel, *The Making of Apartheid 1948–1961* (Oxford: Clarendon Press, 1991).
2. Stanley Trapido, "South Africa in a Comparative study of industrialization," *Journal of Development Studies* vii (1970–1971): 371, cited in Tom Lodge, *Black Politics in South Africa Since 1945* (Johannesburg: Ravan Press, 1983), 93.
3. P. Eric Louw, *The Rise, Fall, and Legacy of Apartheid*, 31; Bernard Magubane, "Apartheid," in *The Oxford Companion to Politics of the World, ed.* Joel Krieger (London: Oxford University Press, 2001), 34; Thiven Reddy, *Hegemony and Resistance*, 110; Robert Davies, "Class Struggle and the Periodization of the South Africa State," *Review of African Political Economy* 7 (Sep-Dec 1976); C. W. de Kieweit, *A History of South Africa: Social and Economic* (London: Oxford University Press, 1975); Frederick A. Johnstone, "White Prosperity and White Supremacy in South Africa," *African Affairs* 69 (April 1970): 124–40; Martin Legassick, "The Dynamics of Modernization in South Africa," *Journal of African History* 13 (1972): 145–50; T. R. H. Davenport, *South Africa: A Modern History* (Toronto: University of Toronto Press, 1977).
4. Leon Louw and Frances Kendall, *South Africa: The Solution*, 29–31; David Welsh, *The Roots of Segregation: Native Policy in Natal (1945–1910)*; Calvin, *The Life of Jameson C Edward* (London: Arnold & Co., 1922), Some authors have drawn parallels between apartheid and Nazism. See, for example, Alexander Hepple, *Verwoed* (Baltimore: Penguin Books, 1967); Sipho E. Mzimela, *Apartheid: South African Nazism* (New York: Vantage Press, 1983); Brian Bunting, *The Rise of the South African Reich* (London: International Defence Fund & Aid for Southern Africa, 1986); Edgar H. Brookes, *Apartheid: A Documentary Study of Modern South Africa* (New York: Barnes and Noble, 1968), 19.
5. Baruch Hirson, *Year of Fire, Year of Ash* (London: Zed Press, 1975), 45.
6. Reddy, 135; M. M. Balintulo, "The Black Universities in South Africa" in J. Rex, *Apartheid and Social Research* (Paris: UNESCO, 1981), 148; Mbulelo Vizihugo Mzamane, *Children of Soweto* (New York: Longman, 1982); Martin Meredith, *The Fate of Africa: A History of Fifty Years of Independence* (New York: Public Affairs, 2005); Anne Marie du Preez Bezdrob, *Winnie Mandela: A Life* (Cape Town: Zebra Press, 2003);

Charles H. Feinstein, *An Economic History of South Africa* (Cambridge, UK: Cambridge University Press, 2005).

7. "Prime Minister addresses the Nation," in *Weekly Newsletter* 465 (November 1, 1948), 7; On education, see Eric Molobi, "From Bantu Education to a Peoples' Education," in *Popular Struggles in South Africa, ed.* William Cobbert and Robin Cohen (New Jersey: Africa World Press, 1988), 166;.

8. Trevor Huddleston, *Naught for your Comfort* (London: Collins, 1956), 121–22; Tom Lodge, *Black Politics in South Africa Since 1945* (Johannesburg: Ravan Press, 1983), 91–110.

9. Miriam Tlali, *Muriel at Metropolitan* (Johannesburg: Ravan Press, 1975), 70.

10. Gerald W. Broomfield, *Colour Conflict, Race Relations in Africa* (London: Edinburgh House Press, 1934), 88; on apartheid see Adamastor, *White Man Boss: Footsteps to the South African Volk Republic* (Boston: The Beacon Press, 1951), 24; Edgar H. Brookes, *Apartheid: A Documentary Study of Modern South Africa*, 6 R. H. Du Pre, *The Making of Racial Conflict in South Africa* (Johannesburg: Skotaville Publishers, 1992); Clifton Crais, "Prophecies of Nation" (Paper presented at the 45th Annual Meeting of the African Studies Association, Washington, DC, December 5–8, 2002).

11. P. Eric Louw, *The Rise, Fall, and Legacy of Apartheid* (Westport, Connecticut: Praeger, 2004), 29.

12. cited in *Weekly Newsletter* (Pretoria: State Information Office), 486; see also William J. Pomeroy, *Apartheid, Imperialism and African Freedom* (New York: International Publishers, 1986), 11.

13. Thiven Reddy, *Hegemony and Resistance*, 153.

14. P. Eric Louw, *The Rise, Fall, and Legacy of Apartheid*, 34; On this period see Thomas G. Karis and Gail M. Gehart, *From Protest to Challenge: A Documentary History of African Politics in South Africa, 1882–1990 Nadir and Resurgence, 1964–1979* volume 5, 157; William Minter, "Destructive Engagement: The United States and South Africa in the Reagan Era" in *Frontline Southern Africa: Destructive Engagement*, ed. Phyllis Johnson and David Martin (New York: Four Walls eight Windows, 1988); Robert Price and Carl G. Roseberg, ed., *Apartheid Regime: Political Power and Racial Domination* (Berkeley: University of California, 1980); Robert Price, *The Apartheid State in Crisis: Political Transformation in South Africa 1975–1990* (New York: Oxford University Press, 1991); Wilmot G. James, "The State of Apartheid: An Introduction," in *The State of Apartheid*, ed. Wilmot James (Boulder, Colorado: Lynne Rienner Publishers, 1987), 1–4.

15. P. Eric Louw, *The Rise, Fall, and Legacy of Apartheid*, 86–87.

16. Ibid., 34; Brian Bunting, *The Rise of the South African Reich*, 406; Naboth Mokgatle, *The Autobiography of an Unknown South African* (Los Angeles: U. C. Berkeley, 1971); See also William Miller Macmillan, *Bantu, Boer and Britain: The Making of the South African Native Problem* (London: Faber & Guyer, 1929), 309; Bernard Magubane, "The Political economy of South African Revolution," in *Whither South Africa?, ed.* Bernard Magubane and Ibbo Mandaza (Africa World Press, 1988), 51–87; Thiven Reddy, *Hegemony and Resistance*, 123; *The Rise, Fall, and Legacy of Apartheid*.

17. Antony Altbeker and Jonny Steinberg, "Race, Reason and Representation in National Party Discourse 1990–1992," in *South Africa in Transition: New Theoretical Perspectives*, ed. David R. Howarth and Aletta J. Norval (London: Macmillan Press, 1998), 49–71; on this period see Joe Slovo, "The Working Class & Nation-Building," in Maria van Diepen, *The National Question*, 146; Heribert Adam, "The South African Power-Elite: A Survey of Ideological Commitment," in *South African Sociological Perspectives*, ed. Heribert Adam (London: Oxford University Press, 1971) cited in Thiven Reddy, *Hegemony and*

Resistance, 123; Robert M. Price, *The Apartheid State in Crisis: Political Transformation in South Africa 1975–1990* (New York: Oxford University Press, 1991). In contemporary South Africa the belief that whites should not engage in manual labor is entrenched in the system. The white minority represents itself as thinkers. In 1996, a caucasianAmerican friend visited this writer in a Cape Town suburb. African laborers were working nearby and were, at times, singing or talking to each other. As soon as they saw the American, they were silent. A few days later, a biracial salesman knocked on this writer's door, and when she answered, he demanded to see the "*baas*"; See also, Bloke Modisane, *Blame me on History* (London: Thames and Hudson, 1963).
18. F. W. de Klerk, "Speech Delivered at Davos," February 2, 1992; Pik Botha, "Speech to Hans Seidel Stiftung, Munich," November, 20 1990 cited in Antony Atlbeker and Jonny Steinberg, Race, Reason and Representation in National Party Discourse 1990–1992": 65; F. W. de Klerk, "75th Anniversary of the Cape National Party," Middleburg, 15 September 1990 cited in Antony Atlbeker and Jonny Steinberg, "Race, Reason and Representation in National Party Discourse, 1990–1992," 64; F. W. de Klerk, Speech to Swiss-South Africa Association, Zurich, 23 May 1990;
19. F. W. de Klerk, Speech to Swiss-South Africa Association, Zurich, May, 23 1990.
20. F. W. de Klerk, Speech to the Johannesburg Afrikaans Business Chamber, Kempton Park (translated from the Afrikaans), November 21, 1990; see also Antony Atlbeker and Jonny Steinberg, "Race, Reason and Representation in National Party Discourse, 1990–1992," 66.
21. Ibid.; see also Adriaan Vlok, "Press conference held at Union Buildings, Pretoria," October 1, 1992; F. W. de Klerk, "Address to the National Press Club, Washington, D. C.," September 25, 1992; on other political parties see Alister Sparks, *Tomorrow is Another Country: The Inside Story of South Africa's Negotiated Revolution* (Johannesburg: Struik Book Distributors, 1994).
22. Thiven Reddy, *Hegemony and Resistance*, 182–96.
23. G.M. Gerhart, *Black Power in South Africa*, 98; ANC "The Freedom Charter," June 26, 1955, in *Soul of a Nation: Constitution-Making in South Africa*, Hassen Ebrahim (Cape Town: Oxford University Press, 1998), 415–19; "The Road from Nonviolence to Violence," Speech by Z. K. Matthews, Thomas Karis, and Gail Gerhart, *From Protest to Challenge 1882–1990; Nadir and Resistance vol. 5*, 355; ANC *Strategy and Tactics*, cited in Francis Meli, "South Africa and the Rise of African Nationalism," in *The National Question in South Africa, ed.* Maria van Diepen (London: Zed Books, 1988), 71; See also S. Hassim, J. Metekerkamp, and A. Todes, "A bit on the Side: Gender Struggle in the Politics of Transformation," *Transformation* 5 (1987): 3–32; Thomas Karis and Gail Gerhart, *From Protest to Challenge 1882–1990: Nadir and Resistance vol. 5:.* 16; Nelson Mandela, cited in "The Road from Nonviolence to Violence," Speech by Z. K. Matthews, Thomas Karis, and Gail Gerhart, *From Protest to Challenge 1882–1990; Nadir and Resistance*, vol. 5, 354.
24. Howard Barrell, "The Turn to the Masses: the African National Congress" Strategic Review of 1978–79," *Journal of Southern African Studies* 18, no.1 (March 1992): 71.
25. ANC *Strategy and Tactics*, cited in Francis Meli, "South Africa and the Rise of African Nationalism," in *The National Question in South Africa*, ed. Maria van Diepen (London: Zed Books, 1988), 71; See also Nelson Mandela, *Long Walk to Freedom* (London, 1993); Tom Lodge, "Mandela, Nelson," *The Oxford Companion to Politics of the World, ed*. Joel Krieger (London: Oxford University Press, 2001), 520–21.
26. G. M. Gerhart, *Black Power in South Africa* (Berkeley: University of California Press, 1978), 159.

27. G. M. Gerhart, *Black Power in South Africa*, 206; see also, R. M. Sobukwe, "Future of the Africanist Movement," in Karis and Carter, *From Protest*, vol. 3, 508.
28. Bernice Reagan quoted in Nancy Hartsock, "Foucault on Power," in *Feminism /Postmodernism, ed.* Linda J. Nicholson (New York: Routledge, 1994), 163; See also Thiven Reddy, *Hegemony and Resistance*, 193.
29. G. M. Gerhart, *Black Power in South Africa*, 247.
30. Thiven Reddy, *Hegemony and Resistance*, 194; On PAC see Thomas Karis and Gail Gerhart, *From Protest to Challenge A Documentary History of African Politics in South Africa, 1882–1990 vol. 5*; Mokgethi Motlhabi, *Black Resistance to Apartheid*, 40; Gail M. Gerhart, *Black Power in South Africa*; James Leatt, Theo Kneifel & Klaus Nuremberger, eds., *Contending Ideologies in South Africa* (Cape Town: David Phillip, 1986).
31. Gail M. Gerhart, *Black Power in South Africa*, 269.
32. Hendrik W. van der Merwe, Nancy C. J. Charton, D. A. Kotze and Ake Magnussen, eds., SASO Policy Manifesto, *African Perspectives on South Africa: Speeches, articles and documents* (Stanford: Hoover Institute, 1978), 99; Strini Moodley, *What is Black Consciousness* (Durban: Azapo publications, 1983); See also Thomas Karis and Gail Gerhart, *From Protest to Challenge A Documentary History of African Politics in South Africa 1882–1990* vol. 5.
33. Steve Biko, *I Write What I Like*, 63; On BCM see J. Leatt, T. Kneifel, and K. Nurnberger, *Contending Ideologies in South Africa*; Millard Arnold, *Steve Biko: Black Consciousness in South Africa* (New York: Vintage Books, 1979).
34. Steve Biko, *I Write What I Like* (London: The Bowerdean Press, 1978), 76.
35. Frantz Fanon, *The Wretched of the Earth* (New York: Grove Press, INC., 1963), 45.
36. Thiven Reddy, *Hegemony and Resistance Contesting Identities in South Africa*, 220.
37. J. Leatt, T. Kneifel, and K. Nurnberger, *Contending Ideologies*, 112; Baruch Hirson, *Year of Ash: The Soweto Revolt: Roots of a Revolution?* (London: Zed Publications, 1979); Alan Brooks and Jeremy Brickhill, *Whirlwind before the Storm* (London: International Defence and AID Fund for Southern Africa, 1980); D Du Toit, *Capital and Labour in South Africa: Class Struggles in the 1970's* (London: Kegan Paul, 1981); John Kane-Berman, *Soweto: Black Revolt White Reaction* (Johannesburg: Ravan Press, 1978).
38. Rian Malan, *My Traitor's Heart*, 300; See Francis Meli, "South Africa and the Rise of African Nationalism," in *The National Question in South Africa, ed.* Maria van Diepen (London: Zed Books, 1988), 66–75; Tom Lodge, *Black Politics in South Africa since 1945*; J. Leatt, T. Kneifel, and K. Nurnberger, *Contending Ideologies in South Africa*; Heribert Adam, *Modernizing Racial Domination: The Dynamics of South African Politics*; See also Vladimir Shubin, *ANC View From Moscow*, 91; Thomas Karis and Gail Gerhart, *From Protest to Challenge: A Documentary History of African Politics in South Africa, 1882–1990 vol. 5*.
39. Z. Pallo Jordan, "Socialist Transformation and the Freedom Charter," in *Whither South Africa?* ed. Bernard Magubane and Ibbo Mandaza, 95 (Trenton, NJ: Africa World Press, 1988); on AZAPO see Document 126, "Resolution adopted at the inaugural conference of the Azanian People's Organisation, Roodepoort September 29–39, 1979"; In *From Protest to Challenge: A Documentary History of African Politics in South Africa, 1882–1992, vol.5*, 761–63.
40. Heribert Adam and Kogila Moodley, *South Africa Without Apartheid*, 56.
41. "A Reply to Dr. Dadoo Through Steve Biko," *Ikwesi: A Pan Africanist Socialist Journal of Azanian Black and First World Liberation* 11 (March, 1979): 39–43.
42. "Struggling Shoulder to Shoulder," in *30 Years of the Freedom Charter*, ed. Raymond Suttner and Jeremy Cronin (Johannesburg: Ravan Press, 1986), 186.

43. Debby Bonin, Roger Deacon, Robert Morrell and Jenny Robinson, "Identity and the Changing Politics of Gender in South Africa," in *South Africa in Transition*, 119; Elaine Unterhalter, "Class, Race & Gender," in *South Africa in Question*.
44. Elaine Unterhalter, "Class, Race & Gender," *South Africa in Question*, 162; De Klerk, *The Puritans in Africa*
45. Ibid., 165; John Fisher, *The Afrikaners*.
46. Debby Bonnin et. al., "Identity and the Changing Politics of Gender in South Africa," 115; Raymond Suttner & Jeremy Cronin, *30 Years of the Freedom Charter*.
47. *Sechaba*, March 1981, 17–18.
48. Elaine Unterhalter, "Class, Race & Gender," 168; *Voice of Women* (First Quarter, 1986): 2.
49. Ibid., 115.
50. Teresa Marcus, "The Women's Question and National Liberation in South Africa," *The National Question in South Africa*, 100.
51. Elaine Unterhalter, "Class, Race & Gender," in *South Africa in Question*, 155.
52. Jeremy Seekings, "The Origins of Political Mobilisation in the PWV Townships," in ed. William Cobbert & Robin Cohen, *Popular Struggles in South Africa*, 65.
53. Elaine Unterhalter, "Class, Race & Gender," in *South Africa in Question*, 155.
54. Editorial, The *Guardian*, August 19, 1985.
55. S. Hassim and C. Walker, "Women's Studies and the Women's Movement in South Africa: Defining a Relationship," *Women's Studies International Forum*, 16, no.5 (1993): 523–34; J. Robinson, "White Women Researching /Representing Others: From Anti-Apartheid to Postcolonialism?" in *Writing Women and Space*, ed. G. Rose and A. Blunt (London: 1996), 197–226; Debby Bonnin, Roger Deacon, Robert Morrell, and Jenny Robinson, "Identity and the Changing Politics of Gender in South Africa," 124; C. Albertin, "Women and the transition to democracy in South Africa," in *Gender and the New South African Legal Order*, ed. C. Murray (Cape Town, 1994), 39–63; Joe Slovo, "South Africa-No Middle Road," in *Southern Africa: The New Politics of Revolution, ed.* Basil Davidson, David Wilkinson, and Joe Slovo (Harmondsworth: Penguin Books, 1976); Joe Slovo, "Has Socialism Failed?" *African Communist* 121 (1990); Joe Slovo, "Negotiations: What room for Compromise?" *The African Communist* 130 (Third Quarter: 1992); and his "Beyond the Stereotype: the SACP in the Past, Present and Future," *The African Communist* (Second Quater, 1992); J. Steinberg, "Leninist Fantasies and SACP Illusions," *Work in Progress* 74 (May, 1991); Dale T. Mckinley, *The ANC and the Liberation Struggle: A Critical Political Biography* (London: Pluto Press, 1997).

Chapter 4

1. Rachel L. Swanns "After Apartheid: White Anxiety," *New York Times* November 14, 1999, 1, 4; Mark Devenney, "South African Literature, Beyond Apartheid' in *South Africa in Transition: New Theoretical Perspectives, ed.* David R. Howarth & Aletta J. Norval (New York: Macmillan Press Ltd, 1998), 165–81.
2. Njabulo S. Ndebele, "Fools" in *Fools and other Stories*, ed. Njabulo S. Ndebele (Johannesburg: Ravan Press, 1983), 278.
3. Ibid., 225, 273.
4. Ibid., 273.
5. Ibid., 275.
6. Ibid., 276.
7. Ibid.

8. Mtutuzeli Matshoba, "My Friend, The Outcast" in *Call Me Not a Man*, ed. Mtutuzeli Matshoba(London: Longman, 1979), 1–17.
9. Ibid., 12.
10. Ibid., 13.
11. Ibid., 8.
12. Ibid., 17.
13. Etienne van Heerden, *Ancestral Voices*, trans. Malcolm Hacksley (Cape Town: Tafelberg Publishers, 1986).
14. Ibid., 179
15. J. M. Coetzee, *Age of Iron* (New York: Penguin Books, 1990), 50.
16. Ibid., 70.
17. Ibid., 70.
18. Ibid., 68.
19. Ibid., 48.
20. Ibid., 50
21. Ibid., 198.
22. Mark Behr, *The Smell of Apples* (London: Abacus, 1995).
23. Ibid., 124.
24. Ibid., 199
25. Ibid., 107.
26. Sindiwe Magona, "The Hand That Kills" in *Push-Push & Other Stories, ed. Sindiwe Magona* (Cape Town: David Phillip, 1996), 131.
27. Ibid., 128.
28. Ibid., 128
29. Ibid., 139
30. Mandla Langa, *The Naked Song & Other Stories* (Cape Town: David Phillip, 1996), 85.
31. Ibid., 83.
32. Ibid., 71.
33. Ibid., 79
34. Ibid., 90
35. Ibid., 90.
36. Ibid., 91
37. Mark Devenney, "South African Literature, Beyond Apartheid" in *South Africa in Transition: New Theoretical Perspectives, ed.* David R. Howarth & Aletta J. Norval (New York: Macmillan Press Ltd, 1998), 165–81.
38. Marlene van Niekerk, *Triomf.* Trans. Leon de Kock (Great Britain: Little, Brown and Company, 1999); See also, Shauna de Waal, "A Novel That Finds Adversity in Triomf," *Mail & Guardian*, April 9–15, 22–23, 1999 http://www.mg.co.za
39. Marlene van Niekerk, *Triomf,* 512–13.
40. Marlene van Niekerk, *Triomf,* 169.
41. Ibid., 30
42. Ibid., 30.
43. Ibid., 29.
44. Ibid., 522.

CHAPTER 5

1. Robert M. Price, *The Apartheid State in Crisis: Political Transformation in South Africa 1975–1990* (New York: Oxford University Press, 1991), 72.

2. Hermann Giliomee, "Broedertwis: Intra-Afrikaner Conflicts in the Transition from Apartheid 1969–1991," *African Affairs* 364 (1992): 349.
3. Hein Marais, *South Africa Limits to Change: The Political Economy of Transformation* (Cape Town: University Cape Town Press, 1998), 20.
4. Stephen Gelb, *South Africa's Economic Crisis* (Cape Town: David Philip, 1991), cited in Hein Marais, *South Africa: Limits to Change: The Political Economy of Transformation*, 21.
5. Hermann Giliomee, "Broedertwis," 399.
6. Heribert Adam and Hermann Giliomee, *Ethnic Power Mobilized: Can South Africa Change?* (New Haven: Yale University Press, 1979), 169.
7. William Pomeroy, *Apartheid Imperialism and African Freedom* (New York: International Publishers, 1986), 10; Vishnu Padayachee, "Private International Banks, The Debt Crisis and the Apartheid State, 1982–85," *African Affairs* (London), 1988; 87: 361–76.
8. Dan O' Meara, *Volkskapitalisme: Class, Capital and Ideology in the Development of Afrikaner Nationalism 1934–1948* (Johannesburg: Ravan Press, 1983), 250–54; Dan O'Meara, "'Muldergate' and the Politics of Afrikaner Nationalism," *Work in Progress* 22 (1982): 1–18.
9. Herman Giliomee, "Afrikanerdom Today: Ideology and Interests," unpublished manuscript (1987), 17.
10. J. Saul & S. Gelb, *The Crisis in South Africa: Class Defence and Class Revolution* (New York: Monthly Review Press, 1981), 23.
11. Hein Marais, *South Africa: Limits to Change*, 30.
12. Ibid., 117.
13. Vella Pillay, "Rising Cost of Apartheid," *Frontline Southern Africa: Destructive Engagement* ed. Phyllis Martin and David Martin (New York: Four Walls Eight Windows, 1988), 314–15.
14. Ibid., 317.
15. Ibid., 317
16. Robert M. Price, *The Apartheid State in Crisis*, 33; Merle Lipton, "Capitalism & Apartheid," in *South Africa in Question*, ed. John Lonsdale (London: James Currey, 1988), 52.
17. James Leatt, Theo Kneifel & Klaus Nuremberger, eds., *Contending Ideologies in South Africa* (Cape Town; David Philip, 1986), 82.
18. Hermann Giliomee, "Broedertwis," 346.
19. Charles H. Feinstein, *An Economic History of South Africa* (Cambridge, UK: Cambridge University Press, 2005), 213; Robert M. Price, *The Apartheid State in Crisis*, 32.
20. Charles H. Feinstein, *An Economic History of South Africa*, 213.
21. Anna Starcke, *Survival* (Tafelberg, Cape Town, 1978), 23. Quoted in Hermann Giliomee, "Broedertwis," 345.
22. Ibid., 345.
23. Merle Lipton, "Capitalism & Apartheid," 52.
24. Hermann Giliomee, "Broedertwis," 350.
25. Merle Lipton, "Capitalism & Apartheid," 57.
26. Vella Pillay, "Rising Cost of Apartheid," 323
27. Merle Lipton, "Capitalism & Apartheid," 57
28. Leonard Thompson, *A History of South Africa* (New Haven: Yale University Press, 2001).
29. Robert M. Price, *The Apartheid State in Crisis*, 84.
30. Craig Charney, "The National Party, 1982–1985: A Class Alliance in Crisis," 24. In ed. Wilmot James and Craig Charney, *The State of Apartheid* (Boulder: Lynne Rienner, 1987), 5–36.
31. Ibid., 24.

32. *The Guardian*, 30 October 1985, *The State of Apartheid*.
33. *Sunday Times*, 17 June 1984.
34. *Rapport* 28 April 1985; *The Star* 27 May 1985. See also Hermann Giliomee, "The Growth of Afrikaner Identity," in ed. Hermann Giliomee and Heribert Adam, *Ethnic Power Mobilized*.
35. Vella Pillay, "Rising Cost of Apartheid," 315.
36. Hermann Giliomee, "Broedertwis," 363. According to Nolutshungu, "The Verligte and Verkrampte represent two inherent contradictory tendencies of exclusivism and accommodation within the nationalist Afrikanerdom. While the Verligtes see themselves as white men (as well as Afrikaners) the Verkramptes see themselves as Afrikaners first and insist that it is their detailed dissimilarity from other white groups in Africa which accounts for their survival in a hostile Africa." Sam Noltshungu, "Issues of Afrikaner Enlightenment" *African Affairs* 70 (1971), 28.
37. Du Pisani, *Vorster en die Verlig/Verkrampstryd*, 178, quoted in "Broedertwis," 348.
38. Craig Charney, "The National Party, 1982–1985: A Class Alliance in Crisis," 9.
39. Ibid., 15
40. Vladimir Shubin, *ANC: A View From Moscow* (Cape Town: Mayibuye Books, 1999), 309; see also *Pravda*, 5 November 1986.
41. Hermann Giliomee, "Broedertwis," 360.
42. "Political Values for the Survival of the Afrikaner," unpublished document of the Afrikaner Broederbond, ca July 1989; cited Hermann Giliomee "Broedertwis," 360.
43. Hermann Giliomee, "Broedertwis," 361.
44. Hein Marais, *South Africa: Limits to Change*, 38.
45. Counter Information Services, *Black South Africa Explodes* (London: Counter Information Services, 1977), 44–45; On Sophiatown see Bloke Modisane, *Blame me on History* (London: Thames and Hudson, 1963); Trevor Huddleston, *Naught for Your Comfort* (Glasgow: William Sons & Sons, 1987).
46. Ibidem.
47. Robert M. Price, *The Apartheid State in Crisis*, 57.
48. Ibid., 54; Alan Brooks and Jeremy Brickhill, *Whirlwind Before the Storm: Origins and Development of the Uprising in Soweto and the Rest of South Africa, June–December 1976* (South Africa: Mayibue Books, 1978), 179.
49. All the information for housing in this section are reproduced from: *World Bank, Economics and Finance Division Technical Department, African Region, Iintra-Regional Trade in Sub-Saharan Africa* (Washington DC: World Bank, May 1991). Reproduced from Microeconomic Research Group, *Making Democracy work*, 124–25.
50. Vella Pillay, "The Rising Cost of Apartheid," 327.
51. Source SAIRR (National Housing Forum-South Africa Institute of Race Relations) "Making Democracy Work: A Framework for Macroeconomic Policy in South Africa," 124.
52. William Minter, "Destructive Engagement: The United States and South Africa in the Reagan Era," in *Frontline Southern Africa: Destructive Engagement*, 406; John Kane Berman, *Soweto; Black Revolt White Reaction* (Johannesburg: Ravan Press, 1981); Guy Martin, *Africa in World Politics: A Pan-African Perspective* (Trenton, NJ: Africa World Press, 2002), 159–61 with 159–63 William Pomeroy, *Apartheid, Imperialism and African Freedom*, 40; Vella Pillay, "The Rising Cost of Apartheid," 318.
54. William Pomeroy, *Apartheid, Imperialism and African Freedom*, 40.
55. Robert M. Price, *The Apartheid State in Crisis*, 43; David Harrison, *The White Tribe of Africa: South Africa in Perspective* (Berkeley: University of California Press, 1981), 227–60.
56. *Rapport*, January 2, 1977; Quoted in Hermann Giliomee, "The Growth of Afrikaner Identity," in Hermann Giliomee and Heribert Adam, *Ethnic Power Mobilized*, 130.
57. Dan O'Meara, Rob Davies, and Sipho Dlamini, *The Struggle for South Africa: A Reference Guide to Movements, Organizations, and Institutions* (London: Zed Press, 1984), 123, cited in

William Minter, *King Solomon's Mines Revisited: Western Interests and the Burdened History of Southern Africa* (New York: Basic Books, 1986), 285–86.
58. Craig Charney, "The National Party, 1982–1985," 10.
59. Ibid., 10.
60. Leonard Thompson, *A History of South Africa* (New Haven, CT: Yale University Press, 2000), 224–25; William Minter, *King Solomon's Mines Revisited*, 250
61. Hein Marais, *South Africa: Limits to Change*, 42.
62. *South Africa Limits to Change*, 43.
63. Republic of South Africa, *Report of the Commission of Inquiry into the Riots at Soweto and Elsewhere (Cillie Commission Report)* (Pretoria: Government Printer, 1980), 604.
64. A. Stadler, *The Political Economy of Modern South Africa* (Cape Town: David Philips, 1987), 160; Vella Pillay, "The Rising Cost of Apartheid," 330; M. Morris & P. Padayachee, "Hegemonic Projects, Accumulation Strategies and State Reform Policy in South Africa," *Labour, Capital and Society*, Vol. 22 No. 1 (1989).
65. Army Chief of Staff (later Defence Minister) General Magnus Malan, cited in Hein Marais, *South Africa: Limits to Change*, 42; Wilmot G. James, "The State of Apartheid: An Introduction," 1–4.
66. Hermann Giliomee, *The Parting of the Ways*, 35.
67. David Harrison, *The White Tribe of Africa: South Africa in Perspective* (Berkeley: University of California Press, 1981), 248.
68. Vella Pillay, "Raising Cost of Apartheid," 331
69. M. Morris, "State, Capital and Growth; *The Political Economy of the National Question*," in *South Africa's Economic Crisis*, ed. Stephen Gelb, 51; Hermann Giliomee, "Broedertwis: Intra-Afrikaner Conflicts in the Transition from Apartheid 1969–1991," 354.
70. Vella Pillay, "Rising Cost of Apartheid," 330; Macroeconomic Research Group, *Making Democracy Work: A Framework for Macroeconomic Policy in South Africa*, 150.
71. Macroeconomic Research Group, *Making Democracy Work*, 150.
72. Reproduced from Vella Pillay "The Rising Cost of Apartheid,"331; D. Budlender, "Women and the Economy," Women and Gender in South Africa conference (paper no. 7, 1991), 12; see also A Bird and C. Lloyd "The Role of Education and Training in Industry and Economic Policy-A South African Trade Union Perspective," Conference Paper for Economic Trends (Mimeo, 1992), 3.
73. Senior NSMS official, quoted in *Weekly Mail*, 3 October 1986, cited in Hein Marias, *South Africa Limits to Change*, 62
74. David Ottaway, *Chained Together*, 232.
75. Ibid., 233.
76. UN World Economic Survey, 1992, cited in Hein Marias, *South Africa: Limits to Change*, 121.
77. Hein Marias, *South Africa: Limits to Change*, 125.
78. S. Lall in A. Baker, A. Borraine & W. Krafchik eds., *South Africa and the World Economy in the 1990s* (Cape Town: David Phillip, 1993), 61–62, cited in *South Africa: Limits to Change*, 128.
79. *Ibid.*, 64.
80. United Nations Security Council, *Resolution 392 South Africa* (June 19, 1976), *Situation in South Africa: Killings and Violence by the Apartheid Regime in South Africa in Soweto and other Areas*
81. Robert M. Price, *The Apartheid State in Crisis*, 63.
82. Martin Bailey, "Foreign Loans are Drying up for White South Africa," *New African* (June 1977), 575.
83. Ibid., 575.
84. Vella Pillay, "The Rising Cost of Apartheid," 310.

85. *The Guardian* 15 September 1985.
86. William Minter, "Destructive Engagement: The United States and South Africa in the Reagan Era," in ed. Phyllis Johnson and David Martin *Frontline Southern: Destructive Engagement* (New York: Four Walls Eight Windows,1988), 428.
87. Ibid., 70.
88. G. Starushenko, Problems of the Struggle against Racism, Apartheid and Colonialism in South Africa (Africa Institute, Moscow, 1986):12; Izvestiya, 4 August 1987. Quoted in Vladimir Shubin, *ANC: A View from Moscow*, 309.
89. African National Congress, *Unite for Freedom: Statement by the African National Congress on the Question of Unity and Anti-Apartheid Coalition 1985–1990* (ANC DIP, Lusaka: 1987): 1.
90. Hermann Giliomee, "Broedertwis" 358; Hermann Giliomee is not the only author for understanding the reasons for negotiations. Various authors have addressed this process. See; Heribert Adam & Kogila Moodley, *The Negotiated Revolution: Society and Politics in Post-Apartheid South Africa* (Johannesburg: Jonathan Ball, 1993); Wilmot G. James, ed., *The State of Apartheid* (Boulder: 1987); Vladimir Shubin, *ANC: A View From Moscow* (Cape Town: Mayibuye Books, 1990; Steven Friedman and Doreen Atkinson, *South African Review 7: The Small Miracle South Africa's Negotiated Settlement* (Johannesburg: Ravan Press, 1994); David Ottaway, *Chained Together: Mandela, De Klerk, and the Struggle to Remake South Africa* (New York: Times Books, 1993); Patti Waldmeir, *Anatomy of a Miracle: The end of Apartheid and the Birth of the New South Africa* (New Jersey: Rutgers University Press, 1997); Allister Sparks, *Tomorrow is Another Country: The Inside Story of South Africa's Negotiated Revolution* (Johannesburg: Struik Book Distributors, 1994); Johannes Mutshutshu Rantete, *The African National Congress and The Negotiated Settlement in South Africa* (Pretoria: J. L. van Schaik, 1998).
91. Hermann Giliomee, "Broedertwis" 358
92. Martin Meredith, *The Fate of Africa: A History of Fifty Years of Independence* (New York: Public Affairs, 2005), 435–36.

Chapter 6

1. David Ottaway, *Chained Together: Mandela, De Klerk and the Struggle to Remake South Africa* (New York: Times Books, 1993);88; William Mervin Gumede, *Thabo Mbeki and the Battle for the Soul of the ANC* (Cape Town: Zebra Press, 2005); Martin Meredith, *The Fate of Africa: A History of Fifty Years of Independence* (New York: Public Affairs, 2005); Anne Marie du Preez Bezdrob, *Winnie Mandela: A Life* (Cape Town: Zebra Press, 2003); P. Eric Louw, *The Rise, Fall and Legacy of Apartheid* (London: Praeger, 2004).
2. David Ottaway, *Chained Together: Mandela, De Klerk and the Struggle to Remake South Africa*, 88.
3. *The Secretary-General's Report*, ANC National Conference, July 1991, 28.
4. David Ottaway, *Chained Together*, 101.
5. Ivor Sarakinsky, "Rehearsing Joint Rule: The Transitional Executive Council," in ed. Steven Friedman and Doreen Atkinson. *The Small Miracle: South Africa's Negotiated Settlement* (Johannesburg: Raven Press, 1994), 69.
6. Simon Adams, *Comrade Minister: The South African Communist Party and the Transition from Apartheid to Democracy* (New York: Nova Publishers, 2001), 110.
7. On the transition see, Richard Spitz with Mathew Chaskalson, *The Politics of Transition: a Hidden History of South Africa's Negotiated Settlement* (Johannesburg: Witwatersrand University Press, 2000), 72.

8. Roger Southall, "The Contradictory State! The Proposals of the National Party for a New Constitution," *Monitor* (October 1991): 90–91; Mathew Chaskalson, *The Politics of Transition*, 16.
9. Raymond Suttner, "Progress in talks" (paper presented to the PWV Regional Workshop, November 17, 1990) and his "Do we Continue the Talks?" *New Era* 5(3) (Summer, 1990): 5; On MK's reaction, see P. Bulger, "Township calls for MK's help growing loud," *Business Day*, January 15, 1991; C. Mathews, "Hani proposes Self Defence Units," *Business Day*, August 27, 1990; D. Beresford, "ANC suspends armed struggle in Peace deal," *Guardian Weekly*, August 12, 1990; According to Mandela Joe Slovo first introduced the idea of abandoning the armed struggle. Mandela's *Long Walk to Freedom*, 701–2. This information is borrowed from Simon Adams, *Comrade Minister*, 112.
10. Johannes J. Mutshtshu Rantete *The African National Congress and the Negotiated Settlement in South Africa* (Pretoria: J. L. Van Schaik Academic, 1998), 196.
11. Ibid., 193.
12. Johannes Rantete, *The African National Congress*, 196.
13. Ralph Lawrence, "Introduction: From Soweto to CODESA" in eds. Steve Friedman and Doreen Atkinson, *South African Review 7 The Small Miracle*, 9
14. *Sunday Times*, October 13, 1991; William Mervin Gumede, *Thabo Mbeki and the Battle for the Soul of the ANC*. Cape Town: Zebra Press, 2005.
15. Richard Spitz and Mathew Chaskalson, *The Politics of Transition*, 17.
16. ANC, "Guidelines on Strategy and Tactics of the ANC," February 1991 http://www.ANC.org.ZA/Ancdocs/history/keydocs.html; see also Richard Spitz and Mathew Chaskalson, *The Politics of Transition*, 17; P. Laurence, "Mandela adamant on Nationalisation," *The Star*, January, 26 1990; K. Nyarsumba, "ANC Flexible on Economy-Mandela," *The Star*, November 21, 1991; S. Johnson, "Nationalisation only one option-ANC," *The Star*, April 29, 1992; J. Batterby, "Mandela Nationalisation call Shakes S. African Market," *Christian Science Monitor*, February 16, 1990; S. Russels, "ANC Shifts Economic Stand," *Business Day*, May 7, 1990; C. Smith, "The Nightmare Recedes," *Financial Mail*, October 5, 1990; P. Laurence, "ANC Nationalisation U-Turn," *Guardian Weekly* March 5, 1991; "C. Ceruti, "How and Why the ANC's Nationalisation Policy Changed: Economic Nationalisation and the Changing State-Capital Relation" (MA Thesis, University of Witwatersrand, 1995); Joe Slovo, "SACP Backs Mixed Economy, Says Slovo," *The Citizen*, June 29, 1990.
17. David Ottaway, *Chained Together: Mandela, De Klerk and the Struggle to Remake South Africa*, 113.
18. Simon Adams, *Comrade Minister*, 112.
19. Johannes Rantete, *The African National Congress*, 182.
20. Thula Bopela and Daluxolo Luthuli, *Umkhonto we Sizwe: Fighting for a Divided People* (Alberton, South Africa: Galago Publishing, 2005); Anthony Minnaar, "The Impact of Political Violence Since 1990 on the Transition to Democracy in South Africa," unpublished paper, June 1994, cited in Mark Shaw, "The bloody Backdrop: Negotiating Violence," in ed. Steven Friedman and Doreen Atkinson *South African Review 7. The Small Miracle: South Africa's Negotiated Settlement*, 182.
21. Doreen Atkinson, "Principle Born out of Pragmatism?"*in* ed. Steven Friedman, and Doreen Atkinson. *South African Review 7, The Small Miracle: South Africa's Negotiated Settlement*, 94.
22. Ibid., 100;
23. Johannes Rantete, *The African National Congress*, 208; *Questions and Answers on Interim Government*, An ANC information pamphlet, January 1991.

24. Claire Robertson, "Contesting the Contest: Negotiating the Election machinery," in ed. Steven Friedman, and Doreen Atkinson. *South African Review 7, The Small Miracle: South Africa's Negotiated Settlement*, 46; Joe Slovo, "Negotiations: What Room for Compromise?" *The African Communist* Fourth Quarter (1992): 40; During the first days of CODESA, Thabo Mbeki had also spoken of 'sun-set clauses'
25. Harry Gwala,"Negotiations as Presented by Joe Slovo," *The African Communist* Fourth Quarter (1992): 28; For the other critics of this process see Blade Nzimande, "Let us Take the People With Us: A Reply to Joe Slovo," *The African Communist* Fourth Quarter (1992): 20; Pallo Jordan, "Strategic Debate in the ANC: A Response to Joe Slovo," *The African Communist* Fourth Quarter (1992): 8–9.
26. Barnabas Wondo *Interview*, 21 July 1995 cited by Simon Adams, *Comrade Minister*, 154.
27. Joe Slovo cited in T. Mali, *Chris Hani: The Sun that Set Before Dawn* (Johannesburg: Sacked, 1993), 91 see also obituaries by Slovo, Nelson Mandela, and Fidel Castro in "Tribute to a Fallen Hero," *Umsebenzi* 9, no.1 (1993); Simon Adams, *Comrade Minister*, 152.
28. Anthony Minnaar, "The Impact of Political Violence Since 1990 on the Transition to Democracy in South Africa," unpublished paper, June 1994, cited in Mark Shaw, "The bloody Backdrop: Negotiating Violence," *The Small Miracle*, 182.
29. Ibid., 182.
30. J. Cronin, "We Need More than Group Therapy," *Work in Progress* (June 1993), 14; Mark Shaw, "The Bloody Backdrop: Negotiating Violence" in ed. Steven Friedman, and Doreen Atkinson. *South African Review 7, The Small Miracle: South Africa's Negotiated Settlement*, 182.
31. Johannes Rantete, *The African National Congress*, 257.
32. Ibid., 205.
33. Greg Mills and Geoffrey Wood, "Ethnicity, Integration and the South African Armed Forces," *South African Defence Review 12* (1993), cited in Mark Shaw, "Biting the Bullet: Negotiating Democracy's Defence," in ed. Steven Friedman, and Doreen Atkinson. *South African Review 7: The Small Miracle: South Africa's Negotiated Settlement* 230.
34. Mark Shaw, "Biting the Bullet: Negotiating Democracy's Defence," ed. Steven Friedman, and Doreen Atkinson. *South African Review 7: The Small Miracle: South Africa's Negotiated Settlement*, 232; See also Laurie Nathan, *The Changing of the Guard: Armed Forces and Defence Policy in a Democratic South Africa* (Pretoria: HSRC, 1994); This process is reminiscent of what happened during Kenya's independence, when former freedom fighters were integrated into the colonial army where they were taught "professional" standards, which, in essence, meant buying them off by wrapping them in the colonial army's ethics and values. As a result, these freedom fighters became the "oppressor" under the new regime; see Horace Campbell, "The Popular Demand for Dismantling of the Apartheid Military Machine and Problems of Conversion of the Military Industrial Complex" in *The Military and Militarism in Africa*, ed. Eboe Hutchful and Abdoulaye Bathily (Dakar: CODESRIA, 1998), 541–87.
35. Mark Shaw, "Biting the Bullet: Negotiating Democracy's Defence," in ed. Steven Friedman, and Doreen Atkinson. *South African Review 7, The Small Miracle: South Africa's Negotiated Settlement*, 233;
36. Ibid., 246.
37. Ibid., 247; see also *SADF Internal Communication Bulletin*. "Achievements by the SADF in the Negotiating Process,:" January 2, 1994, no.2

38. Doreen Atkinson, "Brokering a Miracle? The Multiparty Negotiating Forum," in ed. Steven Friedman, and Doreen Atkinson. *South African Review 7, The Small: Miracle South Africa's Negotiated Settlement*, 14.
39. Doreen Atkinson, "Brokering a Miracle: The Multiparty Negotiating Forum," in ed. Steven Friedman, and Doreen Atkinson. *South African Review 7, The Small Miracle: South Africa's Negotiated Settlement?*" 14.
40. Doreen Atkinson, "Brokering a Miracle? The Multiparty Negotiating Forum," in ed. Steven Friedman and Doreen Atkinson. *South African Review 7, The Small Miracle: South Africa's Negotiated Settlement*, 16
41. Ivor Sarakinsky, "Rehearsing Joint Rule: The Transitional Executive Council" in *The Small Miracle Steven, ed. Friedman and Doreen Atkinson*, 72.
42. Johannes Rantete, *The African National Congress*, 169.
43. Anne Marie du Preez Bezdrob, *Winnie Mandela: A Life* (Cape Town: Zebra Press, 2003), 160–61; See also *This writer's personal interview with Dinesh Prashad* July 15, 1998.
44. David Ottaway, *Chained Together*, 162–63.
45. Harry Gwala cited in R. Mkhondo, *Reporting South Africa* (London: James Currey, 1993), 162; see also "The Role of the SACP in the Transition to Democracy and Socialism," *African Communist* 133 (Second Quarter, 1993); T. Molaba, "Letter of Resignation," *African Communist* 135 (Fourth Quarter 1993): 16–17; F. Abdullah, "A Response to Theo Molaba's letter of Resignation," *African Communist* 135 (Fourth Quarter, 1993); S. Shilowa, "Working Class Unity . . . not a Separate Party," *Weekly Mail & Guardian*, August 12, 1993; Kasrils from R. Hartley, "Unions at Odds over New Workers' Party," *Sunday Times*, July 11, 1993; F. Haffajee, "Workers Party: Jumping the Gun?" *Weekly Mail*, July 23, 1993; J. Cronin, "Workers' Party Plays into Nat Hands," *Weekly Mail*, July 23, 1993; M. Mayekiso, "Reinventing the Hammer and Sickle," Work In Progress, 37–39; C. Louw, "Killing Highlights ANC and NP rifts," *Weekly Mail*, April 16–22, 1993.
46. Johannes Rantete, *The African National Congress*, 211.
47. *The Star*, January 24, 1993; on COSATU's position see C. Ramaphosa, "The Role of Unions in the Transition," *African Communist* 133 (Second Quarter, 1993); J. Moleketti, "Is a Retreat from National Democratic Revolution to National Bourgeois Revolution Imminent?" *African Communist* 133 (Second Quarter, 1993), 11–19.
48. Heribert Adam, Frederick Van Zyl Slabbert, and Kogila Moodley, *Comrades in Business*, 58; see also Simon Adams, *Comrade Minister*, 147–65.
49. Saki Macozoma, "Black Economic Empowerment: A New Covenant Forged in Hope" *Optima* 50 no. 2 (May 2004).
50. Doreen Atkinson, "Brokering a Miracle?," in ed. Steven Friedman and Doreen Atkinson. *South African Review 7, The Small Miracle: South Africa's Negotiated Settlement?*" 35.
51. Johannes Rantete, *The African National Congress*, 212.

Chapter 7

1. Frantz Fanon, *Les Damnés de la Terre* (Paris: François Maspéro, 1961), 122–24.
2. Rita Abrahamsen, *Disciplining Democracy* (London: Zed, 2001), xi–xv, 109.
3. Patrick Bond, *Elite Transition: From Apartheid to Neoliberalism in South Africa* (Scottsville: University of Kwa-Zulu Natal Press, 2005), 19.
4. Sebastian Mallaby, *After Apartheid: The Future of South Africa* (New York: Times Books, 1992), 60.
5. Jeremy Seekings and Nicoli Nattrass, *Class, Race, and Inequality in South Africa* (New Haven: Yale University Press, 2005), 17.

6. Ibid;17
7. Ibid., 47.
8. Ibid., 343.
9. Rita Abrahamsen, *Disciplining Democracy*,79–80
10. Jeremy Cronin, "Neo-Colonials and Mint Imperials,' *Mail and Guardian* (March 13–19, 1998), 20
11. Ibid.,20
12. Pallo Jordan "Soul-Brother Talk of Empowerment?" *Mail and Guradian* (March 20–26 1998),26
13. "Ex-activist Contemplates What it means to Become Filthy Rich," *The Sunday Independent* (May 3 1998), 26.
14. John Pilger,"Outcry over My Film Proves it Hit Home," *The Sunday Independent* (May 3,1998),11
15. Heribert Adam, "Empowering the Black Fat Cats," *Mail and Guardian* (April 9–16 1998), 22.
16. Heribert Adam, F. Van Zyl Slabbert, and Kogila Moodley, *Comrades in Business: Post–Liberation Politics in South Africa* (Cape Town: Tafelberg, 1997), 187
17. Ibid., 163.
18. Stephen Gelb and Lael Bethlehem, "Micro-Economics for the Masses?" *Siyaya!* (no.1. Autumn 1998), 14.
19. Heribert Adam, F. Van Zyl Slabbert, and Kogila Moodley, *Comrades in Business: Post–Liberation Politics in South Africa*, 155.
20. Patrick Bond, *Talk Left Walk Right: South Africa's Frustrated Global Reforms*,(Scottsville, South Africa: University of Kwazulu Natal Press, 2004).
21. Heribert Adam, F. Van Zyl Slabbert, and Kogila Moodley, *Comrades in Business: Post–Liberation Politics in South Africa*, 157.
22. Ibid., 144.
23. William Mervin Gumede, *Thabo Mbeki and the Battle for the Soul of the ANC*, 67–68
24. Hein Marais, *South Africa: Limits to Change-the Political Economy of Transition* (Cape Town: University of Cape Town, 2001), 123.
25. Phillip Dexter, 'The RDP," *South African Labour Bulletin*, September 1995, 58.
26. Editorial, "Taking a Stand But How Could the ANC Deliver?" *Mail and Guardian* (November 13–19, 1998),6–7
27. Ibrahim A. Elbadawi and Trudi Hartzenberg "Introduction and Overview" in ed. Ibrahim A. Elbadawi and Trudi Hartzenberg, *Development Issues in South Africa* (New York: St Martins Press, 2000),1–13
28. *The RDP Programme* (Johannesburg: Umanyano Publications, 2000); Ishamel Lesufi, "Six Years of Neoliberal Socio-Economic Policies in South Africa" *Journal of Asian and African Studies* (vol.31, no. 3–5 2002), 286–298.
29. Michael Morris, "Rich get Richer, But now They're Black," *Cape Argus* (March 8, 1999),11
30. Editorial, *Mail and Guardian* (November 13–19 1998),6
31. Editorial, "Taking a Stand But How Could the ANC Deliver?" *Mail and Guardian*, 7.
32. Jaspreet Kindra, "ANC Might Oust Communist Party Officials," September 21, 2001, http://www.allafrica.com.
33. Irene Louw "South Africa: COSATU Anti-Privatization Strike Could be Delayed," *Business Day*, http://www.labournet; "Accelerating Transformation: COSATU's Engagement with Policy and Legislative Processes during South Africa's first Term of Democratic Governance," http://www.COSATU.ORG.ZA.

34. Sampie Terreblanche, *A History of Inequality in South Africa 1652–2002* (Petermaritzburg: University of Natal Press, 2003), 304.
35. Michael Morris, "Rich Get Richer, But Now They're Black," 11. In 1996 the ANC, GNU, Labor agreed to a "National Framework Agreement (NFA) on the Restructuring of State Assets" which specified sectors of the economy that would be restructured under GEAR. Its goals included the reduction of state debt and a focus on economic growth, among other aspects. NFA was reaffirmed in 2000.
36. Renosi Mokate, "Macro-Economic Context," 58.
37. J. Cronin "Why the SACP Rejects GEAR" *Mail & Guardian*, July 10–16, 1998, 34.
38. Thabo Mbeki, "State of the Nation Address," February 14, 2003. See also, Henri E. Cauvin, "Privatization Snag in South Africa," November 2, 2001, http://query.nytimes.com.
39. Renosi Mokate, "Macro-Economic Context," 57.
40. Stephen Gelb and Laelethlehem, "Macro-Economics for the Masses?" *Siyaya!* 17; "Taking a Stand But How Could the ANC Deliver?" *Mail & Guardian*, Editorial, 7.
41. Ashwin Desai, "Racism Just Donning a New Guise in "New" SA," *Saturday Argus* March 7–8, 1998; Martin Wittenberg, "Growth, Demand and Redistribution: Economic Debates, Rhetoric and Some Food for Thought," in *The Political Economy of South Africa's Transition*, 167; see also Ibrahim A. Elbadawi and Trudi Hartzenberg, ed., *Development Issues in South Africa*; John Ernstzen, "Affirmative Action in Public Sector Employment," Conference on Affirmative Action (Belleville: Centre for Development Studies, 1992); Thabo Mbeki, "State of the Nation Address," February 14, 2003; "Privatisation," *The Sunday Independent*, June 27, 1999, 4; 50 percent of South Africa's economy depends on foreign trade; see also Greg Mills, Growth and Stability Top Foreign Agenda," *The Sunday Independent*, June, 27 1999, 9.
42. Ashwin Desai, "Racism Just Donning a New Guise in "New" SA," *Saturday Argus*, March 7–8, 1998.
43. Ferial Haffajee, "Tapping into Real Change: Taking Stock," *Mail and Guardian*, February 5–11 1999), 11.
44. Jeremy Seekings and Nicoli Nattrass, *Class, Race and Inequality in South Africa* (New Haven: Yale University Press, 2005), 133.
45. Ibid., 135; E. Malherbe, *Education in South Africa*, vol. 2, *1923–1975* (Cape Town: Juta, 1977), 722; P. Pillay, "The Development of Underdevelopment of Education in South Africa," in *Education: From Poverty to Liberty, ed.* W. Nassan and J. Samuel (Cape Town: David Phillip, 1990).
46. *Edusource Data News*, July 1996, 20.
47. Debbie Budlender, "Human Development," in *Poverty Inequality in South Africa*, 100; Debbie Budlender 'Patterns of Poverty in South Africa" *Development Southern Africa* (vol. 16, 3 1999), 197–219
48. Debbie Budlender, "Human Development," in *Poverty Inequality in South Africa*, 100
49. William Mervin Gumede, *Thabo Mbeki and the Battle for the Soul of The ANC*, 113.
50. Ann Eveleth, "Cinderella' Promises Must Wait for Funds" *Mail and Guardian* (October 23–29 1998),37
51. Julian May, Ingrid Woolard and Stephen Klasen, "The Nature and Measurement of Poverty And Inequality," in *Poverty Inequality in South Africa*, 20–48
52. Cornia Pretorius, Prega Govender, Ayesha Ismail, and Henry Ludski,"Curriculum 2005 Fails Grade 1," *Sunday Times* (May 17, 1998),13

53. Linda Chisholm, "The State of South Africa's Schools," in *State of the Nation South Africa 2004–2005*, ed. John Daniel, Roger Southall and Jessica Lutchamn (Cape Town: HRSC, 2005), 203.
54. Ibid., 217; C. Soudien notes that this pattern is followed throughout South Africa where students are confronted by racist teachers and administrators; see also C. Soudien, "Constituting the Class: An analysis of the Process of 'integration' in South African schools," in *Changing Class: Education and Social Change in Post-apartheid South Africa*, ed. L. Chisholm (Pretoria: HSRC Press, 2004).
55. N. Hunter, J. May, and V. Padayachee, "Lessons for PRSP From Poverty Reduction Strategies in South Africa" (paper presented to the Economic Commission for Africa, Addis Ababa, Ethiopia, December 3, 2003); cited in Patrick Bond, *Elite Transition*, 270; on school disparity see Albert van Zyl, "Easing the Education Crisis," *Cape Times*, May 27, 1998, 19; Because of the introduction of fee paying, privileged schools have retained their status since they can afford better trained teachers. School governing bodies have the right to set fees that depend on the wealth of the community. As a result, some schools, especially in the townships and rural areas, have remained exclusively African and very poor with unqualified teachers; see also E. Fiske and H. Ladd, "Balancing Public and Private Resources for Basic Education: School Fees in Post-apartheid South Africa," in *Changing Class: Education and Social Change in Post-Apartheid South Africa*, ed. Linda Chisholm (Pretoria: HSRC, 2004); B. Fuller, P. Pillay and N. Sirur, "Literacy Trends in South Africa: Expanding Education While Reinforcing Unequal Achievement," Harvard University and University of Cape Town, May 31, 1995.
56. Jeremy Seekings and Nicoli Nattrass, *Class, Race and Inequality in South Africa* (New Haven: Yale University Press, 2005), 136; D. McIntyre, "Heath Care Financing and Expenditure in South Africa: Towards Equity and Efficiency in Policy Making" (PhD diss., University of Cape Town, 1997).
57. Macroeconomic Research Group, *Making Democracy Work*, 107.
58. Ferial Haffajee, "Nation Passes Medical Exam," *Mail & Guardian*, January 29 to February 4, 1999, 34; http://196.36.153.56/doh/docs/reports/2000/hivreport.html; Year 2001, http://196.36.153.56/doh/docs/sum-report.html; Year 2002, http://196.36.153.56/doh/docs/reports/2002/hiv-syphilis.pdf
59. Ferial Haffajee, "Nation Passes Medical Exam," *Mail & Guardian*, 34.
60. Patrick Bond, *Talk Left Walk Right: South Africa's Frustrated Global Reforms* (Scottsville, South Africa: University of KwaZulu-Natal Press, 2004), 84; P. Bond and G. Dor, "Uneven Health Outcomes and Political Resistance under Residual Neoliberalism in Africa," *International Journal of Health Services 33* (2002): 3; Patrick Bond and G. Dor, "The Residual Dominance of Neoliberalism in Africa," in *Transforming South Africa*, ed. A. Osmanovic (Hamburg: Institute of African Affairs, 2003).
61. Macroeconomic Research Group, *Making Democracy Work*, 108.
62. Macroeconomic Research Group, *Making Democracy Work*, 108
63. Ibid., 110
64. Charlene Smith, "AZT Case Put on the Test" *Mail and Guardian* (Feburary 28-March 26 1999),10; Aaron Nicodemus "The New South Africa's Silent Killer," *Mail and Guardian* (April 30-May 6 1999), 41
65. Patrick Bond, *Elite Transition: From Apartheid to Neoliberalism in South Africa*, 284–286
66. Ibid.,285; The debt repayment is a major contrast with the amount that government paid to the victims of apartheid death and torture ($85 million); see also Naomi Klein, *The Shock Doctrine: The Rise of Disaster Capitalism* (New York: Metropolitan Books, 2007), 212.

67. *Wall Street*, 16 April 2002 cited by Patrick Bond, *Elite Transition*, 286.
68. *Financial Times*, 18 September 2003 cited by Patrick Bond, *Elite Transition*, 287.
69. Ibid., 288.
70. Ibid., 288.
71. Andrew Geoghegan, "Correspondent's Report-South Africa Struggles to Cut HIV/AIDS Rates," December, 10 2006, available at http://www.abc.net.au; William Mervin Gumede, *Thabo Mbeki and the Battle for the Soul of the ANC*.
72. Macroeconomic Research Group, *Making Democracy Work*, 82; Race Relations Survey (Johannesburg, 1993),
73. National Housing Forum, "Land and Services-Executive Summary of Consultants," Report, Working Group 1, May 1993.
74. Bill Keller, "After Apartheid, Change Lags Behind expectations," *New York Times* (April 27, 1995), A1, A6.
75. Lizeka Mda, "Sweating it out in Diepsloot No. 1," *Mail and Guardian* (April 3–8 1998), 11; Mandla Mnyakama, 'Police Open Fire on 'Illegals' During Eviction," *Cape Argus* (Feburary 26, 1999), 5
76. Patrick Bond, *Elite TransitionFrom Apartheid to Neoliberalism in South Africa*, 271;Ferial Hafajee, "Sankie Shows Women can Build," *Mail and Guardian* (April 30-May 6 1999),43; *Mail and Guardian* Reporters, "Whatever Happened to the Dream of Low-Cost Housing?" *Mail and Guardian* (Feburary 20–26 1998), 4; Sven Lunsche, "ANC Good Deeds Come to Greif at Local Level" *Sunday Times* (May 30 1999), 10
77. David Hemson and Michael O'Donovan, "Putting Numbers to the Scorecard: Presidential Targets and the Sate of Delivery" in ed. Sakhela Buhlungu, John Daniel, Roger Southall and Jessica Luthman.,*South Africa 2005–2006 State of the Nation* (Cape Town: Human Sciences Research Council, 2006),19,24
78. Ferial Hafajee, "Sankie Shows Women can Build" *Mail and Guardian*, 43
79. Ferial Hafajee, "Homeless Seize High Ground," *Mail and Guardian* (June 5–11 1998), 5
80. Jon Jeter,"For South Africa's Poor, a New Power Struggle," *The Washington Post*, available at http://www.Washingtonpost.com
81. Patrick Bond, *Elite Transition: From Apartheid to Neoliberalism in South Africa*, 272
82. William Gumede, *Thabo Mbeki and the Battle for the Soul of the ANC*, 109;Based on a Telkom Report 2001/2 'only 667 039 of the 2.67 million lines installed in poor areas were still in service"; Shaun Johnson, "Mandela, Handbook of Hope is Food for Skeptics," *The Sunday Independent* (February 7, 1999), 8;Editorial, "Mandela to Highlight ANC Successes, Nation-Building in Historic Address," (February 4, 1999),5
83. David Hemson and Michael O'Donovan, "Putting Numbers to the Scorecard: Presidential Targets and the State of Delivery," 24 in ed. Sakhela Buhlungu, John Daniel, Roger Southall and Jessica Luthman.,*South Africa 2005–2006 State of the Nation*
84. Sven Lunsche, "ANC's Good Deeds Come to Grief at Local Level," *Sunday Times* (May 30 1999), 10
85. Sipho Maseko, "Looking Back" *Siyaya* (no.1 Autumn 1998), 5–6
86. Sven Lunsche, "ANC's Good Deeds Come to Grief at Local Level," 10
87. William Mervin Gumede, *Thabo Mbeki and the Battle for the Soul of the ANC*, 77
88. Norman Levy, "Affirmative Interventions" in ed. Patrick Fitzgerald, Anne McLennan and Barry Munslow, *Managing Sustainable Development in South Africa* (Cape Town: Oxford University Press, 1995), 323
89. Norman Levy, "Public Sector Training and the Role of HDIS," unpublished paper, 1
90. Patrick Bond, *Elite Transition*,274

91. Vino Naidoo, "The State of the Public Service" in ed. John Daniel, Roger Southall and Jessica Lutchman, *State of the Nation; South Africa 2004–2005*, 119
92. Manon Edmunds, "Black Navy Recruitment at Sea," *Mail & Guardian*, October 24 to October 30, 1997), 13
93. *Focus Letter*, Helen Suzman Foundation, February 1996
94. Heribert Adam, Van Zyl Slabbert and Kogila Moodley, *Comrades in Business*, 184
95. *Focus Letter*, Helen Suzman Foundation, February 1996
96. Heribert Adam, Van Zyl Slabbert and Kogila Moodley, *Comrades in Business*, 184; on the gender and racial composition on of the military see Len Roux and Henri Boshoff, "The State of the Military," in *The State of the Nation: South Africa 2004–2005, ed.* John Daniel, Roger Southall and Jessica Lutchman (Cape Town: HRSC,2005), 188.
97. Sabine Cessou, "Malaise dans L'armee Sud-Africaines," *Liberation*, July 11, 2001;
98. *Ibid.;* Maisela admits that "he is extremely disappointed by the politicians and he feels "betrayed"; see also Vishwas Satgar, "Is the Multi-Billion Rand Arms Deal in the Interest of the Working Class?" 53.
99. "South Africa: Your Friends the Police," *The Economist* (February 15, 1997, 44.
100. Estelle Randall, "Black Cops in Bid to Arrest Racism in Jobs," *Cape Argus*, February 28–March 1, 1998, 10.
101. Patrick Bond, *Elite Transition*, 222; Dan Motaung, "Animals Surpass Africans in South Africa," *Mail & Guardian*, July 16–22 1999, 18.
102. "Workers Living Hell on Farms of Shame," *Cape Argus*, March 5, 1999, 3.
103. Editorial, *Mail & Guardian*, May 14 to May 20, 1999, 6; Ian Clayton, "Life Gets Tougher in the New SA," *Mail & Guardian*, April 9–15, 1999, 32; In September 1998, an African worker labored for a full day for his white employer. When he asked for his pay, the latter refused. The worker went to the local police station to report the issue. At the police station the police called the employer who claimed that the African had stolen his goods and was a bad worker. As a result, the African was jailed for two months after failing to pay what the employer was asking for R 500. *Author's personal interview with Dan Maskela, Cape Town, May 1999.*
104. Ann Eveleth, "Sadist Grins at Light Fine," *Mail and Guardian* (November 7–13 1997), 6; Ian Clayton, "Key Challenges Lie Ahead for Women," *Mail and Guardian* (April 30-May 6), 45
105. In 1999, of the one hundred and eight five judges nationally, One hundred and forty four were white men, seven white women, thirty African men and four African women; Josey Ballenger, 'Transformation with a Just Cause," *The Sunday Independent* (28 February 1999)
106. Abel Mputing, "To Pin Down a Rainbow," *Cape Times*, May 14, 1998, 13; Blackman Ngoro, "SANDF Commandos' Conducting Reign of Terror," *The Sunday Independent*, December 1, 1996, 7.
107. Events in Zimbabwe have also influenced Thabo Mbeki's land reform; Editorial, "Africa's own Mussolini" *The Economist* (February 24, 2001), 48; Henry Bernstein, *Land Reform and Agrarian Change in South Africa* (Belleville, South Africa: University of the Western Cape, 1997).
108. Lungisile Ntsebeza, *Land Tenure Reform, Traditional Authorities and Rural Local Government in Post Apartheid South Africa: Case Studies From the Eastern Cape,*(Belleville, South Africa: University of the Western Cape, Programme for Land and Agrarian Studies, 1999); ed. Lungisile Ntsebeza and Ruth Hall, *The Land Question in South Africa: The Challenge of Transformation and Redistribution* (Pretoria: HSRC, 2007); Lungisile

Ntsebeza, *Democracy Compromised: Chiefs and the Politics of Land in South Africa* (Amsterdam: Brill Academic Publishers, 2005).
109. Henry Bernstein, *Land Reform and Agrarian Change in South Africa*,7.
110. M. de Klerk, "A Qualifying Perspective," in ed. Merle Lipton and M. de Klerk, *Land, Labour and Livelihoods in Rural South Africa vol.2* (Durban; Indicator Press, 1996),xxi
111. Anna Kimanzi, *Personal Interview* with this author (Machakos, Kenya June 30, 1999)
112. Anne Eveleth, "Land Affairs Divides and Conquers," *Mail and Guardian*, April 30–May 6, 1999, 47; On workers see J. Bakin, ed., *Against the Current: Labour and Economic Policy in South Africa* (Johannesburg: Ravan Press, 1996). Ann Eveleth, "Farm Workers Fight Back with New Charter," *Mail & Guardian*, April 30–May 6, 1999, 46; *Tenure Newsletter*, 2 no.1 (1998): 14; *Tenure Newsletter*, 2 (1), 1998, 14.
113. Landless People's Movement, "LPM to Sue as Protea 7 Acquitted," Johannesburg, Feburary 22, 2004; Patrick Bond, *Elite Transition*, 297.
114. South African Press Association, "Report on Media Briefing by Minister of Agriculture and Land Affairs," Feburary 2, 2005, available at http://www.itweb.co.za/office/Sabinet.
115. Janette Bennett, "SA's Gulf in Facilities Between Rich and Poor: a New Report Points out the Strengths and Weaknesses of the Country's Services." *Sunday Times Business* (November 8, 1998), 5.
116. Jon Jeter, "Whites Feel Excluded in the New South Africa: They have Retreated, and Believe they are Second Class Citizens in their own Land," *Cape Argus*, July 14, 1999, 16; see also Robert Price, "The Political Economy of Growth and Democracy," in *South Africa: The Political Economy of Transformation*, ed. Stephen John Stedman (Boulder, CO: Lynne Rienner publishers, 1994), 81.
117. Julian May, Ingrid Woolard, and Stephen Klasen, "The Nature and Measurement of Poverty and Inequality," 26; Charlotte Mathews, "Black-Empowerment Groups on a Bumpy Ride," *Business Day*, February 6, 2002, allAfrica.com.
118. Patrick Bond, *Elite Transition*, 39;black as used here includes Africans, Indians and biracial people.
119. John Pilger, "Outcry Over My Film Proves it Hit Home," *Sunday Independent*, 11; Heribert Adam, F.Van Zyl Slabbert, and Kogila Moodley, *Comrades in Business*, 160–86 Heribert Adam, F. Van Zyl Slabbert and Kogila Moodley, *Comrades in Business*, 168.
120. Heribert Adam, F. Van Zyl Slabbert and Kogila Moodley, *Comrades in Business*, 174
121. Ibid., 168.
122. John Pilger, "Outcry Over my Film Proves it Hit Home," *Sunday Independent*, 11
123. Shamil Ismail, "Flaws in Black Empowerment Must Not Stop the Process," *Business Report* (10 June 1999).
124. Heribert Adam, "Empowering the Black Fat Cats," *Mail and Guardian* (April 9–16 1998),22
125. William Pomeroy, "Black Empowerment" in South Africa: Democratic Advance or Creation of an Elite? "*People's Weekly World*", December 21, 1996 available at http://www.hartford-hwp.com.
126. Ashwin Desai, "Racism Just Donning a New Guise in "new" South Africa," *Saturday Argus* (March 7–8, 1998), Even the Truth and Reconciliation Commission described the past in individual terms; evil psychotic men who ran amok.
127. Heribert Adam, F. Van Zyl Slabbert and Kogila Moodley, *Comrades in Business*,183.
128. Ibid.,The ANC held such a gala in Robben Island where for several thousand dollars celebrities were mingling with former prisoner Nelson Mandela for fund-raising. Not only is the choice of the island in poor taste, it mocks the whole liberation struggle.

129. Since 1994, attacks on Africans from the rest of the continent by South Africans have substantially increased. The ANC government has consistently ignored these attacks, which are sometimes carried out in the presence of the police. These attacks are similar to the ones carried out in Germany by neo-Nazi elements against Africans, Arabs, Indians and Turks. While both Nelson Mandela and Thabo Mbeki have acted as spokespersons for the continent, they have dismally failed to address this cancer of hate that is festering in their own back yard.
130. Patrick Bond, *Elite Transition*, 275.
131. Amanda Gouws, "The State of the National Gender Machinery: Structural Problems and Personalized Politics," in *South Africa 2005–2006:State of the Nation*, ed. Sakhela Buhlungu, John Daniel, Roger Southall and Jessica Lutchman, 143–66.
132. J. May *Poverty inequality in South Africa: Meeting the Challenge* (Cape Town: David Phillip Publishers, 2000), 34.
133. Macroeconomic Research group, *Making Democracy Work*, 115
134. Statistics South Africa, "The South African Labour Market," (Pretoria, 2002), 147.
135. Shireen Hassim, "A Virtuous Circle? Gender Equality and Representation in South Africa" in ed. Roger Southall and Jessica Lutchman, *State of the Nation: South Africa 2004–2005* (Cape Town: HSRC,2005), 336–359.
136. Patrick Bond, *Elite Transition*, 274–275.
137. Ibid.274–275; Zubeida Jaffer, "The Heart of Politics," *Cape Times* (June 23 1999), 15.

Conclusion

1. Naomi Klein, *The Shock Doctrine: The Rise of Disaster Capitalism* (New York: Metropolitan Books/Henry Holt & Co. 2007), 203-4.
2. Ibid., 194-97
3. Ibid., 199. Nelson Mandela cited the debt burden as the single greatest obstacle to keeping the promises of the Freedom Charter: "That is 30 billion [rand] we did not have to build houses as we planned, before we came into government, to make sure that our children go to the best schools, that unemployment is properly addressed and that everybody has the dignity of having a job, a decent income, of being able to provide shelter to his beloved, to feed them. . . We are limited by the debt we inherited" (Nelson Mandela, unpublished interview with filmmaker Ben Cashdan [2001]; quoted in Klein, 212).
4. Ibid., 204
5. Ibid., 213
6. Sebastian Mallaby, I After Apartheid: The Future of South Africa (New York: Times Books, 1992), 60
7. Jonathan Katzbellenbogen. "Country Still provides Lion's Share of Investment in Africa." *Business Day* (July 3, 2003) available at http://allafrica.com/stories
8. William Pomeroy, *Apartheid, Imperialism and African Freedom*, 74; Interestingly, in early 1994 (just before the elections) the new ANC government signed a USD$ 850 million deal with the IMF promising "wage restraint" Naomi Klein, *The Shock Doctrine*, 203
9. Anne Marie du Preez Bezdrob, *Winnie Mandela: A Life* (Cape Town: Zebra press, 2003), 271.
10. Naomi Klein, *The Shock Doctrine*, 215.
11. Claude Ake, *The Feasibility of Democracy in Africa* (Dakar, Senegal: Council for the Development of Social Science Research in Africa (CODESRIA), 2000), 136.

BIBLIOGRAPHY

Abrahamsen, Rita. *Disciplining Democracy: Development Discourse and Good Governance in Africa*. New York: Zed Books, 2000.
Abrahams, Peter. *Wild Conquest*. New York: Doubleday, 1971.
———. *Tell Freedom: Memories of Africa*. New York: Alfred A. Knopf, 1954.
Adam, Heribert. *Modernizing Racial Domination: The Dynamics of South African Politics*. Los Angeles: University of California Press, 1971.
———. "Empowering the Black Fat Cats." *Mail & Guardian*, April 9–16, 1998, http://www.mg.co.za
———, ed. *South African Sociological Perspectives*. London: Oxford University Press, 1971.
Adam, Heribert, and Kogila Moodley. *The Negotiated Revolution: Society and Politics in Post-Apartheid South Africa*, Johannesburg: Jonathan Ball, 1993.
———. *South Africa Without Apartheid: Dismantling Racial Domination*. Cape Town: Longman, 1986.
Adam, Heribert, and Herman Giliomeee. *Ethnic power Mobilized: Can South Africa Change?* New Haven, CT: Yale University Press, 1979.
Adam, Heribert, Frederik Van Zyl Slabbert, and Kogila Moodley. *Comrades in Business: Post-Liberation Politics in South Africa* Cape Town: Tafelberg Publishers, 1997
Adamastor. *White Man Boss: Footsteps to the South African Volk Republic*. Boston: The Beacon Press, 1951.
Adams, Simon. *Comrade Minister: The South African Communist Party and the Transition from Apartheid to Democracy*. New York: Nova Publishers, 2001.
African National Congress. *Unite For Freedom: Statement by the African National Congress on the Question of Unity and Anti-Apartheid Coalition 1985–1990*. Lusaka, 1987.
———. "*The Secretary–General's Report.*" ANC National Conference Report, July 1991.
———. *Questions and Answers on the Interim Government*. Informational pamphlet, 1991.
———. National Executive Committee "Negotiations: A Strategic Perspective." African National Congress, *Unite for Freedom: Statement by the African National Congress on the Question of Unity and Anti-Apartheid Coalition 1985–1990* Lusaka: DIP, 1987
———. *The Reconstruction and Development Programme*. Johannesburg: ANC, 1994
Ake, Claude. *The Feasibility of Democracy in Africa*. Dakar, Senegal: Council for the Development of Social Science Research in Africa (CODESRIA), 2000.
Alperson, Myra. *Foundations For a New Democracy: Corporate Social Investment in South Africa*. Johannesburg: Ravan Press, 1995.
Alten, Peter. *Nationalism*. New York: Edward Arnold, 1989.
Anderson, Benedict. *Imagined Communities*. London: Verso, 1991.

Andreski, Stanislave. *The African Predicament: A Study in the Pathology of Modernisation.* New York: Atherton Press, 1968.

Anthony, David, H. "Max Yergan in South Africa: From Evangelical Pan Africanism to Revolutionary Socialist." *African Studies Review* 34, no. 2 (1991): 27–55.

Arnold, Guy. *South Africa: Crossing the Rubicon.* London: Macmillan, 1992.

Arnold, Millard. *Steve Biko: Black Consciousness in South Africa.* New York: Vintage Books, 1979.

Azikwe, Nnamdi. *Renascent Africa.* London: Frank Cass & Co., 1937.

Balibar, Etienne, and Immanuel Wallerstein. *Race, Nation, Class: Ambiguous Identities.* London: Verso, 1991.

Baker, Pauline H., Alex Boraine, and Warren Krafchik, eds. *South Africa and the World Economy in the 1990s.* Cape Town: David Philip, 1993.

Bakin, J., ed. *Against the Current: Labour and Economic Policy in South Africa.* Johannesburg: Ravan Press, 1996.

Banton, Micheal. *White and Colored: The Behavior of British People Towards Colored Immigrants.* London: Jonathan Cape, 1959.

Barber, James. *South Africa in the Twentieth Century: A Political History in Search of a Nation State.* Cambridge, MA: Blackwell Publishers, 1999.

Barberton, C, M. Blake, and H. Kotze, eds. *Creating Action Space: The Challenge of Poverty and Democracy in South Africa.* Cape Town: IDASA & David Phillip Publishers, 1998.

Barrell, Howard. "The Turn to the Masses: The African National Congress: Strategic Review of 1978–1979." *Journal of Southern African Studies* 18, no. 1 (1992): 64–92.

Barrow, John. *An Account of Travels into the Interior of Southern Africa in the Years 1797 and 1798.* 2 vols. London: Cadell & Davies, 1801–04.

Behr, Mark. *The Smell of Apples.* London: Abacus, 1995.

Bell, Terry, and Ntsebeza, Buhle Dumisa. *Unfinished Business: South Africa, Apartheid and Truth.* London: Verso, 2003.

Bennet, Janette. "SA's Gulf in Facilities Between Rich and Poor: A New Report Points Out the Strengths and Weaknesses of the Country's Services." *Sunday Business Times*, November 8, 1998.

Benson, Mary. *South Africa: The Struggle for A Birthright.* London: International Defence and Aid Fund For Southern Africa, 1985.

Beresford, Belinda. "Domestic Workers and the Law." *Mail & Guardian*, October 16–22, 1998, 35.

Berger, Peter L., and Bobby Godsell. *A Future South Africa: Visions, Strategies and Realities.* Cape Town: Human Rousseau Tafelberg, 1988.

Berghe, Pierre van den. *South Africa: A Study in Conflict.* Berkeley, CA: University of California Press, 1970.

Berman, John Kane. *Soweto: Black Revolt White Reaction.* Johannesburg: Ravan Press, 1978.

Bermeo, Nancy. "Myths of Moderation: Confrontation and Conflict During Democratic Transitions." *Comparative Politics* 29, no. 3 (April 1997): 305–22.

Bernstein, H., ed. *The Agrarian Question in South Africa.* Durban: Indicator Press, 1996.

Bernstein, Henry. *Land Reform and Agrarian Change in Southern Africa.* Belleville, South Africa: University of the Western Cape, 1997.

Bezdrob, Anne Marie du Preez. *Winnie Mandela: A Life.* Cape Town: Zebra Press, 2003.

Biko, Steve. *I Write What I like: A Selection of His Writing.* Randburg, South Africa: Ravan Press, 1996.

Bloomberg, Charles. *The Afrikaner Broederbond in South Africa 1918–48.* Bloomington, Indiana: Indiana University Press, 1989.

Bond, Patrick. *Talk Left Walk Right: South Africa's Frustrated Global Reforms.* Scottsville, South Africa: University of KwaZulu-Natal Press, 2004.

———. *Elite Transition: From Apartheid to Neoliberalism in South Africa.* Scottsville, South Africa: University of Kwazulu-Natal Press, 2005.

Bopela, Thula, and Luthuli Daluxolo. *Umkhonto we Sizwe: Fighting for a Divided People.* Alberton: Galago Books, 2005.

Borraine A., and W. Krafchik, eds. *South Africa and the World Economy in the 1990s.* Cape Town: David Phillip, 1993.

Botha, Jan. *Verwoerd is Dead.* Cape Town: Books of Africa, 1967.

Bozzoli, Belinda, *The Political Economy of a Ruling Class: Capital and Ideology in South Africa, 1890–1933.* London: Routledge & Kegan Paul, 1981.

———. "Marxism, Feminism and South African Studies." *Journal of Southern African Studies* 9, no. 2 (April 1983): 139–71.

———, ed. *Town and Country in the Transvaal: Capitalist Penetration and Popular Response.* Johannesburg: Ravan Press, 1983.

Brass, Paul. I. *Ethnicity and Nationalism: Theory and Comparison.* New Bury Park, CA: Sage, 1992.

Bray, Grantland. *Rebel with a Cause: Letters to the Editor, or, A Neo-Conservative Agenda for a Post-Apartheid South Africa.* Johannesburg: Thorold's Africana Books, 1994.

Broderick, Jim, Gary Burford, and Gordon Freer. *South Africa's Foreign Policy: Dilemmas of a New Democracy.* New York: Palgrave McMillan, 2001.

Brooks, Alan, and Jeremy Brickhill. *Whirlwind before the Storm.* London: International Defence and AID Fund for Southern Africa, 1980.

Brooks, Edgar H. *Apartheid: A Documentary Study of Modern South Africa.* New York: Barnes & Noble, 1968.

Broomfield, Gerald W. *Colour Conflict, Race Relations in Africa.* London: Edinburgh House Press. 1934.

Bruielly, John. *Nationalism and the State.* Chicago: The University of Chicago Press, 1993.

Bundy, Colin. *The Rise & Fall of the South African Peasantry.* Cape Town: David Phillip, 1988.

Bunting, Brian. *The Rise of the South African Reich.* London: International Defence Fund & Aid for Southern Africa, 1986.

———. *Moses Kotane: South African Revolutionary.* Cape Town: Mayibuye Books, 1998.

Butchart, Alexander. *The Anatomy of Power: European Construction of the African Body.* London: Zed Books, 1998.

Cabral, Amilcar. *Revolution in Guinea: An African People's Struggle.* London: Monthly Review Press, 1969.

———. *Unity and Struggle.* New York: Monthly Review Press, 1979.

———. *Return to the Source: Selected Speeches of Amilcar Cabral.* New York. Africa Information Service, 1973.

Cadman, C. F. Miles. *Socialism For South Africa.* Johannesburg: South African Labour Party, 1942.

Callinicos, Alex, and John Rogers. *Southern Africa After Soweto.* London: Pluto Press, 1977.

Callinicos, Luli. *Oliver Tambo: Beyond the Engeli Mountains.* Cape Town: David Philip Publishers, 2004.

Carlson, Joel. *No Neutral Ground.* New York: Thomas Y. Crowell Co., 1973.

Carter, Gwendolyn, and Thomas Karis. *From Protest to Challenge.* Vol. 1. Pallo Alto, CA: The Hoover Institution, 1971.

Carton, Benedict. *Blood From Your Children: The Colonial Origins of Generational Conflict in South Africa.* Charlottesville: University Press of Virginia, 2000.

Ceruti, C. "How and Why the ANC's Nationalisation Policy Changed: Economic Nationalisation and the Changing State-Capital Relation." Masters thesis, University of Witwatersrand, 1995.
Chabra, Hari Sharan. *New South Africa: Problems of Democratic Transition*. Johannesburg: Thorold's Africana Books, 1994.
Charney, Craig. *Voices of a New Democracy: African Expectations in the New South Africa*. Johannesburg: Centre for Policy Studies, 1995.
———. "Pixley Seme '06: Father of the African National Congress." *Columbia College Today* 19 (Spring/ Summer): 14–17.
Clayton, Ian. "Life Gets tougher in the New South Africa." *Mail & Guardian*. April 9–15, 1999.
Cobbert, William, and Robin Cohen, eds. *Popular Struggles in South Africa*. New Haven, CT: Yale University Press, 1988.
Coetzee, J. M. *White Writing: On the Culture of Letters in South Africa*. New Haven: Yale University Press, 1988.
———. *Age of Iron*. New York: Penguin Books, 1990.
———. *Disgrace*. United Kingdom: Vintage, 2000.
Cohen, Robin. *Endgame in South Africa?* London: James Currey, 1986.
Cohen, Robin, and William Cobert, eds. *Popular Struggles in South Africa*. New Haven, CT: Yale University Press, 1988.
Coleman, Max ed. *A Crime Against Humanity: Analysing the Repression of the Apartheid State*. Johannesburg & Cape Town: Human Rights Committee/Mayibuye Publishers, 1998.
Comaroff, Jean. *Body of Power Spirit of Resistance: The Culture and History of a South African People*. Chicago: The University of Chicago Press, 1985.
Comaroff, Jean, and John Comaroff. *Of Revelation and Revolution: Christianity, Colonialism, and Consciousness in South Africa*. Vol. 1. Chicago: University of Chicago Press, 1991.
Conversi, Daniele, "Reassessing Current Theories of Nationalism: Nationalism as Boundary Maintenance and Creation." *Nationalism and Ethnic Politics* 1 (Spring 1995): 73–85.
Coverlid, D. R. *Richard H. Samuel: Selected Writings*. Melbourne: Melbourne University Press, 1963.
Counter Information Services. *Black South Africa Explodes*. London: Counter Information Services, 1977.
Crais, Clifton. "Prophecies of Nation." Paper presented at the 45th Annual Meeting of the African Studies Association, Washington, D. C., December 5–8, 2002.
———. *The Making of the Colonial Order: White Supremacy and Black Resistance in the Eastern Cape, 1770–1865*. Johannesburg: Witwatersrand University Press, 1992.
Cronin, J. "Neo-Colonials and Mint Imperials." *Mail & Guardian*. March 13–19, 1998.
Croty, Ann. "JCI Deal Takes Black Empowerment Another Step Forward." *The Sunday Independent*. August 3, 1999, 15.
Cuvier, Georges. *Animal Kingdom*. 16 vols. London: Geo. B. Whittaker, 1827–53.
Dalhbour, Omar, and Micheline R. Ishay, eds. *The Nationalism Reader*. New Jersey: Humanities Press International, 1995.
Daniel, John, Roger Southall, and Jessica Luthman, eds. *South Africa: State of The Nation: South Africa 2004–2005*. Cape Town: HRSC, 2005
Davenport, T. R. H. "The South African Rebellion of 1914." *English Historical Review* 78, 1963: 73–94.
———. *South Africa: A Modern History*. Toronto: University of Toronto Press, 1977.
Davidson, Basil. *The Black Star: A View of the Life and Times of Kwame Nkrumah*. Boulder, CO: Westview Press, 1989.

———. *The Liberation of Guinea: Aspects of an African Revolution*. Baltimore, MD: Penguin Books, 1969.

———. *Which Way Africa? The Search for A New Society*. England: Middlesex, 1971.

Davis, R. Hunt. "School vs. Blanket and Settler: Elijah Makiwane and the Leadership of the Cape School Community." *African Affairs* 78, no. 310 (January 1979): 12–27.

———. "John L. Dube: A South African Exponent of Booker T. Washington." *Journal of African Studies* 2, no. 4 (1976: 497–528.

Davis. R. Hunt. *Bantu Education and the Education of Africans in South Africa*. Athens, OH: Center For International Studies, 1973

Davis, R. *Capital, State and White Labour in South Africa, 1900–1960*. London: Harvester, 1979.

Davis, Miranda. "Women in Struggle: An Overview." *Third World Quarterly* 5, no. 4 (October 1983): 874–914.

Davis, Stephen M. *Apartheid Rebels: Inside South Africa's Hidden War*. New Haven, CT: Yale University Press, 1987.

———. *The Afrikaner Bond (1880–1911)*. Cape Town: Oxford University Press, 1966.

Dacalo, Samuel. *Psychoses of Power: African Personal Dictatorships*. Boulder, CO: Westview Press, 1989.

De Klerk, W. A. *The Puritans in Africa: A Story of Afrikanerdom*. London: Rex Collings, 1975.

———. *The Last Trek A New Beginning: The Autobiography*. New York: St. Martins Press, 1999.

Dexterr J., ed. *Christianity and the Natives of South Africa: A Yearbook of South African Missions*. Lovedale, ND: New Nation, 1968.

Diepen, Maria van, ed. *The National Question in South Africa*. London: Zed Books, 1988.

Diop, Cheikh Anta. *Black Africa: The Economic and Cultural Basis of a Federated State*. Trenton, NJ: Africa World Press, 1987.

Du Toit, Pierre. *Capital and Labour in South Africa: Class Struggles in the 1970s*. London: Kegan Paul, 1981.

———. *Power Plays Bargaining Tactics for Transforming South Africa*. Natal, South Africa: Southern Book Publishers, 1991.

Eades, Lindsay M. *The End of Apartheid in South Africa*. Westport, CT: Greenwood Press, 1999.

Edgar, Robert R., and Lynada Ka Msumza. *Freedom in our Lifetime: The Collected Writings of Anton Muziwakle Lembede*. Athens, OH: Ohio University Press, 1996.

Edgar, Robert R. "Garveyism in Africa: D. Wellington and the American Movement in Transkei." *Ufahamu* 1, no. 3 (1976): 31–57.

———, ed. *Sanctioning Apartheid*. (Trenton, NJ: Africa World Press, 1990)

Edwards, John *Reminiscences of the Early Life and Missionary Labours of the Rev. John Edwards*. Grahamstown, South Africa: T. H. Grocott, 1886.

Elbadawi, Ibrahim A., and Trudi Hartzenberg, eds. *Development Issues in South Africa*. New York: St. Martins Press, 2000.

Eldredge, Elizabeth A, and Fred Morton. *Slavery In South Africa: Captive Labor on the Dutch Frontier*. Pietermaritzburg, South Africa: University of Natal Press, 1994.

Eley, Geoff, and Ronald Grigor Sunny, eds. *Becoming National*. New York: Oxford University Press, 1996.

Elphick, Richard, and Hermann Giliomee, eds. *The Shaping of South African Society, 1652–1840*. South Africa: Maskew Miller Longman, 1988.

Emmanuelson, O. E. "A History of Native Education in Natal Between 1835–1927." Masters thesis, Natal University College, 1927.

Emerson, Rupert. *From Empire to Nation: The Rise to Self-Assertion of Asian and African Peoples.* Cambridge, MA: Harvard University Press, 1960.

———. "Nationalism and Political Development." *Journal of Politics* (February, 1960): 3–28.

Eveleth, Ann. "'Cinderella' Provinces Must Wait for Funds." *Mail & Guardian.* May 16–22, 1997.

———. "Sadist Grins at Light Fine." *Mail & Guardian.* November 7–13, 1997.

———. "Help us, Say Rural Poor." *Mail & Guardian.* April 3–8, 1997.

———. "Land Affairs Divides and Conquers." *Mail & Guardian.* June 11–17, 1999, 47.

Fatton, Robert. *Black Consciousness in South Africa: The Dialectics of Ideological Resistance to White Supremacy.* New York: State University of New York Press, 1986

Fanon, Frantz. *The Wretched of the Earth.* Translated by Constance Farrington. New York: Grove Press, 1968.

———. *Black Skin and White Masks.* New York: Grove press, 1967.

———. *A Dying Colonialism.* New York: Grove Press, 1967.

Fatton, Robert. *Black Consciousness in South Africa: The Dialectics of Ideological Resistance to White Supremacy.* New York: State University of New York, 1986.

Feinstein, Charles H. *An Economic History of South Africa.* Cambridge, UK: Cambridge University Press, 2005.

Feit, Edward. *South Africa: The Dynamics of the ANC.* London: Oxford University Press, 1962.

Figlio, Karl. "The Metaphor of Organization: An Historiographical Perspective on the Bio-Medical Sciences of the Early Nineteenth Century." *History of Sciences* 15 (1976): 17–35.

Fisher, John. *The Afrikaners.* London: Cassell, 1969.

Fitzgerald, Patrick, Anne McLennan, and Barr Munslow, eds. *Managing Sustainable Development in South Africa.* Cape Town: Oxford University Press, 1995.

Flood, Tania, Miriam Hoosain, and Natasha Primo. Beyond Inequalities: *Women in South Africa.* Bellville, South Africa: University of the Western Cape, 1997.

Forman, Lionel. *Chapters in the History of the March to Freedom.* Cape Town: New Age, 1959.

Frankenberg, Ruth. *White Women, Race Matters: The Social Construction of Whiteness.* Minneapolis, MN: University of Minnesota Press, 1993.

Freddberg, Lois. "Too Little Land, Too Late." *Mail & Guardian.* June 11–17, 1999, 41. http://wwwmg.co.za

Fredrickson, George M. *White Supremacy: A Comparative Study in American & South Africa History.* New York: Oxford University Press, 1981.

Friedman, Steven, and Doreen Atkinson. *The Small Miracle: South Africa's Negotiated Settlement.* Johannesburg: Ravan Press, 1994.

Freire, Paulo. *The Pedagogy of the Oppressed.* New York: The Seabury Press, 1974.

———. *The Politics of Education: Culture, Power and Liberation.* Massachusetts: Bergen & Garvey Publishers, 1985.

Freund, Bill. *The Making of Contemporary Africa: The Development of African Society Since 1800.* Bloomington: Indiana University Press, 1984.

Fry, Ruth A. *Emily Hobhouse.* Cape Town: Jonathan Ball, 1929.

Fukuyama, Francis. "The Next South Africa." *South Africa International* 22, no. 2 (October 1991): 71–81.

Geen, M. S. *The Making of South Africa.* Cape Town: Maskew Miller LTD, 1971.

Gelb, Stephen. *South Africa's Economic Crisis.* Cape Town: David Philip, 1991.

Gellner, Ernest. *Nations and Nationalism.* Cambridge, MA: Basil Blackwell, 1987.

———. *Encounters with Nationalism.* Cambridge, MA: Blackwell, 1994.

Geismar, Peter. *Fanon the Revolutionary as Prophet.* New York: Grove Press, 1971.

Gendzier, Irene L. *Frantz Fanon.* New York: Vintage Books, 1973.

Gerhart, Gail. *Black Power in South Africa: The Evolution of an Ideology.* Berkeley, CA: University of California, 1978.

Gerth, Hans H., and C. Wright, eds. *From Max Weber: Essays in Sociology.* New York: Oxford University Press, 1976.

Giliomee, Hermann. "Constructing Afrikaner Nationalism." *Journal of Asian and African Studies* 18 (1983): 83–98.

———. *The Parting of the Ways.* Cape Town: David Phillip, 1983.

———. "Afrikanerdom Today: Ideology and Interests." Unpublished manuscript, 1987.

———. "Broedertwis: Intra-Afrikaner Conflicts in the Transition from Apartheid 1969-1991." *African Affairs* 91, no. 364 (July 1992): 339–64.

———. *The Afrikaners: Biography of a People.* Charlottesville, VA: University of Virginia Press, 2003.

Gilroy, Paul. *There Ain't No Black in the Union Jack: The Cultural Politics of Race and Nation.* Chicago: University of Chicago Press, 1991.

Golan, Daphna. *Inventing Shaka: Using History in the Construction of Zulu Nationalism.* Boulder, Co: Lynne Rienner Publishers, 1994.

Goldberg, David Theo, ed. *Anatomy of Racism.* Minneapolis, MN: University of Minnesota Press, 1990.

———. "Modernity, Race, and Morality." *Cultural Critique* (Spring 1993): 193–227.

Gouws, Piet, and P. H. Tiene. "Farm Killings: Enough is Enough." *Mail & Guardian.* August 21–27, 1998, 24.

Greenberg, Stanley. *Race and State in Capitalist Development: Comparative Perspectives.* New Haven, CT: Yale University Press, 1980.

Grimes, Allan P., and Robert H. Horowitz. *Modern Political Ideologies.* New York: Oxford University Press, 1959.

Guelke, Andria. *South Africa in Transition: The Misunderstood Miracle.* New York: Taauris Publishers, 1999.

Gurr, Robert Ted. *Why Men Rebel?* Princeton: Princeton University Press, 1970.

Gutteridge, William. *South Africa: From Apartheid to National Unity, 1981–1994.* Brookfield, VT: Dartmouth, 1995.

Hadland, Adrian, and Rantao Jovial. *The Life and Times of Thabo Mbeki.* Rivonia: Zebra Press, 1999.

Haffajee, Ferial. "Tapping in Real Change: Taking Stock." *Mail & Guardian.* February 5–11, 1999. http://www.mg.co.za

———. "The Meteoric Rise of South Africa's Black Middle Class." *Mail & Guardian.* April 1–8, 1999, 10–11. http://www.mg.co.za

———. "City Streets: Where SA's Economy is Thriving." *Mail & Guardian.* July 3–9, 1998, 25. http://www.mg.co.za

Ha-Minha, Trinh T. *Woman, Native, Other: Writing Postcoloniality and Feminism.* Bloomington, IN: Indian University Press, 1989.

Halisi, C. R. D. *Black Political Thought in the Making of South African Democracy.* Bloomington, IN: Indiana University Press, 1999.

Hansen, Emmanuel. *Frantz Fanon: Social and Political Thought.* Athens, OH: Ohio University Press, 1977.

Harrison, David. *The White Tribe of Africa: South Africa in Perspective.* Berkeley, CA: University of California Press, 1981.

Hassim, S., J. Metekerkamp, and A. Todes. "'A Bit on the Side': Gender Struggle in the Politics of Transformation." *Transformation*, no. 5 (1987): 3–32.

Hassim, S., and C. Walker. "Women's Studies and the Women's Movement in South Africa: Defining a Relationship." *Women's Studies International Forum* 16, no. 5 (1993): 523–34.

Hawkins, Anthony. "Corporate Strategy in South Africa." *South Africa International* 22, no. 2 (October 1991): 133–36.

Hayes, Carlton T. H. *Essays on Nationalism*. London: Macmillan, 1937.

Heidegger, Martin. *The Question Concerning Technology, and Other Essays*. Translated by W. Levitt. New York: Harper & Row, 1977.

Heerden, Etienne van. *Ancestral Voices*. Translated by Malcolm Hacksley. Cape Town: Tafelberg Publishers, 1986.

Headlam, C. *The Milner Papers*. Vol. 2. London: Caswell & Company, 1933.

Hepple, A. *Verwoerd*. London: Harmondsworth, 1967.

Hexham, Irving. *The Irony of Apartheid: The Struggle for National Independence of Afrikaner Calvinism Against British Imperialism*. New York: Edwin Mellen, 1981.

Heyningen, Elizabeth, B. "The Social Evil in the Cape Colony 1868–1902: Prostitution and the Contagious Diseases Acts." *Journal of Southern African Studies* 10, no. 2 (April 1984): 170–97.

Holland, Heidi. *The Struggle: A History of the African National Congress*. London: Crafton Books, 1989.

Horrell, Muriel. *African Education: Some Origins and Development Until 1953*. Johannesburg: South African Institute of Race Relations, 1963.

Horowitz, R. *The Political Economy of South Africa*. London: Oxford University Press, 1967.

Horst Van der S., and J. Reid, eds. *Race Discrimination in South Africa: A Review*. Cape Town: David Phillip, 1981.

Horwath, David R. and Aletta J. Norval, eds *South Africa in Transition: New Theoretical Perspectives*. London: Macmillan Press Ltd., 1998.

Huddleston, Trevor. *Naught for Your Comfort*. London: Collins, 1956.

Hunt, W. R. *The Economics of the Colour Bar*. London: Deutsch, 1964.

Hunter, N., J. May, and V. Padayachee. "Lessons for PRSP From Poverty Reduction Strategies in South Africa." Paper Presented to the Economic Commission for Africa, Addis Ababa, December 3, 2003.

Huttenback, Robert A. *Racism and Empire, White Settlers and Coloured Immigrants in the British Self-Governing Colonies 1830–1910*. Ithaca, New York: Cornell University Press, 1976.

Hutchful, Eboe, and Bathily Abdoulaye, eds. *The Military and Militarism in Africa*. Dakar, Senegal: CODESRIA, 1998.

Jacobs, S., and R. Calland. *Thabo Mbeki's World*. Pietermaritzburg: University of Natal Press, 2002.

Jaffer, Zubeida. "The Heart of Politics." *Cape Times*, June 23, 1999, 14.

Jinadu, L. Adele. *Fanon: In Search of the African Revolution*. London: Routledge & Kegan Paul, 1986.

Johnson, Phyllis, and David Martin, eds. *Frontline Southern Africa: Destructive Engagement*. New York: Four Walls Eight Windows, 1988.

Johnson, Frederick A. "White Prosperity and White Supremacy in South Africa." *African Affairs* 69 (April 1970): 124–40.

Johnson, R. W., and L. Schlemmer. *Launching Democracy in South Africa: The First Open Election, April 1994*. New Haven, CT: Yale University Press, 1996.

Johnson, R. W., and David Welsh. *Ironic Victory: Liberalism in Post-Liberation South Africa*. Cape Town: Oxford University Press, 1998.

Jon, Jeter. "Whites Feel Excluded in the New South Africa: They have Retreated, and Believe they are Second-Class Citizens in their Own Land." *Cape Argus*. July 14, 1999, 16.
Jordan, Pallo. "Soul–Brotherly Talk of Empowerment." *Mail & Guardian*. March 20–26, 1998.
Joseph, Helen. "Women and Passes." *Africa South* 3, no. 1 (October-December, 1958): 20–28.
———. *Side by Side: The Autobiography of Helen Joseph*. London: Zed Books, 1986.
Juckes, Tim J. *Opposition in South Africa: The Leadership of Z. K. Mathews, Nelson Mandela, and Stephen Biko*. Westport, CT: Praeger, 1995.
Kahanovitz, Colin. *Appointment to the Public Service in the Post-Apartheid and the Need for Constitutional Checks and Balances*. Johannesburg: University of Witwatersrand: Center for Applied Legal Studies, 1993.
Karis, Thomas, and Gail Gerhart. *From Protest to Challenge 1820–1990: Nadir and Resurgence*. South Africa: Unisa Press, 1997.
Kasrils, Ronnie. *Armed and Dangerous: My Undercover Struggle Against Apartheid*. London: Heinemann, 1993.
Kathrada, Ahmed. *Memoirs*. Cape Town: Zebra Press, 2004.
Kedourie, Ellie. *Nationalism*. London: Hutchinson, 1961.
Keegan, Timothy. *Colonial South Africa and The Origins of the Racial Order*. Cape Town: David Philip, 1996.
Kesteven, G. R. *The Boer War*. London: Ghatto & Windus, 1970.
Kiewiet, C. W. de, *A History of South Africa: Social and Economic*. London: Oxford University Press, 1941.
Klerk, M. de, and Merle Lipton, eds. *Land, Labour and Livelihoods in Rural South Africa. Vol. 2*. Kwazulu-Natal and Northern Province, Durban: Indicator Press, 1996.
Kohn, Hans. *Nationalism: Its Meaning and History*. New York: Van Nostrand, 1965.
———. *The Idea of Nationalism*. New York: Random House, 1998.
Kreiger, Joel, ed. *The Oxford Companion to Politics of the World*. London: Oxford University Press, 2001.
Krog, Antjie. *Country of My Skull*. New York: Random House, 1998.
Kunnie, Julian. *Is Apartheid Dead? Pan Africanist Working Class Cultural Critical Perspectives*. Boulder, CO: Westview Press, 2000.
Kuper, Leo. *An African Bourgeoisie: Race, Class, and Politics in South Africa*. New Haven, CT: Yale University Press, 1965.
———. *Passive Resistance in South Africa*, New Haven, CT: Yale University Press, 1957.
Kuzwayo, Helen. *Call Me Woman*. Randburg, South Africa: Ravan Press, 1996.
Laband, John. *Rope of Sand: The Rise and Fall of the Zulu Kingdom in the Nineteenth Century*. Johannesburg: Jonathan Ball, 1995.
Langa, Mandla. *The Naked Song & Other Stories*. Cape Town: David Phillip, 1996.
Leatt, James, Theo Kneifel, and Klaus Nuremberger, eds. *Contending Ideologies in South Africa*. Cape Town: David Phillip, 1986.
Legassick, Martin. "The Dynamics of Modernization in South Africa." *Journal of African History* 13 (1972): 145–50.
——— "South Africa: Capital Accumulation and Violence." *Economy and Society* 3, no. 3 (August 1974): 253–91.
———. "Legislation, Ideology and Economy in Post-1948 South Africa." *Journal of Southern African Studies* 1 (October 1974): 5–35.
Leroy, Vail, ed. *The Creation of Tribalism in Southern Africa*. Berkeley, CA: University of California Press, 1989.

Lerumo, A. *Fifty Fighting Years: The South African Communist Party 1921–1971*. London: Inkululeko Publications, 1987.

Levin, R., and D. Weiner, eds. *Community Perspectives on Land and Agrarian Reform in South Africa*. Johannesburg: University of the Witwatersrand, 1994.

Lewis, Jon. *Industrialization and Trade Union Organization in South Africa, 1924–55: The Rise and Fall of the South African Trades and Labour Council*. Cambridge, UK: Cambridge University Press, 1984.

Lichtenstein, Henry W. H. C. *Travels in Southern Africa in the Years 1803, 1804, 1805 and 1806. 2 vols. Translated* by A. Plumptree. Cape Town: The Van Riebeeck Society, 1928–30.

Lipton, Merle. *Capitalism and Apartheid: South Africa `1910–1986*. Cape Town: David Phillip, 1985.

Lipton, Michael, M. de Klerk, and Merle Lipton, eds. *Land, Labour and Livelihoods in Rural South Africa*. Vol. 2. Durban: Indicator Press, 1996.

Livingstone, David. *Missionary Travels and Reaches in South Africa*. London: Murray, 1857.

Lodge, Tom. "Mandela, Nelson." *The Oxford Companion to Politics of the World*. Edited by Joel Krieger. London: Oxford University Press, 2001, pp. 520–21.

———. *Black Politics in South Africa Since 1945*. Johannesburg: Ravan Press, 1983.

Lodge, Tom, and Bill Nasson. *All Here and Now: Black Politics in South Africa in the 1980s*. Cape Town: David Phillip, 1991.

Lonsdale, John, ed. *South Africa in Question*. London: James Currey, 1988.

Louw, Eric P. *The Rise, Fall and Legacy of Apartheid*. Westport, CT: Praeger, 2004.

Louw, Leon, and Frances Kendall. *South Africa: The Solution*. Bisho, South Africa: Amagi Publishers, 1986.

Luckhardt, Ken, and Brenda Will. *Organize or Starve!: The History of the South African Congress of Trade Unions*. London: Lawrence & Wishart, 1980.

Macmillan, William Miller. *Bantu, Boer and Britain: The Making of the South African Native Problem*. London: Faber & Guyer, 1929.

Magona, Sindiwe. *Push-Push & other Stories*. Cape Town: David Phillip, 1996.

MaGregor, Karen. "Plan for Black Universities to Rise Above Their Second Class Legacy." *The Sunday Independent*. August 3, 1997.

———. "Businesses Plan to Pour R 1 Billion in Education in This Year." *The Sunday Independent*. June 7, 1997.

Magubane, Bernard. *The Making of a Racist State: British Imperialism and the Union of South Africa 1875–1910*. Trenton, NJ: Africa World Press, 1996.

Magubane, Bernard, and Ibbo Mandaza, eds. *Whither South Africa?* Trenton, NJ: Africa World Press, 1988.

Malan, Rian. *My Traitor's Heart*. New York: Vintage International, 1990.

Mallaby, Sebastian. *After Apartheid: The Future of South Africa*. New York: Times Books, 1992.

Malherbe. E. *Education in South Africa, 1923–1975*. Vol. 2. Cape Town: Juta, 1977.

Mali T. *Chris Hani: The Sun that Set Before Dawn*. Johannesburg: Sached Books, 1993.

Mamdani, Mohamood. *Citizen and Subject: Contemporary Africa and the Legacy of Late Colonialism*. Cape Town: David Phillip, 1996.

Mandela, Nelson, *The Struggle Is My Life*. London: International Defence & Aid Fund, 1986.

———. *Long Walk to Freedom*. London: ABACUS, 1994.

Manzo, Kathryn, A. *Creating Boundaries: The Politics of Race and Nation*. Boulder, CO: Lynne Rienner, 1996.

———. *Domination, Resistance and Social Change in South Africa: The Local Effects of Global Power*. New York: Praeger, 1992.

———. "Modernist Discourse and the Crisis of Development Theory." *Studies in Comparative International Development* 26 (Summer 1991): 3–36.

Marais, Hein. *South Africa: Limits to Change: The Political Economy of Transformation.* Cape Town: University Cape Town Press, 1998.

Marge, Bernard. *Ethnicity and Politics in South Africa.* Atlantic Highlands, NJ: Zed Books, 1993.

Marks, Shula. *The Ambiguities of Dependence in South Africa: Class, Nationalism and the State in Twentieth-Century Natal.* Baltimore: John Hopkins University Press, 1986.

Marks, Shula, and Anthony Artmore, eds. *Economy and Society in Pre-Industrial South Africa.* London: Longman, 1980.

Marks, Shula & Stanley Trapido, eds. *The Politics of Race, Class and Nationalism in Twentieth Century South Africa.* London: Longman, 1993.

Martin, Guy. *Africa in World Politics: A Pan-African Perspective.* Trenton, NJ: Africa World Press, 2002.

Marx, Anthony. *Making Race and Nation: A Comparison of the United States, South Africa and Brazil.* New York: Cambridge University, 1999.

Masebe, Thabo. "Grassroots Challenge Betrays the Culture and Traditions of the ANC." *Sunday Independent.* October 12, 1997, 11.

Mathews, Charlotte. "Black-Empowerment Groups on a Bumpy Ride." *Business Day.* February 6, 2002, http://www.allAfrica.com.

Mathian, Nomavenda. *South Africa: Diary of Troubled Times.* London: Freedom House, 1989.

Matshoba, Mtutuzeli. *Call Me Not a Man.* London: Longman, 1979.

May, Julian, ed. *Poverty and Inequality in South Africa: Meeting the Challenge.* Cape Town: David Philip, 2000.

Mazrui, Ali A., and Michael Tidy. *Nationalism and New States in Africa: From About 1935 to the Present.* Nairobi: Heinemann, 1984.

Mbeki, T. *Africa Define Yourself.* Johannesburg: Tafelberg, 2003.

Mbongowa, Shimane. "Whites are Lucky to be Alive." *Mail & Guardian.* April 4–10,1997. http://www.mg.co.za

Mboya, Tom. *The Challenge of Nationhood.* London: Heinemann, 1970.

McClintock, Anne, Aamir Mufti, and Ella Shohat, eds. *Gender, Nation & Postcolonial Perspectives.* Minneapolis, MN: University of Minnesota Press, 1997.

McFarlan, S. Neil. *Superpower Rivalry and 3rd World Radicalism: The Ideas of National Liberation.* London: Groom Helm, 1985.

McIntyre, D. "Heath Care Financing and Expenditure in South Africa: Towards Equity and Efficiency in Policy Making." PhD. diss., University of Cape Town, 1997.

Mckinley, Dale T. *The ANC and the Liberation Struggle: A Critical Political Biography.* London: Pluto Press, 1997.

Mda, Lizeka. "Making a Stand in Vrededorp." *Mail & Guardian.* April 3–8, 1998, 32. http://www.mg.co.za

Meer, Fatima. *Higher Than Hope: The Authorized Biography of Nelson Mandela.* New York: Harper & Row, 1988.

Meintjes, Sheila. *Gender, Citizenship & Democracy in Post-Apartheid South Africa.* Johannesburg: University of the Witwatersrand, 1995.

Memmi, Albert. *The Colonizer and the Colonized.* Boston: Beacon Press, 1967.

Meredith, Martin. *South Africa's New Era: The 1994 Election.* London: Mandarin, 1994.

———. *The Fate of Africa: A History of Fifty Years of Independence.* New York: Public Affairs, 2005.

Mervin Gumede, William. *Thabo Mbeki and the Battle for the Soul of the ANC*. Cape Town: Zebra Press, 2005.

Merwe, W. van der Hendrik, Nancy C. J. Charton, D. A. Kotze, and Ake Magnussen, eds. *SASO Policy Manifesto African Perspectives on South Africa: Speeches, Articles and Documents*. Stanford: Hoover Institute, 1978.

Microeconomic Research Group (MERG). *Making Democracy Work: A Framework for Macroeconomic Policy in South Africa*. Johannesburg: Centre for Development Studies, 1993.

Migdal, Joel S. *Strong Societies and Weak States: State-Society Capabilities in the Third World*. Princeton, NJ: Princeton University Press, 1988.

Miller, Christopher, L. *Nationalists and Nations: Essays on Francophone African Literature and Culture*. Chicago: The University of Chicago Press, 1998.

Minter, William. *King Solomon's Mines Revisited: Western Interests and the Burdened History of Southern Africa*. New York: Basic Books, 1986.

Mitchie, Jonathan, and Vishnu Pedayachee, eds. *The Political Economy of South Africa's Transition: Policy Perspectives in the Late 1990s*. New York: The Dryden Press, 1997.

Mkhondo, R. *Reporting South Africa*. London: James Currey, 1993.

Mncwabe, M. P. *Post-Apartheid Education: Towards Non-Racial, Unitary, and Democratic Socialization in the New South Africa*. Lanham, MD: University Press of America, 1993.

Modisane, Bloke. *Blame me on History*. London: Thames and Hudson, 1963.

Modlane, Eduardo. *The Struggle for Mozambique*. Baltimore, MD: Penguin Books, 1969.

Mokgatle, Naboth. *The Autobiography of an Unknown South African*. Los Angeles: University of California Press, 1975.

Molaba, T. "Letter of Resignation." *African Communist*, no. 135 (Fourth Quarter 1993): 16–17.

Moleketti, J. "Is a Retreat from National Democratic Revolution to National Bourgeois Revolution Imminent?" *African Communist*, no. 133 (Second Quarter 1993): 11–19.

Moodie, Dunbar T. *The Rise of Afrikanerdom*. Berkeley, CA: University of California Press, 1975.

Moodley, Strini. *What is Black Consciousness?* Durban: Azapo Publications, 1983.

Mokgatle, Naboth. *The Autobiography of An Unknown South African*. Berkeley, LA: University of California Press, 1975

Morris, Donald. *The Washing of the Spears: A History of the Rise of the Zulu Nation Under Shaka and Its Fall in the Zulu War of 1879*. London: Jonathan Cape, 1966.

Morris, Michael. "Big-Spending Blacks Dominate Wealthy Elite." *Cape Argus*, March 8, 1992, 2.

Mosieleng, Percy, and Temaba Mhambi, eds. *Contending Voices in South African Fiction*. Johannesburg: Lexicon Publisher, 1993.

Mphahalele, Ezekiel. *The African Image*. New York: Frederick A. Praeger, 1962.

Mufson, Steven. *Fighting Years: Black Resistance in the Struggle for a New South Africa*. Boston: Beacon Press, 1990.

Muiu, Mueni Wa. "The African National Congress' Economic and Social Policy Changes in South Africa (1994–2004): Another African Straightjacket Independence?" *African and Asian Studies 3, no. 3–4*: 273–94.

Munger, Edwin S. *Afrikaner and African Nationalism: South African Parallels and Parameters*. London: Oxford University Press, 1967.

Murray. C., ed. *Gender and the New South African Legal Order*. Kenwyn: Juta, 1994.

Murray, Martin J. *Revolution Deferred: The Painful Birth of Post-Apartheid South Africa*, New York: Verso, 1994.

Muthien, Yvonne. *Democracy South Africa: Evaluating the 1999 Election.* Pretoria: Human Research Council, 1999.

Mzamane, Mbulelo Vizihugo. *Children of Soweto.* New York: Longman, 1982.

Mzimela, Sipho E. *Apartheid: South African Nazism.* New York: Vantage Press, 1983.

Nassan, W., and J. Samuel, eds. *Education: From Poverty to Liberty.* Cape Town: David Phillip, 1990.

Nathan, Laurie. *The Changing of the Guard: Armed Forces and Defence Policy in a Democratic South Africa.* Pretoria: HSRC, 1994.

National Institute for Economic Policy (NIEP). *From RDP to GEAR: The Gradual Embracing of Neo-Liberalism in Economic Policy.* Johannesburg: NIEP, 1996.

Ndebele, Njabulo S. *Fools and other Stories.* Johannesburg: Ravan Press, 1983.

Nicholson, Linda J., ed. *Feminism /Postmodernism.* New York: Routledge, 1994.

Niekerk Marlene van. *Triomf.* Translated by Leon de Kock. Great Britain: Little, Brown and Company, 1999.

Nigel, Harris. *National Liberation.* Las Vegas: University of Nevada Press, 1990.

Nina, Daniel. "Beyond the Frontier: Civil Society Revisited." *Transformation* (1992): 61–73.

Nolutshungu, Sam. *Changing South Africa: Political Considerations.* Manchester: Manchester University Press, 1982.

Norval, Alletta, J. *Deconstructing Apartheid Discourse.* London: New Left Books, 1996.

Ntsebeza, Lungisile. *Land Tenure Reform, Traditional Authorities and Rural Local Government in Post Apartheid South Africa: Case Studies From the Eastern Cape.* Belleville, Cape Town: University of the Western Cape Programme for Land and Agrarian Studies, 1999.

Ntsebeza, Lungisile and Ruth Hall. ed., *The Land Question in South Africa: The Challenge of Transformation and Redistribution.* Pretoria: HSRC, 2007

Ntsebeza, Lungisile. *Democracy Compromised: Chiefs and the Politics of Land in South Africa.* Amsterdam: Brill Academic Publishers, 2005.

Nuremberger, Klaus. *An Economic Vision for South Africa: The Task of the Church in the Post-Apartheid Economy.* Pietermaritzburg, South Africa: Encounter Publications, 1994.

Nzula, A. T., I. Potekhin, and A. Z. Zusmanovich. *Forced Labour in Colonial Africa.* London: Zed Press, 1979.

Odendaal, Andre. *Black Protest in South Africa to 1912.* New Jersey: Barnes & Noble, 1984.

O'Donnell, O. Guillermo, Phillipe C. Schmitter, and Laurence Whiteheads, eds. *Transitions from Authoritarian Rule: Prospects for Democracy.* Baltimore: John Hopkins University Press, 1986.

Oliver, Nic. "ANC Constitutional Proposals and State Reaction." *South Africa International* 22, no. 2 (October 1991): 55–64.

O'Meara, Dan. *Volkapitalisme,* London: Cambridge University Press, 1983.

———. "'Muldergate' and the politics of Afrikaner Nationalism." *Work in Progress,* no. 22 (1982): 1–18.

———. *Forty Lost Years: The Apartheid State and the Politics of the National Party, 1948–1994.* Athens, OH: Ohio University Press, 1996.

O'Meara, Dan, R. H. Davies, and Sipho Dlamini. *The Struggle for South Africa: A Reference Guide to Movements, Organizations, and Institutions.* London: Zed Press, 1984.

Onwulanibe, Richard C. *A Critique of Revolutionary Humanism: Frantz Fano.*, St. Louis, MO: Warren H. Green, 1983.

Ottaway, David. *Chained Together: Mandela, De Klerk, and the Struggle to Remake South Africa.* New York: Times Books, 1993.

Otutei, Adu. *The Cross & the Beast of the South.* Accra, Ghana: Assempa Publishers, 1989.

Overberg, Henrik, trans. *The Jew's State.* Jerusalem: Jason Aronson Inc, 1997.

Pakenham, Thomas. *The Boer War*. New York: Random House, 1979.

Perinbam, Marie B. *Holy Violence: The Revolutionary Thought of Frantz Fanon*. Westport, CT: Greenwood Press, 1997.

Peron, Jim. *Die, the Beloved Country?* Johannesburg: Amagi publishers, 1999.

Pilger, John. "Outcry over My Film Proves it Hit Home." *Sunday Independent*. May 3, 1998. http://www.sundayindependent.co.za.com

Pityana, Barney, M. Ramphele, M. Mpumlwana, and L. Wilson. *Bounds of Possibility: The Legacy of Steve Biko and Black Consciousness*. London: Zed Books, 1991.

Plaatje, Sol T. *Native Life in South Africa*. Johannesburg: Ravan Press, 1982.

———. *Mhudi: An Epic of South African Native Life a Hundred Years Ago*. Jeppestown, South Africa: AD Donker Publishers, 1989.

Pomeroy, William J. *Apartheid, Imperialism, and African Freedom*. New York: International Publishers, 1986.

Posel, Deborah. *The Making of Apartheid 1948–1961*. Oxford: Clarendon Press, 1991.

Pre, Du R. H. *The Making of Racial Conflict in South Africa*. Johannesburg: Skotaville Publishers, 1992.

Price, Robert M. *The Apartheid State in Crisis: Political Transformation in South Africa 1975–1990*. New York: Oxford University Press, 1991.

Price, Robert, and Carl G. Roseberg, eds. *Apartheid Regime: Political Power and Racial Domination*. Berkeley, CA: University of California, 1980.

Ralston, Richard D. "American Episodes in the Making of an African Leader: A Case Study of Alfred B. Xuma (1893–1962)." *International Journal of African Historical Studies* 6, no. 1 (1973): 72–93.

Ramphele, Mamphela. "Citizenship Challenges for South Africa's Young Democracy." *Daedalus: Journal of the American Academy of Arts and Sciences* 130, no. 1 (Winter 2001): 1–17.

Rantete, J. Mutshtshu. *The African National Congress and the Negotiated Settlement in South Africa*. Pretoria: J. L. Van Schaik Academic, 1998.

Rantete, Johannes, and Hermann Giliomee. "Transition to Democracy Through Transaction?: Bilateral Negotiations Between the ANC and NP in South Africa." *Africa Affairs 91* (1992): 515–42.

Reddy, Thiven. *Hegemony and Resistance: Contesting Identities in South Africa*. Burlington, VT: Ashgate, 2000.

Republic of South Africa. Cillie Commission. *Report of the Commission of Inquiry into the Riots at Soweto and Elsewhere*. Pretoria: Government Printer, 1980.

Republic of South Africa. *The Constitution of the Republic of South Africa*. Pretoria: Government Printer, 1996.

Reynolds, Andrew, ed. *Election 94 South Africa: The Campaigns, Results and Future Prospects*. Cape Town: David Philip, 1994.

———. *Election 99 South Africa: From Mandela to Mbeki*. New York: St. Martins Press, 1999.

Rex, J. I. *Apartheid and Social Research*. Paris: UNESCO, 1981.

Rhoodie, Nic, and Ian Liebenberg, eds. *Democratic Nation-Building in South Africa*. Pretoria: HSRC Publishers, 1994.

Robertson, H. M. "150 Years of Economic Contact Between Black and White: A Preliminary Survey Part 1." *The South African Journal of Economics* 2 (1934): 403–25.

Rogers, Barbara. *Divide and Rule: South Africa's Bantustans*. London: International Defence & Aid Fund, 1976.

Rose, B., and R. Tunmer, eds. *Documents in South African Education*. Cape Town: Ad Donker, 1975.

Roux, Edward. *Time Longer Than Rope: The Black Man's Struggle For Freedom in South Africa.* Madison, WI: The University of Wisconsin Press, 1964.

Sachikonye, L. *Democracy, Civil Society and the State: Social Movements in Southern Africa.* Harare: SAPES, 1995.

Said, Edward. *Culture and Imperialism.* London: Vintage Books, 1994.

———. *Orientalism.* New York: Vintage, 1979.

Sampson, Anthony. *Mandela: The Authorized Biography.* New York: Alfred A. Knopf, 1999.

———. "Out of the Shadow of Mandela." *Mail & Guardian.* June 11–17, 1999, 30. http://www.mg.co.za

Saul J., and S. Gelb. *The Crisis in South Africa: Class Defence and Class Revolution.* New York: Monthly Review Press, 1981.

Saul, John. *Recolonization and Resistance: Southern Africa in the 1990s.* Trenton, NJ: Africa World Press, 1993.

Schapera, I., ed. *David Livingstone: South African Papers, 1849–1853.* Cape Town: The Van Riebeeck Society, 1974.

Scott, James. *Domination and the Arts of Resistance: Hidden Transcripts.* New Haven, CT: Yale University Press, 1990.

Seekings, Jeremy. *The UDF.* Cape Town: David Phillip, 2000.

Seekings, Jeremy, and Nicoli Nattrass. *Class, Race and Inequality in South Africa.* New Haven, CT: Yale University Press, 2005.

Semmel, Bernard. *Imperialism and Social Reform: English Social Imperial Thought* 1895–1914. New York: Doubleday, 1960.

Seton-Watson, Hugh. *Nations and States.* Boulder, CO: Westview Press, 1977.

Shillington, Kevin. *An African Adventure: A Brief History of Cecil Rhodes* Bristol: Jenny Lee Publishers, 1993.

Shubin, Vladimir. *ANC: A View From Moscow.* Cape Town: Mayibuye Books, 1999.

Simons, Jack, and Ray Simons. *Class and Color in South Africa 1850–1950.* London: IDAFSA, 1983.

Smith, Anthony D. *Democratization in South Africa: The Elusive Social Contract.* Princeton, NJ: Princeton University Press, 1995.

Sithole, Ndabanigi. *African Nationalism.* London: Oxford University Press, 1959.

Slabbert, Frederick van zyl. *The Last White Parliament.* Johannesburg: Jonathan Ball Publishers, 1985.

Slovo, Joe. *The South African Working Class and the National Democratic Revolution.* Cape Town: South African Communist Party, 1989.

———. "Has Socialism Failed?" http://www.shodalap.com.

———. "Negotiations: What room for Compromise?" *The African Communist*, no. 130 (Third Quarter 1992): 36–40.

———.Smith, Anthony D. *National Identity.* Las Vegas: University of Nevada Press, 1991.

———. *Theories of Nationalism.* London: Duckworth, 1971.

———. *The Ethnic Origins of Nations.* Cambridge, MA: Basil Blackwell, 1988.

———. *Nationalism in the Twentieth Century.* New York: New York University Press, 1979.

Sono, Themba. *Race Relations in Post-Apartheid South Africa.* Johannesburg: South African Institute of Race Relations, 1999.

Sparks, Alistar. *The Mind of South Africa.* London: Mandarin, 1990.

———. *Tomorrow is Another Country: The Inside Story of South Africa's Negotiated Revolution.* Johannesburg: Struik Book Distributors, 1994.

Spitz, Richard, and Mathew Chaskalson. *The Politics of Transition: a Hidden History of South Africa's Negotiated Settlement.* Johannesburg: Witwatersrand University Press, 2000.

Starushenko, G. *Problems of the Struggle against Racism, Apartheid and Colonialism in South Africa*. Moscow: Africa Institute, 1986.

Stedman, Stephen John, ed. *South Africa: The Political Economy of Transformation*. Boulder, CO: Lynne Rienner publishers, 1994.

Suttner, Raymond, and Jeremy Cronin. *30 Years of the Freedom Charter*. Johannesburg: Ravan Press, 1986.

Swanns, Rachel L. "After Apartheid: White Anxiety." *New York Times*. November 14, 1999, 1, 4.

Switzer, Les. "Bantu World and the Origins of a Captive African Commercial Press." *Journal of South African Studies* 14, no. 3 (April 1988): 351–70.

Taylor, Viviene. *Social Mobilisation: Lessons From the Mass Democratic Movement*. Cape Town: Mega Print, 1997.

Thomas, Anthony. *Rhodes: The Race for Africa*. Middlesex, England: Penguin Books, 1997.

Thompson, Leonard. *The Political Mythology of Apartheid* New Haven, CT: Yale University Press, 1985.

———. A History of South Africa, New Haven: Yale University Press, 2000

———, ed. *African Societies in Southern Africa*. New York: Praeger Publishers, 1969.

Thompson, L., and Jeffrey Butler, eds. *Change In Contemporary South Africa*. Berkeley, CA: University of California Press, 1975.

Thompson, L., and Andrew Prior. *South African Politics*. Cape Town: David Philip, 1982.

Tlali, Miriam. *Muriel at Metropolitan*. Johannesburg: Ravan Press, 1975.

Toit, Andre du. "No Chosen People: The Myth of the Calvinist Origins of Afrikaner Nationalism and Racial Ideology." *The American Historical Review* 88. no. 4 (October 1983): 920–52.

Toit, Andre du. "South Africa as Another Case of Transition from Authoritarian Rule." Occasional papers from the *Institute for a Democratic South Africa* (IDASA), May 1987.

Toit, Pierre du. *Power Plays: Bargaining Tactics for Transforming South Africa*. Natal, South Africa: Southern Books Publishers, 1991.

Trapido, Stanley, and Shula Marks. *The Politics of Race, Class and Nationalism in Twentieth Century South Africa*. London: Longman, 1993.

Trollope, Anthony. *South Africa: A Report of the 1878 Edition*. Cape Town: A. A. Balkema, 1878.

Turok, Ben. *Nothing but the Truth: Behind the ANC's Struggle Politics*. Johannesburg: Jonathan Ball Publishers, 2003.

Ucko, Peter. "The Politics of the Indigenous Minority." *Journal of Biosocial Science. Supplement* 8 (1983): 25–40.

Uys, Stanley. "Can a Democratic Constitution Take Root in South Africa?" *South Africa International* 22, no. 2 (October 1991): 82–85.

Verscholes, F. *Cecil Rhodes: His Political Life and Speeches*. London: Chapman & Hall, 1900.

Vestergraard, Mads. "Who's Got the Map? The Negotiation of Afrikaner Identities in Post-Apartheid South Africa." *Daedalus: Journal of the American Academy of Arts and Sciences* 130, no. 1 (Winter 2001): 19–44.

Villakazi, B. W. *Ama'zulu*. Johannesburg: Witwatersrand University Press, 1945.

Villiers, Marq de. *White Tribe Dream: Apartheid's Bitter Roots Notes of an Eighth Generation Afrikaner*. Toronto, Canada: Macmillan, 1987.

Vindix [Rev. F. Verscholes]. *Cecil Rhodes: His political Life and Speeches*. London: Chapman & Hall, 1900.

Vroom, Eugen. *The Helpless Boers*. New Jersey: Flanders Hall, 1940.

Waal, Shaun de. "A Novel that Finds Adversity in Triomf." *Mail & Guardian*. April 9–15, 1999, 22–23. http://www.mg.co.za

Waldmeir, Patti. *Anatomy of a Miracle: The End of Apartheid and the Birth of the New South Africa*. New Jersey: Rutgers University Press, 1997.
Walker, Cheryl. *Women and Resistance in South Africa*. Cape Town: David Philip, 1982.
———, ed. *Women and Gender in Southern Africa*. Cape Town: David Phillip, 1990.
Walker, Eric A. *A History of Southern Africa*. London: Longman, 1957.
Wallerstein, Immanuel. *The Politics of the World Economy: The States, the Movements and the Civilizations*. Cambridge, UK: Cambridge University Press, 1984.
———. *Africa: The Politics of Independence*. New York: Vantage Books, 1961.
Walshe, Peter. *The Rise of African Nationalism in South Africa*. London: C. Hurst, 1970.
Ward, David. *Chronicles of Darkness*. London: Routledge, 1990.
Watson, Michael. *Contemporary Minority Nationalism*. New York: Routledge, 1990.
Weber, Max. *The Protestant Ethic and the Spirit of Capitalism*. New York: Charles Scribner, 1958.
Welsh, David. *The Roots of Segregation Native Policy in Natal 1845–1910*. Cape Town: Oxford University Press, 1971.
Welsh, Frank. *A History of South Africa*. London: Harper Collins, 1998.
Who ought to Win? Oom Paul or Queen Victoria: The South African Struggle. South Africa: Laid & Lee Publishers, 1900.
Wilkins, Ivor, and Hans Strydom. *The Super-Afrikaners: Inside the Afrikaner Broederbond*. Johannesburg: Jonathan Ball Publishers, 1978.
Wilkinson, David, and Joe Slovo, eds. *Southern Africa: The New Politics of Revolution*. Harmondsworth, England: Penguin Books, 1976.
Wilmot, Alexander. *The Story of the Expansion of South Africa*. London: Juta Co., 1895.
———. *The History of Our Own Times in South Africa: 1880–1888*. Cape Town: 1898.
Wilmot, James, ed. *The State of Apartheid*. Boulder, CO: Lynne Rienner Publishers, 1987.
Wilmot, James, Daria Caliguire, and Kerry Cullinan, eds. *Now That We Are Free: Coloured Communities in a Democratic South Africa*. Boulder, CO: Lynne Rienner, 1996.
Wilson, Monica, and Leonard Thompson. *A History of South Africa to 1870*. Cape Town: David Phillip, 1982.
———, eds. *The Oxford History of South Africa*. London: Oxford University Press, 1971.
Wolpe, Harold. *Race, Class, and the Apartheid State*. London: James Currey, 1988.
Wooddis, Jack. *New Theories of Revolution*. New York: International Publishers, 1972.
Woods, Donald. *Biko*. New York: Paddington Press, 1978.
Worden, Nigel. *The Making of Modern South Africa*. Cambridge, MA: Blackwell Publishers, 1994.
Worden, Nigel, and Clifton Crais, eds. *Breaking the Chains: Slavery and its Legacy in the Nineteenth-Century Cape Colony*. Johannesburg: Witwatersrand University Press, 1994.
Young, Crawford. *Ideology and Development in Africa*. New Haven, CT: Yale University Press, 1982.
———. *The African Colonial State in Comparative Perspective*. New Haven, CT: Yale University Press, 1994.
Yudelman, David. *The Emergence of Modern South Africa: State, Capital, and the Incorporation of Organized Labour on the South African Gold Fields, 1901–1939*. Cape Town: David Phillip, 1984.

NEWSPAPERS AND MAGAZINES

Business Day
Cape Argus

Cape Times
Christian Science Monitor
City Press
Eastern Province Herald (Port Elizabeth)
Economist
Financial Mail
Financial Times
Guardian Weekly
Ilanga LaseNatal
Inkanyiso
Izvestiya
Liberation
Mail & Guardian
Natal Witness
New York Times
Pravda
Rapport
Siyaya!
Sowetan
Sunday Independent
Sunday Star
Sunday Times
The African Communist
The Citizen
The Economist
The Guardian
The Star
Time
Wall Street
Weekly Mail & Guardian

Index

Afrikaner Broederbond, 54, 64, 70–71, 83, 87, 115, 116, 135, 154
Afrikaner Weerstand Beweging (AWB/Afrikaner Resistance Movement), 132, 143
AIDS. *See* HIV/AIDS
Anglo-Boer war, 36, 62
Azanian People's Liberation Army (APLA), 142, 143
Azanian People's Organization (AZAPO), 81

Bantu, 1–4, 8, 13, 28, 30, 43, 65–66, 69, 93, 109
Bantustans, 13, 70, 85, 109, 138, 168
Biko, Steve, 79, 146
Black Consciousness/Black Consciousness Movement (BC/BCM), 10, 35, 63, 74, 75, 76, 78–80, 87, 89, 104, 116–17, 143, 182
Boers, 32, 35, 48, 91–92
Boesak, Allan, 147, 148
Botha, Pieter Willem (P. W.), 55, 69, 71, 73, 111, 115, 120, 121, 122–24, 127, 129, 133, 135, 173
Bourgeoisie. *See* middle class
Britain (British), 5, 13, 22–23, 26, 36, 44, 51, 53, 62, 64, 70, 71, 81, 82, 112, 114, 126, 154, 175, 176, 180, 181, 182, 185
Buthelezi, Mangosuthu, 144
bywoners, 50, 54

Cabral, Amilcar, 8–9
Congress Youth League. *See* Youth League

Convention for a Democratic South Africa (CODESA), 87, 137–40
Congress of South African Trade Unions (COSATU), 123–24, 132, 137, 144, 147–48, 154, 156–57, 158, 160, 174
Conservative Party (CP), 69, 111, 113, 114, 132, 133, 134, 140, 145

De Klerk, F. W., 71, 73, 116, 123–25, 128, 132–33, 135, 137, 146–48
Democratic Party (DP), 134, 159
Development Bank of South Africa (DBSA), 158, 171
Dutch, 4, 5, 22–23, 25, 49, 51, 82
Dutch East India Company (DEIC), 48, 64
Dutch Reformed Church (DRC), 60, 115

Ethiopia, 33–34, 76–77

Fanon, Frantz, 7–9, 17–19, 152
Freedom Charter, 3, 39, 74, 76, 84, 151, 155, 174, 183

gender, 40–45, 47, 56–60, 61, 83–87, 94, 96, 175–76
Government of National Unity (GNU), 140, 155, 159, 168
Growth, Employment and Redistribution (GEAR), 17, 152, 154, 157, 158–60, 161, 163

INDEX

Hani, Chris, 132, 136, 141, 142
HIV/AIDS, 163–65, 186
housing, 85–86, 117, 165–67

Industrial and Commercial Workers' Union of South Africa (ICU), 37–38
Inkatha Freedom Party (IFP), 3, 8, 15, 49, 73, 134, 140, 142–43, 144, 145, 184
Independent Election Commission (IEC), 146
International Monetary Fund (IMF), 17, 19, 118, 153, 154–56, 158, 176, 183, 184, 185

Kaffir, 22, 26–29, 31–33, 43, 48, 50, 53, 66, 96, 101–2, 104
Kholwa, 30, 33–34, 37, 41–43, 181
Khoikhoi, 22
Khoisan, 22, 24, 64
Kraal Kaffirs (Red People), 33

land reform, 156, 166, 171–72
late nationalism, 1–3
Lembede, Anton Muziwakhe, 6, 38, 77, 78
liberal democracy, 1–4, 8, 87, 151, 177, 179, 185–86
Liberal Party, 77

Malan, D. F., 36–37, 53, 54, 55, 66, 69, 71
Mandela, Nelson, 4, 40, 71, 125–26, 128, 132, 135–37, 141, 144, 146–49, 169, 173, 176, 184
Mandela, Winnie Madikizela, 63, 118, 125, 131, 132, 141, 147–48, 171, 173, 186
Mass Democratic Movement (MDM), 72, 119
Mbeki, Govan, 131
Mbeki, Thabo, 131, 132, 135, 149, 150, 158, 167, 168, 176, 183, 184, 187
middle class, 7–9, 114, 151–52, 173–75, 180
Milner, Alfred, 51, 58
missionary, 10, 21, 27, 30–36, 40–42
multiracial, 1–5, 11, 14, 29, 39, 72, 80, 114, 151, 179

National Council of African Women (NCAW), 43
National Party, 3, 5–6, 15, 18, 51–53, 55–56, 63, 66–67, 70, 71–73, 79, 80–81, 82, 87, 94, 99–100, 102, 107, 108, 112–13, 115, 128, 129, 132–33, 146, 181, 187

Pan Africanist Congress (PAC), 10, 15, 39, 63, 69, 74–80, 82, 87, 89, 104, 133–34, 144, 146, 149, 168–69, 181–82, 184
Poqo, 77, 144, 169
Purified National Party (PNP), 54–55, 61

Ramaphosa, Cyril, 146, 160
Reconstruction and Development Programme (RDP), 17, 152, 154, 156–58, 183
Reserve Bank of South Africa, 137, 156, 158, 183
Rhodes, Cecil, 6, 36

Shaka, 80
Shepstone, Theophilus, 6, 29, 33, 64
Sisulu, Walter, 131, 141, 176
Slovo, Joe, 10, 140–41, 144, 146, 154, 165
Sophiatown, 67, 116
South African Agricultural Union (SAAU), 111
South African Communist Party (SACP), 2, 39, 45, 74, 75, 82, 87, 132, 137, 141, 144, 145, 146, 147, 148, 156–58, 174
South African Defense Force (SADF), 125, 142–43, 144, 150, 156, 168, 169
South African National Defense Force (SANDF), 99, 143–44, 150, 168, 184
South African Native National Congress (SANNC), 31, 36–38
South African Students' Organization (SASO), 78
Soviet Union, 2, 19, 70, 72, 75, 87, 107, 119, 127–28, 179, 183
Soweto revolt, 4, 66, 80, 90, 107, 120, 117–18, 121, 126–27, 129, 135

Tambo, Oliver, 98, 115, 127–28, 142
Transitional Executive Council (TEC), 145, 146
Trekboers, 48–50
Truth and Reconciliation Commission (TRC), 170

Umkhonto we Sizwe, 70, 75, 98, 131, 136, 142–43, 149, 169, 184
United Democratic Front (UDF), 72, 76, 81, 85–86, 119, 124, 131, 132

verligte, 69–71, 109–10, 113–15, 121, 133
verkrampte, 69–71, 113–15, 121
Verwoerd, Hendrik, 65
Vorster, John, 71, 120, 129, 135

white supremacy, 25–28, 54–55
Women's National Coalition, 86–87
World Bank, 17, 19, 149, 153, 154–56, 158, 171, 176, 183, 184, 185

Xhosa, 27, 29, 31–32, 77

Youth League, 38–40, 77, 79, 147

Zulu, 27, 30–31, 35, 40–41, 80, 144, 161